# Beyond Slavery

# Jaguar Books on Latin America Series
## William Beezley and Colin MacLachlan, Series Editors

# Beyond Slavery

## The Multilayered Legacy of Africans in Latin America and the Caribbean

Edited by
Darién J. Davis

ROWMAN & LITTLEFIELD PUBLISHERS, INC.
*Lanham • Boulder • New York • Toronto • Plymouth, UK*

ROWMAN & LITTLEFIELD PUBLISHERS, INC.

Published in the United States of America
by Rowman & Littlefield Publishers, Inc.
A wholly owned subsidary of The Rowman & Littlefield Publishing Group, Inc.
4501 Forbes Boulevard, Suite 200, Lanham, Maryland 20706
www.rowmanlittlefield.com

Estover Road, Plymouth PL6 7PY, United Kingdom

British Library Cataloguing in Publication Information Available

**Library of Congress Cataloging-in-Publication Data**

Beyond slavery : the multilayered legacy of Africans in Latin America and the
  Caribbean / edited by Darién J. Davis.
      p.   cm.—(Jaguar books on Latin America series)
  Includes bibliographical references and index.
  ISBN-13: 978-0-7425-4130-6 (cloth : alk. paper)
  ISBN-10: 0-7425-4130-4 (cloth : alk. paper)
  ISBN-13: 978-0-7425-4131-3 (pbk. : alk. paper)
  ISBN-10: 0-7425-4131-2 (pbk. : alk. paper)
  1. Blacks—Latin America—History. 2. Blacks—Race identity—Latin
America.   3. Latin America—Civilization—African influences.   4. Marginality,
Social—Latin America—History.   5. African diaspora.   I. Davis, Darién J.,
1964–   II. Series: Jaguar books on Latin America.
F1419.N4B49 2007
305.89608—dc22

                                                               2006014833

Printed in the United States of America

♾ ™The paper used in this publication meets the minimum requirements of
American National Standard for Information Sciences—Permanence of Paper for
Printed Library Materials, ANSI/NISO Z39.48-1992.

# Contents

# Acknowledgments

I wish to thank editors Colin MacLachlan and William Beezley and the editorial and production team at Rowman & Littlefield for their help preparing this manuscript for publication. Special thanks goes to Susan McEachern, editorial director at Rowman & Littlefield; Jenn Nemec, associate editor; and Sarah Wood, editorial assistant.

I am also grateful to Ashley Kerry, my research assistant at Middlebury College, for her help and comments. I must also thank the contributors to this volume for their knowledge and patience, and especially for the dialogue that we have begun. Finally, I am indebted to my family (Karin Hanta, Caetano Hanta-Davis, and Marcelo Hanta-Davis) for their support during the organization, writing, and editing of this work.

# Introduction

Africa and its people have played critical roles in shaping the course of history in Latin America. The continent's incredible political, economic, and cultural diversity has marked the people and custom of Latin America in multiple ways. The present-day country of Nigeria, for example, the largest African nation and the ancestral home of thousands of black Latin Americans, was once the home of more than two hundred ethno-linguistic groups. European colonization in the nineteenth century destroyed or subjugated thousands of diverse African polities from religious imperial kingdoms in north Africa to local autonomous governments in the south and central regions of the continent. European domination and exploitation of Africa did not begin in the nineteenth century, however. Rather, the roots of conquest are to be found in the African slave trade, which began in the early sixteenth century. The enslavement and forced migration of Africans between 1513 and 1850 constitutes one of the greatest human rights tragedies of human history. For most of this history, European conquerors and settlers in Latin America treated the majority of Africans and their progeny as chattel, dispersing them throughout western Europe and the Americas. In Latin America, Africans were deprived of a multitude of dignities, robbed of their identities, and treated as pawns in an emerging capitalist system.

Despite these historical abuses, Africans and their descendants had an impact on many Latin American structures and peoples and on the institutions that oppressed them. In many cases, Africans and their descendents courageously fought against and resisted the institutions of conquest. But many men and women also accommodated or adapted to the emerging societies in the Americas. Africans and their descendants found ways of celebrating their cultures; recreating and reconstituting African customs and beliefs; and passing down religious, aesthetic, musical, and other social and cultural values from one generation to another. Africans not only intermin-

1

gled with Europeans and native populations, but they also mixed with one another in ways impossible in Africa, helping to create a vibrant new mestizo, or mixed, cultures. As Sidney Mintz and Richard Price have argued, no group can transfer its way of life and cultural beliefs intact from one place to another. Yet the diverse Africans who entered Latin American society were not all brainwashed into adhering to European rules that deprived them of their links to their ancestral home. Indeed, the multifaceted legacies of Africans in Latin America are testaments to their ingenuity and creativity in a world in which their freedoms were severely restricted.[1]

Africans of the diaspora and their descendants influenced Latin America in multiple and diverse ways. The African presence in many regions may be prominent and continuous, as in areas such as the Caribbean and Brazil, or it might have been limited to specific historical periods, as it was in Chile. Although it may be unusual to observe significant groups of Africans among the populations of some Latin American cities (Mexico City and Buenos Aires, for example), this does not necessarily mean that their historical presence and influence were slight. In some areas of colonial Latin America, Africans outnumbered Europeans fifteen to one. Almost half of the populations of colonial Buenos Aires, Lima, and Mexico City reflected varying degrees of African ancestry. A few scholars have even argued that African influences predated the arrival of Columbus and the Spaniards in 1492, but most historians reject this claim.[2] However, most historians agree that African influences entered the New World first through the Iberian Peninsula and then directly from Africa as a result of the slave trade.

Through most of the colonial era (1492–1800), Iberian imperialism and European racial and religious superiority shaped African behavior and activities. Although thinkers of the European Enlightenment would posit a different relationship between the individual and society in the eighteenth century, the legacy of racial oppression remained surprisingly resilient. Nonetheless, African men and women and their descendants continued to develop new ways to resist, accommodate, or respond to the new political order that would create modern nations. Today, many Latin American and Caribbean nations recognize and celebrate the responses and creations of their African forbearers. In other countries, historians continue to uncover hidden or previously unperceived legacies in spite of the persistent racist traditions that encourage individuals to identify with their white European colonial culture and to denigrate blacks.

In the late 1970s and the 1980s, scholars such as Rebecca Scott, Verena Martínez Alier, and Stuart Schwartz explained that slavery was not merely an economic or moral system but a dynamic way of life that affected and had consequences for all members of society. Indeed, in the evolving societies of Latin America, Africans and their descendents, like their European and native counterparts, formed alliances, utilized and broke laws, and sought and heeded power depending on the opportunities available to them. Enslaved Africans occupied the status of "slave" in Latin American society, but they were also mothers, fathers, carpenters, soldiers, confidants, priests and priestesses, and musicians. Without denying the cruelty of slavery, the legacy of which continues to play an important role in contemporary Latin American societies, this collection of essays focuses on the multiple influences, actions, and contributions of people of African descent beyond the system of slavery that held people of African descent in bondage. We thus hope to provide a window into the multilayered impact and legacy of men and women of African descent in the Americas.[3]

## ORGANIZATION OF THE VOLUME

The chapters are organized and divided into four distinct chronological and thematic parts. All four chapters in part 1 treat the multiple issues related to independence, freedom, and national identity and emphasize the place and role of freed and enslaved blacks in the revolutionary wars of independence, republicanism, and the periods of national consolidation. Although these essays focus primarily on the late eighteenth and nineteenth centuries, the authors show how and why these issues continue to be important in the contemporary era. Readers will note the multiplicity of racial terms that reflect shifting ideas of racial, cultural, and national identities in all four essays. Nations and individuals utilized and evoked racial identities in general and blackness in particular in multiple ways and for many purposes. Part 2 includes three chapters that discuss ideologies of inclusion and exclusion from the end of the nineteenth century to the 1950s. These chapters explore issues such as the meaning of abolition, national and race consciousness, protest, and access to full citizenship. Part 3 looks at issues of black displacement, transnationalism, and migration. These chapters also examine black marginalization, difference, and diasporic consciousness from the end of World War II to the present. Finally, the volume closes with a resources section that considers blacks in Latin American cinema and offers other sources for consultation.

## UNDERSTANDING THE COLONIAL ERA

Although this work focuses on the modern era, it is important to examine briefly the African impact on the colonial past. Europeans were familiar with Africa long before making contact with the New World in 1492. Many Africans had been involuntarily settled in the Iberian Peninsula prior to the conquest of the Western Hemisphere. In 1455, Pope Nicholas V gave the

Portuguese the right to enslave those inhabitants of the southern coast of Africa who resisted the introduction of Christianity, thus making themselves the enemies of Christ. As a consequence, the Iberians began a modest slave trade on the western coast of Africa. Distinguishing themselves from their Spanish counterparts, the Portuguese set up factories, or trading posts, to trade with local middlemen and African tribal chiefs. Africans contributed to the diversity of Iberian cities such as Seville and Lisbon, both of which were already inhabited by Jews, Arabs, and Christians. Small communities of Afro-Iberians thus emerged.

African slavery met a steady, but limited, demand in Europe, as neither Spain nor Portugal could profitably absorb a large number of slaves into their peninsular economies. Indeed, the Portuguese realized the independent sovereign existence of many African rulers and sought to establish political and cultural alliances with them. The institution of slavery, although long present both in Europe and Africa, continued to occupy a relatively minor position in both regions until its abolition in the early nineteenth century.

The initial period of conquest relied upon Africans residing on the peninsula to supplement the limited number of Europeans in their effort to subdue the native population of the New World to the new economic and political order. The Spanish respected and rewarded their contributions. Thus Juan Valiente, a fugitive slave who fought along the conquistadors in Chile, received an *encomienda* in the 1550s for his bravery. Other men of African ancestry, such as Juan Beltrán and Juan Fernandez, also took part in the conquest of Chile. The activities of Africans during exploration and conquest in other regions remain to be explored, but indigenous groups clearly recognized them as part of the conquering party. Miguel León Portilla, a prominent Mexican historian, reports that Aztecs referred to the Afro-Iberians who arrived with the Spaniards to Mexico as "soiled gods."[4]

Juan Garrido, known simply as Handsome John, participated in the conquest of Mexico. Both Manuel Orrozco y Berra and Bernal Díaz del Castillo noted his arrival with the conquistadors.[5] Garrido, who lived in Castile and considered himself a devout Christian, arrived first in Santo Domingo. After participating in several exploratory trips to other islands, he traveled to New Spain with one of the first groups of conquistadors. He did not receive the same benefits of conquest as other Spanish conquistadors but settled outside the city. Nevertheless, in 1525, he became a respected *vecino*, or citizen.

Following the conquest, the new overlords began the task of constructing colonial economies and societies. At the same time, cultural disruption, exploitation of the indigenous populations, and epidemic diseases caused a drastic decline of the Native American populations, resulting in a severe shortage of labor and slowing the rate of European development and exploitation of the newly conquered territories. In some areas, such as Brazil, it became evident that the native populations would not become efficient laborers for the Portuguese-controlled economy. Consequently, Europeans turned to African slavery, in some areas as a supplement to scarce indigenous labor, and in other areas as the main source of workers. Henceforth, European-African relations centered on slavery and the slave trade—a reality that endured for over three hundred years.

Characterized by distinct ethnic groupings with varying religions, customs, and practices, west Africa's inhabitants included the Ashanti, the Yoruba, the Ibo, and the Dahomey, all of whom subsequently contributed to culture in the Western Hemisphere. Tribes from the Muslim area of north Africa such as the Hausa, the Amalinke, and the Mandingo, in addition to tribes from the central Congo region, such as the Bantu, also influenced culture in the New World.[6] Despite their subjugated position, Africans played diverse roles in Latin America and would have an enduring effect on the region's culture and society. Africans and their descendants often resisted white domination, while others accommodated to the rules of European colonialism.

The institution of slavery adapted to the needs of the particular region, the demographic reality, and the nature of the work being performed. Slaves performed a variety of tasks from pearl fishing, mining, and carpentry to sharecropping and domestic chores. Slavery in Mexico, Argentina, and Chile differed substantially from the plantation economies of the Caribbean and Brazil. Urban slave labor also differed from plantation life, which had its own set of laws. Enforcement of the laws of manumission, marriage, and the general treatment of slaves depended on regional and local considerations rather than theoretical codes of conduct. Martínez Alier, the author of several works focusing on slavery in Cuba, has pointed out, for example, that although there were rigid laws that prohibited interracial marriage, widespread cohabitation occurred.[7]

## AFRICANS AND THEIR DESCENDANTS IN THE MODERN ERA

The racism that institutionalized European superiority over Africans and natives did not cease with the dawn of the modern era. Yet Africans and their descendants played key roles in the wars of independence and national liberation. The first Latin American nation to declare independence from a European power was the former French colony of Haiti. Inspired by the ideas of the 1789 French Revolution, which set the standards of modern nationhood based on radical calls for freedom, equality, and liberty, African slaves rose up against their French overlords. In 1791, chaos broke out on the island after the execution of Vincent Ogé, a mulatto who, encouraged by the French-based Les Amis des Noir, led a demonstration against the governor. The emergence of the figure of the former African slave Toussaint Louverture would help to channel the discontent through an organized effort that would become the Haitian Revolution. On January 1, 1804, Jean-Jacques Dessalines declared political independence, creating the first black republic in the Atlantic world until the early twentieth century.

The Haitian Revolution and independence would have reverberations throughout the Atlantic world. Haiti's economy suffered as a result of almost a decade of fighting in addition to its isolation after centuries of exploitative agricultural practices that depleted the land of a vast amount of resources. Both France and the United States banned trade with the island in 1806, aggravating the situation. Haiti nonetheless became an important point of reference for enslaved and free blacks throughout the Western Hemisphere. In chapter 1, "The Sounds and Echoes of Freedom: The Impact of the Haitian Revolution on Latin America," David Geggus documents the varied impact of the events in Haiti on Latin America. Geggus highlights the challenges of the Haitian people, who struggled to construct a state apparatus in a world dominated by European powers. "News of the Haitian Revolution spread wide and fast; nothing remotely like it had happened before, and nobody could think about slavery in quite the same way again," Geggus observes. Furthermore, enslaved Africans around the hemisphere were inspired by the events in Haiti, while white slaveholders complained of a new "insolence" on the part of their slaves, which they attributed to their awareness of the successful black revolution.

Geggus documents the impact of the first independent black nation on neighboring countries such as the Dominican Republic and Cuba, as well as the more distant countries of South America such as Venezuela and Brazil. Two centuries after the Haitian Revolution, Haiti remains a symbol of black pride. At the same time, Haiti's unfortunate distinction as one of the poorest nations in the Western Hemisphere is a vivid reminder of the legacies of racial oppression, colonialism, and the cost of resistance. It is without a sense of irony that in response to the brutal massacre of 111 prisoners at the Carandiru penitentiary in São Paulo, singer-song writers Caetano Veloso and Gilberto Gil recorded the song "Haiti," which connected the massacre with oppression and Brazil's complex system of racial identity.

Unlike Haiti, almost all Spanish- and Portuguese-speaking Latin American countries (with the exception of Cuba) attained political independence from Europe before outlawing slavery. Indeed, for South American independence fighters such as Simón Bolívar, this strategy was essential. Independence meant freedom from colonial government, not necessarily universal liberty. Thus, even after national liberation in the first three decades of the nineteenth century, slavery constituted a vital aspect of most of Latin America's political economy. While many Africans and their descendants resisted white domination in multiple ways, others utilized the emerging national constitutional and legal frameworks to secure rights and to improve their well-being.

In chapter 2, "In Search of Liberty: The Efforts of the Enslaved to Attain Abolition in Ecuador, 1822–1852," Camilla Townsend examines the actions of a group of the enslaved to attain greater freedom in Ecuador prior to that nation's abolition of slavery and highlights the role of Afro-Ecuadorians who contributed to the patriot army. Some used the language of citizenship employed by the new republic, while many others presented petitions to masters, the courts, or the government at strategic moments when they would most likely be viewed favorably. Townsend illustrates that many enslaved men and women were in tune with the political climate and used their knowledge of Ecuador's political system to their advantage. Paralleling cases in Mexico, Brazil, Peru, and elsewhere, individuals often touched the sensibilities of the new patriotic republican government to secure rights and privileges, thus setting precedents for others to follow. Today, Afro-Ecuadorians continue to speak out for their rights while forging alliances with indigenous groups and local and national governments. In August 2005, for example, UNESCO and the city's authorities in Esmeraldas supported the creation of the Esmeraldas International Center for Cultural Diversity to promote cultural development among the Afro-Ecuadorian populations.

The period of national independence in the nineteenth century was followed by a period of consolidation. Independence meant that European powers would have no explicit political authority over Latin American political institutions, but it did not ban their influences in other areas.

Although historians believe that we may be able to understand the present by reconstructing the dynamics and realities of the past, they understand that we cannot make assumptions about the past based on contemporary realities. This lesson is acutely apparent in cities such as Buenos Aires, where the contemporary Afro-Argentine population represents a fraction of what it represented in the early and middle nineteenth century after independence and through the period of national consolidation. During the age of caudillos, military strongmen unified their nations under strong patriarchal governments of the liberal and conservative persuasions. Some caudillos treated the poor and the African descendent and indigenous populations with disdain, while others called upon the masses for support. Juan Manual Rosas of Argentina (1829–1852) developed a special rapport with the popular masses, including the black and *pardo* populations of the city and the gauchos of the pampas. Rosas earned sharp criticism from liberal intellectuals such as Domingo Faustino Sarmiento and Estéban Echevarría because of his brutal political and military tactics, which drove them into exile, but they also criticized and mocked his relationship with the black and mestizo masses. Argentine historiography remains divided on Rosas's impact on Argentine history. Some continue to view him as a brutal dictator while others point to his promotion of local culture and his relatively positive relationship with the masses.

In chapter 3, "Integral Outsiders: Afro-Argentines in the Era of Juan Manuel Rosas, and Beyond," Ricardo Salvatore focuses on the role of the flourishing Afro-Argentine culture during the Rosas's dictatorship. While discussing Rosas's and his daughter Manuelita's relationship to the black community, Salvatore documents black agency and the white response to it in nineteenth-century Argentina. Africans and their decedents all over the region understood how to forge alliances and function within newly created national institutions. Like most alliances based on personal power, however, dynamics may change in the absence of power. Salvatore demonstrates how that happened to Afro-Argentines after the Rosas regime.

While racial and cultural intermingling constituted important social and cultural realities throughout the region, national politicians and intellectuals neither promoted nor celebrated these trends until the 1920s. Ironically, throughout the nineteenth century, the Creole elite's desire for European economic and cultural connections became patently clear. While Rosas and his regime may have represented an exception to this rule, most Latin American nations aimed to present themselves as "modern" and "civilized," and this often meant highlighting the European legacy while downplaying the African and indigenous roots and influences. Portuguese and Spanish authorities often promoted miscegenation as a population policy in under populated regions. Expressions such as *el que no tengo dingo tiene mandingo* (he who doesn't have dingo has mandingo) and *com um pé na cozinha* (with a foot in the kitchen), which seemingly denote the black ancestry of Latin Americans, often overlook the racist intonations that stress the importance of assimilating the African into the broader mestizo, or racially mixed, society. A psychologically important caste system based on color emerged in which blacks occupied the lowest rung. Such a system collided with an emerging class system based on economic considerations. As a result, miscegenation engendered a flexible system in which race as well as an individual's socioeconomic position determined social status.

By the end of the nineteenth century, most Latin American societies had become decidedly mestizo or mulatto. The mestizo became the majority in areas with high concentrations of indigenous communities such as the Andes, Central America, and Mexico. In regions with small native populations, including newly formed Spanish cities African populations were greater and mulattoes or *pardos* became a dominant force. In these regions, mulattoes and mestizos became a middle class that served as a buffer between the oppressed lower classes of blacks and natives and those who identified themselves as upper-class whites, many of whom had indigenous or African ancestry.

In small countries like Honduras, which witnessed the intermingling of Africans, Spanish, and natives in addition to the extraordinary presence of the Black Caribs or Garifuna, an exile community from the island of St. Vincent, the discourse of national consolidation and modernity presents several interesting variations. In chapter 4, "Free *Pardos* and Mulattoes Vanquish Indians: Cultural Civility as Conquest and Modernity in Honduras," Dario Eraque discusses the notion of civility and modernity and its relationship to the perceptions and place of race in nineteenth-century Honduras. He focuses on the foundation and subsequent perceptions of the town of Olanchito by mulatto and *pardo* descendants of enslaved African taken to Honduras in the sixteenth century. Eraque documents the shifting views of Honduran perceptions of the town from the nineteenth century, when notions of civility and citizenship prevailed, to the 1920s, when models of *mestizaje* began to come into vogue, particularly after the abolition of slavery.

By the late 1880s, all Latin American nations had abolished slavery. Of all of Spain's colonies, Puerto Rico and Cuba were the only two not to have declared republics before the beginning of the new century. Cuba and Brazil continued to rely heavily on slave labor after the British abolition of the slave trade in 1820 and were the last two countries to abolish slavery. Enslaved Africans continued to arrive on Cuban shores long after Ecuador and Honduras had abolished slavery, for example. Abolition finally came to Cuba in 1886 and to Brazil in 1888, one year before the declaration of the republic. By the time of abolition both Cuba and Brazil possessed a significant free population of color. Thus, in the second half of the nineteenth century, Latin America witnessed diverse struggles against slavery and efforts for inclusion and integration by men and women of African descent and their allies. The freed and the enslaved continued to struggle to increase their well-being in diverse ways: from serving in national armies and local militias to sexual alliances and personal ties of loyalty that enabled them to mitigate the impersonal cruelty of slavery and racism. Stories of suicide, escape, sabotage, and acts that defied European laws of social conduct and religion abound. Some people sought to preserve their culture while adapting to the new social and cultural order, while others organized rebellions and resisted European authorities in a myriad of ways.

On the verge of abolition, resistance against slavery continued to take various forms and often appeared in unexpected places. By the late nineteenth century the abolitionist movement, comprised of diverse men and women from various backgrounds, political persuasions, and races, orchestrated numerous campaigns that led to slavery's demise. In many countries, enslaved Africans played important roles in the abolitionist movements. Students of abolition in Brazil have often overlooked the role of *quilombos*, self-emancipated communities of enslaved Africans and Afro-Brazilians, in the struggle for abolition and instead have focused on their role in resisting slavery, or what Eduardo Silva calls the "break-away *quilombo* model." Indeed, *quilombos* played significant roles in the preservation of African culture in the Americas because they remained beyond the control of the Europeans. The most famous American settlement was the Republic of Palmares (1630–1682), established in a remote region of Portuguese America. At least 20,000 people lived within its boundaries, governed by west African customs, particularly Bantu, and cultural elements drawn from the Portuguese slave society from which they had fled. Other black settlements ranged from the small encampment of runaways, the *palenques* in Spanish America, and the *quilombos* in Portuguese America, to the Maroons in Jamaica and Guyana.

Some *quilombos*, as Eduardo Silva explains in "Black Abolitionists in the *Quilombo* of Leblon, Rio de Janeiro: Symbols, Organizers, and Revolutionaries" (chapter 5), were not so remote and played critical roles in the abolitionist struggle. He describes this type of *quilombo* as a abolitionist *quilombo*. Silva's research underscores the role of black Brazilians in the abolitionist movement. By focusing on this hitherto unknown *quilombo* in one of the most exclusive neighborhoods in Rio de Janeiro, Silva also emphasizes the fact that African influences in Brazil are everywhere. Close analysis of this "suburban" *quilombo* indicates how closely the enslaved in Brazil participated in their own emancipation. It also reveals their connections to allies and sympathizers, including many liberal abolitionists and Princess Isabela, daughter of Emperor Pedro II, who eventually signed the abolition decree on May 13, 1888.

In the nineteenth century, liberal elites preferred to focus on development issues rather than race relations or racial origins. Most did not question the premise of inferior and superior races but hoped that miscegenation would eliminate the issue. Many abolitionists opposed slavery for economic reasons and believed that European migration would promote progress and alleviate racial problems. Implicit in this stand was the Brazilian notion of *embranquecimiento*, the process of "whitening" and becoming more European. Thus, liberals such as Joaquim Nabuco advocated an end to slavery in Brazil because, among other things, it repelled potential European immigration. Moreover, Nabuco believed that without slavery, Brazil could have been another Canada or Australia. Nabuco's arguments are reflected in the writings of a wide range of Latin American commentators. Intellectuals such as José Martí took the nationalists' rhetoric one step further by negating racial difference and conflict so as to focus on what united blacks, whites, and mulattoes. Despite this rhetoric and the varied contributions to key national struggles, in the wake of independence blacks were categorically marginalized or ignored, as Aline Helg explains in chapter 6, "To Be Black and to Be Cuban: The Dilemma of Afro-Cubans in Post-independence Politics." Helg documents both the contributions of Afro-Cubans and their systematic marginalization by white elites from political and economic advancement.

Despite their lack of political and economic power, black Latin Americans nonetheless influenced all aspects of regional and local society. While music and food are the most obvious areas of influence to the casual observer, Afro-Latin Americans exerted a strong influence on social values and attitudes conveyed through religious beliefs and practices. The Cuban anthropologist Fernando Ortiz was one of the first to explain African transculturation, or the transfer of cultural values and rituals from Africa, to Cuba. In Brazil, enslaved Africans from what is modern-day Nigeria and Angola brought with them a philosophy and concept of the cosmos that provided the religious basis of Latin American religions such as *Umbanda* and *Candomblé*. When forced to acknowledge European saints and follow the Roman Catholic liturgical calendar, they associated African deities with Catholic saints. In west Africa, the Yoruban people used anthropomorphic images to interpret and to organize their world. This practice, which has continued in the Americas to the present day, was facilitated by Catholicism, which organized the saints in a pantheon similar to the Yoruba religion.

In the 1920s, nationalist writers began to recognize the contribution of previously ignored racial sectors to the formation of national identity. Latin Americans began to project positive racial images, celebrating the *mestizaje* of native, European, and African traits. In this era, the Mexican writer and educator José Vasconcelos noted that miscegenation had created what he called a "cosmic race."[8] Similar theories arose in the 1920s and 1930s throughout Latin America. Writers such as the Brazilian Gilberto Freyre and the Cuban Elías Entralgo wrote about miscegenation between the European and the African in a positive manner. These views, in part, reflected the twentieth-century nationalists' attempts to view their Latin American identity and development in positive terms. Intellectual recognition by whites of African contributions did not necessarily signal the widespread acceptance of black culture on equal terms by white or mestizo masses or equal treatment of blacks, although it did influence the emergence of black consciousness.[9]

Cultural rejuvenation and racial and ethnic pride on the part of Afro-Latin Americans after World War I represented a major shift in race relations in the Atlantic world in the first half of the twentieth century. The writings of intellectuals such as the Martinican Aimé Césaire, the Cuban Nicolás Guillén, and the Brazilian Abdias do Nascimento were instrumental in raising black consciousness prior to the North American civil rights movements of the 1960s. Cultural movements such as Negritude, Negrismo, and Rastafarianism have connected blacks in Africa and throughout the diaspora in multiple ways. The period following World War I saw the rise of popular black social movements that challenged the status quo. Their emergence was due to a combination of international and national factors. Since then, black consciousness movements have emerged in virtually every region of the Americas. Chapter 7, "Pan-Africanism, Negritude, and the Currency of Blackness: Cuba, the Francophone Caribbean, and Brazil in Comparative Perspective, 1930–1950s" by Darién J. Davis and Judith Michelle Williams, provides a comparative analysis of three cultural movements, and their major protagonists, that aimed to promote black pride, defend the rights of blacks, and promote black culture within their distinct national political, economic, and social frameworks. The authors highlight a currency of blackness that found forms in the national milieu but that nonetheless dialogued with issues and struggles throughout the diaspora.

Diasporic thinkers such as Césaire helped to begin a multinational dialogue with other thinkers and writers in the African diaspora, including Marcus Garvey and Langston Hughes. All three found ways to celebrate blackness and to call for equal rights. The Afro-Brazilian activist Abdias do Nascimento followed in this tradition. Nascimento was one of the founders of the Black Experimental Theater (TEN), which became the major consciousness-raising organization of the 1940s and 1950s. Although the agenda and programs of TEN emerged out of the uniquely Brazilian milieu, Nascimento saw a connection with other types of cultural activity throughout the diaspora. Despite Woodrow Wilson's post–World War I insistence on the importance of the nation-state to global affairs, pan-Africans such as Césaire, Nascimento, and Garvey, along with their African American counterparts such as W. E. B. DuBois, indirectly highlighted the limitations of the nation-state. Africans of the Diaspora had an intimate understanding of transnationalism.

## POST–WORLD WAR II AND THE CONTEMPORARY ERA

Part 4 of this work looks more closely at issues of transnationalism, displacement, and culture across national borders in the middle and late twentieth century. Latin Americans of African decent have continued to cross national borders for a variety of reasons. At the turn of the twentieth century, for example, black migrants from the Caribbean islands flocked to Central America by the thousands to work on various projects on railroads, on plantations, and on the building of the Panama Canal. These migrations transformed the demographic composition of countries such as Panama and Costa Rica, although the new arrivals and their descendants were not always welcome. Panama, for example, denied citizenship to the offspring of Caribbean immigrants for decades, and many returned to the islands or migrated to the United States.

Regional and civil wars have also led to dislocation and displacement. During the cold war, thousands of Latin Americans were displaced or went into exile. Nowhere has the impact of civil war affected black Latin Americans more than in Colombia. Chapter 8, "The Logic of Displacement: Afro-Colombians and the War in Colombia," by Aviva Chomsky, focuses on the impact of the Colombian civil war on Afro-Colombians from the 1950s to the present day. Colombia is one of the few Latin American countries that recognizes Afro-Colombians as a distinct ethnic community and guarantees their political representation in the country's National Congress. Colombia's 1993 Federal Law 70 assigns seats in its national House of Representatives to Afro-Colombians, for example, and secondary school students are required to learn Afro-Colombian history. Despite these positive developments, Chomsky's essay shows that in addition to the tragedies of the civil war between government forces and guerrillas, the displacement of Afro-Colombian communities has been accelerated by the implementation of large-scale agricultural projects promoted by the government in the lands where they live. The national disasters of the war affect those on the economic and political periphery, and this means many Afro-Colombians.

The dispersal of cultural products and customs has accompanied the contemporary dislocation, exile, and emigration of peoples of African descent. Travel, mass media, and new technologies have also played crucial roles in the spread of international cultural products, particularly popular music. Music inspired and created by people of African descent is no exception. For centuries, musicians, performers, and singers from around the globe have borrowed from and been influenced by African and African-derived rhythms and styles. Black musicians in Latin America have not only preserved and propagated the music of their ancestors, but they have also celebrated and borrowed from a host of other diasporic traditions.

The performance of black music has also played an implicit and explicit part in Afro-Latin American resistance in the face of white dominance and oppression. The aesthetic and musical articulation of that resistance has taken on many formats and has been influenced by styles and musicians throughout the globe. The currency of blackness expressed by pan-African intellectuals from the 1930s to the 1950s found voices in popular musical forums throughout the Americas since the 1960s. Syncretism and cultural intermingling were not only a privilege of Europeans with conquered people. From colonial times, different African ethnic groups influenced and borrowed from one another as they did with indigenous populations. In the modern and contemporary era, peoples of African descent throughout the diaspora have continued this process across national and regional boundaries. Despite their disadvantaged position in North American society, African Americans have benefited from the United States' global media reach by promoting a number of popular musical and dance forms, from jazz to rap music. In chapter 9, Sujatha Fernandes and Jason Stanyek explore those transnational links through a comparative analysis of the emergence of hip-hop in three Latin American countries. "Hip-Hop and Black Public Spheres in Cuba, Venezuela, and Brazil" references and makes explicit comparisons with the emergence of hip-hop in the United States. Given the endemic marginalization of the black youth in Latin America, the authors argue that hip-hop provides a vital voice for expression and protest in Latin America. In many instances, Latin American hip-hop has retained its close association with the urban poor and disenfranchised blacks in ways similar to earlier hip-hop artists in the United States.

The speed of communication and the forced and voluntary dispersal of people across national boundaries have led to multiple cross-hybridization and influences in a process that has benefited artists and musicians for centuries, as evidenced by Picasso's cubism, Maranhão and Bahia's reggae traditions, and capoiera's influence on and dialogue with break dancing. These processes have also allowed us to entertain questions about ownership and authenticity and have helped us to challenge modes of thinking and heretofore seemingly stagnant identities based on one nation's experience. The United States, which possesses the largest economy in the world, has also been the recipient of thousands of diverse immigrants. Unlike the majority of Latin America nations, which officially recognized, encouraged, or promoted miscegenation and cultural syncretism at one time or another, nineteenth-century U.S. authorities relied on legal segregation and the one-drop rule, which defined blackness though ancestry. Although these policies have defined race and racial politics ever since, the increasing heterogeneity of the immigrant pool in North America and the diversity among minority peoples have challenged historical notions of blackness. This has been acutely apparent among Latin American populations of mixed ancestry in the United States.

Early Puerto Rican migrants to New York, for example, identified closely with African Americans. Indeed, pioneers such as Arthur Schonberg are revered as icons of the black community in New York City. The U.S. government was slow to recognize racial and ethnic distinctions among its Latino population in the United States. Only in 1980 did official U.S. census reports introduce the "Hispanic" category, for example. Official ethnic categories such as "black, non-Hispanic" indicate the growing awareness of the fluidity of racial and ethnic categories, but they also institutionalize potentially divisive boundaries within racial groups.[10] Because Africans have played such an important role in Latin American societies, it follows that a significant number of Latino immigrants have African ancestry. They may also have European and indigenous ancestry, and this is also the case for African Americans, many of whom have European, Chinese, and indigenous—as well as African--roots. North Americans recognize the influence of African culture in immigrants from Brazil and in Caribbean societies such as Cuba, Puerto Rico, and the Dominican Republic, but few associate blackness with Mexican immigrants, for example, who make up the majority of the Latino population in the United States.

Africans, as we have seen, played an important role in Mexican history beginning with the exploration and conquest. As in other regions, however, Mexicans of African decent remain marginalized both politically and economically. Afro-Mexicans make up a part of the vast working-poor populations across Mexico, and many of them have crossed into the United States. However, no major study has ever been conducted on Afro-Mexican migration. Bobby Vaughn and Ben Vinson III's timely study is a call to further research. In "Unfinished Migrations: From the Mexican South to the American South—Impressions on Afro-Mexican Migration to North Carolina" (chapter 10), the authors provide a preliminary ethnographic picture of the Afro-Mexican community in North Carolina. This chapter highlights the intercommunity relations between African Americans and Afro-Mexicans and discusses issues of class and national representation.

The final section in this volume groups together a number of resources for the study and analysis of the African impact on Latin America and the Caribbean. Chapter 11 provides a historical assessment of the contribution of Africans and their descendents to film and cinema in Latin America and in the Latino community in the United States. "Fading In: Race and the Representation of Peoples of African Descent in Latin American Cinema" documents black marginalization in the media but also highlights the role of black filmmakers, producers, and actors who have helped transform images of blackness on the silver screen. This chapter also provides sources for visual material for use in the classroom. In many respects, the African legacy and influence has yet to be documented on film for the vast majority of Latin American nations. Yet African cultural, economic, social, and political traits are undeniable. The purpose of this volume is to aid students of Latin America and of the African diaspora in general to engage in the multidimensional arguments that have emerged in the study of those influences. The volume closes with a glossary of terms used throughout the text and a brief chronology of major watersheds created by and affecting Afro-Latin Americans. This is followed by a list of selected readings, and a list of North American and international NGOs (for English speakers) and resources for future research on the African dimension in Latin America.

# NOTES

1. Sidney Mintz and Richard Price, *The Birth of African-American Culture: An Anthropologic Perspective* (Boston: Beacon University Press, 1992), 1

2. See, for example, Ivan Van Sertima, *They Came before Columbus* (New York: Random House, 1976), and *The African Presence in Early America* (New Brunswick, NJ: Transaction Publishers, 1987).

3. See, for example, Stuart B. Schwartz, "Resistance and Accommodation in Eighteenth Century Brazil: The Slaves View of Slavery," *Hispanic American Historical Review* 57, no. 1 (1977): 69–81; Verena Martínez Alier, *Marriage, Class, and Colour in Nineteenth-Century Cuba: A Study of Racial Attitudes and Sexual Values in a Slave Society* (Ann Arbor: University of Michigan Press, 1989), 12; Rebecca Scott, *Slave Emancipation in Cuba* (Princeton, NJ: Princeton University Press, 1985).

4. Miguel León Portilla, *Broken Spears: The Aztec Account of the Conquest of Mexico* (Boston: Beacon Press, 1992), 34.

5. Francisco de Icaza, *Diccionario autobiográfico de conquistadores y pobladores de Nueva España* (Madrid, Spain: El Adelantado de Segovia, 1923), vol. 1, entry 169. See also Hubert Howe Bancroft, *History of Mexico* (San Francisco: A. L. Bancroft, 1883–1886), 2:423n. Some scholars report that Cortéz's exhibition included four hundred Spaniards and three hundred blacks. In *La Corona española y los foraneos en los pueblos de indios de America* (Stockholm: Latinamerikanska-institutet i Stockholm, Almqvist & Wiksell, 1970), Magnus Mörner argues that many more blacks participated.

6. Philip D. Curtin in *The Atlantic Slave Trade* (Madison: University of Wisconsin Press, 1969) identified the eight major regions in West Africa: Gambia and Senegal, Sierra Leon, Ivory Coast and Liberia, the Gold Coast (modern-day Ghana), Togo and Dahomey, the Bight of Biafra, Angola, and Southern Africa.

7. Alier, *Marriage, Class, and Colour*, 12.

8. José Vasconcelos, *La Raza cósmica: Misión de la raza iberoamericana* (Mexico City: Aguilar S. A. de Ediciones, 1961).

9. See Gilberto Freyre's Brazilian classic *The Masters and the Slaves* (1933; repr., New York: Knopf, 1964), in which he developed his theory of lusotropicalism, crediting Portuguese racial tolerance as critical to their colonization efforts. Elías Entralgo proposed his ideas about *mestizaje* and miscegenation in *La Liberación étnica cubana* (Havana, Cuba: Imprenta de la Universidad de la Habana, 1953).

10. The definition of "Hispanic" has been modified in every U.S. census since 1970. The 1970 U.S. Census defined "Hispanic" in three ways, leading to widespread confusion. In 1980, the term was modified and since then has been used interchangeably with the "Latino," although many Latin American, and particularly Brazilian, immigrants who utilize terms of U.S. origin prefer "Latino." Others continue to define themselves by the country of origin (i.e., Colombian, Brazilian, Cuban).

# I

## STRUGGLES FOR INDEPENDENCE: REPUBLICANISM AND THE AGE OF CAUDILLOS

# 1

# The Sounds and Echoes of Freedom

## The Impact of the Haitian Revolution on Latin America

*David Geggus*

*Predating the wars of Spanish American independence by some two decades, the Haitian Revolution was the single most important international event of the early modern era. Enslaved Africans rebelled against European authority and created the first black republic in the world. The second would not come until the foundation of Liberia in west Africa in 1847. The impact of the revolution was immediate and widespread. David Geggus demonstrates how the revolution inspired peoples of African descent throughout the diaspora and affected the behavior of white slave owners. He compares and contrasts the impact of the revolution on countries near the island republic, such as Cuba and the Dominican Republic, as well as those farther afield such as Brazil, Venezuela, and Colombia.*

*The Haitian Revolution influenced freed and enslaved Africans outside Haiti, but it also had an impact on whites throughout the region.*

The revolution of 1789–1803 that transformed French Saint Domingue into the Republic of Haiti was an object of fear and inspiration in the American colonies of Spain and Portugal during the period when they pursued their own independence. The Haitian Revolution began, like the earlier revolt of Britain's thirteen colonies, as a bid for greater autonomy by the colony's white elite but quickly expanded into a more complex social revolution. It ended by destroying the most productive colonial export economy of its time. Massive rebellions by free people of color and by slaves

19

forced Saint Domingue in 1792 to become the first American colony to establish racial equality, and in 1793, the first major slave society to abolish slavery. France, then in the midst of its own revolution, was obliged to extend these reforms to its other colonies. Through the 1790s, former slaves led by Toussaint Louverture consolidated their power in Saint Domingue under the aegis of the French republic and inflicted costly defeats on British and Spanish forces sent to seize the colony and restore slavery. An attempt by Napoleon Bonaparte to reestablish the colonial status quo precipitated a vicious war of independence in 1802–1803 that led to the elimination of the white population. If Saint Domingue is considered part of Latin America by virtue of its Catholic absolutist institutions and linguistic affiliation, Haiti was the region's first independent state.[1]

Having defeated armies of the three main colonial powers, France, Spain, and Britain, the former slaves and free people of color turned to making laws for themselves and building a state apparatus. A symbol of black freedom and anti-imperialism, Haiti's first constitution defiantly prohibited landownership by whites and soon was amended to offer citizenship to anyone of African or Native American descent who settled in the country. These events took place in an Atlantic world dominated by Europeans, where slavery and the slave trade were at their peak, and where ideas about racial hierarchy were gaining in legitimacy. Because of its primacy in the struggle for freedom and equality, because it involved by far the largest of American slave uprisings, and because it took place in the world's major producer of tropical produce, the Haitian Revolution had a significance reaching well beyond its modest geographic dimensions. Yet it is not easy to define how it affected the wider world. Its repercussions were felt in a number of domains, from the economic to the intellectual; they were sometimes ambiguous or contradictory, and in the slave-owning Americas, they were not always easy to disentangle from the effects of the French Revolution.

## EARLY REACTIONS OF PEOPLE OF COLOR

News of the Haitian Revolution spread wide and fast; nothing remotely like it had happened before, and nobody could think about slavery in quite the same way again. Whites in many parts of the Americas began complaining of a new "insolence" on the part of their slaves, which they attributed to awareness of the successful black revolution. In 1795 Cuba's governor wrote bitterly that the name of Jean-François, leader of the insurgent slaves, "resounds in the ears of the lower classes like that of an invincible hero and redeemer of the slaves," and a local magnate reported that, since the Saint Domingue uprising, "The insolence [of Havana's blacks and mulattoes] no longer knows any bounds." This opinion was echoed three years later by the island's governor, who commented on the excitement created by news of blacks' growing power over whites in the neighboring colony.[2] In 1806, a British visitor to Rio de Janeiro speculated that "the secret spell that caused the Negro to tremble at the presence of the white man [had been] in a great degree dissolved" by the spectacle of "black power."[3]

Just weeks after Toussaint Louverture occupied Spanish Santo Domingo, early in 1801, free blacks and slaves in the hills above Coro in western Venezuela rejoiced at the news and sang a refrain that punned on the leader's name, "Look to the firebrand [*Tisón*]. . . . They'd better watch out!"[4] In distant Rio de Janeiro, some free black and mulatto militiamen were found in 1805 to be wearing around their necks medallion portraits of Emperor Dessalines, Haiti's first head of state, who had been crowned the year before. Nine years later, Bahian merchants complained that slaves were talking openly about local revolts, Haiti, and the elimination of all whites and mulattoes.[5] Long after the revolution at Bayamo, Cuba produced a more subtle example when, in 1836, local officials found that the banner of the town's Carabalí *cabildo* (an African association) no longer bore the royal crown symbolic of the Spanish monarchy, but a plumed cocked hat representative of Haitian heads of state.[6] How much news penetrated rural regions remains unclear, and how news traveled from the Caribbean to Brazil is a mystery. But the basic facts of the Haitian Revolution appear to have been rapidly disseminated along maritime trade routes by sailors, refugees, and proselytizing privateers of diverse origins.[7]

## SLAVE RESISTANCE

If the French Revolution proclaimed the ideals of liberty and equality, the Haitian Revolution proved to African Americans these ideals could be won by force of arms, and that things were perhaps not so immutable as they seemed. However, if the revolution was an inspiration, did it also serve as an object lesson, or source of support, for insurgents in other places? To what extent did it play a causal role in the numerous slave rebellions and conspiracies of these decades?[8]

The answer to this question depends not only on an empirical accumulation of evidence but on one's individual understanding of the perpetually elusive issue of why people suddenly choose to risk their lives at a particular moment. Both contemporary observers and historians have therefore disagreed about how much "Haitian influence" there was in the many rebellions of the period. The frequency of slave revolts and conspiracies in the Americas certainly reached a peak in the 1790s, and the largest rebellions all occurred in the forty years following the Saint Domingue uprising of

1791. But there were many other influences at work in the rebellions of the period, both internal to the societies concerned and deriving from revolutionary France or from the antislavery movement. Eugene Genovese's argument that the Haitian Revolution marked a turning point in the character of slave resistance does not seem borne out by the evidence from Latin America or elsewhere.[9] In the Spanish Empire, we find two striking upsurges in slave and free colored resistance in the years 1795 and 1811–1812. In the aggregate, these reflected an increase in the sales tax and rumors of emancipation that derived from the *gracias al sacar* reform (in 1795) and from the discussions (in 1811–1812) of the Cortes of Cádiz, as much as from news arriving from Haiti.[10] In Brazil, the pattern of slave revolt reflected the rhythms of the slave trade and seems to have owed nothing to the Haitian example.[11]

There existed, nevertheless, several types of connections between the Haitian Revolution and slave resistance elsewhere. Transplanted "French" slaves and free coloreds show up in several rebellions in Spanish-, Dutch-, and English-speaking territories from the 1790s to the 1820s. It is not certain that all these French blacks were from Saint Domingue, and, despite the exaggerations of some scholars, they did not necessarily play key roles in these events. The several small Spanish West Indian revolts and conspiracies of the mid-1790s provide a case in point. Moreover, the once-supposed contact between Haiti and maroons in eastern Cuba no longer appears very likely.[12]

Slaves taken to Puerto Rico from Saint Domingue used a nonviolent tactic. In 1796, the island's governor complained that local law courts were daily being bothered by French slaves who claimed they were really free, and that they were encouraging local slaves to do the same.[13] In Cuba, too, around the same time, some bold spirits among the slaves of French refugees similarly insisted they were free by virtue of the events in Saint Domingue, "maliciously" confusing, in one official's words, the French emancipation decree of February 1794 with a local deportation order.[14]

Joaquín Chirino, a sharecropper of Coro, Venezuela, exemplifies another type of linkage with the French colony. He was not from Saint Domingue, but he had visited the colony with his owner before launching a bloody revolt in May 1795, supposedly demanding "the law of the French," which meant slave emancipation. (One should note, however, that the traditional interpretation that links the revolt to French/Haitian influences has been recently challenged.)[15] The example of Saint Domingue was more explicitly invoked two years earlier by a Creole slave conspirator in neighboring Santo Domingo who declared that local slaves were fools for doing nothing while slaves in the French colony were killing whites. He further claimed (falsely) that Jean-François, the leader of the 1791 insurrection, was already preparing an uprising in the Spanish colony. That plot came to nothing, but when in 1796 Africans organized a slave rebellion in Boca Nigua, Santo Domingo, they sought to learn directly about the Saint Domingue uprising from some of its former participants who had settled nearby.[16]

The case with the most impressive Haitian linkage is the 1812 conspiracy of the free black carpenter José Antonio Aponte of Havana.[17] He promised his followers that Haitian soldiers would come to their aid when they plotted to take over the island of Cuba. Similar promises had been made the previous year in Santo Domingo in the multiracial conspiracy of Manuel del Monte and would be made again in the Escalera conspiracy three decades later.[18] Such predictions seem to have been a device employed by leaders for winning recruits and stiffening resolve in the face of overwhelming odds. One of Aponte's fellow urban conspirators appears to have visited plantation slave quarters, pretending to be Jean-François, the main leader of the 1791 insurrection, who had long been an object of pride for blacks in Havana. Jean-François was in fact already dead, but some of his former officers were passing through Havana at this time, and they were approached by the conspirators, who wanted them to join the conspiracy, but they apparently refused.

Most interesting of all is that Aponte, who was an artist, used a sketch book that contained paintings or drawings of Toussaint Louverture, Jean-Jacques Dessalines, and Henry Christophe, who had been crowned king of Haiti the previous year. The crowning of a black king and the creation of a black aristocracy in the heart of the slave-owning Caribbean assuredly caught the imagination of many black people across the Americas. Yet, even in this conspiracy where Haitian influence was most visible, other major causal factors were in play, such as the considerable decline in Cuba's military garrison during the previous decade, and the rumors of slave emancipation issuing that year from the Cortes of Cádiz, which also sparked resistance in Puerto Rico and Santo Domingo (as well as Martinique).

Although Aponte's promises of Haitian help were bogus, there were a few instances of direct participation from Saint Domingue in resistance to slavery elsewhere. One involved the participation of mulatto and black privateers from the French colony in a revolutionary plot in 1799 in Maracaibo, Venezuela, where their intermediary was a local *pardo* tailor named Francisco Pirela.[19] During the presidency of Alexandre Pétion (1807–1818), Haitian soldiers also fought alongside Spanish American Creoles for the independence of (a slavery-free) Venezuela.[20] The politics of survival, however, generally prevented Haitian statesmen from seeking to spread slave rebellion overseas; they could not risk a retaliatory maritime blockade that would cut off their source of arms. Beginning with the declaration of independence itself, Haitian governments disavowed such intentions, even if Dessalines' early proclamations did express sympathy for those still enslaved in the remaining French colonies. The annexation of Spanish

Santo Domingo, attempted by Dessalines in 1805 and achieved by President Boyer in 1822, which ended slavery in Hispaniola, strengthened fears of Haitian aggrandizement and subversion, but it was primarily motivated by the defensive concern of denying a convenient base to potential invaders.

Into the 1840s and beyond, rumors circulated regarding the activity of "Haitian agents," and these have been taken seriously by some scholars. Although Haitian governments attacked slavery vigorously in print, there is no evidence they engaged in the sort of activism that characterized the French Jacobin regime on Guadeloupe, which in the mid-1790s helped foment uprisings in neighboring British colonies. Surprisingly, perhaps, those who did most to export liberty from Saint Domingue were not the ex-slave rulers who dominated northern Haiti, but former freemen of color based in the south who had no inhibiting links with the British.

It is entirely possible, even so, that Haitian individuals ventured where Haitian governments feared to tread. The most intriguing example is perhaps the case of Luis Gigaut and the Escalera conspiracy of 1843 in Cuba. Though some historians have doubted the existence of both Gigaut and the conspiracy, in Robert Paquette's masterful reconstruction he appears as a key player, although his identity as Haitian is not clearly demonstrated.[21]

## RACE AND RACE RELATIONS

Did the Haitian Revolution help change ideas about racial difference or merely reinforce existing preconceptions? The revolution occurred at a critical juncture in European thought, when libertarian ideology and humanitarianism were gaining ground, but when the beginnings of biological science were weakening Christian teachings about the oneness of humankind and preparing the way for the so-called scientific racism of the nineteenth century. The epic struggle for Saint Domingue fed both sides of this debate. The spectacle of a people freeing itself from bondage, waging a successful war, and establishing an independent state certainly inspired many existing opponents of slavery and racial discrimination. Other commentators, however, found it easy to rationalize the successes of the Haitians, and a selective reporting of the revolution's numerous atrocities provided vivid propaganda for diatribes about civilization and barbarism. Moreover, the sharp contrast between the mortality rates suffered by white and black soldiers in the tropics, which was highlighted by the conflict, may also have encouraged people to think in terms of immutable racial differences.[22] In Hispanic America, where this epidemiological gap was narrower and where secularism made slower progress, modern racism was perhaps less widespread than among Anglo-Saxons. Some Cubans claimed this was so, but

others among its most liberal thinkers dismissed Haiti for having a "stupid
. . . impotent government of orangutans."[23]

Race relations in Latin America and the Caribbean were characterized by
two contrary developments during the half-century following the Haitian
Revolution. In the new Spanish American republics the legal caste system
of the colonial era gave way before official ideologies of racial democracy,
and institutionalized racial discrimination was ended in the British, Dutch,
Danish, and French Caribbean around 1830. In the Spanish West Indian
colonies, on the other hand, the legal situation for free blacks tended to
worsen with the introduction of harsher regulation, less frequent manumission, declining use of black militia, forced labor in Puerto Rico, and fero-
cious repression in Cuba after the Escalera conspiracy of 1843.[24]

Both positive and negative influences on these divergent trends have
been attributed to Haiti and its revolution. Its impact is thus ambiguous
and uncertain. The worsening climate for free blacks in the Spanish West
Indies, especially the growing hostility to the black militia that emerged in
the 1790s, doubtless owed something to Haitian-inspired fears, but it could
also be explained simply by the growth of the slave economy in these decades, especially as comparable developments had occurred in French and
British colonies a century earlier. Even in the Dominican Republic, where
the Haitian Revolution had its most direct impact, the revolution's influence remains unclear. Some twentieth-century Dominican historians have
accorded to massacres supposedly perpetrated by Haitian invaders in 1802
and 1805 a major role in generating the much-publicized antipathy
between the two nations of Hispaniola.[25] However, as some white Dominican revolutionaries hoped for Haitian aid in 1811, and others in 1821
chose to name their briefly independent state Haití Español—something
unimaginable for later generations—it may be that this enmity did not
develop before the Haitian annexation of 1822–1843, if not later. Indeed,
as the Dominican population was largely of African descent, there is reason
to think the Haitian occupation enjoyed widespread support at least initially.[26]

On the mainland, the Spanish Creole revolutionaries' sudden acceptance
of racial equality after 1810—in striking contrast to their hostility to the
*gracias al sacar* law of 1795—surely was informed by their reaction to events
in Haiti, even if the military and demographic circumstances they faced
provided sufficient cause for the change, and disputes over the franchise for
the Cortes of Cádiz provided the occasion.[27] As far away as Michoacán, the
local bishop cited the case of Saint Domingue and his desire to avoid a local
race war when in 1810 he advocated abolition of racially discriminatory
taxation.[28] On the other hand, the Haitian example of racial conflict and
political instability, which the Coro revolt of 1795 brought even closer to
home, perhaps more obviously inflected Simón Bolívar's private fears of

*pardocracia*, which led to his execution of his nonwhite allies and potential rivals, Píar and Padilla. In Bolívar's correspondence, Haiti frequently appeared as an example to be avoided and, at least once, as a direct threat.[29] Such fears were doubtless strengthened by the popular republicanism that developed among nonwhites in Gran Colombia, which expressed itself in rhetorical appeals to the Haitian Revolution during several local conflicts with the post-revolutionary elite.[30]

The meaning of Haiti was of course radically different for whites and blacks. At the same time that Gaspar de Betancourt was holding forth about Haitian orangutans, he also noted that Haiti was an object of pride for black Cubans. Along with news of government reforms and abolitionist activity, he thought it responsible for their "swagger."[31] Even among Cuban insurgents of the 1890s, blacks and whites differed in their tendencies to make positive or negative references to Haiti.[32] Yet opinion among blacks was not uniformly positive. Although the image of King Christophe resonated strongly in Cuba, Brazil, and elsewhere, Haiti's three periods of monarchy (1804–1806, 1811–1820, 1848–1859) could hardly inspire enthusiasm among those with republican sympathies.

Nonwhite public figures also found that the black state's example was used against them by their opponents. In 1824 the light-skinned Brazilian politician Antonio Rebouças was accused of praising the king of Haiti and stirring up hostility toward whites by saying that "any mulatto or black could become a general."[33] Cyrille Bissette and other free black activists were deported from Martinique the same year under similar circumstances. Down to the end of the century, black leaders like George William Gordon in Jamaica and Antonio Maceo in Cuba would be accused by their white enemies of seeking to emulate and being secretly in league with the black republic.[34]

Evidently some free persons, inspired by the events in Saint Domingue, were willing to turn to violent resistance, as is shown by the cases of Chirino, Pirela, Aponte, and other free blacks who organized slave rebellions. However, no such Haitian connection emerges in those cases where free coloreds conspired with whites rather than with slaves, such as the Gual and España plot in La Guaira in 1797, the Bahian Tailors' Rebellion of 1798, or Cuba's Masonic plots of 1810 and the 1820s, the principal points of reference of which were the French and mainland American revolutions.[35] As for the conspiracy of mulatto farmer Nicolás Morales that was uncovered near Bayamo, Cuba, in August 1795, we may assume that Morales was encouraged by the achievements of his counterparts in Saint Domingue. Yet the surviving sources provide no certain evidence of this, whereas they do demonstrate the critical impact of local issues (land, tax, and racial discrimination). It seems a safe counterfactual proposition that the conspiracy could well have occurred without the Haitian Revolution, but not without the *gracias al sacar* law and its local suppression.[36]

Here we confront an epistemological or methodological problem. Since it is scarcely credible that Nicolás Morales did not know of the Saint Domingue Revolution, some may feel it beyond question that the unprecedented success of black rebels in the French colony must have played a major role in motivating his resistance, and that of any protagonists in later black-white conflicts. Others may feel that historians should not put into the historical record what is not there, and that it was not simply the arbitrariness of colonial document making that has linked Aponte and Chirino but not Morales to Haiti. Similarly plausible, but lacking documentary support, is the idea that the revolution had a conservative impact not just on whites but on many free people of color, too. Since the revolution divided free blacks in Saint Domingue itself and caused the migration of several thousands, the idea is worth pondering. Moreover, as Aponte, Morales, and Pirela were each betrayed by *pardo* militiamen, and colored militia generally were involved in suppressing the rebellions of the period, there is ample reason to think that the entire nonwhite population did not respond enthusiastically to the Haitian spectacle of slave emancipation and black power.

All in all, it seems difficult to argue that the creation of Haiti had a decisive impact, either on the activities of Latin American free blacks or on the political or social climate in which they lived. Just as it proved to be a widespread—but not the most important—influence on slave resistance, so too was it a contributory factor reinforcing other influences affecting free populations of color, but not one of unique significance. Its impact, moreover, was ambiguous; it stimulated contrary tendencies. However, if this meant the revolution's impact was not clear cut, it also gave it greater intensity.

## MIGRATION AND ECONOMICS

As Saint Domingue had been the world's major producer of both sugar and coffee, the collapse of its economy shocked the world market, encouraging others to profit from the prices it sent soaring. New frontiers opened to slavery in central Brazil, eastern Cuba, and Louisiana, and long-established sugar-growing regions like northeast Brazil underwent a revival. Increasing world demand for tropical staples and the liberalization of trade laws probably meant these developments would have occurred anyway, but not so quickly. Spanish West Indian sugar exports tripled in the quarter-century ending in 1815, and blacks became the majority of the population of Cuba as the slave trade boomed.

Another way the Haitian Revolution stimulated Latin American economies was by creating a refugee diaspora. Throughout the revolution, waves of refugees and deportees left Saint Domingue and neighboring Santo Domingo, seeking temporary shelter or new homes elsewhere in the Caribbean or in North America. Intermittently, governments sought to restrict immigration from Saint Domingue and from the other French colonies, and to expel refugees, particularly if they were of African descent.[37] Nevertheless, such restrictions often were bypassed, especially when immigration promised economic rewards. Carlos Deive estimates that 4,000 Dominicans settled in Cuba, and perhaps 6,000 more in Venezuela, Colombia, and Puerto Rico. The number of French who came to Cuba from Saint Domingue has been put as high as 30,000.[38] By no means were they all of European descent. Blacks, equally divided between slaves and free men and women, formed 70 percent of the 10,000 who migrated from the French colony to Cuba and, in 1809–1810, were deported to Louisiana because of the Napoleonic invasion of Spain.[39] The proportion of nonwhites among the Spanish who left Santo Domingo for Cuba was probably similar.[40]

Men of color were also prominent among the POWs who were packed into the region's jails and prison ships. Within months of the outbreak of war in 1793, more than 900 were sent to La Guaira, Venezuela, where their "subversive shouts from inside the prison" greatly annoyed the captain-general. Thousands more were shipped in the following decade to Vera Cruz, Havana, and Puerto Rico, where they were accused of spreading "French principles."[41] Slaves from Saint Domingue who had borne arms or were just war booty or who migrated with refugees were sold in Cuba and the south Caribbean.[42] Other groups of blacks, impossible to sell, were relocated from Saint Domingue and other revolutionary hot spots to Central America, or simply abandoned on its coast or that of New Granada.[43]

This very diverse group of people affected local populations in different ways, but all made more palpable the drama of what was happening in Saint Domingue. Probably the most feared groups of migrants were the men Spain had recruited as auxiliary troops among the original slave insurgents during its failed attempt to conquer the French colony (1793–1795). In 1796, after the loss of Santo Domingo to France, the Spanish government agreed to relocate an elite group of 800 (including women and children). Fearing they would end up in his colony, Governor Las Casas of Cuba warned: "The appearance of these persons, who yesterday were miserable slaves and today are decorated heroes of a revolution, triumphant and wealthy: such are not objects to be viewed by a people composed for the most part of men of color who live beneath the oppression of a smaller number of whites." He imagined them "parading with astonishing luxury in a magnificent coach with six horses, [their] elaborate households and dining, etc., much superior to that ever seen by the public in the chief officer of this island."[44]

Though the governor succeeded in keeping the group out of Cuba, where the slave economy was booming, more than three hundred former insurgents and family members were resettled in Guatemala, more than one hundred in Campeche, and smaller groups in Panama and Florida. Most became farmers or followed the trade they had previously practiced. In Guatemala and Florida, they provided valuable service as militiamen, but everywhere they settled, they created considerable unease among whites, despite their ostentatious royalism, and great curiosity among blacks. Their pride was often singled out for criticism. The pension paid "General" Georges Biassou, one of the leaders of the 1791 slave revolt, in St. Augustine, Florida, was almost as much as the local governor's salary.[45]

The economic impact of the Saint Domingue diaspora was felt chiefly in Cuba and Jamaica through its contribution of skilled personnel to the sugar industry and especially through its expansion of coffee production on the two islands. Coffee cultivation had been almost a French monopoly until the revolution, but, stimulated by high prices and new migrants, Jamaica and Cuba would largely fill the shortfall in world production until Brazil overtook them in the 1820s. Among the owners of the new plantations that sprang up, French blacks could be found in Cuba's Oriente, where many fled after defeat by Toussaint Louverture in the War of the South (1799–1800). A few also acquired properties in western Cuba. Free blacks were more commonly artisans; one worked as a refiner on the famous Ninfa sugar estate; their womenfolk did laundry and sewing.[46] The greatest infusion of labor came from the slaves the refugees brought with them. The newcomers' harsh exploitation of slave workers attracted comment from the Spanish and perhaps also left its mark on the evolution of Cuban mores.[47]

Plantations where Domingan slaves predominated became islands of French Creole culture. The French Creole legacy in eastern Cuba extends to onomastics, religion, music, and dance, notably the carnival *tumba francesa*. However, a later influx of French migrants to the region in the 1830s, and the migration of Haitians in the early twentieth century, makes it difficult to assess precisely the Haitian Revolution's influence on regional culture.[48] Puerto Rico also received a substantial number of Francophone migrants, but fewer than 40 percent of those who arrived during the revolutionary wars came from Saint Domingue.[49]

The main American migration movement during the Haitian Revolution continued to be the Atlantic slave trade. The revolution considerably changed distribution patterns in the trade by removing the trade's major market (the destination of a third or more of incoming Africans in 1785–1790) and encouraging plantation development elsewhere, but it had little impact on the total American demand for slaves. Despite the near closure of the huge Saint Domingue market, the inflow of enslaved Africans into the Caribbean declined in the 1790s by less than 20 percent, while arrivals in Brazil greatly increased.[50] In contemplating the lure of the world market, colonists in Puerto Rico and Cuba certainly debated the wisdom of turning their islands into full-fledged plantation colonies, in view of what had happened to their powerful neighbor. In both cases, however, they concluded, in the famous words of Francisco Arango y Parreño, that "the hour of our happiness has arrived."[51] Only Spanish Louisiana tried suspending the influx of Africans, and then only briefly.[52] Only in the next decade, with the ending of the British, U.S., Dutch, and Danish slave trades, did the volume of the Atlantic slave trade appreciably decline. However, it is by no means certain that the Haitian Revolution was an influential factor in this development.

## ABOLITION, EMANCIPATION, AND DECOLONIZATION

Did the violent self-liberation of Haiti retard, or advance, the struggle to end slavery and the slave trade elsewhere? As in the debate about race, the revolution provided propaganda to both sides in the antislavery debate and had paradoxical results. During the 1790s, the uprising in Saint Domingue caused the success of abolitionism in France, yet it was a significant factor in its failure in Britain. In Cuba, it apparently assisted the thousand or so *Cobreros* in gaining ratification of their freedom in 1800,[53] but in the Cortes of Cádiz and in nineteenth-century Cuba, the dangers supposedly demonstrated by the Haitian example tended to be used as an argument for abolishing the slave trade and for not abolishing slavery. That argument seems to have helped Spanish ministers agree in 1817 to end the slave trade.[54] Yet strong financial inducement from the British government was perhaps a more influential factor, and the decision anyway had no practical effect; Spanish officials allowed the trade to continue illegally for another half-century. Furthermore, the argument that stresses fear of rebellion was clearly not an essential part of the abolitionist case, even for those like José Antonio Saco, who switched when it was convenient from predicting racial war to arguing enslaved Africans were not dangerous, but inefficient.[55]

Fear does seem to have motivated Venezuela's governor in 1804 to quietly prevent slave imports, but the regional trade had already ceased several years before, to the dismay of the planter class.[56] Whether the revolutionary congress in Caracas was similarly motivated when it definitively banned the slave trade in 1811 is unclear, but the ban was likewise an event after the fact, and like similar abolitions in the southern cone, it probably owed more to liberal ideology and the desire for British support than to fear.

Haiti's most direct contribution to ending slavery elsewhere concerns

President Pétion's assistance to Simón Bolívar when he took refuge in Haiti in 1815–1816. The payment Pétion stipulated for the arms, supplies, and soldiers he provided to Bolívar's two expeditions of 1816 was the future abolition of slavery in the liberated colonies. Creole revolutionaries in other parts of Latin America (Chile, Buenos Aires, Antioquia) had already passed emancipation laws, but they were unsuccessful or had very limited impact. Bolívar's belated adoption of abolitionism, though similarly piecemeal, was a more significant turning point. But how much did it owe to Haiti? One can argue that Bolívar's acceptance of an antislavery stance was essentially mandated by the military and political situation he confronted within Venezuela, that it was the logical development of the military manumission with which both insurgents and royalists had experimented from the beginning of the independence wars. An alternative view is that no other Venezuelan leader showed Bolívar's commitment to slave emancipation, and that, whatever the political dynamics within Venezuela, he might never have returned there without Haitian help.[57]

This question of Pétion's aid to Bolívar is also central to assessing Haiti's contribution to the process of decolonization. As Bolívar already had ships at his disposal, and the Haitian government was hardly his sole source of arms and soldiers, the episode was perhaps not indispensable to the liberation of Spanish America. On the other hand, it is difficult to see how else these two expeditions could have been launched from within the Caribbean at a time when the European colonies were hostile to the insurgents' presence.[58] Furthermore, this was not Haiti's only role in the Spanish American independence struggle. Pétion had already given modest assistance to Francisco Miranda's abortive invasion of Venezuela in 1806, and he and his successor, Boyer, helped equip other insurgent expeditions between 1816 and 1819, including that of Francisco Mina to Mexico. Numerous Haitians also took part as private individuals in the revolution in New Granada and Venezuela. They participated as seamen, shipowners, and soldiers. The printer of Venezuela's first constitution (whose first book was *The Rights of Man*) was also a Haitian citizen.[59]

On the other side of the balance sheet, it may be said that the Haitian Revolution indirectly contributed to keeping Cuba a colony through the nineteenth century in that memories of the revolution reinforced the fears of slave rebellion and racial war that deterred and divided Creole resistance. The revolution's example was also used as an excuse in Spain not to extend political liberties to the island.[60] Finally, although President Geffrard assisted the Dominican Republic win its independence from Spain in the war of 1863–1865, it was ironically the Haitian annexation of forty years earlier that extinguished the Dominicans' first brief experience of independence, as well as their far longer experience of slavery.

Saint Domingue's fifteen-year struggle for racial equality, slave emancipation, and colonial independence had a complex and multifarious impact on Latin America. Its influence was often ambiguous; its repercussions, contradictory. From Rio to Spanish New Orleans, it rapidly became an object of pride for many, though surely not all, people of color. The revolutionaries and the state they created served quite frequently as a stimulus to slave resistance, though rarely as an actual source of support. The revolution's impact on race relations was both positive and negative and thus remains elusive. Although it destroyed the main slave market in the Americas, the revolution did little to reduce the volume of the Atlantic slave trade; while liberating a half-million slaves from bondage, it simultaneously encouraged the spread and intensification of slavery elsewhere. At the same time, it both encouraged and impeded in different ways the development of antislavery discourse and of the impetus toward independence of other colonial subjects.

## NOTES

1. This chapter draws extensively on David Geggus, "The Influence of the Haitian Revolution on Blacks in Latin America and the Caribbean," in *Blacks, Coloureds and National Identity in Nineteenth-Century Latin America*, ed. Nancy Naro (London: Institute of Latin American Studies, 2003), 38–59; and David P. Geggus, ed., *The Impact of the Haitian Revolution in the Atlantic World* (Columbia: University Press of South Carolina, 2001).

2. Archivo General de Indias, Seville (hereafter AGI), Estado 5, exp. 176, Las Casas to Príncipe de la Paz, December 16, 1795; Alain Yacou, "Le Projet des révoltes serviles de l'île de Cuba dans la première moitié du XIXe siècle," *Revue du CERC* (Guadeloupe) 1 (1984): 50–51; AGI, Estado 1, exp. 80, Conde de Santa Clara to Príncipe de la Paz, November 29, 1798.

3. John Barrow, *A Voyage to Cochin China in the Years 1972 and 1973* (London: Cadell, 1806), 117–18.

4. Academia Nacional de la Historia, Caracas, Sección Civiles, Signatura A13-5159-2, report of February 24, 1801. I am indebted to Jeremy Cohen of the University of Florida for this reference.

5. Luiz Mott, "A Revolução dos negros do Haiti e o Brasil," *Mensario do Arquivo Nacional* (Rio de Janeiro) 13, no. 1 (1982): 3–10.

6. José Luciano Franco, *Ensayos históricos* (Havana, Cuba: Editorial de Ciencias Sociales, 1974), 185.

7. Julius S. Scott III, "The Common Wind: Currents of Afro-American Communication in the Era of the Haitian Revolution" (PhD diss., Duke University, 1986).

8. This section is primarily based on David Geggus, "The French and Haitian Revolutions, and Resistance to Slavery in the Americas: An Overview," *Revue française d'histoire d'outre-mer* 76 (1989): 107–24; and Geggus, "Slavery, War, and Revolution in the Greater Caribbean, 1789–1815," in *A Turbulent Time: The French*

*Revolution and the Greater Caribbean,* ed. David Barry Gaspar and David Patrick Geggus (Bloomington: Indiana University Press, 1997), 1–50.

9. Eugene Genovese, *From Rebellion to Revolution: Afro-American Slave Revolts in the Making of the Modern World* (Baton Rouge: Louisiana State University Press, 1979).

10. David Geggus, "Slave Resistance in the Spanish Caribbean in the Mid-1790s," in *A Turbulent Time,* 136, 139; Geggus, "Slavery, War, and Revolution," 8–10.

11. Stuart B. Schwartz, *Sugar Plantations in the Formation of Brazilian Society: Bahia, 1550–1835* (Cambridge: Cambridge University Press, 1985), chap. 17.

12. Geggus, "Slave Resistance in the Spanish Caribbean," 142; Gabino La Rosa Corzo, *Los Palenques del Oriente de Cuba: Resistencia y acoso* (Havana, Cuba: Editorial academia, 1991), 115–18.

13. AGI, Estado 10, exp. 12, Ramón de Castro to Príncipe de la Paz, June 15, 1796.

14. Geggus, "Slave Resistance in the Spanish Caribbean," 137.

15. For contrasting assessments, see Pedro Arcaya, *La Insurrección de los negros de la serranía de Coro* (Caracas, Venezuela: n.p., 1949); Federico Brito Figueroa, *Las Insurrecciones de los esclavos negros en la sociedad colonial venezolana* (Caracas, Venezuela: Cantaclaro, 1961); Pedro Gil Rivas, Luis Dovale Prado, and Lidia L. Bello, *La Insurrección de los negros de la serranía coriana: 10 de mayo de 1795* (Caracas, Venezuela: n.p., 1996).

16. Geggus, "Slave Resistance in the Spanish Caribbean."

17. José Luciano Franco, *La Conspiración de Aponte* (Havana, Cuba: Consejo Nacional de Cultura, 1963); Matt Childs, "'A Black French General Arrived to Conquer the Island': Images of the Haitian Revolution in Cuba's 1812 Aponte Rebellion," in Geggus, *Impact of the Haitian Revolution,* 135–56; Sybil Fischer, *Modernity Disavowed: Haiti and the Cultures of Slavery in the Age of Revolution* (Durham, NC: Duke University Press, 2004), 41–56.

18. AGI, Santo Domingo 1000, August 3, 1811, José Nuñez de Cáceres to Secretario de Estado, with enclosures; Robert Paquette, *Sugar Is Made with Blood: The Conspiracy of La Escalera and the Conflict between Empires over Slavery in Cuba* (Middletown, CT: Wesleyan University Press, 1988), 242. In late 1825, the Cuban planter intellectual Francisco de Arango expressed fear that a victorious Simón Bolívar might invade Cuba in alliance with President Boyer and 30,000 "hombres terribles": *Obras de D. Francisco de Arango y Parreño* (Havana, Cuba: Ministerio de Educación, 1952), 2:401.

19. Brito Figueroa, *Las Insurrecciones,* 79; Aline Helg, "A Fragmented Majority: Free 'of All Colors,' Indians, and Slaves in Caribbean Colombia during the Haitian Revolution," in Geggus, *Impact of the Haitian Revolution,* 159–60.

20. Paul Verna, *Petión y Bolívar: Cuarenta años de relaciones haitiano-venezolanas* (Caracas, Venezuela: n.p., 1969), 201–98.

21. Paquette, *Sugar Is Made with Blood,* 246–48, 255.

22. David P. Geggus, *Slavery, War and Revolution: The British Occupation of Saint Domingue, 1793–1798* (Oxford: Oxford University Press, 1982), 287.

23. Paquette, *Sugar Is Made with Blood,* 115, 180.

24. Paquette, *Sugar Is Made with Blood*, 119–27; Schmidt-Nowara, *Empire and Antislavery*, 41.

25. Emilio Rodríguez Demorizi, *Invasiones haitianas de 1801, 1805 y 1822* (Ciudad Trujillo, Dominican Republic: Editora del Caribe, 1955).

26. AGI, Santo Domingo 1000, August 3, 1811, José Nuñez de Cáceres to Secretario de Estado, with enclosures; David Geggus, "The Naming of Haiti," *New West Indian Guide* 71 (1997): 56; Fischer, *Modernity Disavowed*, 146–52, 181–82.

27. Jaime E. Rodríguez O., *The Independence of Spanish America* (Cambridge: Cambridge University Press, 1998), 115–16; Manuel Chust, *La Cuestión nacional americana en las Cortes de Cádiz* (Valencia, Spain: Centro Francisco Tomás y Valiente, 1999), 54–55, 71–74, 150–57, 164–67; John Lynch, *The Spanish American Revolutions, 1808–1826* (London: Weidenfeld & Nicolson, 1973), 21–22, 196, 210–12, 263, 332–33.

28. David Brading, *The First America: The Spanish Monarchy, Spanish Patriots, and Liberal State, 1492–1867* (New York: Cambridge University Press, 1991), 570–71.

29. Simón Bolívar, *Selected Writings*, ed. Harold A. Bierck (New York: Colonial Press, 1951), 140, 229, 267–68, 307–8, 499, 624.

30. Marixa Lasso, "Haiti as an Image of Popular Republicanism in Caribbean Colombia: Cartagena Province (1811–1828)," in Geggus, *Impact of the Haitian Revolution*, 176–90.

31. Paquette, *Sugar Is Made with Blood*, 179.

32. Ferrer, *Insurgent Cuba*, 134.

33. Mott, "A Revoluçao," 7–8; Lawrence C. Jennings, "Cyrille Bissette, Radical Black French Abolitionist," *French History* 9, no. 1 (1995): 48–66.

34. Ada Ferrer, *Insurgent Cuba: Race, Nation, and Revolution, 1868–1898* (Chapel Hill: University of North Carolina Press, 1999), 59–60, 94; Aline Helg, *Our Rightful Share: The Afro-Cuban Struggle for Equality, 1886–1912* (Chapel Hill: University of North Carolina Press, 1995), 48–54.

35. Pedro Grases, *La Conspiración de Gual y España y el ideario de la Independencia* (Caracas, Venezuela: Academia Nacional de la Historia, 1997); Kenneth Maxwell, *Conflicts and Conspiracies in Brazil and Portugal, 1750–1808* (Cambridge: Cambridge University Press, 1973), 218. José Luciano Franco, *Las Conspiraciones de 1810 y 1812* (Havana, Cuba: Editorial de Ciencias Sociales, 1977); Franco, *Ensayos históricos*, 23–29.

36. Geggus, "Slavery, War, and Revolution," 16; Franco, *Ensayos históricos*, 93–100.

37. A Spanish decree of May 21, 1790, banned immigration of blacks from French colonies and any other nonwhites viewed as dangerous. The next year, a treaty with the Dutch sought to close the Orinoco to fugitives. See AGI, Estado 5, Las Casas to Príncipe de la Paz, January 3, 1796; Alvin Thompson, *Some Problems of Slave Desertion in Guyana, c. 1750–1814* (Cave Hill, Barbados: University of the West Indies, 1976), 27.

38. Carlos Esteban Deive, *Las Emigraciones dominicanas a Cuba: 1795–1808* (Santo Domingo, Dominican Republic: Fundación Cultural Dominicana, 1989), 132; Jorge Domínguez, *Insurrection or Loyalty: The Breakdown of the Spanish American Empire* (Cambridge, MA: Harvard University Press, 1980), 161.

39. Paul Lachance, "Repercussions of the Haitian Revolution in Louisiana," in Geggus, *Impact of the Haitian Revolution*, 214.

40. In a sample of 683 Spanish refugees on five ships only 26 percent were white and 2 percent were *indios blancos*. AGI, Estado 5, expedientes 95, 99, 138, 187, 189.

41. Angel Sanz Tapia, *Los Militares emigrados y los prisioneros franceses en Venezuela durante la guerra contra la revolución* (Caracas, Venezuela: Instituto Panamericano, 1977), 77–80, 103n, 147, 263–64.

42. David Geggus, "The Great Powers and the Haitian Revolution," in *Tordesillas y sus consecuencias: La Política de las grandes potencias europeas respecto a América Latina (1494–1898)*, ed. Berntd Schröter and Karin Schüller (Frankfurt, Germany: Vervuert, 1995), 121, n. 43; AGI, Estado 5, Las Casas to Príncipe de la Paz, January 3, 1796.

43. Geggus, "Slavery, War, and Revolution," 26–27; Geggus, *Haitian Revolutionary Studies* (Bloomington: Indiana University Press, 2002), chap. 7; Helg, "A Fragmented Majority."

44. AGI, Estado 5, Las Casas to Príncipe de la Paz, December 16, 1795.

45. Geggus, *Haitian Revolutionary Studies*, chap. 12; Jane Landers, "Rebellion and Royalism in Spanish Florida: The French Revolution on Spain's Northern Colonial Frontier," in *A Turbulent Time*, 156–77.

46. Alain Yacou, "Esclaves et libres français à Cuba au lendemain de la Révolution de Saint-Domingue," *Jahrbuch für Geschichte von Staat, Wirtschaft und Gesellschaft Lateinamerikas* 28 (1991): 163–97; Alain Yacou, "La Présence française dans la partie occidentale de l'île Cuba au lendemain de la Révolution de Saint-Domingue," *Revue française d'histoire d'outre-mer* 84 (1987): 149–88.

47. Yacou, "Esclaves et libres français," 184; Gabriel Debien, "Les Colons de Saint-Domingue réfugiés à Cuba, 1793–1815," *Revista de Indias* 13, no. 1 (1987): 559–605 ; 13 (2): 11–36.

48. Jean Lamore, ed., *Les Français dans l'Oriente cubain* (Bordeaux, France: Maison des Pays Ibériques, 1993); Judith Bettelheim, ed., *Cuban Festivals: An Illustrated Anthology* (New York: Garland, 1993); Carlos Padrón, *Franceses en el suroriente de Cuba* (Havana, Cuba: Ediciones Union, 1997); Fernando Ortiz, *Los Negros esclavos* (Havana, Cuba: Editorial de Ciencias Sociales, 1975), 216–18.

49. María Luque de Sánchez, "Colons français réfugiés à Porto Rico," in *De la Révolution française aux révolutions créoles*, ed. Michel Martin and Alain Yacou (Paris: Editions Caribéennes, 1989), 41–48.

50. David Eltis, *Economic Growth and the Ending of the Transatlantic Slave Trade* (New York: Oxford University Press, 1987), 37–38, 243–45, 249.

51. Arango y Parreño, *Obras*, 1:134; Michael Zeuske, Clarence Munford, "Die 'Grosse Furcht' in der Karibik: Saint Domingue und Kuba (1789–1795)," *Zeitschrift für Geschichtswissenschaft* 39, no. 1 (1991): 51–59; Manuel Moreno Fraginals, *El Ingenio: Complejo económico social cubano del azúcar* (Havana, Cuba: Editorial de Ciencias Sociales, 1978), 2:108; Schmidt-Nowara, *Empire and Antislavery*, 2:40–41.

52. Paul Lachance, "The Politics of Fear: French Louisianians and the Slave Trade," *Plantation Society in the Americas* 1 (1979): 162–97.

53. José Luciano Franco, *Las Minas de Santiago del Prado y la rebelión de los Cobreros, 1530–1800* (Havana, Cuba: Editorial de Ciencias Sociales, 1975), 131,

142. The *Cobreros* were descendants of royal slaves attached to abandoned copper mines.

54. Hubert H. S. Aimes, *The History of Slavery in Cuba, 1511–1868* (New York: Octagon, 1967), 64, 73.

55. *José Antonio Saco: El Autor y su obra* (Havana, Cuba: Dirección Nacional de Educación General, 1973), 6, 35–36; Schmidt-Nowara, *Empire and Antislavery*, 8–9, 24, 31.

56. Domínguez, *Insurrection*, 99–100.

57. John Lombardi, *The Decline and Abolition of Negro Slavery in Venezuela, 1820–1854* (Westport, CT: Greenwood, 1961), 13, 41; Robin Blackburn, *The Overthrow of Colonial Slavery* (London: Verso, 1988), 340–50; Verna, *Petión y Bolívar*, 228–35, 257–59.

58. Rodríguez O., *Independence of Spanish America*, 185–87; Verna, *Petión y Bolívar*, 175–77, 257–59.

59. Verna, *Petión y Bolívar*, 92–100, 299–321; Grases, *Conspiración de Gual y España*, 67, 75.

60. Ferrer, *Insurgent Cuba*, 8, 94, 112; Schmidt-Nowara, *Empire and Antislavery*, 25.

# 2

# In Search of Liberty

## The Efforts of the Enslaved to Attain Abolition in Ecuador, 1822–1852

*Camilla Townsend*

*Independence in Latin America did not mean freedom and liberty for all who resided within the newly created national boundaries. Moreover, independence was primarily a Creole idea that promoted Creole economic and social power. The former French colony of Haiti was an anomaly in the pattern of Latin American independence, since abolition preceded the creation of a republican state there. In most of Spanish and Portuguese America, abolition was a slow, protracted process put into place after the consolidation of independence from Spain or Portugal. Creoles nonetheless employed the values of republicanism and the rhetoric of citizenship from the French Revolution to legitimize and consolidate their new governments. Enslaved Africans all over Latin America were acutely aware of these contradictions. In this chapter, Camilla Townsend highlights the ways in which enslaved Ecuadorian men and women dialogued with the language of republicanism to better their position in society and ultimately secure abolition.*

Of the six slaves who gathered on August 23, 1822, to sign their petition to the *intendente* of Guayaquil, not one needed to use a mark: Francisco Rosi, Bernardino Arboleda, José María Macsimo, José Chavarría, Simón Camba, and José Ignacio Cortazar could all write their own names.[1] "A love of liberty being natural in all creatures in us is even more vehement, in that our captivity, our painful duties and our labors are so absolute and dismal." They had had a truly wonderful idea—despite their "stolid minds," they tactfully hastened to add, "Every captive who has a trade and work will manage to save one or two *reales* daily from what he earns, with the object of contributing it to a liberty fund."[2] As soon as they had five hundred pesos, "freedom would immediately be given to one or two captives." They thought they could find five hundred slaves who would want to join the "voluntary cooperative," each of whom would promise to deliver one real daily until *all* participants were purchased from their owners. They could thus liberate two or perhaps even three of their number per week, using a lottery to determine the order of manumissions. They would not desist until every member who had signed up was free.

The slaves claimed that their contributions would cause them no hard-ship (read: debilitating hunger or illness that would decrease their produc-tivity), as the money would probably otherwise be wasted (*se hubiera disipado*), but in fact they were promising to make Herculean efforts to save so much: most urban slaves earned three or four *reales* per day, from which they had to pay for their keep if they lived on their own and turn over a share to their masters. They could not possibly have been in the habit of "wasting" one-third of their income. Clearly they were willing to go to extraordinary lengths to attain their freedom.

The first step was to use all their knowledge of the current political envi-ronment and their combined eloquence to try to secure the legalization of their cooperative. They astutely played on the sensibilities of the new patri-otic republican government: "Liberty for captives has always been a privi-leged concept; we hope it will be even more so under the just, humane and honorable government we now enjoy." So as not to appear ungrateful, they profusely thanked the young government for certain legal changes that had already been made in favor of the slaves and explained that they were impelled to ask for more due to "extremely urgent circumstances." By the latter, it turned out, they meant the ironically unpleasant side effects of the new laws. First, because of the recently enacted Law of the Free Womb, babies born to slave women henceforth would be free when they reached their eighteenth birthday, but the slaves' older children saw the contrast in their fates and cried out to their parents for help, which at this point they could not give. And second, because such legal changes seemed to suggest that abolition might follow shortly, the slaves were finding that it was impossible to change masters as they had been accustomed to doing, for, they said, "There is no one who wants to buy us."[3] In a final effort to ensure the acceptability of their proposal, the six petitioners added that they would take full responsibility for the orderly conduct and good behavior of all slaves involved in the project. By implication, of course, they could promise nothing should the slaves be denied their only hope of salvation. In a time of political turmoil and war with Spain, trouble with the slaves loomed as a particularly ominous specter.

The *intendente* first showed the document to Simón Bolívar, who was quartered just outside the city gathering an army to attempt to liberate Peru. He approved a plan "so analogous to his own sentiments" and returned it to the *intendente,* who assigned it to a commissioner to draw up specific rules and regulations.[4] In his introduction to the final posting, José Leocadio Llona defended it by borrowing several of the arguments that the petitioning slaves had used. He said (1) that slavery is barbarous and should not exist in a new republican nation, (2) that this plan guaranteed the maintenance of good order amongst a people who might well otherwise be restive, and (3) that this plan would not undermine the rights of property holders.[5] This last point was of course extremely important: it was the elites' unwillingness to compromise on this issue that prevented an earlier abolition of slavery. And although the slaves had not addressed it directly in their document, the very nature of their proposal indicates that they realized there would be no deal if the owners were not paid every peso they felt they were owed.

The slaves' remarkable petition, although unique in some ways, brings to the foreground many of the most common tactics and concerns of the various parties involved in the political struggles that finally culminated in the abolition of slavery in Ecuador in 1852. Unfortunately, the ensuing failure to implement the plan on the grand scale envisioned was also typical. Although some slaves may have contributed to a "freedom lottery," they apparently did not do so by the hundreds, as I have found no other mention of this plan in the archival record. For many slaves, it would have been impossible to come up with a spare real every day. Yet the fact that such a scheme was envisioned, and probably to some limited extent implemented, is in itself significant: it demonstrates that the enslaved were indeed active agents in seeking to end slavery—and not merely their own individual bondage, but that of all their fellows.

The current historiography on slavery and abolition certainly emphasizes activities of the enslaved on their own behalf, and this is no less true in the Andean nations than elsewhere. However, the jury is still out concerning the *effectiveness* of the slaves' efforts. Did they or did they not ultimately make a difference? Were economic shifts in fact determinant of the political decision makers' actions? Was resistance to slavery on the part of Francisco Rosi and his fellow petitioners relevant to the system's demise? Slavery, after all, was not abolished in Ecuador for another thirty years. Rebecca Scott has said in a recent debate in the *American Historical Review* that "the problem of incorporating an understanding of slave agency into a system-wide analysis remains to a large extent unresolved."[6] The Haitian Revolution of course offers a thrilling and dramatic example of a situation in which the slaves clearly were able to take matters into their own hands, but what, Scott asks, do we make of "agency that operates less epochally"?

Indeed, the very nature of a systematic and comparative approach to the study of slavery draws attention to the "bankers and traders and planters" who operated on a large scale. Yet if we resist this tendency and focus on the actions of slaves and free blacks, we run into other problems: "The term 'agency' . . . has become a bit shopworn, and holds its own methodological pitfalls in encouraging the scholar to emphasize fragments of autonomy even in situations of what we know to have been extreme constraint." What can we make of this puzzle, and where does a place like Ecuador fit?

## THE ECUADORIAN CASE

It is a truism that slavery was abolished first in those areas where it was structurally least important (New England, for example, or Chile), and retained longest where it was a crucial element of the economy (the southern United States, Brazil, and Cuba). Enslaved people were able to make more successful efforts on their own behalf in the former areas than in the latter, and white abolitionist movements were likewise proportionately stronger. Ecuador, however, resembles those many regions that fall somewhere in between, where slavery was neither integral to the economy nor easily expendable, such as in the mid-Atlantic region of the United States, Peru, Argentina, and Venezuela.

An in-depth study of the Ecuadorian case suggests that in these areas, two elements were required to be present at the same time in order for slavery to end: (1) market changes rendering the most profitable export crop one that did not need year-round attention, making plantation slavery somewhat less appealing to landowners, and (2) insistent and demanding strategizing on the part of slaves themselves—which efforts were most successful in cosmopolitan cities. The first element—structural changes that make slavery less necessary on large estates—was not in itself enough. Left to their own devices, owners would not simply sacrifice their property but rather would find some other way to profit from it, either through selling their slaves to another region, or contracting out their bondsmen's labor as paid workers in a city. Similarly, the second element—adamant resistance on the part of the slaves—was alone not enough. Owners would simply have been far more draconian in their punishments rather than partially receptive to slaves' proposals if structural changes had not pressured them to consider either selling off their human property or allowing slaves to have an urban lifestyle as artisans and day laborers.

These ideas have been demonstrated in other areas. In the mid-Atlantic region of the United States, as tobacco soils were depleted in the late eighteenth and early nineteenth centuries, and grain emerged as the dominant export crop, owners came to be more willing to allow self-purchase or to consider manumitting favored slaves in their wills. Traditionally, this fact has been interpreted as evidence that the structural changes alone favored abolition, regardless of any actions on the part of the slaves. T. Stephen Whitman, however, has recently made some remarkable discoveries: first, while the proportion of slaves decreased in the Maryland countryside, it at first increased in the city of Baltimore, where slaves were profitably employed as artisans and workers in manufactories; and secondly, owners who allowed a self-purchase were just as likely as not to immediately replace that slave by buying another. In fact, argues Whitman, owners were using the prospect of freedom after many years of hard work as a "carrot" to stabilize their workforce and had no intention of abolishing the labor form as a whole. What made it impossible for the owners to continue with this plan were the actions of the slaves themselves: the stream from the countryside to the city continued, swelling the number of slaves who interacted with the growing ranks of the already free, and increasing their discontent and legal demands faster than the masters could defuse them.[7]

A glance at the Ecuadorian situation confirms that similar events were occurring there, at least on the coast. In 1828, the New Granadan government seat at Bogotá sent a special letter to the *intendente* of Guayas, insisting that he do something about what was by all accounts a dire situation in his capital city, given the large and growing number of slaves living there apart from their masters, working for wages and setting a bad example for the others.[8] Rural slaves were drawn to this mecca and strategized how to end up there. When a master proved willing to sell, for example, husbands thought it best to buy their wives and send them to the city, where they could work to earn more money for the families.[9]

Such anecdotes were part and parcel of broader changes. In the latter part of the eighteenth century, due to the opening in trade brought about by the Bourbon reforms, the food crop and tobacco plantations of the Guayas River had turned increasingly to cacao, which was used for making the popular European beverage. This crop did not require year-round attention: it was often just as profitable for an owner to let his slaves buy themselves and then hire them to work for wages during the seasons of the year when he needed them. Between 1780 and 1820 it is estimated that several hundred slaves took advantage of this new reality.[10] Similar changes, however, did not occur everywhere in Ecuador (see table 2.1). In the highland region of Imbabura slavery remained central to the economy. There the Jesuits had established a constellation of plantations and workshops in the sixteenth century that remained viable over the long term specifically because of their variegated nature, somewhat reminiscent of the Incas' style of settling a wide array of ecological niches. If the price of sugar went down, the Jesuits could transfer labor to their other enterprises, including some tobacco farming and textile production. When Britain flooded the market with cheap cloth, the fathers still had their sugar mills. The relative stability meant that the slaves, in turn, were able to protect deep and intricate family connections over the course of generations.[11]

This statement as to where in Ecuador slavery did and did not decline should *not* lead us back to a belief that it began to die out "naturally" where it had become less profitable, without any help from the slaves. It did decline in Guayas in the wake of the cacao boom, but it did not have to. Owners could have turned their human property into profits in some new way, and indeed, they started down that road. Like slave owners elsewhere, they first considered selling their slaves to other regions: they sold them, for example, to Barbacoas (in present-day Colombia) and to the gold mines at Zaruma.[12] They also sold them in the coastal province of Manabí: while the slave population declined overall everywhere else on the coast, there it rose from a mere handful in 1780 (127) to nearly four hundred in 1831.[13] The records do not tell us what work the new Manabí slaves were engaged in, but the region was not known for its cacao, as the crop did not grow well there. It is possible in fact that the indigenous bourgeoisie in Jipijapa and Montecristi were buying up slaves, as they themselves were doing exceedingly well in this era, feeding and supplying the cacao regions and exporting their cottage-industry straw hats.[14] Mostly, however, slave owners transferred their human property to the city of Guayaquil, where the numbers of slaves in fact continued to rise until 1790 and the shipyards and incipient industries depended on them.[15] There in the city it was people like our six petitioners who made it nearly impossible for elites to assume that they could continue to rely indefinitely on a slave labor force.

## THE BATTLE OF THE ENSLAVED

The slaves' battle to win their own freedom began even before the independence era provided the apt language that we saw the petitioners use. It began as soon as there was any visible rift among the elites that the enslaved could turn to their advantage. Sherwin Bryant points out that the continental-wide expulsion of the Jesuits in 1767 would have had special reverberations in Ecuador, in that the Jesuits there had operated the largest and most successful slave plantations.[16] They were masters par excellence who had now been declared personae non gratae. Furthermore, the break-up of some of their plantations led to sales that caused painful dislocation in the slaves' lives and family networks, exacerbating the resentments of the enslaved population.

A generation later, as part of the Bourbon reforms, the Spanish Crown issued the *Real Cédula de 1789*, a set of rules regarding the actual practices of slave-holding. The new law stipulated, among other things, that owners were bound to provide religious instruction, encourage matrimony, and keep punishments within certain limits. The underlying goal was not to improve the slaves' quality of life for their own sake but rather to remove potential "fault lines" and make the system more durable. Owners were not, for example, supposed to set their slaves to work in the cities, where they would be exposed to Enlightenment ideas. "The first and principal occupation of the slaves ought to be agriculture and other labors of the countryside, and not the trades of sedentary [urban] life."[17] One historian has aptly and sarcastically called the *cédula* an "owners' manual" issued by the state.[18] Still, there is no doubt that it led to a discursive opening that worked to the slaves' benefit: "The reformist normative diminished the power that the slaveowner exercised, and increased slightly that of the representatives of the state whose task it was to oversee the behavior of the owner and protect the slave."[19]

Planter aristocrats felt so threatened at having their power eroded before the eyes of their slaves that they protested until the law was revoked. Public discussion of the law had already done damage, however. Through their white advocates, slaves became familiar with the legal debate, and in the later part of the eighteenth century, they sued their masters in record numbers. Occasionally they demanded freedom that had been promised them, or that was due them because their owners had broken the law in some way. María Chiquinquirá Díaz, for instance, pursued her case in the Guayaquil court system through to an appeal in Quito, basing her claim on the fact that her mother, as a leper, had been abandoned by her owner even before she was born.[20] Usually they sued to improve the conditions of their lives within the confines of slavery—demanding that certain behaviors cease, that their purchase price be lowered, and the like. More and more often, they demanded the right to be sold to a new master—one who would treat them better or allow them to hire themselves out or reunite them with other family members. Bernard Levallé has pointed out that almost no slaves demanded a different master in the middle of the eighteenth century, but they did so increasingly in the period under discussion, until, in the decade between 1801 and 1810, there were thirty such cases in the city of Quito alone. By then, one-third of all slavery-related lawsuits were actually between current and former masters disputing the physical conditions and personality types of slaves they had been induced to buy or sell, usually with the slaves happily keeping certain secrets.[21]

The real discursive opening for the enslaved came with the wars for independence.[22] The era was indeed a heady one for all involved, white and black. At first many of the young Creoles who had been exposed to Enlight-

enment thinking preferred to participate in reforming the Spanish government rather than break away from it: they were often more liberal than the
majority of their peers and had their most exciting conversations in Europe.
In 1809, the *quiteño* Antonio de Villavicencio, then living in Spain, made
an impassioned plea to the Cortes of Cádiz for the abolition of slavery. The
*guayaquileño* poet José Joaquín Olmedo was later elected to the Cortes, and
he eventually showed himself to be committed to the cause of abolition.[23]
After he returned home in 1816, Olmedo ceased to believe that the best
course was to work with liberals in Spain; instead he espoused the patriot
cause and became a leader in the *independentista* movement. In 1820, the
governing assembly of the province of Guayas declared their home a sovereign city-state, and it remained so until pressured to join Gran Colombia
in 1822, when Bolívar arrived at the head of his army. In the current political climate, a popular language of "liberty" reigned, and there arose among
enthusiastic white patriots like Olmedo a certain discomfort with slavery.
Did people fighting tyranny have the right to tyrannize others? In the same
year that the six petitioners presented their idea, the *procurador* general was
pleased to remind his listeners that it was the defeated Spaniards who had
introduced slavery into the New World. He spoke of "the unhappy people
whose liberty was so barbarously snatched away by the Spaniards."[24] As
part of a ruling triumvirate, Olmedo helped to push through two measures
regarding slavery, one outlawing participation in the international slave
trade, and the other declaring that all children born to slaves henceforth
would be free themselves, although they would live with their masters until
the age of eighteen. These laws, in fact, were what the six petitioners referred
to in their statement of August 1822.

At that moment, Guayaquil was in the process of being annexed to the
state of Quito, in the nation of Gran Colombia. In Gran Colombia the
recently enacted laws concerning slavery that had passed in 1821 were similar to those of Guayaquil, except that they also provided for the foundation
of local *fondos de manumisión*, based on a small tax on inheritance. During
the period of political uncertainty, almost no slaves were bought or sold in
Guayas, but there now occurred a flurry of sales by some owners who
"feared that the Decree of Liberty was shortly to be announced" (*temiendo
los titulados amos que en breve se pronuncie el Decreto de la Libertad*) to others
who were reassured by the idea of joining Colombia and were convinced
slavery was there to stay.[25]

It would be a major error to assume that the Enlightenment and independence movement automatically brought abolition with them in their wake
if the structural conditions were right. Despite the lofty ideals of men like
Olmedo, most wealthy *costeños* resisted abolition with a stunningly unem-
barrassed tenacity. One woman publicly complained that the local priests

and a slave mother claimed the latter's baby daughter should be free, though she was born before the publication of the Law of the Free Womb. She spoke as if the child had been born to her. "A little slave girl having been born to me on the 16th of the present month, before the pronouncement of the decree . . . the sacristans are claiming the right to list her in the baptismal record as free, when only because of a coincidence in the family was there a delay [in the ceremony], and she could have been baptized four days earlier." Olmedo responded that the little girl should be considered free, but he ordered that the treasury pay the owner fifty pesos to sweeten his decision.[26] Slave trader José Maruri arrived in port several months after the law banning the trade had taken effect. He found it easy to skirt: he claimed that he had been ignorant of the law when he sold the first part of his cargo, and so the sales already made were allowed to stand, provided he took the rest of his cargo and left quickly—that is, within thirty days.[27] The law requiring that an inheritance tax be used to create a manumission fund was so thoroughly ignored in various locales that Bolívar reissued the edict later in the decade. After Ecuador declared independence from Gran Colombia in 1830, the Quito legislature, even when under the leadership of the liberal *guayaquileño* Vicente Rocafuerte, regularly chiseled away at the law, reducing the taxes designed to replenish the fund and obfuscating the language clarifying how manumission of real individuals would actually come about. "We can say," wrote Julio Tobar Donoso, "that the country's first administrations, those of General Flores and don Vicente Rocafuerte, were not propitious for the manumission of the slaves."[28]

One can only assume that the majority of the Ecuadorian lawmakers would have been delighted to do away with the manumission fund imposed on them by liberal Colombians if they could have: but by now the slaves knew of the law and relied on it. There would have been vehement and perhaps dangerous protests had it been absolutely annulled. The masters were certainly concerned about the slaves' attitude. In 1823, when a white man named Francisco Cora was accused of having said, "Shit on the patria" (*que se caga en la Patria*), and that "it was better under the king" (*mejor era el Gobierno del Rey*), his action was considered doubly criminal because he spoke his words in front of slaves making weekly self-purchase payments at the Casa del Gobierno.[29] Even more threatening, in 1831— after the famous Nat Turner rebellion in the United States—someone denounced the free blacks Francisco Paredes and Bernardo Villamar for having uttered "subversive words against the white class" (*palabras subversives contra la clase de blancos*) at a baptism party.[30] The planters and their colleagues in the legislature clearly understood that backsliding laws would have to be subtle.

It seems clear that had the enslaved not made their voices heard, thus alerting their owners to their potential rage, little change would have come about in the years following independence. In the cities the slaves were not willing to simply wait and see what would happen. There was even enough of a critical mass in Quito to allow for some legal protests, but it was in the port city of Guayaquil, situated in the midst of cacao country, that the demands were transformed from a trickle to a flood.[31]

Some of the enslaved protested their condition by fleeing. Indeed, the frequency of flight in this period became a major preoccupation on the part of owners. Those who sold their slaves now often insisted that they be absolved of all responsibility not only if the slave died, but also if he or she should run away. And potential purchasers did not hesitate to ask about a slave's background in this regard. One ad read: "Needed: A robust slave without vices about fourteen years who has never fled from his owners."[32] Sometimes urban slaves absented themselves in order to stay with friends elsewhere in the city, or "to traffic freely in the street," in the words of one furious owner, but in such a small world they were usually found straight away.[33] Slaves from the countryside had greater success in hiding in the city, where few people knew them. One free woman of color was punished with a fine of four pesos for having hidden just such a runaway.[34] Though some slaves did find freedom in this way, it was a dangerous path. They were usually indefatigably hunted down. In 1834, *El Colombiano* began to publish the names of apprehended slaves, at least two per month. Owners had long memories. On one occasion, a planter mentioned that he had just seen a peon and a slave of his who had run off twelve years earlier. We probably will never know if he succeeded in capturing them or not, but it was clearly his agenda to do so.

Given the impermanence of any freedom gained through flight, the enslaved preferred to use legal methods to release themselves from bondage. And in the independence era, there were several such paths accessible to them. Supposedly each region had its own manumission committee (*junta*), which met at least once per year to determine which slaves were to be freed by means of the funds in the manumission bank. In Guayaquil, the bank's resources supposedly included an inheritance tax, as well as weekly contributions from slaves themselves. However, it seems that the first source of revenue existed only in theory and not in practice, as there is no evidence that it was ever really collected regularly. And even the weekly contributions made by slaves at the government office at the Plaza de San Francisco often went astray and were lost or simply were used up before all hopeful contributors could be aided. "I have contributed half my value," raged Petra Iler, "and after all that I have attained nothing as I hear that the bank is destitute."[35]

In January of 1826, after many such complaints, the government addressed the problem of administering the funds. From Bogotá came a letter to the *intendente* about the "abuses" related to the inheritance tax that was supposed to be collected for the bank of manumission.[36] After that date, an effort was made to collect the taxes, but in 1830, the great majority of the files still read "pending" rather than "paid."[37] In 1827 there appeared in the newspapers, by order of the Liberator Simón Bolívar, an announcement of the refoundation of the bank under a new name—the Bank of Amortization. The slaves could still visit the *Casa de Gobierno* on the plaza to pay a minimum of one peso per week toward their own self-purchase. A committee of five men of the master class named by the governor had the responsibility of choosing which of the slaves would be freed first and would make their selections using as their criteria who had contributed most, who had fought for the Patria, and who had the best recommendations.[38]

No one, however, could be selected if the committee never met, which they tried to avoid doing. Thus did the local elites circumvent the new rules in a masterstroke of passive aggression. After hearing complaints from slaves, the abolitionist Francisco de Icaza wrote to the governor, begging him to appoint substitutes to the *junta* who were actually present in the city and would be able to hold a meeting.[39]

Despite all obstacles, however, the enslaved continued to take advantage of the new law with great determination. Every Christmas, just before the meeting of the committee, numerous petitions would arrive, some very eloquent. Many of the authors already considered themselves no longer to be slaves. "I, slave that was," they would begin (*yo, esclavo que fui*). Others described themselves simultaneously as slaves and citizens: "I, Petra Iler, *vecina* of this city and *esclava* of my mistress Francisca Ayala. . . ."[40]

The majority of the men who presented petitions had fought in the patriot army. In 1825, Alejandro Campusano still remembered the day he left his master's house: "There came to my ears the sweet voice of the patria, and desiring to be one of her soldiers both to shake the yoke of the general oppression as well as to free myself from slavery, I quickly ran to present myself to the liberating army."[41] Some of the petitioners, like Campusano, had to fight hard against their former owners; others were actually able to get a recommendation for liberty from those who had once claimed the right to dominate them.[42] Theoretically it did not matter how a former owner felt about the situation if the petitioner could prove he had been in the army, but in some cases the owners did everything possible to convince the judges that their former slaves had only joined for a very short time or that they had not fought with true dedication, or even that they had been too young to fight with any effectiveness. The widow of General Juan Paz de Castillo, for example, argued that the slave who had followed her husband into battle could never have wielded weapons, that he was still too young "even to serve as a drummer boy."

Still, others besides Alejandro Campusano were able to defeat obstinate owners. Pedro Franco, another former soldier, moved between adept manipulation of his audience's concerns and heartrending expressions of his belief in a freer world. He began with the very practical reminder that the country was still dependent on men like himself. "The claims of the owners do not seem right to me, because I am free, and ready to take up arms [again] as a faithful Colombian soldier." Then he put in a plea for liberalism and the rights of man. He did not simply say that he desperately wanted to be free. He said, "Sir, I have committed no crime other than not wanting to be a slave again, and for this reason they have me a prisoner in this jail."[43] In this new republican world it was not supposed to be a crime, an offense punishable with imprisonment, for a man to want to be free. This was what the elites had themselves argued in defending their own honor not so long ago. If these words had been radical coming out their mouths, they were the more so from Pedro Franco's.

Each of the successful petitioners linked his own cause with the cause of the liberal patriots in their ongoing struggles with closet royalists, hoping in this way to gain supporters. Alejandro Campusano wrote of his would-be master: "He was crazy enough to say to me that the Patria does not have the authority to command regarding the issue of slaves," underlining the last phrase noticeably. Would the republican government allow such a challenge to its authority to stand? Pedro Franco went further and actually accused his pretended master of treason to the new republic, so that the latter was forced to gather several statements from prominent citizens attesting to his good name.

Women could not base their claims on armed service but instead scrimped and saved their money, negotiating constantly with the bank and their owners. In 1825, for example, Estefana García, who clearly must have had some extraordinarily marketable skill, patiently explained that she had managed to pay the bank three pesos a week for almost a year, one for herself, and two for her two children. When she had saved a total of one hundred pesos, her owner said she could have her freedom *if* the bank would award her the two hundred remaining pesos of her three hundred-peso asking price. The bank proposed that she continue paying the owner weekly instead, but the mistress said that in that case she would prefer to retain García. García took the case to court, and a compromise was reached that she would continue paying weekly until the following Christmas, at which point the bank would give her owner her remaining value in the desired lump sum. Valued slaves could refuse to perform desperately needed services if their owners would not lower their asking price: one woman consented to act as a wet nurse for her owner's friend's child if and only if he would lower her purchase price, and he quickly agreed.[44] In 1822 and 1823, a majority of the cases in the *corte de conciliaciones* were between masters and slave women over a just sale price. Generally, the owner and the slave signed a *papel de venta*, and according to its terms, the slave would then leave the owner's house to work and support herself, paying an agreed-upon sum to the owner every week.[45]

Many slave women, however, were not in a position to save any money and could not even argue with the bank. Instead, they sued for their freedom without any reference to the bank, using an array of linguistic and political strategies. Their local urban culture indeed offered them a litigious tradition with which they were quite familiar. We saw that even before the independence period, in the opening provided by the *Cedula* of 1789, some had begun to sue for their freedom rather than merely ameliorate their living conditions. The post-independence period, however, provided a wealth of new material and tactics to the politically conscious slaves, which they did not hesitate to use.

Angela Batallas presented an illustrative case in 1823. She claimed that her master had convinced her to enter into a sexual relationship with him by promising that he would free her. At least one other woman had in the past unsuccessfully sued on the basis of a similar broken promise.[46] In this case, however, the master who made the promise, Ildefonso Coronel, had been a leader in the patriot cause and was now working actively to promote the new government. She declared that a man who had declared himself free of colonial shackles could not become physically one with a person who was not free:

> The union of two people of opposite sex renders them one, for from this act regularly results issue: *et erum duo in carne una*. And is it possible to believe, using good judgment, that Ildefonso Coronel, when he proposed such a union to me, wanted half his body to be free, the other half enslaved, subject to servitude, sale and other hatefulness, which some disgraced people cling to as relics of the feudal system that has enveloped us for nearly three centuries?[47]

The united bodies of the one couple in some ways symbolized the body politic: for the whole to be free, all its parts would have to be liberated. Angela Batallas and her attorney went on to say very specifically that a government promoting itself as republican, and demanding popular loyalty on those grounds, was going to have to side with liberty in order to retain its internal logic and widespread support. One might wonder what proportion of these visible strategies were really those of an uneducated slave, and what proportion were those of a white lawyer with abolitionist sympathies. A close textual analysis of the entire case, however, provides convincing evidence that the ideas were first articulated by Batallas in her depositions, although in less elegant form. Furthermore, Batallas herself later decided to visit the Liberator in his military barracks, where she enlisted his political support.[48]

## THE LAST ACT

Enslaved people continued to bring cases embedded in the notion of independence through the 1820s and 1830s. By the 1840s, however, rupture with Spain and the breaking of shackles were no longer dominant metaphors in their cultural milieu. After years of strain between two political factions, a compromise had been reached in 1835: the presidency would alternate between the more liberal *costeños* and the more conservative highlanders. The concept of accord thus became the notion of the day. In 1843, however, while serving his second term, the Venezuelan-born Juan José Flores, who had married into the *quiteño* elite, attempted to make changes that would ensure his reelection. A constitution called by liberals "the Charter of Slavery" spelled out his ideas, and resistance to it grew not only in Guayaquil but also in Quito. Most of the political agitation was on the part of educated elites, but there was strong popular protest against a new head tax that was included in the Floreanista package. It may also have been relevant that an insidious law of 1843 that reaffirmed that the importation of new slaves was illegal nonetheless added a proviso that exceptions could be made when absolutely necessary. Additionally, although children were of course born free, they now needed to serve their parents' masters until the age of twenty-five rather than eighteen. In March of 1845, *guayaquileño* elites, including Olmedo, managed to gather an army to lead against Flores's forces at Babahoyo. Their army was made up of many men who either were former slaves themselves or were related to slaves and former slaves. In May, the largely black coastal city of Esmeraldas joined the revolt, and even the conservatives who had assumed they held the reins of power securely began to fear "bloodshed and destruction of property."[49]

The March Revolution drove Flores from office and ushered in major political change. Still, many of the coastal liberals were themselves slaveholders, and abolition was not immediate. Article 108 of the new constitution first reaffirmed the original republican laws of the early 1820s regarding human bondage: "Nobody is born a slave in the Republic, nor can anybody be brought into her in such a condition without becoming free."[50] The age at which children born to slaves could leave the service of their parents' masters was returned to eighteen from the twenty-five years declared in the 1843 law. The manumission committees were reactivated in many locales: in 1846, the new government counted 3,452 slaves in the country, and they had reduced that number to 2,484 by 1852.[51]

Most importantly, there occurred a marked shift in debate over the final abolition of slavery: in the context of the recent, even decisive, victory of the liberals, and the apparent support of the popular classes, not one of the legislative representatives argued that slavery should be retained. Instead, the debated issue was whether owners had to be fully recompensed before all slaves were freed, whether the concept of property itself would be threatened if they were not. In response to a speech by President Urvina, Assembly members expressed their hope that his "philanthropic desires would be realized, so that slavery would disappear from the nation, but without losing sight of the sacred respect for private property, so that it would not be violated."[52]

The elites were apparently relatively evenly divided on this question as to whether it was more useless to retain slavery (waging an uphill battle against unwilling workers) or more dangerous to free them without recompense to the owners (sending a message that coerced labor had been inherently wrong). The assemblyman from Guayaquil, another member of the Icaza family, made impassioned speeches against slavery. Finally, on September 27, 1852, the Assembly voted nineteen to seventeen to abolish all slavery in the land as of March 6, 1854 (in honor of the March Revolution), whether or not all owners had been paid. In the meantime, as a compromise, they increased the tax revenues available for repayment. It was perhaps not unrelated that the very next day, the Jesuits, who had been readmitted to the country since independence, were reexpelled. They had been, after all, the largest slaveholders in the nation. Interestingly, it was their expulsion, rather than abolition, that aroused most comment in the nation's newspapers that week.[53] Whether the papers' editors were unsurprised by abolition, having known it must come soon, or whether they were deeply shaken by it and preferred not to discuss such matters in public is difficult to determine. Both may well have been true at once. The pressure the elites had felt from the slaves themselves might well have led to both reactions.

That matters had been tense for some time is evidenced not only by the hundreds of slaves who had sought manumission since 1846, but also by an event that took place in July of 1852, only two months before the final vote was taken in the Assembly and while debates were still occurring. An enslaved man who apparently found his relationship with his master more and more unbearable as events dragged out obtained a gun and killed his owner in public, in front of at least one other wealthy gentleman. The master had been a direct descendant of the conquistador Belalcázar. The slave attempted to win clemency by claiming that he was a patriot, and that his master had been plotting to aid the exiled General Flores, who was planning to invade the nation (as indeed he was). The white judges chose not to believe him. "This invention," fumed the future president García Moreno, "worthy of a Negro, shows you the state of immorality into which the populace [*populacho*] has fallen with democratic clubs and societies offering them socialistic chimeras."[54]

Structural changes had cleared the way for at least some Ecuadorian elites—primarily those on the coast—to consider altering their relationship with labor. There is no evidence, however, to indicate that they would have been disposed to abolish slavery absolutely rather than simply using the workers in new ways if the slaves themselves had not suggested it repeatedly—by suing and buying themselves in droves and hence reducing their own numbers, by becoming involved in national politics in times of upheaval, and even by speaking out directly against slavery as did our six petitioners. They made it impossible for the master class to assume that things could continue as they were. That slavery did not end for another thirty years after Francisco Rosi and his cohort made their statement does not mean that words like theirs were lost. A thirty-year struggle to end a three hundred-year-old institution does not in fact seem so terribly long.

If the slaves in some regions were louder and more active in their protests than the slaves in other areas, the Ecuadorian case suggests that we look for an explanation in the presence or absence of a city drawing them together as well as a shifting countryside. Actions taken against slavery on the part of the enslaved began to increase in Guayaquil after 1790, the year during which their numbers peaked, as their owners transferred them from the countryside to the urban shipyards and artisan shops. They learned from each other; they learned from white sympathizers; they learned from sailors in the port. They were ready when the rhetoric of "liberty" began to pervade the air in the independence era. In Imbabura, on the other hand, a stable constellation of varied plantations continued to rely on slave labor, and when slaves did on occasion move to a nearby city, there were others to choose from besides Quito. Thus the highland slaves had fewer chances to develop their own intellectual world. Although there were suits for freedom in Quito, their numbers and frequency never matched those in Guayaquil. Nor did the number of manumissions. Between the 1790s and the 1840s, the slave population of Guayas was reduced from approximately 2,000 to approximately 700; of these, the 1,250 who had lived in Guayaquil declined to about 380. In the highlands, on the other hand, the 2,800 slaves of 1780 had held their number nearly constant with the 2,400 counted in the 1840s; of these, about 1,200 had lived and continued to live on the Jesuit lands.[55] Historians have shown that these same slaves were active in creating and re-creating family ties and cultural identities; they were by no means passive. They did not, however, have the same opportunities to develop strategies as did those living with freed slaves and others of diverse backgrounds in a cosmopolitan port city. In Guayaquil, they worked tirelessly—in the words of our six petitioners—to "extinguish the indecency of slavery quickly and directly."[56]

**Table 2.1.   Slave Population in Ecuador**

| Departments | C.1780 | C.1845 |
|---|---|---|
| Guayas | 1,980 | 696 |
| *Guayaquil only* | 1,251 | 378[a] |
| Manabí | 127 | 195[b] |
| Imbabura | 1,203 | 1,186 |
| Northern Sierra | 1,099 | 730 |
| *Quito only* | 550 | 683 |
| Cuenca | 254 | 92 |
| Loja | 312 | 553[c] |
| Total | 4,975 | 3,452 |

*Sources:* Archivo Nacional de Historia (Quito), Empadronamientos, Padrones de 1779 y 1780. Archivo de la Biblioteca Municipal de Guayaquil, Diversos Funcionarios, "Censos Generales de las Poblaciones de 1840." Cited in Michael Hamerly, *Historia social y económica de la antigua provincia de Guayaquil, 1763–1842* (Guayaquil, Ecuador: Archivo Histórico del Guayas, 1987) and Kenneth J. Andrien, *The Kingdom of Quito, 1690–1830: The State and Regional Development* (Cambridge: Cambridge University Press, 1995); Memoria del Ministerio del Gobierno de 1846. Cited in Julio Tobar Donoso, "La Abolición de la esclavitud en el Ecuador," *Boletín de la Academia Nacional de Historia* 34 (1959): 5–30.

[a] The number of slaves in Guayaquil peaked in 1790 at 1,345. The count for 1845 is missing. The estimate of 378 was obtained by taking the total count for the province of Guayas and subtracting the number of slaves recorded in the *censos jenerales de cantones* recorded for the entire province, except the city, in 1840.
[b] The Loja region included several mines, which explains the increase.
[c] The number of slaves in Manabí peaked in 1831 at 373.

# NOTES

1. "Expediente sobre establecimiento de un sistema mutalista o cooperativo voluntario entre los esclavos para su liberación con la intervención de una Junta de Manumisión, 23.XIII.1822," printed in *Revista del Archivo Histórico del Guayas* 5 (1974): 115–16.

2. "Todo cautivo de oficio y de trabajo procurará economizar uno o dos *reales* diarios de lo que gana con el objeto de contribuirlo a la Caja fondo de su libertad."

3. The six only referred to and did not explain the misery of their older children and the shortage of willing purchasers, but the legal changes of 1822 surely explain their comments.

4. Oruna Lara, "La Place de Simon Bolivar dans le procès de destruction du système esclavagiste aux Caraïbes," *Cahiers des Amériques latines* 29–30 (1984): 213–40.

5. "Expediente sobre establecimiento," 122.

6. Rebecca Scott, "Small-Scale Dynamics of Large-Scale Processes," *American Historical Review* 105, no. 2 (2000): 473–74.

7. T. Stephen Whitman, *The Price of Freedom: Slavery and Manumission in Baltimore and Early National Maryland* (Lexington: University Press of Kentucky, 1997), especially chap. 4.

8. Archivo de la Biblioteca Municipal de Guayaquil (henceforth BMG), vol. 77, "Ministerios y secretarías" (1828).

9. Archivo Histórico del Guayas, Sección Escribano Público (henceforth AHG),

doc. 784, "Procurador general en defensa de Josef Hurtado, etc. contra Francisco Granja" (1823).

10. Nick D. Mills, "Economía y sociedad en el periodo de la independencia (1780–1845): Retrato de un país atomizado," in *Nueva historia del Ecuador*, ed. Enrique Ayala (Quito, Ecuador: Grijalbo, 1983), 6:155–56; Michael Hamerly, *Históira social y económica de la Antigua provincia de Guayaquil, 1763–1842* (Guayaquil, Ecuador: Archivo Histórico del Guayas, 1987), 102–3. For an overview of the economic situation, see Kenneth A. Andrien, *The Kingdom of Quito, 1690–1830: The State and Regional Development* (New York: Cambridge University Press, 1995), or Maria Luisa Laviana Cuetos, *Guayaquil en el siglo XVIII: Recursos naturales y desarrollo económico* (Seville, Spain: Escuela de Estudios Hispano-Americanos, 1987).

11. Sherwin Bryant, "Slavery and Slave Life in the Kingdom of Quito, 1600–1800" (MA thesis, Ohio State University, 2000). On other aspects of the Jesuits' endeavors, see Nicholas Cushner, *Farm and Factory: The Jesuits and the Development of Agrarian Capitalism in Colonial Quito, 1600–1767* (Albany: State University of New York, 1982).

12. Bernard Levallé, " 'Aquella ignominiosa herida que se hizo la humanidad': El Cuestionamiento de la esclavitud en Quito a finales de la época colonial," *Procesos: Revista ecuatoriana de historia* 6 (1994), 42–44.

13. Hamerly, *Históira social*, 92; Carmen Duenas de Anhalzer, *Soberanía e insurrección en Manabí* (Quito, Ecuador: Abya-Yala, 1991), 87.

14. Maritza Aráuz, *Pueblos de Indios en la Costa Ecuatoriana: Jipijapa y Montecristi en la Segunda mitad del siglo XVIII* (Guayaquil, Ecuador: AHG, 1999).

15. Hamerly, *Históira social*, 92; Camilla Townsend, *Tales of Two Cities: Race and Economic Culture in Early Republican North and South America* (Austin: University of Texas, 2000), 95–98. On the importance of black workers in the shipyards, see Lawrence Clayton, *Caulkers and Carpenters in a New World: The Shipyards of Colonial Guayaquil* (Athens: Ohio University, Center for International Studies, 1980).

16. Bryant, "Slavery and Slave Life," 68.

17. "La Primera y principal ocupacion de los esclavos debe ser la agricultura y demas labores del campo, y no los oficios de vida sedentaria." Instrucción de 1789, "Ocupación de los esclavos."

18. Bryant, "Slavery and Slave Life," 40.

19. Chaves, *María Chiquinquirá*, 116.

20. Chaves, *María Chiquinquirá*, 116. María Chinquinquirá won her case.

21. Levallé, "Aquella ignominiosa herida," 26, 36. See also Bryant, "Slavery and Slave Life," and older pieces by David Chandler, such as "Slave over Master in Colonial Colombia and Ecuador," *Americas* 38, no. 3 (1982): 315–26, and Juan Villegas, *Negros y mulatos esclavos: Audiencia de Quito* (Montevideo, Uruguay: Centro de Estudios de História Americana, 1992). The evidence from the *guayaquileño* archives mirrors that of Quito in this regard.

22. Sherwin Bryant reminds us that it is a mistake, however, to assume the radicalism on the part of the enslaved appeared in this period for the first time. "Enslaved Rebels, Fugitives and Litigants: The Resistance Continuum in Colonial Quito," *Colonial Latin American Review* 13, no. 1 (2004): 7–46. On this subject, see also Kris Lane, *Quito, 1599: City and Colony in Transition* (Albuquerque: University

of New Mexico Press, 2002), and, for Mexico, Herman Bennett, *Africans in Colonial Mexico: Absolutisim, Christianity, and Afro-Creole Consciousness* (Bloomington: Indiana University Press, 2003).

23. Julio Tobar Donoso, "La Abolición de la esclavitud en el Ecuador," *Boletín nacional de historia* (Quito) 39 (1959): 11; Margarita Gonzalez. *Ensayos de historia colonial colombiana* (Bogotá, Colombia: El Ancora Editores, 1984); Julio Estrada Ycaza, *La Lucha de Guayaquil por el estado de Quito* (Guayaquil, Ecuador: Archivo Histórico del Guayas, 1984).

24. "Los Infelices de dicha clase [de esclavos] cuya libertad fue arrebatada tan barbaramente por los Españoles." AHG, doc. 1546, "Causas varias" (1822), 11. The legal documents of the 1820s are replete with hundreds of examples of such language.

25. "Los Infelices," 11.

26. *El Patriota de Guayaquil*, May 4, 1822.

27. AHG, doc. 985, "Sobre la introducción de esclavos en Guayaquil" (1821). See also Mariano Fazio Fernandez, *Ideología de la emancipación guayaquileña* (Guayaquil, Ecuador: Banco Central del Ecuador, 1987), 105–15.

28. Tobar Donoso, "La Abolicion de la esclavitud," 17–18.

29. AHG, doc. 609, "El Ciudadano Francisco Cora sobre falso calumniante" (1823).

30. BMG, vol. 104, "Causas criminales" (1831).

31. The "Esclavos" Record Group of the Archivo Nacional de Historia in Quito has been examined by several historians previously cited (Bryant, Chandler, Chaves, Levallé, and Villegas).

32. AHG, doc. 3477, "Fernando Pareja contra José Pío Rodriguez" (1830); *El Patriota de Guayaquil*, February 1, 1832.

33. Some examples are in the AHG, docs. 894, "Sra. Juana Avellana contra del Dr. José Mascote" (1827) and 1546, "Causas varias" (1822).

34. *El Colombiano del Guayas*, January 7, 1830.

35. AHG, doc. 6145, "Petra Iler, sobre 50 pesos" (1824).

36. BMG, vol. 61, "Gobernaciones" (1826).

37. BMG, vol. 71, "Diversos funcionarios" (1827).

38. *El Patriota de Guayaquil*, January 6, 1827.

39. BMG, vol. 71 (1827); Townsend, *Tales of Two Cities*, 77.

40. AHG, doc. 672, "El Señor procurador municipal en defensa de un esclavo sobre se le declare libre de esclavitud" (1831).

41. AHG, doc. 5996, "El Procurador municipal en defensa de Alexandro Campusano" (1826).

42. AHG, doc. 6196, "El Procurador municipal en defensa de Diego Pinedo" (1826).

43. AHG, doc. 501, "Sr. José Santa Coloma reclama la entrega de su esclavo" (1830).

44. AHG, doc. 769, "Testamentarios" (1823).

45. David Chandler found that just before independence in the city of Quito, the royal courts were most likely to split the difference between the price the slave demanded and that desired by the owner. It was not then, however, assumed that

the slave would want to leave the owner's home while earning the money. See Chandler, "Slave over Master," 320–21.

46. Levallé, "Aquella ignominiosa herida," 33.

47. AHG, doc. 698, "Angela Batallas contra su amo" (1822).

48. Camilla Townsend, "'Half My Body Free, the Other Half Enslaved': The Politics of the Slaves of Guayaquil at the End of the Colonial Era," *Colonial Latin American Review* 7, no. 1 (1998): 105–28.

49. Frank M. Spindler, *Nineteenth Century Ecuador* (Fairfax, VA: George Mason University Press, 1987), 37.

50. "Nadie nace esclavo en la República, ni puede ser introducido en ella en tal condición sin quedar libre."

51. Informes del Ministro de Gobierno, 1846 and 1853. Tobar Donoso suggests that some of these counts may have been inflated: he suspects some hacendados of listing as "slaves" men and women who were already manumitted, in hopes of being recompensed by the government. "La Abolición de la esclavitud," 15.

52. Cited in Tobar Donoso, "La Abolición de la esclavitud," 21.

53. Tobar Donoso, "La Abolición de la esclavitud," 24.

54. Cited in Wilfrido [sic] Loor, *Cartas de Gabriel García Moreno* (Quito, Ecuador: La Prensa Católica, 1935), 1:252.

55. See appendix.

56. *Extinguir muy breve y facilmente la indecorosa esclavitud*, in "Expediente sobre establecimiento," 115.

# 3

# Integral Outsiders

## Afro-Argentines in the Era of Juan Manuel de Rosas and Beyond

*Ricardo D. Salvatore*

*Born to a Creole family of Argentine landowners and political officials, Juan Manuel de Rosas (1829–1852) became a protypical Latin American caudillo, or military strongman, interested in consolidating and establishing political and social order during the region's turbulent transition from colonies to independent nations. Race played a critical role in the creation of the new nations. Caudillos such as Simón Bolívar in Venezuela, José Gaspar Rodríguez de Francia in Paraguay, and Rosas in Argentina often relied on the popular classes for military and political support. Rosas utilized and identified with gauchos, or Argentine cowboys; Afro-Argentines; and other popular forces to promote his personal political ideology of Rosismo.*

*Under Rosas, Afro-Argentines, who organized in associations called "African nations," contributed to his federalist cause in a number of ways. Many Afro-Argentines also established personal relationships with the Rosas family, particularly with Rosas's daughter Manuelita and with the governor himself. Rosas understood that his political authority was tied to the survival of the Afro-Argentine community. On the other hand, local communities often viewed Rosas's federal militias, which were comprsied of Afro-Argentines, as outsiders. Upon them fell the community's suspicions about sexual and property crimes. Not pressured by the question of military service, black women acted more independently, although their language, dress, and public behavior often offended the conservative mores of the Argentine elite. The African influence under Rosas was, nonetheless, undeniable,*

*at least in Buenos Aires. After the triumph of the liberals over Rosas at the 1852
Battle of Caseros, Afro-Argentines suffered political exclusion and greater discrimination.*

This chapter examines the role of black men and women during and within
the Rosas regime, focusing on their subjugated condition and on the ways
in which Afro-Argentines challenged the attributes and behaviors associated
with their unfavorable social position. Using records taken from the state
archives, this essay revisits the old question of the role black subjects played
in the making of the Rosas regime. This perspective allows us to understand
the Rosas regime and the role of Afro-Argentines in a new light. My main
contribution in this regard is an attempt to rescue the voices of Afro-
Argentines as political interventions in the making of the federalist republic
and to suggest that the justice system served as space for airing the grievances of Afro-Argentines about mistreatment and abuse. Though reduced
in numbers, blacks and mulattoes had gained a new space in the society of
the period, perhaps due to their own interventions (many of them individual, not through ethnic communities) in the judicial and military spheres.

Afro-Argentines addressed state authorities, masters, and employers but
also considered themselves part of the federalist fatherland and, consequently, entitled to the rights of social equality, personal respect, and the
possibility of redressing injustice. With a careful reading of recent historiography, this chapter also reexamines the condition of "withdrawal" and
"invisibility" that Afro-Argentines experienced during the transition
between 1852 and 1900. Having been mobilized into political participation during the Rosas period, the African nations gradually fragmented
themselves into a myriad of cultural enterprises attempting inclusion and
recognition under the banner of liberalism.

## HISTORIANS, ROMANTICS, AND
## INFLUENCES FROM BELOW

The intellectuals who fought against Rosista federalism presented Afro-
Argentines as the main instruments of an oppressive and tyrannical regime.
To writers such as Domingo F. Sarmiento, José Mármol, Felix Frías, and
many others, black servants were spies of the regime operating within the
households of "decent people" to denounce any symptom of antifederalist
opposition. Sarmiento clearly stated this indictment in *Facundo* (1845),[1]
and the accusation was repeated by Mármol in his novel *Amalia* (1851) and
later spread by the *criollista* literature of the 1890s in their promotion of
national and local culture.[2]

In *La Gloria del tirano Rosas* (1847), Felix Frías saw the red federalist flag presiding over the festivities of May 25, 1838, as a blemish and insult to the May revolutionary tradition. As revolting was the fact that "bands of African Negroes paraded through the streets of Buenos Aires," stopping at Victory Square to dance "immodest dances." Mármol extended the moral condemnation of the "decent people" to Manuelita Rosas for involving herself in African dances, which he considered lascivious and repugnant.[3] During Rosas's times and afterward, the intelligentsia denied any political agency to Afro-Argentines. To Frías, the regime's persistence was based upon the "blind obedience" of slaves and illiterate gauchos, people who did not have the autonomy or instruction to become true citizens. To Juana Manso, it was the obsequious behavior of *pardos* and *morenos*, and their irrational loyalty, that sustained the tyranny.[4] At the end of the century, J. M. Ramos Mejía presented the Rosista plebe as an irrational mass attracted to Rosas by sexual instinct, adulation, and propaganda. He reduced the attraction of a black woman to basic sexual drives and spoke of the *mulata* as a seducing beauty able to extract all family secrets for the benefit of Don Juan Manuel.[5]

Nineteenth-century and early twentieth-century interpretations of the relations between Rosas and Afro-Argentines appear as a condemnatory, schizophrenic discourse. By presenting Afro-Argentines as abject spies and as indecent dancers, romantic intellectuals placed Afro-Argentines simultaneously within and outside politics. While denying reasoned agency to blacks and mulattoes, they affirmed that Africans' political and military support was crucial to the endurance and popularity of the Rosas regime.[6] Irresponsible for their irrationality, they were guilty by being participants in the making of tyranny. Historians have been gradually modifying this view of Rosas and his policies (better known as Rosismo), yet little has been done to deconstruct the implications of these renditions of caudillismo upon the identity and struggles of Afro-Argentines.

In the last fifteen years, traditional views of caudillismo and so-called cattle-ranching feudalism have come under increasing criticism. To begin with, cattle ranchers were not as powerful as they were previously believed to be. The fuzziness of property boundaries, the erratic enforcement of vagrancy laws, and the mobility of peasants and peons prevented the emergence of an effective system of labor control. Landowners had to rely on the labor market to recruit their needed peons and laborers. Different means of coercion (so-called debt peonage, Indian servitude, and imported Spanish laborers) proved ineffective to channel sufficient workers to their estancias. In spite of the continuity of vagrancy and passport laws, contractual relations grew to become the prevalent form of labor relations.[7]

Also discredited is the notion of an all-powerful Rosas who managed at will his own ranches and those of his associates (the *Anchorenas*). Rosas's rewards to Spanish peons, his payment for overtime and night work, and his recurrent advice to his personal servants to make efficient use of the labor force demonstrate that his predicament (in an economy with severe labor shortages) was similar to that of other cattle ranchers. Rosas himself was forced to negotiate with intruders on his own lands, granting them permission to stay as well as other benefits.[8]

The new historiography has questioned the traditional view that Rosas used the style of governance that he learned on his own land to govern the nation. Governing a province presented a completely different challenge than managing a cattle ranch. Moreover, Rosas's alleged capacity for mobilizing gaucho militias did not continue during his governorship: he was forced to organize a regular army, recruiting free men of peasant origins (white, *trigueño*, and black). The militias played a crucial role in the fight against *unitarios*, but only because they became disciplined military units.[9] More and more the question of political persuasion and Afro-Argentine involvement has come to the attention of historians.[10] The "order" established by Governor Rosas appears to be the product of protracted and widespread contention about rights and responsibilities. Within the rhetoric of federalism, Afro-Argentines negotiated their own understanding of war, nation, and self. Looked at from an Afro-Argentine perspective, there were multiple meanings and possibilities to being a federalist.

Historian P. González Bernaldo, for example, presents Rosas's relations with the African societies as mainly a clientelistic one based upon an exchange of loyalty for political protection. The patron (Rosas) granted his clients (African societies) a series of gifts: public lands, financial assistance, and legal favoritism. In return, black societies provided political mobilization and military service to the federalist cause. In the public sphere the relationship appeared as one of reciprocity: Rosas gave black Argentines a crucial role in civic celebrations, while the African nations accepted Rosas and his family into their community festivities. But the reciprocity was only apparent. Rosas used the African societies to mobilize black Argentines in support of the federalist cause and, by doing so, spread fear among his political enemies, the *unitarios*.[11]

By regarding the relationship between Governor Rosas and the African nations only as a form of clientelism, we fail to understand the activities and struggles of Afro-Argentines as choices through which they exerted their self-interest. While distinct from the indictment of the generation of romantic writers of the nineteenth century, González Bernaldo's rendition continues to assume an elitist perspective to post-independence history. Her account assumes a premodern (corporatist) engagement of blacks into federalist politics. In order to restore the political agency of blacks, we need to revise their interventions in the sphere of justice, their contestation of authority in military barracks, and their individual and group pursuit of freedom in the context of the federalist republic.

## SLAVERY IN THE LATE COLONIAL AND INDEPENDENCE PERIODS

Late colonial Buenos Aires was a multiracial town in which whites constituted a minority. The majority of the population, composed of blacks,
mulattoes, and a variety of other *castas*, did most of the work. In the countryside, a limited number of slaves planted the land and harvested the crops
with primitive tools. Foreign observers attributed this propensity to let so-
called people of color do most of the work to Spanish disdain for manual
labor. The continued inflow of imported slaves (as contraband for the most
part) permitted a racial division of labor. Buenos Aires was also a city where
white *peninsulares* failed to impose exclusive racial control over the trades.[12]

Scholars have noted the peculiar nature of slavery in late colonial Buenos
Aires. Under the system of stipendiary slavery, men and women in bondage
looked for jobs in the open market, negotiated wages, and worked outside
the master's home, paying their masters a portion of their earnings. Most
slaves were household servants or craftsmen.[13] Their masters were men and
women of modest means, highly dependent on the wages generated by
their slaves. In most workplaces (brick kilns, bakeries, stockyards, and construction sites) slaves and free men worked and slept together.[14]

The law obliged slaves to provide a daily payment to their masters. "For
thousands of slaves in late colonial Buenos Aires," writes Lyman Johnson,
"slavery meant weekly or, less commonly, monthly, cash payments paid to
the owners." This had important implications for the sustainability of slavery, for wage-earning slaves were naturally in the business of purchasing,
little by little, their freedom. The city of late colonial Buenos Aires had one
of the highest rates of annual manumissions, be it by purchase or by master's will.[15]

The almost contractual nature of domestic slavery limited the possibilities of coercion open to masters. Hired-out slaves were almost free from
surveillance from owners. Slaves had to adjust only to the provisions of
their craft and to the desires of their masters. Domestic slaves living in their
masters' houses were subject to closer supervision and coercion. Though
laws restricted whipping, masters could, if they wished, put their servants
to humiliating and unwanted tasks, lock them up at night, and reduce their
food and clothes provisions. Few of them actually did, preferring instead
the use of incentives in order to get good service and deference. They hired
the slaves out, sent them to a farm or ranch, and allowed them to keep their
savings, promised them some inheritance or reward after the master's death
or, more commonly, made arrangements for the future manumission of the
slave.

During the post-independence period, masters' repertoires of coercion
experienced further reductions. The 1813 Assembly declared the freedom

of slaves' newborn children and established a transition regime by which these children (*libertos*) were put under the custody of masters. At the age of twenty (males) and sixteen (females), these children were to gain their freedom. Meanwhile they had to provide services to their custodians in exchange for education and food. After age fifteen (males) or fourteen (females), they were entitled to earn a salary. While not abolishing slavery, the Law of the Free Womb destabilized relationships between masters and slaves, creating an issue (the custody of *libertos*) over which slaves could take their masters to court.

Contemporaneously, the state purchased slaves for military purposes (*rescates*). This gave adult slaves an opportunity to escape bondage. These "rescued" slaves were to serve five years in the army, after which time they would be freed.[16] In the late 1810s, as a result of their participation in the defense of Buenos Aires (1806–1807) and in the independence wars, free blacks were allowed to enter the militias, a situation that caused resentment among the white militias. As various racial incidents indicate, in 1817–1818 new winds of equality blew, as white and *trigueño* officers defended the rights of their young black comrades. During the war with Brazil (1825–1828), black soldiers made prisoners by the Argentine army and those who escaped from the Brazilian forces created additional problems to local slave owners. New regulations were established to distinguish between Brazilian slaves (whose status was in doubt) and African slaves already residing in Buenos Aires.

With an increasing number of manumissions (by purchase or by reward) and relatively few additional imports (most of them illegal), the numbers of slaves declined. If the rates of manumission continued as they had in the late colonial period, few slaves must have remained in bondage by 1853 (the year the constitution abolished slavery).[17] True, some legislative measures prolonged the demise of slavery,[18] but the importance and viability of slavery had declined significantly by the 1840s.

Particularly in the city, it became increasingly difficult to retain slaves, who were attracted by the freer social environment of the countryside. Those slaves who were in a position to negotiate their place of residence asked to be relocated in the countryside. In the country, slaves could pass for free, and colored individuals could "whiten" themselves. This was particularly true for males. Once they acquired property and social connections, it was difficult to subject them to bondage. Those who found themselves mistreated were able to force their sale in court. More commonly, slaves (male and female) escaped to the southern frontier of the emerging Argentine nation-state, where, with a different identity, they could make a new start.[19] The wars of independence, with their *rescates* and acts of confiscation, encouraged slaves to make demands on their masters. Many of the latter, in order to retain their servants, issued "promises of freedom," which transformed labor relations during the transition period. Some slaves went to the courts seeking the fulfillment of promises of freedom made by their masters.[20]

In 1831 a mandatory registration of *libertos* tried to protect the rights of sons and daughters of slaves born after 1813. This protection was extended in part because the government authorized the internal selling of adult slaves not included in the Law of the Free Womb.[21] The justices of the peace, searching for *libertos* in ranches and farms, caused significant resentment among masters or custodians.

The intense use of slaves by the military, manumissions, and the masters' practice of sending their slaves to the countryside ended up reducing significantly the number of men under bondage. Hence, during the time of Rosismo (1829–1852) there were clear signs that this human "resource" had been overused. In the city of Buenos Aires, the African population (free and slave) declined from 29.5 percent in 1810 to 26 percent in 1836. Still a significant minority, they entered into the political game siding with the Federalist Party, which was supported if not controlled by Rosas. Few, in fact, joined the *unitario* militias, Rosas's sworn enemies. In the 1840s, perhaps because African males were fighting the war, Afro-Argentines lost some of their visibility.[22] Population lists (*padrones*) taken in the southern frontier showed also that *pardos* and *morenos* were already a small minority in the mid-1840s.[23]

## AFRO-ARGENTINES DURING THE ROSAS REGIME

Individual struggles by black servants and black soldiers carved out spaces for respect, freedom, and legality. A continuation of similar struggles during the post-independence period, these activities now became more productive to the extent that they enjoyed greater sympathy from state functionaries (military officers and judges). Afro-Argentines directed their grievances to Governor Rosas as well as to the justice system and, on occasion, used the newspapers to express their views. Contemporary political poetry shows the extent to which the emergence of Rosista federalism was seen as an opportunity to affirm the double identity of African and patriot. More importantly, judicial records present us with a silent rebellion within the households of the so-called high brow: black male and female servants were actively questioning the authority of heads of households and, in some cases, leaving the house.

### Afro-Argentine Political Voices

To better understand the political agency of Afro-Argentines, we need to recuperate some fragments of writings, songs, and paintings that present an alternative view of the federation, Rosas, and the question of slavery. One of them was the "Hymn to Da. Manuela Rosas," sung by African women on the occasion of Manuelita's birthday.[24] In the poem-song the Conga women proclaim Manuelita their "queen," "mother," and "loyal protector" and lament that their ancestors died in Congo without seeing Manuelita's beauty. The song presents the federation as the true fatherland of Africans, the place where they had found solace, freedom, and peace. Rosas's daughter is credited with having thrown to the abyss the "diabolical Union." Manuelita is a "moon" that radiates beauty, joy, and light, guiding *felices morenas* throughout their journey. While the elite deprecated Manuelita's *trigueño* complexion, Conga women celebrated her skin tonality, asking the sun not to "eclipse the color."

Another instance of black federalist pride is the poem "¡Viva la Patria!" published in the newspaper *La Negrita* in July 1833.[25] In the poem, Juana Peña, a *negrita federal*, expresses her loyalty to Rosas and the federation. She is free, wears the adornments of a lady, and considers herself attractive. Though coming from the core of African societies (being in the front line of *candombes*), she has taken the bold step of writing for a political cause. And she does so only to prove that "although black, I am a true patriot." She calls on young blacks (*negritos*) to save the menaced fatherland, the same land that has given Africans their freedom. The *negrita* probably refers to the 1813 Law of the Free Womb and to the 1831 protection of *libertos*—in her mind there is continuity between the independence leadership and Rosas. She directs her call to her compatriots, the *negritos defensores* (black defenders), those who already support the law and its restorer. They are the "true patriots" who will kill or die in defense of "Don Juan Manuel."

The diminutive used to refer to her male compatriots (*negritos*) finds its correlate in the colloquial manner in which she addresses Rosas: *mandame mi general*. (Command me, *mi general*—using the familiar form *tú* for "you.")[26] As a free woman now engaged in politics, she awaits Rosas's orders to continue the struggle against the *unitarios*. The question of color difference (Rosas was seen as "blond") is suppressed in the poem. Juana Peña is proud of being both black and a federalist. Here the hyphenation (*negrita-federal*) produces a new subjectivity: a black woman mobilized into politics and acting in the public sphere.

A third representation that provides insight into the relationship between Rosas and the black community is a painting dated May 1841, which depicts the freed women's gratitude toward Governor Rosas for abolishing the slave traffic (1839). In the painting, Rosas presents a group of Africans (most of them women) with a document that proclaims that federation amounts to liberty. The meaning of this liberty is made clear by the broken chains on the floor and by the words of an angel that trumpets the end of slavery.[27] In exchange for freedom, the *morenas* show the symbols of federalism on their clothes and carry banners saluting the federation, its restoration, and liberty. The sacrifice made by Africans to the defense of the federation is underscored by the absence of adult males in the picture—they are in the federalist armies. Though some historians have seen here another sign of Rosas's semantic manipulation and purposeful ambiguity,[28] it is possible to interpret this painting as a leveling of two distinct political subjects: Rosas and the *morenas*.

Both political actors are joining forces in the struggle for "freedom," something that for one actor means the consolidation of legitimate government and independence, while for the other it means the institutional context in which it is possible to cease being a slave. In fact, the freedom that Rosas speaks of is still in the future: it came two years after the abolition of the slave traffic; when the federalist armies restored internal peace, defeating Lavalle's invasion.

It is difficult to extricate the voice of Afro-Argentines from the rhetoric of federalism. The freedoms gained by Afro-Argentines (by manumission, the Law of the Free Womb, or military *rescate*) remained illusory if the legal order were broken. If an illegitimate military government, not elected by the majority, took control of public decisions, slavery could be reestablished, regardless of the liberal rhetoric of this government. Thus, the restoration of the federalist government was to Afro-Argentines the continuity of the promise made by the earlier republican leaders that the independence of the country would also mean freedom for Africans. Rather than a manipulated confusion, the equation between federation and freedom was a rational discursive option. Pressed between a leadership that considered Africans spies for a tyrannical government, and a government that promised the continuity of the institutional frame that slaves had used to free themselves, the preferred option was quite clear.

### Black Servants' Silent Insurrection

The control of masters over domestic servants, already diminished in the late colonial period, became highly contested during the Rosas period. Indeed, one could argue that, as a result of this intensified tension within the household, master-slave relations adopted a new contractual basis functional to the gradual emancipation of slaves.

Many slave servants purchased their freedom with savings obtained from work or theft. Lacking other employment opportunities, they remained with their prior masters as wage earners. For female servants, the transition toward paid labor was perhaps the most important change during this period. As they tried to behave as free wage earners, servants faced opposition from the heads of households. At the core of these conflicts were the new conditions of wage contracts. Mistresses expected their female servants to perform the same duties and to be as deferential as they had been under slavery, whereas servants instead wanted the respect deserved by free men and women. The introduction of salaries to labor relations brought about increased tensions within the household—tensions that revolved around questions of petty theft, and the quantity and quality of work.

Masters were able to send their rebellious servants to be "corrected" in the prison at the Cabildo: one month in prison and a few whippings—the masters thought—would restore the slave's deferential attitude.[29] Many *morenas* and *pardas* were sent to jail for correction on charges of theft, insolent answers, and insults. Theft was the single most common cause of arrest of female servants. Urged to dress up in order to gain respectability, or simply trying to raise money to help relatives or lovers, female servants felt entitled to money or clothes belonging to their masters. At the interior of the household, tensions continued unabated, despite the punishment. In a political context in which the word "liberty" saturated political discourse, the imposition of domestic work and deference had become highly contested. Masters' threats of corporal punishment, household confinement, and sale carried a less menacing tone—they were now ineffective and impractical.

Judicial records bring to light moments of generalized confrontations between masters and slaves on the domestic domain. Perhaps we are in the presence of a silent rebellion by black servants that contributed to easing the transition toward free labor and, to a certain extent, to the alleviation of corporal punishment. A few examples will serve to prove this point.

Punishment and abuse continued to characterize the relations between masters and slaves, but Afro-Argentines could now resort to the courts to stop or reduce the abuse. In 1831 the *morena* Juana María went to the justice to accuse Doña Cipriana Barcalá of mistreatment of her daughter, the *negrita* Agustina (apparently a *liberta* placed under the care of this lady). She presented witnesses who testified that Doña Barcalá had subjected the young servant to whippings, locked her in a room, and denied her food for days. The judge found the mistress's conduct unacceptable and, to safeguard the child, ordered that the *negrita* Agustina be placed under the care of a more humane master until she reached adulthood.[30]

To defend their freedom, slaves also resorted to judicial authorities. In 1838 the *liberta* Angela, who had passed through the homes of various masters and now was "deposited" in the house of a stranger, asked the judge to recognize her freedom. She alleged that her previous masters had promised her freedom in exchange for services, that she had paid part of the manumission price of $300 and that she was sold on the condition that she would obtain her freedom later, and that her last master had written her freedom into his will. In her petition, Angela declared: "There is no doubt that I am free." Furthermore, she asked the judge to place her with a close relative of her original master, with whom she had already reached a mutually beneficial salaried agreement. The judge confirmed her condition of freedom.[31]

On occasions, domestic slaves who had arranged with their masters a sort of self-imposed servitude to pay for their manumission defaulted on their obligations. This was the case of the *morena* María Melgarejo. Her mistress had lent her $600 to help Melgarejo pay for her freedom—she was supposed to cancel this debt in monthly installments of $10. But, instead of paying her debt, the *morena* engaged in an argument with her mistress, insulted her, and left the house. When the case was presented to the court, the judge ordered Melgarejo to pay $20 as a means of canceling the debt and to be released. In the end, the *morena* had her way: she got rid of the burden of an important debt and of a problematic mistress.[32]

In 1840, Doña Jacinta Laurel denounced her hired servant, the *parda* Petrona, for stealing $1,300 from her chest. She argued that her servant had recently purchased expensive clothes (a new dress, a shawl, and shoes) that were not proper for a servant. Petrona contested that her money was legitimately obtained: it came from her salary and from a gift from her mother. In fact, she vindicated the right to spend her money as she saw fit, transforming a case of theft into an open discussion about servants' rights to income and the disposal of that income.[33]

The same tension could be found in gender relations within the household. The authority of male heads of households over female relatives, laboriously crafted during the colonial period, began to reveal significant cracks in the post-independence period. In particular, men's self-appointed right to correct women became a contested issue as many women took to court cases of abuse by their male partners, finding to their surprise that judges were sympathetic to their demands.[34] Ricardo Cicerchia has shown how poor women went to the courts to redress the abuses of men, demanding economic support or accusing men of ill treatment. In most of these cases, the plaintiffs won their cases. Male abuse of women was particularly violent and cruel in this period—knife wounds often accompanied attempted rape—but women's courage in reporting these cases and fighting in court for the conviction of offenders produced unexpected results. The cases of a battered *mulata* who managed to get her husband exiled and of a poor white women who, with the help of female friends, got a male assailant sentenced to military service are indicative of the opportunities open to women of all classes in the courts. Judges, horrified by the violence perpetuated by lower-class men against women, often sided with the victims.[35]

Through various ways, women contested patriarchal authority. Wives asked for religious courts for separations, challenged the privilege of their husbands in administering inherited wealth, and demanded from them the provision of food and clothes when they avoided their responsibilities.

Women of the lower classes, who had fewer options for paying the expense of a trial, opted for a more expedient solution to their marital difficulties: escape. They ran away to the southern frontier, where the vengeance of husbands and fathers could not reach them. Some women responded in kind to male violence. Women's attacks with knives and guns on their male partners were not uncommon. Lacking the support of church and state, male heads of households saw their means for coercing women greatly reduced.

## Justice and the Color Line

To the confusing racial categories of the colonial order based on purity of blood, the Rosista state added further confusion by utilizing a classification of people's color according to direct observance or appearance. The official categories of the colonial period were replaced by what race one appeared to be to others (usually a state scribe). Some whites were described as *rosados* (pink) or *claros* (light), while the category *trigueño*, originally reserved for sun-burned mestizos, became a catchall label that described complexions ranging from those of "light *pardos*" to blond-haired country people. On occasion, a person classified as *trigueño* by one officer was registered as white by another. Clearly, the democratization of the countryside shook the stability of the inherited racial order. Few authorities were ready to call a person mulatto or *pardo*, particularly if the person was a free man, a citizen. They preferred to register him as a *trigueño*. The word "negro" was probably reserved for people with unambiguous traits of African ancestry. Thus more than 70 percent of the rural population came to be classified under the categories *blanco* or *trigueño*.

Apparently, appearance was not a reliable marker of race. Though Rosas inculcated military recruiters and justices of the peace in the art of seeing— telling them what details in the appearance of detainees their eyes should catch—state officers had difficulties ascertaining the race of a subject just by looking at him or her. In 1841, Nasario Acosta, a man from the city of Cordoba residing in Buenos Aires province, assaulted a house in the town of Lobos and killed an eleven-year-old child. He was tried for this felony and sentenced to the maximum penalty: death by shooting. During the trial, witnesses and judicial officers spoke of him as "the *Indio* Acosta," but his personal dossier presented him as a *moreno aindiado*, that is, as black with Indian traits. Was he an Indian? Was he an Afro-Argentine?

The ambiguity of racial categories extended also to the distinction between gaucho (or *criollo*) and *indio*. H. Armaignac, a French traveler who visited the Buenos Aires pampas in 1870–1871, left readers wondering about the "true color" of gauchos.[36] To the French traveler, there were blond, black, and brown gauchos. As the gaucho's racial identity was hard to establish, Armaignac proposed to distinguish them by their conduct and moral qualities.[37] Immediately after the fall of Rosas, William MacCann described the amazing racial and ethnic diversity of the social landscape of Buenos Aires: "The olive skin tone of the Spaniard, the *cetrino* skin of the French and the pinkness of the English alternate with indigenous, tartars, Jewish and black physiognomies."[38] The various languages, the different styles of dress, and the tonalities of skin confused even the more acute observer.

While the plurality of languages and races presented positive expectations about "progress"—the transformation of Argentine society under the influence of the European presence—in another sense, this plurality was confusing, for the foreign observer could no longer decipher the racial code. Contradicting Sarmiento, MacCann found that European immigration did not bring about "whitening." Around this time, John Brabazon, an Irish immigrant worker, traveled all over the Buenos Aires countryside looking for work. In his journey, he met a mulatto peon who taught him Spanish, worked in a sheep-shearing team that included *criollos* and an Indian family, dealt with a Galician journeyman, met various English ranch owners, and came across many Irish and Scottish shepherds.[39] The Buenos Aires countryside had become a racially diverse landscape.

Within military barracks, the color line was also hard to enforce. Rosas disbanded the old divisions of *pardos* and *morenos*, placing black soldiers in regular divisions, among them the so-called Restorer's Battalion (Batallón de los Restauradores), a term that probably indicated that these were people who participated in some of the pro-Rosas revolts, called *restauraciones*. In this way the regiments acted as levelers of social differences, spaces where whites, *trigueños*, blacks, and mulattoes fought together under the same flag. Although some of the soldiers were ordinary delinquents sent there as a punishment and others were ex-slaves "rescued" from their bondage, in campaign they acquired the same pay, cloth, and rations as the rest of the soldiery. I have argued elsewhere that regiments became contested spaces where soldiers and officers negotiated (sometimes violently) the limits of discipline and "correction."[40] In particular, soldiers resisted the use of corporal punishment and abusive language as proper ways of treating free men. Enlisted ex-slaves participated in these negotiations and struggles. By the mid-1840s, soldiers had achieved a consensus: arbitrary and humiliating treatment was considered intolerable.

Judicial evidence tends to reaffirm the notion that slavery was rapidly disintegrating during the Rosas period. In the countryside, as more blacks and mulattoes passed for *trigueños*, the color barrier became more difficult to impose. Among those arrested in the Buenos Aires countryside, 40 percent were registered as *trigueños*, 32 percent as whites, 8 percent as black, 9 percent as mulatto, 5 percent as *aindiado*, and 3 percent as (pure) Indian. The stigma against people of color probably remained strong, but it mattered less. Greater employment in the countryside generated enhanced mobility and independence to black freedmen and the possibility of countering racial stereotypes. Now black and mulatto veterans could return to their communities with the pride of having served the fatherland. The case of a black peon ascending to the position of *capataz*, having under his command white and *trigueño* peons, was not unusual.[41]

In addition, the justice system provided a sphere in which blacks and mulattoes could redress the injustices suffered under their employers or other members of society, or at least have their complaints heard. Justices of the peace continued to admit evidence and testimony furnished by blacks and mulattoes without suffering from the humiliation of the old colonial *tachas*, an old legal term used to refer to the marks that accompanied a person of color and made him or her unfit to give testimony in court. Black veterans initiated cases for the payment of wages in arrears. Others recounted, with pride, their actions in battle in defense of the federation. Black peons accused their bosses of abusive treatment. The judicial resolution of cases of rape shows the extent to which *morenos* were still associated with uncontained sexual drives. But these cases were few, for the state was more concerned with identifying deserters and draft evaders. The inflow of darker *trigueño* migrants from the interior provinces made racial discrimination quite difficult to implement, even to justices attentive to the color difference.

Due to the peculiar political conditions of the period, two additional means of redress opened to Afro-Argentines: petitions to the government, and notices or ads in the press. In 1837, a free African named Antonio del Valle wrote to the governor requesting his freedom from prison in exchange for service in the armed forces. He had been arrested after a dispute with a white person. He was assaulted with a whip and beaten until his eye bled. In a defensive move, he wounded his attacker with a knife. In his petition to Rosas, he used respectful language, acknowledging that he had used violence. But in his defense, he also asserted his gained rights and the equality of people of other races. He wrote: "Your Excellency, I know that I wounded him in the hand on my own free will and that I have done wrong. But, I would also like to say that the gentleman in question should not assume that because he is white that he is better than me and has the right to punish me as if I were his servant."[42]

Antonio del Valle was expressing a connection that was already part of the understanding of the new conditions after independence. Rejecting corporal punishment as improper and humiliating treatment of a citizen, the African was claiming legitimate self-defense as a natural right. To reaffirm this understanding and remind the state of its promise, he directed his denunciation to Rosas, the highest authority in the province, the person upon whom rested the expectations of justice.

Defiance of authority sometimes took the form of public exposure and humiliation of the judges. In 1830, a reader calling himself "The Lover of Order" sent a letter to the *Gaceta Mercantil* complaining of the abuses of a particular judge. The letter, as it was later discovered, came from a free African who was pursuing the liberation of his spouse (a slave woman) through the courts. In his letter to the press, this anonymous Afro-Argentine implied that the judge was delaying the resolution of his spouse's case (a claim for freedom after the payment of manumission). To save his reputation, the judge was compelled to reply to the ex-slave and explain the reasons for the delay.[43]

## LIBERALISM AND EXCLUSION

In the two decades that followed the fall of Rosas in February 1852, the new liberal leadership strove to hold back the political participation of African societies. At the same time liberals promoted the individual elevation of blacks through education, art, and work. Displaced from the center stage of politics, Afro-Argentines continued to display their music and dances in carnival. Some of their societies embraced the ideology of progress. But even the festive space of carnival became contested. Other participants tried to undo the existing relationship between carnival and blackness. The political importance of blacks, overwhelmed in numbers by European immigrants, diminished, and so did their social visibility. By the 1880s, members of the elite started to articulate the idea that the African community was "vanishing."[44]

George Reid Andrews has examined the integration of Afro-Argentines into the nation as part of a more general process of transition from "caste" to "class" societies. Social integration, in his view, derived from economic mobility. Ever since the 1850s, Afro-Argentines faced particularly favorable conditions for social advancement and integration. The export boom of the period 1870–1914 brought about new sources of wealth and employment, a diversification in labor markets, and ample opportunities for entrepreneurs who offered goods and services to a rapidly expanding urban market.[45] But were they really integrated?

During the period 1852–1880, the carnival, up to that point a festivity controlled by African societies, turned into a space shared by various ethnic groups and different social classes. The *comparsas*, musical associations that emerged during the early liberal period, came to dominate the scene of the carnival. They no longer deployed the aesthetic and spiritual values of African societies but the ideals of "public civility" instilled by the liberal press. Spanish and Italian immigrants joined these *comparsas* together with young members of the Creole elite. These white dancers and musicians painted their faces black and imitated the music and dances of black *candombes*. They Europeanized African music with the introduction of guitars and lutes and asserted a peculiar "right": every white had the right to become black for awhile, as a way of remembering a bygone era.[46]

Why did the vibrant African culture of Buenos Aires suddenly become a relic of the past? The possibility of whites imitating (and mimicking) black music and dance was implicit in the message of liberalism.[47] The liberal carnival would be a space of joy celebrated by all ethnic groups, so much so that even African societies were enticed to participate. And they did. Adopting names that reflected the new ideals of progress, younger Afro-Argentines created new *comparsas* that projected little of their earlier ethnic values. The new associations followed the rules of other civic associations: their members paid dues, elected commissions, and conducted affairs according to bylaws. Apparently, the new dominant ideology of liberalism had so profoundly permeated the public space that it was difficult to resist it from the perspective of African-ness.[48] The liberal elite had perfected a mechanism through which different social and ethnic groups could temporarily share the same public space and still maintain their social identity and separate notions of respectability.

The blending of colors and classes under the banner of liberalism did not last long. In 1881 two *comparsa* clubs tried, unsuccessfully, to ban the entrance of blacks to their societies. In the late 1880s the city prohibited the "playing with water," the traditional carnival practice of throwing water to unsuspecting passerby, pushing them to the peripheral barrios. By 1901 two different carnivals were organized: one was the *corso blanco* in the corridor north of the city, the other the *corso negro* in Monserrat. This put an end to the multiethnic carnival constructed by liberalism at a time during which the Afro-Argentines ceased to be a "threat" to the white nation.

The decline of the Afro-Argentine population in absolute and relative terms made their claims for full citizenship and cultural participation less pressing for the post-Caseros political leadership. From 1838 to 1887 the number of Afro-Argentines in the city declined from 15,000 to 8,000. During this period the city, thanks to European immigration, experienced an extraordinary growth in its population. Consequently, the number of Afro-Argentines declined even further: from 24 percent to less than 2 percent.[49]

In the early 1880s, José Ceppi, an Italian journalist who wrote under the pseudonym of Aníbal Latino, remarked on the cosmopolitan features of Buenos Aires. Hundreds of ethnic groups coexisted in a dynamic social environment. The cultural heterogeneity of the city, he claimed, was greater than in any other European or North American city. Thus, a true rainbow of colors populated the streets.[50] But one of the colors had become invisible to the eyes of this sensitive observer. Ceppi could not find anything to say about Afro-Argentines. Víctor Gálvez, in an essay published in 1883, believed that Afro-Argentines were in the process of disappearing. Hence, they constituted no threat to the formation of the nation. In particular, the remaining black population did not present a challenge to the European immigrant in the competition for jobs, housing, and other resources. This, however, does not fully explain the position of insignificance and invisibility in which Afro-Argentines found themselves after 1880.[51]

## LIVING FRAGMENTS OF THE PAST

Excluded from public-political space and prematurely invisible as a distinctive social group, Afro-Argentines continued to express their demands for inclusion in the body of the nation. Like many others without official power and influence, they used journalistic interventions, poetry, and biographies to reaffirm their belonging to the realms of progress, nation, and culture. Confronting ridicule and disbelief, these writers affirmed an association between country and blackness that was negated by white intellectuals. The attempt to make acceptable the idea of a separate patriotism was evident in the hymn composed by the Sociedad Musical Los Negros (and performed in the Colon theater in 1886) that saluted blacks as privileged members of the Argentine nation.[52]

In 1877 Casildo Thompson, an Afro-Argentine poet, published his "Canto a Africa," a poignant critique of slavery and the white man.[53] In it, Africa is presented as a virgin land violated by the white man; as the cradle of a noble and dignified race, the black man, who enjoyed natural freedom ("as the lion in the jungle") before the arrival of Europeans. The white man, bloodthirsty and cruel, separated families, killed, and punished children in order to establish a new "infamy": slavery. In vain the Negro tried to stop the white man with humane arguments, but he would not understand. The poem then curses those who had enslaved his race ("dammed a thousand times") and promises that the white man's grandsons will carry the stain of infamy on their foreheads. Finally, the poem announces the coming of the day when equality would reunite the human race.

Slavery, the poems implies, was a catastrophe of biblical proportions. While a rich critique of colonialism and slavery, the poem is not clearly connected to the situation of blacks in Argentina.[54] A good reader could see in the poem resonances of the debate about the past "tyranny," but it is difficult to locate the poem in a particular period or time framework. Indeed, the poem is ambivalent about its political project. Whereas Thompson is against slavery in general, it is unclear whether his views are informed by the Brazilian situation or by the quite different reality of slavery in Rio de la Plata.[55] Twenty-four years earlier, the constitution had abolished slavery. But the institution was still running strong in Brazil. Still more remarkable is the lack of repercussion that this poem had on the Argentine intelligentsia. Except for a few commentaries by other Afro-Argentines,[56] the poem went unnoticed.

Before Thompson, other black poets tried to vindicate blackness and denounce the discriminatory activities of whites. Among them was young poet Horacio Mendizábal, who died in 1871 when assisting the victims of the yellow fever epidemic.[57] In a prologue to his *Horas de meditación* (1869), dedicated to President Sarmiento, Mendizábal clearly stated that, despite enjoying formal freedom, blacks were objects of insults, humiliation, and disdain from white Argentines. The rest of Argentine society could not imagine that a black or mulatto man could be appointed to the congress or to the presidency. Virtue and education were not sufficient to produce true equality. Still the word "mulatto" itself disqualified a person for public office. Sharing Sarmiento's anticlericalism, the author expected the president to understand his indignation about racial discrimination. Poetry—the author trusted—could elevate a race condemned by slavery, servitude, and moral decay. And he urged other Argentine poets to feel solidarity for the sordid fate of his race.

The period 1869–1882 saw the emergence of newspapers created to represent the Afro-Argentine community. Among them the best known were *La Broma* and *Los Negros*. While on occasion lending support to groups of workers on strike, *La Broma* tried to distance itself from party politics. In this strategy, they differed from the newspapers of Italian immigrants, which tended to support liberal candidates. The reasons for this editorial policy were clear: no candidate incorporated into his programs the concerns of the Afro-Argentine community.[58] This autonomy gave the newspaper the possibility of criticizing the whole white ruling class. In Argentina, according to *La Broma*, equality was only a formal conquest. In actuality, blacks continued to occupy the worst-paid jobs and were subject to racial discrimination. While pointing out that Africans had contributed, more than other races, to the military efforts that created and sustained Argentine independence, these newspapers emphasized the contemporary marginalization of Afro-Argentines.

In addition to criticizing racial inequality, the editors of *La Broma* promoted the organization of black *comparsas* and, in relation to this activity, raised the issue of language and political participation (c. 1876–1878). They posed the question of whether African songs should be sung in African languages and asked why blacks were excluded from political participation. Toward 1880–1882 the newspaper left aside the issue of the carnival and started to advance the question of freedmen's access to politics. Its editorials spoke of the need to extend public instruction to children of color and defended the rights of women to enter politics.[59]

After having contributed to the birth of the nation, Argentina's black citizens were deprived of the material benefits and social equality promised in the constitution. Women and blacks, argued *La Broma*, shared the same condition of political exclusion. The newspaper *Los Negros* tried to convey a perspective of blackness that could converse with the Europeanized culture of the white elite. Refined spiritualism and aristocratic universalism were combined to project a new engagement between the black community and the project of progress. The black community, the newspaper asserted, could also furnish distinguished and intelligent young men in tune with elite society. Solomianski remarks upon the irony of this project of aristocratic integration: while the editors of the newspaper were trying to organize a national music conservatory, the members of the white elite were negating the existence of blacks in modern Argentina.[60]

Toward the end of the nineteenth century, Gabino Ezeiza, a mulatto *payador*, presented the fatherland as a popular construction and tried to inculcate in his contemporaries the "glories" of the nation. He popularized the *milonga de contrapunto* singing competitions and in 1890 entered the popular circus of the Podestá brothers. He was an admirer of the renowned writer José Hernández and collaborated in the staging of *Martín Fierro* in 1892. In a *payada* (ballad) entitled "La Verdad" (1897) he sang to the battles of independence, reminding readers that his grandfather, also an Afro-Argentine, had fought in these battles. All peoples, regardless of their degree of civilization, he argued in his poetry, have national songs or hymns. This was the way people expressed national belonging. Rather than claiming a particular space for Afro-Argentine traditions, Ezeiza tried to locate them within the emerging popular culture.[61]

In 1899, a collection of short biographies of Afro-Argentines edited by Jorge M. Ford appeared. The book, titled *Beneméritos de mi estirpe*, was an attempt to provide young black Argentines examples that could restore their pride in their race and inspire them to follow the lead of these illustrious (though largely unknown) ancestors. Salient among these biographies were those of black military officers and Afro-Argentine poets and writers. While leaning toward certain positions of socialism, Ford strongly rooted his arguments in a liberal, anticlerical perspective. He paid tribute to the great romantic writers (Mármol, Echeverría, Sarmiento) and condemned the Rosas regime as a tyranny. In fact, he rescued Afro-Argentine officers who had fought against Rosista federalism from oblivion. This stand was probably an attempt to separate his civilizing discourse, directed to young black Argentines, from a past associated with "barbarism."[62]

These poems, journalistic pieces, and short biographies represented attempts to challenge the notion of an "extinguished race." Some of them (that of Mendizábal) made gestures toward inclusion, while others (that of Ezeiza) tried to connect the experiences of black Argentines with the emerging field of *criollismo* and popular culture. They fought against racial discrimination and white disdain from different positions and using different strategies. Their impact in the world of Argentine ideas was minimal, not only because of their negation by the white intelligentsia but also because the Afro-Argentine community, fragmented and partially integrated into mainstream culture, could not present an organized political challenge to elite polices and the immigration wave. Consequently, they turned into an unproblematic and "vanishing" minority.

During the Golden Age (1890–1914) other populations (immigrant workers, recidivist delinquents, anarchists, street children, and prostitutes) attracted the attention of white intellectuals examining national problems. While race became a crucial category under which to examine the question of nationality and progress, the Afro-Argentine community was no longer an important or appealing subject. The indictment against blacks contained in Ramos Mejía's *Las Multitudes argentines* (published around the same time as Ford's *Beneméritos de mi estirpe*) was directed against the past, against an era of tyranny that had created certain types of relationships between cau-dillos and the masses, which were now being reproduced by the immigrant crowds. Ramos Mejía's concerns concentrated on European immigrants because they—the crowds whose politics could derail the twin projects of nationality and progress—were the true obstacles of progress.[63]

While some authors have argued for the persistence of an Afro-Argentine past in culture, these influences did not translate into the recognition of black presence and importance in the shaping of modern Argentina. Main-stream society and culture pushed these fragments of self-expression into a corner of invisibility and insignificance. This, Reid Andrews reminds us, was the result of a long process of forced withdrawal during which Afro-Argentines were pushed out of labor markets, high-ranking positions in the military, political citizenship, and their central location in the city. Around 1900 they also lost visibility in the press. The attempt of black poets, jour-nalists, and *comparsas* societies to integrate Afro-Argentines into the nation proved insufficient to shake off the white indictment of the "vanishing race." In their efforts to negotiate a position in the program of civilization and progress by distancing themselves from the Rosista past, Afro-Argentines failed to attain recognition and inclusion. Viewed in historical perspective, their engagement with liberalism proved very costly, for they ended up more marginalized and invisible than before. One wonders then, whether this was elite culture's payoff for Afro-Americans' direct engage-ment in politics during the Rosas period.[64]

## NOTES

1. Sarmiento's denunciation is worth quoting: "Los Negros, ganados así para el Gobierno, ponían en manos de Rosas un celoso espionaje en el seno de cada familia, por los sirvientes y esclavos, proporcionándole, además, excelentes e incor-

ruptibles soldados de otro idioma y de una raza salvaje." Quoted in Alejandro Solomianski, *Identidades secretas: La Negritud argentina* (Rosario, Argentina: Beatriz Viterbo, 2003), 118.

2. Eduardo Gutiérrez's *Los Dramas del terror* is a case in point.

3. Felix Frías, *La Gloria del tirano Rosas* (Buenos Aires, Argentina: El Ateneo, 1928), 34–35. José Mármol, *Manuela Rosas y otros escritos políticos en el exilio* (1850; repr., Buenos Aires, Argentina: Taurus, 2001).

4. Solomianski, *Identidades secretas,* 106.

5. Frías, *La Gloria del tirano Rosas,* 94–95; José María Ramos Mejía, *Rosas y su tiempo* (Buenos Aires, Argentina: La Cultura Argentina, 1952), 3:32–40.

6. As Solomianski correctly points out in *Identidades secretas,* blacks were at the "center of evil" for the romantic generation (60).

7. As a result, cattle ranches showed a lesser degree of coercion than other fields, such as the military and the state judiciary. Ricardo Salvatore "Repertoires of Coercion and Market Culture in Nineteenth-Century Buenos Aires Province," *International Review of Social History* 45, no. 3 (2003): 408–48; Ricardo Salvatore, *Wandering Paysanos: State Order and Subaltern Experience in Buenos Aires Province during the Rosas Era* (Durham, NC: Duke University Press, 2003); Jorge D. Gelman, "El Fracaso de los sistemas coactivos de trabajo rural en Buenos Aires bajo el Rosismo, algunas explicaciones preliminares," *Revista de Indias* 9, no. 215 (1999): 123–41; Carlos A. Mayo, "Landed but Not Powerful: The Colonial Estancieros of Buenos Aires (1750–1810)," *Hispanic American Historical Review* 71, no. 4 (1991): 761–79.

8. Ricardo Salvatore, "Fiestas federales: Representaciones de la República en el Buenos Aires rosista," *Entrepasados* 5, no. 11 (1996): chap. 2; Jorge D. Gelman, "Un Gigante con pies de barro: Rosas y los pobladores de la campaña," in *Caudillismos rioplatenses: Nuevas miradas a un viejo problema,* ed. Noemí Goldman and Ricardo Salvatore (Buenos Aires, Argentina: Eudeba, 1998), 223–40.

9. Carlos A. Mayo, "Patricio Belén: Nada menos que un capataz," *Hispanic American Historical Review* 77, no. 4 (1997): 597–617; Carlos A. Mayo, "Estructura agraria, revolución de independencia y caudillismo en el Río de la Plata, 1750–1820: Algunas reflexiones preliminares," *Anuario IEHS* 12 (1997): 69–77; see also Mayo, "Landed but Not Powerful," op. cit.

10. Jorge Myers, *Orden y virtud: El Discurso republicano en el régimen rosista* (Buenos Aires, Argentina: Universidad Nacional de Quilmes, 1995); see Salvatore, "Fiestas federales."

11. P. González Bernaldo, *Civilidad y política en los orígenes de la nación argentina* (Mexico: Fondo de Cultura Económic, 2000), 169–72.

12. Alexander Gillespie *Buenos Aires y el interior* (Buenos Aires, Argentina: Hyspamerica, 1986), 61, 115–16.

13. At the beginning of the eighteenth century, nearly 80 percent of all slaves in the city of Buenos Aires were domestic servants; the remaining 20 percent worked in artisan shops and in the nearby farms. Lyman L. Johnson, "The Competition of Slave and Free Labor in Artisanal Production: Buenos Aires, 1770–1815," *International Review of Social History* 40, no. 3 (1995): 411.

14. Eduardo Saguier, "La Naturaleza estipendiaria de la esclavitud urbana colonial: El Caso del Río de la Plata en el siglo XVIII," *Revista Paraguaya de sociología* 26, no. 74 (1989): 45–54; Johnson, "Competition of Slave and Free Labor"; Silvia C. Mallo, "Mujeres esclavas en América a fines del s. XVIII: Una Aproximación histori-

ográfica," in *El Negro en la Argentina: Presencia y negación*, ed. D. Picotti (Buenos Aires, Argentina: Editores de América Latina, 2001).

15. Johnson, "Competition of Slave and Free Labor," 418.

16. Other slaves were simply confiscated from their Spanish masters and transferred to the army. Marta Goldberg and Laura Jany, "Algunos problemas referentes a la situación del esclavo en el Río de la Plata," in *Cuarto Congreso Internacional de Historia de América* (Buenos Aires, Argentina: Academia Nacional de Historia, 1968), 6:61–75.

17. The process had started in the late colonial period, when 1.5 percent of the total slave population was manumitted each year. Lyman L. Johnson, "Manumission in Colonial Buenos Aires, 1776–1810," *Hispanic American Historical Review* 59, no. 2 (1979): 258–79. Total population of blacks and mulattoes in the city of Buenos Aires increased only slightly between 1810 and 1822 and remained stationary from 1822 to 1836. This stagnation might be reflective of the transfers of blacks and mulattoes from city to countryside, parallel to the process of gradual emancipation. See Marta B. Goldberg, "La Población negra y mulata de la ciudad de Buenos Aires: 1810–1840," *Desarrollo Económico* 16, no. 61 (1976): 88.

18. Owners of *libertos* managed to get an extension of their "patronage" of young slaves and, despite the prohibition of the slave traffic, slaves caught from foreign vessels found their way into the local slave market. See Liliana Crespi, "Negros apresados en operaciones de corso durante la guerra con el Brasil (1825–1828)," *Temas de Africa y Asia* 2 (1993): 109–24.

19. Goldberg, "La Población negra y mulata." The proportion of mulattoes was greater among the areas with longer histories of colonization, while the proportion of blacks was larger in areas of recent colonization. This is interpreted by Marta Goldberg as clear evidence that "whitening" was a strategy for gaining freedom among slaves transported to the countryside.

20. Silvia Mallo, "La Libertad en el discurso del Estado, de amos y esclavos, 1780–1830," *Revista de historia de América* 112 (1991).

21. Ministerio de Gobierno, decree of October 15, 1831; AGN (Colección Ruíz-Guiñazú), 16-4-8, no. 1429.

22. Of ninety-four persons taken into custody, only three were slaves. J. P. Manuel Vila to Rosas, San Nicolás, January 15, 1841, AGN 21-7-1.

23. "Padrón de Havitantes qe existen en Bahía Blanca," 1845, AGN X 17-6-4. See also George Reid Andrews, *Los Afroargentinos de Buenos Aires* (Buenos Aires, Argentina: Ediciones de la Flor, 1989), 81.

24. Solomianski, *Identidades secretas*, 112–15.

25. The poem is reproduced in Solomianski, *Identidades secretas*, 116–18. It is a verbatim reproduction of the version published by Luis Soler Cañas, *Negros, gauchos y compadres en el cancionero de la Federación* (Buenos Aires, Argentina: Instituto de Investigaciones Históricas Juan Manuel de Rosas, 1958).

26. In the Indian frontier, Rosas was the general of the expeditionary forces.

27. The angel's message is quite telling: "Ya no gemirá en el Plata en cadenas niún esclavo. Su amargo llanto cesó desde que Rosas humano, de su libertad ufano, compasivo y generoso, prodigó este don precioso al infeliz Africano." Quoted in Fermín Chávez, *Juan Manuel de Rosas, su iconografía* (Buenos Aires, Argentina: Editorial Oriente, 1970), 138.

28. P. González Bernaldo writes: "El Cuadro da testimonio de la confusión deliberada entre régimen de Rosas y libertad de los esclavos: confusión cuyo principal objetivo no es sólo ganar la fidelidad de los africanos sino mostrar al mundo entero—muy en especial a Inglaterra—que el régimen es un régimen de derecho natural." P. González Bernaldo, *Civilidad y política*, 170.

29. In the countryside, female captives freed from the Indian *toldos* (huts) were sometimes reduced to servitude under the custom of *crianza*. In practice, these servants were treated worse than slaves and were subject to punishment and abuse. See Juan Méndez Avellaneda, "Entonces la mujer," *Todo es historia*, 286 (1991): 50–51.

30. Judge Domingo Larrea to chief of police, Buenos Aires, December 2, 1831, AGN X 31-9-5.

31. Petition of ex-slave Angela, Buenos Aires, March 10, 1838, AGN X 43-1-5.

32. "Contra la negra María Melgarejo a pedido de su ama," AHPBA, Juzgado del Crimen (1829), 34-4-85-19.

33. "Contra la parda Petrona Sarratea por robo de dinero a Da. Jacinta Laurel," AHPBA, Juzgado del Crimen (1840), 41-1-130-37.

34. With the help of an *escribiente*, they narrated in detail their husbands' violence, hoping to impress male judges—the narration of sword beatings during pregnancy certainly made a point.

35. Ricardo Cicerchia, "Familia: La Historia de una idea: Los Desórdenes domésticos de la plebe urbana porteña, 1776–1850," in *Vivir en familia*, ed. C. Wainerman (Buenos Aires, Argentina: UNICEF-Losada, 1994), 49–72.

36. "No existe, propiamente, un tipo de gaucho: uno es rubio, otros *morenos*, blancos o un poco cobrizos. Algunos son delgados y barbudos, otros obesos y lampiños, jóvenes y viejos, tienen en el fondo el mismo carácter, con los mismo vicios o cualidades." Henri Armaignac, *Viaje por las pampas de la República Argentina* (La Plata, Argentina: Ministerio de Educación, 1961).

37. Armaignac, *Viaje por las pampas*, 39.

38. MacCann, quoted in Samuel Trifilo, *La Argentina vista por viajeros ingleses: 1810–1860* (Buenos Aires, Argentina: Ediciones Gure, 1959), 65.

39. Due to the Anglo-French blockade (1845–1848), many unemployed foreign sailors were traversing the countryside, looking for employment. John Brabazon, *Andanzas de un irlandés en el campo porteno (1845–1864)*, trans. E. A. Coghlan (Buenos Aires, Argentina: Ministerio de Cultura y Educación, 1981).

40. Salvatore, *Wandering Paysanos*.

41. Mayo, "Patricio Belén."

42. Salvatore, *Wandering Paysanos*, 189.

43. Salvatore, *Wandering Paysanos*, 189.

44. Reid Andrews, *Los Afroargentinos de Buenos Aires*.

45. See James Scobie, *Argentina: A City and a Nation*, 2nd ed. (New York: Oxford University Press, 1971); Roberto Cortés Conde and Ezequiel Gallo, *La Formación de la Argentina moderna* (Buenos Aires, Argentina: Paidós, 1967); George Reid Andrews, "Race versus Class Association: The Afro-Argentines of Buenos Aires, 1850–1900," *Journal of Latin American Studies* 11, no. 1 (1979): 19–39.

46. Oscar Chamosa, "To Honor the Ashes of Their Forebears: The Rise and Crisis of African Nations in the Post-independence State of Buenos Aires, 1820–1860," *Americas* 59, no. 3 (2003): 347–78.

47. On this topic see also John Chasteen, "Black Kings, Blackface Carnival, and the Nineteenth-Century Origins of the Tango," in *Latin American Popular Culture: An Introduction*, ed. William H. Beezley and Linda A. Curcio-Nage (Wilmington, DE: Scholarly Resources, 2000), 43–60.

48. Chamosa, "To Honor the Ashes," 127.

49. Reid Andrews, "Race versus Class Association," 19–39.

50. Aníbal Latino [José Ceppi], *Tipos y costumbres bonaerenses*, 2nd ed. (Buenos Aires, Argentina: Hyspamerica, 1984), 81–87.

51. Latino, *Tipos y costumbres bonaerenses*; Víctor Gálvez [Vicente Quesada], "La Raza africana en Buenos Aires," *Nueva revista de Buenos Aires* 8 (1883): 246–60.

52. The hymn emphasized equality between whites and blacks, presenting the notion that they were only sun-tanned sons of the Argentine nation, marked with special good fortune and hope. Solomianski, *Identidades secretas*, 211–13.

53. The poem is partially reproduced in Solomianski, *Identidades secretas*, 214–15.

54. Solomianski, *Identidades secretas*, 214.

55. At one point the author identifies the master—the white man—with despotism. And, as indicated above, the "Negro" enjoyed his natural freedom before he was enslaved.

56. For example Jorge M. Ford included this poem into his work *Benemeritos de mi estirpe* (1899), thus making the poem available to future generations.

57. See Solomianski, *Identidades secretas*, 201–7.

58. See in this regard an editorial published in September 1879, quoted in Solomianski, *Identidades secretas*, 194.

59. Francine Masiello, "Estado, género y sexualidad en la cultura de fin de siglo," in *Las Culturas de fin de siglo en América Latina*, ed. Josefina Ludmer (Rosario, Argentina: Beatriz Viterbo, 1994), 139–49.

60. Solomianski, *Identidades secretas*, 209.

61. Gabino Ezeiza (1858–1916) was the best known of Afro-Argentine *payadores*. Through his performances, Ezeiza managed to project to Argentine audiences a particular black aesthetic. Solomianski, *Identidades secretas*, 218–23; Nestor Rodrigo Ortiz, *Aspectos de la cultura Africana en el Río de la Plata* (Buenos Aires, Argentina: Plus Ultra, 1974), 116; Beatriz Seibel *Historia del teatro argentino* (Buenos Aires, Argentina: Corregidor, 2002), 202–3. Beatriz Seibel, "La Presencia afroargentina en el espectáculo," in Picotti, *El Negro en la Argentina*, 204.

62. More contradictory was Ford's support of Mitre's war against Paraguay, in which Argentine had allied herself with Brazil, probably the only remaining state supporting slavery. Solomianski, *Identidades secretas*, 197–200.

63. Oscar Terán, *Positivismo y nación en la Argentina* (Buenos Aires, Argentina: Puntosur, 1987); Ricardo D. Salvatore, "Criminology, Prison Reform, and the Buenos Aires Working-Class, 1900–1920," *Journal of Interdisciplinary History* 23, no. 2 (1992); Juan Suriano, ed., *La Cuestión social en la Argentina, 1870–1943* (Buenos Aires, Argentina: La Colmena, 2000).

64. Reid Andrews, *Los Afroargentinos de Buenos Aires*.

# 4

# Free *Pardos* and Mulattoes Vanquish Indians

## Cultural Civility as Conquest and Modernity in Honduras

*Dario Euraque*

*Miscegenation, cultural mestizaje, and religious syncretism played important roles in the formation of Latin American nation-states. Intellectuals, politicians, and ordinary Latin Americans often utilized and transformed these realities into powerful ideologies for a variety of purposes. Thinkers such as the Argentine Domingo Faustino Sarmiento (1811–1888) and the Bolivian Alcides Arguedas (1879– 1946) looked upon black and indigenous influences in a negative light and cited them as responsible for defects in their nation's character. Many others promoted white European immigration as an antidote to so-called racial degeneracy. In the late nineteenth and early twentieth centuries, many countries that could not attract enough European immigrants to whiten their demographics focused on the celebration of mestizaje as a means to promote a mixed, or mestizo, identity. This was the case in Brazil and Mexico. Few countries outside Haiti explicitly promoted or celebrated blackness or their African heritage.*

*In most cases, the celebration of mestizaje as a national symbol implied an acceptance, if not promotion, of "whitening." Patriots viewed mestizo identities as more favorable than black or indigenous ones. Indeed, in Honduras, intellectuals and politicians constructed their national ideology of mestizaje in opposition to a particular type of blackness and Native American identity. In this chapter, Dario Euraque takes us through the slow and complicated process of the forging of a mes-*

81

*tizo national identity in Honduras. Honduran elites employed a "rhetoric of con-*
*quest, civility, and modernity" to promote a unique Honduran mestizo identity that*
*included some selected individuals of African ancestry and excluded others.*

Many contemporary Honduran intellectuals reject the use of race as a primary framework of reference into the Honduran past. Juan Ramón Martínez (b.1941), for example, one of Honduras's best-known intellectuals who
frequently addresses Honduras's history and traditions, often downplays
issues of racial origins in general and Honduras's African roots in particular.[1] This is surprising for two reasons. First, Martínez hails from the town
of Olanchito in the province of Yoro, one of Honduras's Caribbean provinces historically associated with the country's black, mulatto, and *pardo*
populations. Second, Martínez and other Honduran intellectuals largely
ignore the practice of early historians who explicitly acknowledged the
black origins of the founders of the provinces of Yoro and Olancho.[2]
Indeed, free mulattoes from the province of Olancho founded Yoro, the
regional capital of the department of the same name, in 1649.[3] Historically,
black slavery played a more important role in many towns in the province
of Yoro, including Olanchito, than in any other place in Honduras.[4]

This chapter explores the black origins of the town of Olanchito in the
province of Yoro in the context of the shifting debates of Honduran
national identity. It places the foundation of the town into the context of
three historical debates that have affected how Hondurans viewed themselves: the evangelizing discourse of the Spanish missionaries of the eighteenth century, the "civilizing" discourse of the nineteenth-century post-
independence era, and the rhetoric of *civismo* developed by Olanchito's
intellectuals in the early twentieth century. These ideologies, which have
worked together to create an image of a "civilized" mestizo nation, contrast
with the historical record and the memories of many Hondurans.[5] To
understand the construction of this image, it is necessary to examine how
Honduran intellectuals and politicians in the nineteenth and twentieth
centuries helped to revise Honduran history to downplay its African influences and succeeded in locating blackness as an outside force associated
with the Garifuna, an immigrant population that made its way to Honduras
in the late eighteenth and early nineteenth centuries. In exploring these
processes we will gain a fuller understanding of the complex legacy of the
African population in Honduras.

## HISTORICAL BACKGROUND AND TWENTIETH-
## CENTURY IDEAS OF CIVILITY

Honduras as a province of Central America declared its independence from
Spain in 1821. It became a member state of the Central American Federa-

tion in 1824 but separated from it in 1838. Between the 1820s and 1830s, civil wars characterized the political scenario, although stability was restored during the government of Francisco Ferrera (1841–1847). Some kind of stability continued with the governments of Juan Lindo (1848–1852) and José Trinidad Cabañas (1852–1856). General Santos Guardiola, who was supported by Rafael Carrera, the main enemy of Morazán and Cabañas, defeated Cabañas. Guardiola was assassinated and succeeded by José María Medina, who remained in power until 1872, when Celeo Arias, aided by political leaders from El Salvador and Guatemala, defeated him. Civil wars continued until 1876. After that year, Marco Aurelio Soto, supported by Rufino Barrios, president of Guatemala, ruled the country until 1883. Luis Bográn succeeded him and remained in office until 1890.

Throughout the course of the nineteenth century, public education in Honduras did not advance much, even when the state passed laws and regulations to promote education in 1847, 1866, 1875, and 1881.[6] All these legal provisions, and the reforms of the 1890s, charged the political governors of the departments, appointed by executive decree, with supervising elementary schools and teachers, who would be supported with resources granted by municipal authorities. At the close of the nineteenth century, governors shared duties with departmental inspectors and commissioners appointed by municipalities, such as Olanchito. These regional offices hired educators, developed programs, selected texts, and administered exams by executive decrees.

According to prominent intellectuals from Olanchito, this city, which currently has a population of about 80,000 inhabitants, is a peculiar city in Honduras. Juan Ramon Martínez, for example, has argued that the distinctive character of the city is "grounded in the broad affection its inhabitants have always had for 'culture,' and particularly their inhabitants' inclination for 'the word' and literature, prose and poetry. The people of Olanchito are so proud of their affection and inclination for 'culture' that in Tegucigalpa, as well as in other provincial cities, such attitudes are interpreted as boastfulness."[7]

The view that promotes the idea of Olanchito's cultural uniqueness has its roots in the generation of Honduran intellectuals of the early twentieth century. They believed that their ancestors were especially concerned with providing education to the inhabitants as a way to "progress," and they neglected military careers. Local authorities brought schoolteachers to Olanchito and prepared educators who could continue the schooling of more teachers. Furthermore, the vocation for education and culture is explained, according to Martínez, not by "a magical or an improvised act, but as a result of a long anticipated and reiterated collective dream, that existed from the time the Spanish conquerors rode in on horseback, and listened to the vibrations of a culture that would develop along the margins of a river."[8]

For Martínez and others, this meant that the education system introduced by the state in that region during the nineteenth and twentieth centuries built on a "cultural spirit" present in Olanchito prior to the Spanish conquest. However, it was not nature per se that allowed for the fact that in Olanchito military men put down their arms in favor of civilization. "Culture," suggests Martínez, is "a human product, and since Olanchito, from the beginning, was and continues to be, more than a landscape, the sum of actions of those born there[,] . . . the leaders joined in an effort to establish schools, to emphasize the role and prominence of educators, and above all, to place the love for Honduras first."[9]

In the early twentieth century, Juan Ramón Fúnez, author of a *History of Olanchito*, explained the factors that contributed to the development of "cultural civility" in that region. "The people of Olanchito," declared Fúnez, "because of a natural inclination, have abilities when communicating with others. They are excellent speakers, and they have overcome their shyness when expressing their opinions, standing out because of the easy way they relate to other people."[10] According to Fúnez, schooling promoted such faculties beginning first with "civic Saturdays," special days designated by the authorities to celebrate patriotism, national values, the civic calendar, and national heroes. In sum, the authorities promoted campaigns that encouraged attributes that made people value themselves positively. That is how "Olanchito's people forged particular attributes such as good speech, love for reading, love for working, and . . . participated to keep alive the positive values of society. Such activities created the civility of Olanchito."

Local political leaders and astute intellectuals and teachers also played a role in promoting civil pride and culture. According to Fúnez, in 1935, Francisco Murillo Soto (1893–1988) encouraged community leaders and municipal authorities to celebrate the "Week of Civility." During that week, school students would be engaged in civic activities, starting seven days before the Central America Independence Day, September 15. Murillo Soto graduated from the teacher's college in Tegucigalpa in 1915, thanks to a scholarship procured by General Purificación Zelaya (1866–1940), a congressman and native of Olanchito. When Murillo Soto promoted the Week of Civility, he already had twenty years of pedagogical experience, and when Juan Ramón Martínez studied in Olanchito's elementary school in the 1940s, local authorities and intellectuals were already aware of a "natural inclination" for culture and refined speech; by the 1940s they were proud of civic Saturdays and the Week of Civility, which presently distinguishes Olanchito as the so-called City of Civility.[11]

This notion of civility, however, which developed in the early twentieth century and has reverberations in Olanchito today, does not accurately reflect the region's past. Moreover, the modern and contemporary discourse of civility has allowed citizen and historian alike to reinterpret the region's past in a more positive light. This interpretation not only avoids discussions of race, and thus its black heritage, but it also overlooks the eighteenth- and nineteenth-century policies of conquest and evangelization that subdued native populations and allowed intellectuals and politicians to forge a positive "civilized" mestizo identity. Furthermore, the arrival of the Black Caribs (or Garifuna), a population that Hondurans clearly identified as black "outsiders" (through the Honduran term *moreno*), allowed many to relegate blackness outside the national polity.

## REGIONALISM AND THE COMPLEX ETHNO-RACIAL CONTEXT OF OLANCHITO'S PAST

Writing regional histories in Honduras from an ethno-racial point of view is a difficult task because few researchers have dealt with this issue. Table 4.1 is based on the regional divisions made by Francisco Guevara-Escudero. He divides the country at the beginning of the nineteenth century into three geo-economic regions; distinctions are made according to agricultural and pastoral production, and their relation to particular topographic and geographic features. Furthermore, each region was articulated differently based on the import and export systems associated with regional and foreign economies.[12] The sum of these factors differentiates each region. Thus, the history of Olanchito will be placed within this context, as well as the origin of the cultural civility of the community in the eighteenth and nineteenth centuries.

Guevara-Escudero segmented Honduras's territory into three zones: The eastern zone includes the department of Olancho and the eastern part of the department of Yoro, which encompasses what is now the department of Atlántida; the central zone covers the department of Tegucigalpa, today called the department of Francisco Morazán, and includes Choluteca; and the western zone consists of the departments of Comayagua, Gracias, and Santa Bárbara as well as the present-day department of Cortés, and the western part of the department of Yoro. In 1801, the eastern zone, the least populated of the three zones, consisting of 128,353 inhabitants, represented 6 percent of the nation's population; 45 percent of the inhabitants lived in the central zone; and the western zone, the most populated, registered 49 percent of the total population. At that time, the community of Olanchito, consisting of 1,500 inhabitants, was located in the least populated zone, which also experienced the lowest demographic increase during the nineteenth century and at the beginning of the twentieth century.[13]

This geo-economic segmentation had its origins in a convergence of vari-

**Table 4.1.** Demographic Growth by Departments and Regional Zones in Honduras, 1801–1910

| Zones | Years | | | |
|---|---|---|---|---|
| | *1801* | *1855* | *1887* | *1910* |
| **Western** | | | | |
| Comayagua | 13,845 | 50,000 | 16,739 | 26,339 |
| La Paz (1869) | | | 18,000 | 28,764 |
| Intibucá (1883) | | | 17,942 | 27,285 |
| Santa Bárbara | 9,054 | 42,000 | 32,634 | 39,064 |
| Copán (1869) | | | 36,634 | 40,282 |
| Cortés (1893) | | | | 23,559 |
| Lempira | 40,103 | 65,000 | 27,816 | 49,955 |
| Ocotepeque (1906) | | | | 28,190 |
| Gracias a Dios | | | | |
| Subtotal | 63,002 | 157,000 | 150,675 | 263,438 |
| **Central** | | | | |
| F. Morazán | 25,948 | 55,000 | 60,170 | 81,844 |
| El Paraíso (1869) | | | 18,057 | 42,118 |
| Choluteca | 17,308 | 20,000 | 43,588 | 45,817 |
| Valle (1893) | | | | 30,479 |
| Yoro | 14,392 | 18,000 | 13,996 | 18,926 |
| Islas de la Bahía (1892) | | | 2,825 | 4,893 |
| Atlántida (1902) | | | | 11,372 |
| Subtotal | 57,648 | 93,000 | 138,636 | 246,821 |
| **Eastern** | | | | |
| Olancho | 7,703 | 52,000 | 31,132 | 43,368 |
| Colón (1881) | | | 11,474 | 11,191 |
| Subtotal | 7,703 | 52,000 | 42,600 | 54,559 |
| **Total** | **128,353** | **302,000** | **334,742** | **564,818** |

*Sources:* The information for the years between 1801–1910 for most of the departments, not including the Bay Islands, is from Francisco Guevara-Escudero, "Nineteenth-Century Honduras: A Regional Approach to the Economic History of Central America, 1839–1914" (PhD diss., New York University, 1983), 92.

ous factors. First, during the mining boom of the sixteenth century, between 1,000 and 1,500 black slaves were imported into Olancho. After the mining decline, the small population of Spaniards initiated a movement into the interior of the country, at the same time depopulating the few settlements located on the north coast. Within this context, more important than the decline of mining exports was the demographic catastrophe suffered by the indigenous population. For the beginning of the sixteenth century, the Honduran aboriginal population has been calculated at 800,0000 inhabitants, 18 percent of the total Central American population at the end of the fifteenth century.[14] Around 1550 that population fell to 132,000 inhabitants, a radical decrease of 84 percent.[15] This demographic catastrophe continued during the following two centuries and had different regional impacts. At the end of the seventeenth century, the indigenous population has been estimated at 47,544 inhabitants, showing a precipitous decrease of 64 percent between 1550 and the last decades of the seventeenth century.[16] This process explains the following figures for the tributary population of Honduras in different years: 15,000 in 1539; 5,106 in 1582; 4,864 in 1590; 5,701 in 1770; 7,479 in 1801; and 7,898 in 1811.[17] The Olanchito tributary population experienced a similar pattern. Around 1740 this population consisted of 200 Indians; in 1770 it decreased to 100 Indians, and by 1810 there were just 70 Indians paying tribute in Olanchito.[18]

In 1777, Honduras's population consisted of 88,965 inhabitants distributed as follows: 47 percent in the western zone, 47 percent in the central zone, and 6 percent in the eastern zone.[19] The Spanish population moved into the interior and settled in the most favorable lands of the central and western zones; subsequently, the Indians—especially the Lencas—suffered the effects of that slow conquest. The Indians of the northern part of the central zone, those living in the eastern part of the western zone (in the western part of the present-day department of Yoro), and those located in the eastern zone were subjected to a second wave of evangelization and conquest that continued into the end of the eighteenth century.

Olanchito and Yoro, founded in the middle of the seventeenth century by mulattoes and free *pardos*, played an important role in that second evangelization and conquest of the Tolupan Indians. They helped bring Creole values, customs, and government and business practices to the region, to the detriment of the existing indigenous populations.[20]

This appraisal indicates that the process of *mestizaje* deserves a regional and historical analysis, a task up to now not seriously approached by Honduran historians. In fact, the historiography of *mestizaje* in Honduras remains in its infancy. Marvin Barahona has presented a history of racial mixture in two periods: the first between 1520 and the first decades of the eighteenth century, and the second between the middle of the eighteenth century and the first decades of the nineteenth century. According to Barahona, racial mixture during the first period was meager, due primarily to the decline of the Indian population and because of the small number of Spanish immigrants arriving in Honduras. In the eastern zone, racial mixture was low even in the second period.

As Barahona points out, within the context of the Bourbon reforms in the eighteenth century, the recovery of the indigo and silver economies, the prohibition against non-Indian groups living in Indian towns, and the population growth registered during that century, Indian-Spanish *mestizaje* not only increased considerably, but it was concentrated in the present-day province of Francisco Morazán and in the departments of Choluteca and Comayagua. The settlements located within these departments attracted all types of racial mixtures, including mestizos, ladinos, mulattoes, *pardos*, and others different from the indigenous population and concentrated in the western departments and the already largely depopulated north coast or Caribbean coast.

At the end of the eighteenth century, the peninsular and *criollo* families amounted to a minority compared to the population of racial mixture considered ladino, Spanish-speaking Indians or Indian-Spanish mestizos.[21] However, in large areas of the departments of the western and eastern zones, miscegenation was less intense and enjoyed different rhythms compared to the racial mixing in the departments of the central zone, where it is supposed that ladino racial mixture was predominant. When the department of Yoro was created in 1825, the largest population was not ladino but Indian, followed by an important population segment considered mulattoes. At the beginning of nineteenth century, 30 percent of Honduras's population were mulattoes and/or of African ancestry.

Were *pardos* or mulattoes the principal actors in the history of the department of Yoro, and particularly in the municipality of Olanchito after independence in the 1820s? The fact is that in Honduras, a certain elastic racial classification existed in the colonial period, which has not yet been studied with primary documents. This is the case for the town of Olanchito. However, the available documentation rescued by colonial scholars suggests that, even if we do not have foundational documents for Olanchito, like the ones we have for Yoro, it is highly probable that the town was founded by blacks, consistent with the historical memory from the beginning of the twentieth century. According to one woman living at the turn of that century, for example, her grandparents told her that Olanchito was founded "by fugitive blacks from the department of Olancho and La Mosquitia," as was Yoro in 1649, for which we have documents.[22]

The demographic data available for Olanchito for the seventeenth and eighteenth centuries, as well as the data available for the beginning of nineteenth century, show a town whose population was composed mostly of mulattoes and ladinos. Such a characterization was a way to deny the black origins of many urban towns in Honduras in general.[23] For example, the first ethno-racial census for Olanchito shows that in 1683, ten Spaniards, two mestizos, and twenty-four mulattoes lived there. By then, 3 Spaniards and 167 *pardos* inhabited the town of Yoro, 33 years after its establishment by mulattoes.

A century later, in 1876, Olanchito reported 1,478 inhabitants, including 105 Spanish adults, 986 adult ladinos, and 387 Indians. In the same year, Yoro reported 2,761 inhabitants, 48 of whom were adult Spaniards; 2,446 ladinos; and 267 Indians, probably conquered Tolupan and perhaps tribute-paying Indians. By 1801, Olanchito registered a population of 1,692 "souls," divided between Spaniards and ladinos. This last census does not specify categories, but without a doubt, it maintained its historic mulatto predominance. Even so, such a number represented a minority when compared to the number of Tolupan Indians surrounding the mulattoes.

During the eighteenth century and the beginning of the nineteenth century, in Honduras and no doubt in Olanchito, as occurred in others areas of Latin America, deep racist prejudices prevailed not only against Indians but also against those individuals classified under the caste categories created by Spaniards or other whites for peoples with some degree of African ancestry, that is, mulattoes, *pardos*, and the like. Addressing this history for Honduras is difficult because there is a generalized misconception on the matter that has been neatly summarized by an important Honduran anthropologist: "The Honduran black disappeared in the *mestizaje* process. Nothing remains of his culture, but the phonotypical factors present in a great part of the Honduran population."[24] But when, why, and where did blacks disappear?

Mario Felipe Martinez Castillo, one of the most important Honduran historians of the colonial period, provided a partial answer to this question when he stated that "Tegucigalpa never had dominant elite based on blood purity; it was managed by a mining and merchant bourgeoisie for whom ethnic origin was not important."[25] While certain historians could apply this assertion to Olanchito, there is evidence that challenges that assumption there and in other locations in Honduras.[26] Mulattoes and *pardos* played critical roles throughout Honduras, including roles that historians have traditionally attributed simply to mestizos.

## THE HISTORICAL RECORD: MULATTOES AND HONDURAN POLITICS IN THE NINETEENTH CENTURY

Honduran authorities abolished legal slavery in 1824.[27] For the first time, mulattoes and *pardos* became citizens, which gave them the right to vote in the provincial deputy elections of 1820. It was not an easy beginning. Consider the case of José Flamenco, a wealthy mulatto resident in the department of Choluteca, the central zone, who raised a complaint before the Guatemalan provincial deputy because the mayor of Tegucigalpa prevented mulattoes and *pardos* from participating in the municipal elections of that year.[28]

Under these conditions, local mulatto and *pardo* identities would be transformed in provincial municipalities across Honduras in general and in urban towns in the present-day departments of Yoro, Atlántida, Olancho, and Colón. In the process, black influences slowly disappeared from national histories. Not surprisingly, by the 1930s and 1940s, local histories of important municipalities in these regions had already begun promoting *mestizaje* without reference to blackness. One tourist book about the municipality of Olanchito around 1930 states, for example, that Olanchito "was established as a municipality and declared a city the same year of its foundation; its residents are of the Indian and Spanish race; at present the municipality has 10,000 inhabitants, products of the mixture of the two races."[29]

The first Honduran president after the destruction of the Central American Federation in the 1830s was, temporarily, Francisco Zelaya y Ayes, the richest hacendado in the department of Olancho and a descendant of Spanish colonists from the seventeenth century.[30] He became president within the context of the dissolution of the federation and the exile of Francisco Morazán, former president of the federation (1830–1834, 1835–1839). As president of an independent Honduras, Zelaya y Ayes established his office in Juticalpa, considered by the Spanish authorities at the beginning of the nineteenth century a mulatto municipality. In 1821 Juticalpa had 1,200 inhabitants, less than the population of Olanchito in 1800.[31]

Following Francisco Zelaya, General Francisco Ferrera (1794–1851), who ruled Honduras from 1841 to 1847, was the man who played a central role in a newly emerging discourse on race in the first half of the nineteenth century. Ferrera was born in San Juan de Flores, a town close to Tegucigalpa, located within the central zone defined by Guevara-Escudero, and Barahona earlier on. At birth, he was classified as a *pardo*. In fact, he was one of the first *pardos* to enjoy electoral citizenship in 1820, when he was twenty-six years old. He became mayor of his hometown.

Initially Ferrera was linked to the liberal movement of Morazán, but in 1830 he turned against Morazán and authorized the first execution of a Honduran president, Don Joaquín Rivera.[32] Rivera and Zelaya were descendants of important Spanish families who had settled in Tegucigalpa. Ferrera, on the other hand, represented the exact opposite. As Ramón Rosa, the most important intellectual of late nineteenth-century Honduras, wrote in his memoirs, Ferrera was the "mulatto of iron."[33]

Unfortunately, we cannot describe with certainty Ferrera's ethnic or racial identity. However, certain elements indicate that Ferrera was the first powerful individual who addressed the African inheritance that "stained" his own birth and put him in a difficult situation. In 1819, when Ferrera was twenty-five years old, a priest called him "a resident mulatto," and he was subsequently the object of an unfair criminal accusation by the authorities from Tegucigalpa. He was charged with supposed acts of insubordination and scandals due to drunkenness.[34] Colonial authorities described him as "short and fat, of a wheat-colored [*trigueño*] complexion, curly hair and with a scar above his upper lip and another on his cheek."[35]

Such a description introduces another element that complicates the racial prescriptions and classifications used in the immediate postcolonial period in Honduras: the use of the word *mulatto* (*mulato* in Spanish) compared to the use of the term *trigueño*, which in Spanish means the color of wheat and was used then to describe wheat-colored skin. However, the use of such a term did not necessarily imply black or African ancestry, or any other racial classification. In fact we have colonial documents from the 1790s that refer to Spanish individuals disembarking in the port of Trujillo, on the Caribbean coast, with the following phonotypical descriptions: Juan Reyes— short, *trigueño*, bearded, gray haired, and honey-colored eyes—and Josef Herrera—tall, honey-colored eyes, black beard, and clear *trigueño*. Nonetheless, these examples help us to understand that General Ferrera's *trigueño* complexion connoted a different meaning from that used in Spain, and not necessarily because of the color of his complexion, but because of the African ancestry registered in his precolonial *pardo* classification.[36]

More significant is General Ferrera's 1842 decree that ordered "the repatriation of all *morenos* [a racial euphemism for black or negro] and other individuals from the Port of Omoa who abandoned the national territory between 1832 and 1833, as a consequence of the revolutionary movement headed by General Vicente Domínguez."[37] Ferrera was referring to members of a black group currently known in Honduras as Garifuna, but who were then known as Black Caribs, Caribs, or *morenos*. The baptismal records from the 1850s from the town of Trujillo, on the Caribbean coast of the country, are full of records of *morenos*, for example. The presence of Black Caribs in Honduras would play a key role in cementing Honduras's mestizo identity.[38]

## THE HISTORY OF THE GARIFUNA

In 1797, as is well known in the Honduran historiography, the English left 2,000 to 4,000 Garifuna in Roatan, an island off the Caribbean coast of Honduras then controlled by the British, although claimed by the Spanish. Soon after, the Garifuna settled in the old colonial port of Trujillo.[39] The Garifuna represented a mixed people of black African and Indian ancestry from the island of Saint Vincent. The English deported the Garifuna because they resisted subjugation. The resistance against the English has a complicated history dating back to the early eighteenth century. Up to that time, the original Indian-Carib population's contact with outsiders was mostly with French colonists and their African slaves.

By the mid-eighteenth century, in the midst of European imperial rivalries, the British fought the French for control over St. Vincent and the increasingly mixed African-Carib populations, who resisted subjugation of all sorts by all powers. In the process, these Afro-native peoples also made and dissolved alliances with the French and the British. By the 1760s, when the British finally took over Saint Vincent, the Afro-indigenous populations were known to the English-speaking world as Black Caribs. They now defended their lands from the British, who, after a number of wars, made a decision to deport the community to Roatan, which is off the coast of the Honduran mainland. From there, they made their way to Trujillo on the mainland, which by the 1790s had a long history of a largely mulatto and *pardo* pedigree.[40]

From the outset, the Spanish speakers on the Caribbean coast referred to the Black Caribs, or Garifuna, with the term *moreno*, which had a longer history as a euphemism for a black or negro. By the first decades of the nineteenth century, however, especially on the Caribbean coast of Honduras, the euphemistic reference associated with the word *moreno* lost ground to the use of the notion of *moreno* as an ethnic reference for the old Black Caribs. This seems to have been linked to the regional distribution of the *morenos* as they moved west and east from Trujillo. Around 1820, the so-called *morenos*, or *negros caribes* (Black Caribs), began populating the Caribbean coast of Honduras, often coming in contact with Tolupan Indians and others who survived there, but in tiny numbers.[41] Some Garifuna traveled into the interior hinterlands, even as far away as Santa Rosa de Copán, a town located at the extreme west of the country.[42]

The events alluded to in General Francisco Ferrera's 1842 decree actually began in 1831, when Ferrera, then during the government of Francisco Morazán, repressed an initial uprising by General Vicente Domínguez. General Domínguez had been receiving support from the Black Caribs, who had arrived from Saint Vincent. Domínguez and his black allies lost the battle. Black Caribs were persecuted as traitors to the new republic, which forced some of them to flee to Belize. Morazán also suggested transferring the Black Caribs to the Pacific ports, away from their new homes on the Caribbean coast, where they might join other rebellions.[43] Later, in 1832, General Domínguez, again with the help of Black Caribs, but now supported by enemies of Morazán from Guatemala, defeated General Francisco Ferrera.

In 1842, only ten years after General Domínguez's uprising, General Ferrera ordered the repatriation of the *morenos*. Ferrera's use of the term *moreno* was indicative of an emerging, and eventually hegemonic, racial discourse in which the state attributed "real" blackness only to the Black Caribs, the so-called *morenos* who arrived in Honduras in 1797. In Honduras, thereafter the term *moreno* was used as an ethnic reference for the Black Caribs, not to be confused with *moreno* as a euphemism for "black" in some other

Latin American countries, or even in Honduras prior to the early 1800s. Thus, the pre-Garifuna African colonial inheritance, including General Ferrera's mulatto/*pardo* ancestry, was eliminated. In fact, Honduran leaders and many free mulattoes who descended from *cimarrones*, runaway slaves, have historically denied their African ancestry and do not use the term *moreno* to define themselves. This process of denial and whitening was at once an example of a type of republican ethnogenesis and symptomatic of a Latin American "civilizing" conquest, which branded *some* black peoples as outsiders and reinforced the exploitation of native populations such as the Tolupan Indians.[44]

It is important to emphasize that General Ferrera's ascension to power served important sectors of mulattoes and *pardos* who distinguished themselves from *morenos*, and who after the 1830s were more and more often considered *trigueño* citizens in a postcolonial and post-slave society, thus diluting or denying any African ancestry. This enabled the mulattoes and *pardos* to exert and practice forms of a liberal citizenship that, prior to 1820, were denied to free mulattoes and free *pardos*. In Olanchito and Yoro during the 1840s, as well as in other towns that in the past had been populated by mulattoes and *pardos*, provincial intellectuals started to think about the meaning of their black inheritance at a moment when a republican nationality was being constructed in Honduras and elsewhere in Latin America.[45] In Olanchito, such a reflection originated in a particular ethno-racial context, especially because in the 1820s the majority of the population of the department of Yoro consisted of Tolupan Indians who survived the Spanish conquest.

## HONDURAS'S NATIVES AND THE DISCOURSE OF CIVILITY

The Tolupan Indians survived the demographic catastrophe suffered in the sixteenth and seventeenth centuries by other indigenous populations. Only in the eighteenth century did Honduras's indigenous population witness growth especially in the eastern zone of the country. In 1800 almost half of Honduras's population was Indian, even if by then the Tolupan Indians had already abandoned the Caribbean coast. Only at the beginning of the nineteenth century was that region settled by the Black Caribs. The Tolupans remained in the department of Yoro, resisting evangelization efforts by Franciscan missionaries.[46]

In 1813, the Franciscan inspector general declared that the Tolupan Indians not only rejected the priests, but that they also hated "civility."[47] There is no doubt that such so-called civility was grounded in the Christian civility of Saint Augustine and his "City of God." It was not a reference to the civility or civilization of the secular city that later would be championed by the formerly free mulattoes and *pardos*, like General Ferrera, who were converted into republican citizens at the beginning of the nineteenth century. For the Tolupan Indians, both discourses implied a sorrowful and forced acculturation.

Since the end of the sixteenth century, the term *jicaque*, which means "barbarian," "pagan," and "wild," was applied to any seminomadic Indian group that subsisted on hunting and fishing. That term was also used to designate the ancestors of the Tolupan Indians of the eighteenth century and any other seminomadic Indian group resisting evangelization and conquest.[48] During that time, the Tolupan Indians, who resisted forced settlement managed by Franciscan missionaries, were classified as *enmontañados* and *selváticos*, those living in the mountains or in the jungles. Later, in the 1860s, President José María Medina charged departmental governors with the task of civilizing these *enmontañados* and *selváticos*. Efforts continued into the 1870s, and by the end of the nineteenth century, a municipal law charged regional governors with "the protection of the *selváticos* and their civilization."[49]

The civilizing project of the nineteenth century was common in the Americas, and perhaps best expressed in Domingo Sarmiento's *Civilization and Barbarism*, published in 1845. While the Honduran case offers elements of Sarmiento's views, the case of the department of Yoro, and the municipality of Olanchito, offers several interesting distinctions. Nonetheless, it is not possible to deny the possible influence of Sarmiento's ideas among Honduran intellectuals of that time, especially those in Tegucigalpa, including the famous Adolfo Zuñiga (1835–1900).[50] Between the 1860s and the 1880s, Zuñiga was one of the country's most important intellectuals and legislators, especially after the 1870s. His writings demonstrate significant knowledge of Argentinean arguments about the need to attract European immigration to the Americas, the need for a new "civilizing mission," and the need to eliminate the remnants of the "savage tribes" in the region.[51]

The discourse of cultural civility in Olanchito represented not only a regional and provincial civilizing vision to be applied to the Tolupan Indians, the *selváticos*, but it also implied the construction of a subjective regional and provincial cultural citizenship devoid of blackness, even in its colonial pedigrees, that is, as mulattoes or *pardos*. This cultural citizenship denied a strong black, mulatto, and *pardo* ancestry embodied by many thousands of Hondurans who were not as well known as General Ferrera.

This cultural citizenship was in turn radicalized via the word *trigueño* and also juxtaposed to the emerging discourse around blackness associated with *morenos* in the post-1797 world of the Garifuna's arrival in Honduras. To understand the consolidation of such a process in the nineteenth century, in the department of Yoro, and later in the municipality of Olanchito, we have to address the links between the notions of evangelization and civilization and the immediate postcolonial political economy of the region.

## THE POSTCOLONIAL POLITICAL ECONOMY
## OF THE SECOND CONQUEST OF THE
## TOLUPAN INDIANS

In July 1867, the governor of the department of Yoro, General Norberto Martínez, carried out the duties assigned to him by the National Education Law of 1866. He visited the municipal towns of the department and established elementary school examination tribunals. These tasks were carried out with local authorities and individuals selected for these purposes by General Martínez. General Martínez, who had been mayor of Olanchito in 1848, visited Agalteca, an Indian town a few miles from Olanchito. In Agalteca, the examining tribunal tested some "sad" Indians on their knowledge of "urbanity" and sacred and lay history.[52]

By 1867, Agalteca had been in existence for more than 250 years. It originated with an *encomienda* granted to the conquistador Diego López, who was also given fifty-eight tributary Indians to work on his lands.[53] In 1610, a small convent was built there. Later, in 1680, it was the seat of the office of the Doctrine of Religion, and in 1685 Agalteca was mentioned in a list as a town located "scarcely on the hillside of the *camino real* [royal road] behind Olanchito."[54] The Spanish censuses of the late eighteenth century and the early nineteenth century characterized Agalteca as an "Indian town linked with Olanchito.[55]

When General Martínez visited Agalteca, the Indians who were tested were no longer *selváticos* because of the Franciscan evangelization of the eighteenth century. Moreover, General Martínez was no ordinary visitor. He had been in charge of the execution of William Walker, infamous for various military efforts to gain power in Honduras and Nicaragua. By the 1860s and 1870s, General Martínez had become an important landowner in the municipality of Olanchito.[56] Years later, in 1902, he also became president of the Honduran Congress, and in his old age he even served as councilman in the municipal administration of Olanchito during the government of General Purificación Zelaya. General Martínez in 1867 encouraged the Tolupan Indians of Agalteca to dedicate themselves to agriculture.

In June 1867, the auxiliary mayor of Agalteca acknowledged that people from Olanchito were settling in the town's communal lands (*ejidos*), and he decreed an ordinance dealing with the issue. This ordinance established that individuals settling in Agalteca would be under the jurisdiction of the auxiliary mayor, since the municipality of Olanchito encouraged the authorities of Agalteca to allow "residency to some national and foreign immigrants desiring to establish themselves there because they would bring benefits."[57] In this way, Martínez's efforts reflected the ideas espoused by Domingo Sarmiento in Argentina and Adolfo Zuñiga in Honduras. The Tolupan Indians of Agalteca had doubts about such projects because their ancestors had already suffered three centuries of "progress."

At the end of the nineteenth century, the municipality of Olanchito took over the jurisdiction of Agalteca, thus making it subject to mulatto and *pardo* political authority and discourses. Thereafter, little by little the Indians abandoned their ancient town. Some moved to neighboring towns, including the urban settlement of Olanchito itself; others became laborers in the local haciendas, including the ones owned by General Purificación Zelaya. Other Indians, apparently pressured by Olanchito's authorities, moved to a village called Yaruca, which was located far and deep in the western neighboring department of Atlántida.[58] Meanwhile, in 1901 General Purificación Zelaya, who studied military strategy in Tegucigalpa, had requested that the Ministry of Government register sixty-five *manzanas* of communal lands that apparently belonged to the Tolupan Indians of La Carbonera and Agua Caliente.[59]

As late as the 1990s, the issue of land loss remained part of the memories of elderly people in that village. Agueda Cáceres Delarca (b. 1903), a Tolupan Indian whom I interviewed in 1999, remembered that her grandparents had spoken "the dialect," although she and her parents had not.[60] She also remembered that when she was a child people talked about moving to Yaruca, and even to La Ceiba, where a considerable number of people from Yoro, including mulattoes and *pardos*, migrated between the 1850s and 1860s.[61]

Doña Agueda's narrative is crucial in helping us understand the complicated origins of the discourse of cultural civility in Olanchito during the nineteenth century and its connection to the secular implications of the history of evangelization. For example, as we will see soon, Doña Argueda's comment that a certain "Subirana put the Indians in order because they were sorcerers" is best understood within the context of the historiography of public education in the department of Yoro.[62] Doña Agueda was referring to Manuel de Jesús Subirana (1807–1864), a Spanish missionary authorized by President Santos Guardiola to evangelize and civilize the Indians. In 1858 Guardiola informed the Honduran Congress of "the important services carried out by the priest [Subirana] in favor of the State with his evangelizing and civilizing effort in attracting the errant *selvático* Indians to the social State."[63] In 1864, when Subirana died, then President José María Medina recognized "the noble purpose of continuing the Christianization and civilizing of the Indians."[64]

There was a connection between Subirana's religious project, the civilizing efforts of the new nation-state, and the origins of Olanchito's discourse of cultural civility. This connection was reproduced after Subirana's death, which provoked a complicated process of national mystification, including processions that repeatedly reconstructed the friar's steps and wanderings not only in the department of Yoro, but throughout different regions of Honduras.[65] By the 1920s, the Ministry of Education ordered that Subirana's image be installed in the classrooms of all primary schools in the country. While we still lack a serious biography of Subirana, as well as a social history of his time period and the region to help us better understand his significance in the context of Honduras, there is little doubt that Olanchito and its surroundings experienced the discursive implications of his life and death.

The mystification of Subirana coincides with two key processes relevant to the discourse on civility and the role of race in Honduran history and national identity. Subirana understood that his civilizing project was both practically secular and evangelizing in spiritual and religious terms. When Subirana informed President Guardiola in 1859 that he had baptized 4,100 Tolupan Indians, he also declared that the Indians were apt for work and "could be useful to the State." Guardiola also understood Subirnara's civilizing effort in the same terms.[66]

In 1869, four years after Subirana's death, and two years after General Norberto Martínez's visit to Agalteca, President José María Medina decreed a legal system to civilize the Tolupan Indians and to take advantage of their labor. President Medina established the position of an administrator, or curator, to govern the *selvático* Tolupan Indians of Yoro. The position of curator was similar to the system of *encomiendas* and *repartimientos* of the colonial period and was maintained well into the 1870s. For example, the curator in charge of Christianizing and civilizing the Indians was declared the beneficiary of 8 percent of the products cultivated by the Indians

The curator would also appoint guardians for the "moral instruction" and civilization of the Indians. The political governors of the departments where *indios selváticos* lived and resisted the new conquest would supervise the entire system. This secular project followed the discourse of Subirana, who, four months before his death in 1864, had claimed to have rescued 6,000 Indians from their "miserable condition" by baptism, and hence they were to be of "great utility to the Honduras state, especially in years of scarce crops, including corn, tobacco and other agricultural products cultivated by them and that the State needs."[67]

It is important to emphasize that the system established in 1869 originated, in its conceptual and legal sense, with Subirana's religious project. He characterized the Indians as "minors"—children—and designed a *"Reglamento* for newly baptized Indians" and other documents that served as the basis for the laws decreed by the state for its own purposes.[68] This convergence was perhaps not intentional, because in 1858 Subirana denounced the state's exploitation of the Tolupan Indians in the department of Yoro. However, his close links with the protagonists of the political economy that exploited the Tolupans, the descendents of free *pardos* and mulattoes of the eighteenth century, served the lay projects of the governors and other individuals who were obtaining benefits from the export boom of the sarsaparilla collected by the Tolupan Indians.

The sarsaparilla export boom of the nineteenth century underwent a number of fluctuations. The period of major and constant boom took place during the 1850s and 1860s, even though it registered extraordinary growth during the 1840s, that is, during the government of General Francisco Ferrera, "the iron mulatto," and the yesteryear of colonial *pardo* ancestry. Indeed, it is highly probable that, beginning in 1840, the political governors of Yoro started to force the Tolupan Indians to collect sarsaparilla, as was later done in 1860 by Jesús Quiroz. In fact, in 1856 the governor of Yoro informed the authorities in Tegucigalpa that the "sad Indians" suffered not only the burden of cultivating and carrying the "loads of zarza [sarsaparilla] without receiving their wages," but they also "endured the kidnapping and raping of their children and wives."[69] We know that Subirana himself denounced this tragedy as early as 1858.[70]

At the beginning of 1860, Subirana begged the civilizing state for a donation of lands for his baptized Indians. The existing if scanty historiography registers this act. However, the fact is that the governors and other individuals who took advantage of the sarsaparilla boom considered Subirana's project a kind of discourse that supported their secular projects. By the end of the nineteenth century, the Tolupan population, after having been a majority in the department of Yoro in 1800, had fallen to only 20 percent of the population, or about 14,000 Indians.[71] These data must be compared to the growing mulatto and *pardo* populations in the department.

The elite of the town of Olanchito, the majority of mulatto and *pardo* ancestry, like the majority in Yoro, perhaps envisioning productive marriage alliances with the few Spanish whites, actively championed Subirana's civilizing project. The mulatto and *pardo* role in the civilizing of the region and their accumulation of capital through the export of sarsaparilla requires further exploration. Nonetheless, it seems clear that in the nineteenth century, mulattoes and *pardos* became a part of the group of "civilizers" of the native Tolupan "barbarians." (The school for Indians in the community of Lomitas del Oeste was named after General Purificación Zelaya, for example.) Over time, many Hondurans saw them as part of a native Honduran force and racially distinct from the "foreign" *morenos*, later known as the Garifuna.[72]

It is most probable that this ideological discourse, a regional type of cultural "whitening," enjoyed a long trajectory extending back to the end of the eighteenth century. In the department of Yoro, this process generated relationships of ethnic and economic exploitation between Olanchito and Agalteca. By the time of the sarsaparilla boom in the 1850s and 1860s, Agalteca, a former *pueblo de indios*, had already been "civilized," freed of sorcerers.[73] By the end of the nineteenth century, in the regional history of the area, the descendants of the colonial mulattoes and *pardos* considered it natural that individuals like Doña Agueda's father, whose parents still spoke the "dialect," labored on a hacienda owned by General Purificación Zelaya, a man whose black ancestry was apparent.

## CONCLUSIONS: AN ALLEGORY OF CONQUEST

Max Sorto Batres (b.1927), a primary schoolteacher born in Olanchito, has devoted his efforts to writing the history of the town. By 1991 he had written a number of essays, some of them published in national newspapers. One is entitled "Toncontin," and it serves as the final story to this chapter. That word, *toncontin*, apparently of Náhuatl-Aztec origins, referred to an ancient and sacred dance. However, according to Sorto Batres, in Agalteca this term was used to refer to "a musical instrument of Indian manufacture . . . made of a tree commonly called mulatto; the wood is red-colored with yellowish veins." This tree, wrote Sorto Batres, grows along rivers, and for the Indians it was "an enchanted tree," a tree that embodied supernatural and magical powers.

This suggestive ethno-racial allegory helps us understand the history and discourse of cultural civility in Olanchito, and its generalized distribution at the national level by intellectuals such as Juan Ramón Martínez. José Canuto Delarca, an old resident of Agalteca who "used to tell stories to his descendants while drinking chocolate deep into the night," narrated the story a long time ago to Max Sorto Batres. Tío Canuto, as he was affectionately known in the village and beyond, knew the aboriginal inhabitants of Agalteca—Tolupan Indians—well. Tío Canuto, as a young man, had worked on one of General Purificación Zelaya's haciendas; he was also the father of Águeda Cáceres Delarca, the old woman who in 1999 told me, more than one century after Father Subirana's death, that this revered missionary "fixed the Indians" because they practiced sorcery.[74]

Sorto Bartres's rendition of this allegory of conquest in Olanchito should also be located in the more general history of discourses on race in Honduras, especially around the notion of *mestizaje* in the Honduran context. This racialized nationalist discourse achieved hegemony in the country in the 1920s and 1930s and served as the broader context for the discourse of cultural civility that emerged particular to Olanchito and the department of Yoro at the same time. Indeed, the hegemony of the *mestizaje* discourse only began to disintegrate in the 1990s, in part because it enjoyed a deep-rooted history, and in part because a certain historiography promulgated this narrow vision.

After the 1940s, much of the historiography followed William S. Stokes when he argued, "Honduras is not hampered in its organization of government by a political aristocracy of Spaniards, or retarded by a racially inferior Indian or negro proletariat." Stokes also argued other critical points: "the average Honduran admits being a *mestizo* with no loss to his dignity"; "with few exceptions, the Indian is accepted by the Honduran as a Honduran, and as a racial equal"; and "the negroes have not only been accepted into the political pattern on a basis of equality, but in actuality have been represented in Congress and in the executive branch in numbers far out of proportion to their population."[75]

This chapter argues the contrary.[76] Indeed, we have argued that the triumph of a mestizo Honduras by the 1930s was the ideological result of a process of social and economic change that brought foreign capital and foreign immigrants to Honduras's north coast, including Olanchito, and that threatened, on many levels, elites' domination of their country. Elites in Tegucigalpa, and especially within the Honduran state, were too weak politically and economically to challenge or reject foreign capital; thus they attempted to reassert their dominance, at least in the ideological sphere, by asserting a national unity based on a homogeneous Honduran mestizo race (which included or blended in native descendents of black slaves, the *pardos* and mulattoes) but excluding black West Indian immigrants brought in by the banana companies, and the indigenous north coast Garifuna populations, or the *morenos*, as they continued be called into the 1930s and 1940s, and well into the 1960s.[77]

In Honduras, this process reached its culmination in the immigration laws of 1929 and 1934. According to the 1929 legislation, immigrant Arabs, Turks, Syrians, Armenians, blacks, and "coolies" were required to deposit $2,500 when entering the country. Local relatives from these "races" could secure temporary permits for immigrant kinship of the same races. The Immigration Law of 1934 restated many elements of the 1929 legislation. Article 14 of the law simply stated, "The entry of Negroes, coolies, gypsies and Chinese into the territory of the Republic is prohibited."[78]

The anti-immigrant legislation was connected to the emergence of a vision of Honduras as a homogeneous mestizo country, and this construction was connected to the rise of the foreign-owned banana industry on the north coast, of which of course Olanchito was a key urban area. The anti-immigration legislation of 1929 and 1934, as well as anti-black labor legislation introduced into Congress between 1923 and 1925, must be seen in the context of changes in the way that the government counted and classified the population—eliminating entire categories of people, especially the mulatto category still in use in the 1910s, and thus reducing Honduran racial-ethnic references and identities to an all-encompassing indo-Hispanic mestizo.

This, in turn, was connected to intellectuals' and politicians' attempts to define the nation for themselves and for the population in a way that reaffirmed Honduran identity in a society and economy increasingly dominated by foreigners. The legislation established the racial and ethnic parameters for the acceptable homogeneous mestizo Honduras, thus also simplifying a more complicated narrative of colonial and nineteenth-century racial-ethnic history, including that in Olanchito. In this process, the relations of conquest, missionary evangelizing, and civilization that occurred in the department of Yoro in the eighteenth and nineteenth centuries were also eliminated. In this way, the legacy of peoples of African descent also vanished, at least in the public discourse.

## NOTES

1. Martínez is one of Honduras's best-known intellectuals and also was a candidate for the 2005 presidential elections. He has served as president of the editorial board of Honduras's main university press. Over the past two decades he has published an important column in a national newspaper, *La Tribuna*.

2. Rubén Antúnez, *Monografía del Departamento de Yoro* (Tegucigalpa, Honduras: Tipografía Nacional, 1937): 76–77, 127; Mario Posas, *Monografía de la Ciudad de Olanchito* (Olanchito, Honduras: Alcaldía de Olanchito, 1993); Juan Ramón Fúnez, *Historia de San Jorge de Olanchito* (Tegucigalpa, Honduras: Editorial Universitaria, 1995).

3. On the establishment of Yoro by *pardos* and mulattoes, see Mario F. Martínez Castillo, "Proceso de formación de la Villa de Santa Cruz de Yoro," *Historia crítica* 1, no. 2 (1981): 29–34. On *cimarronaje* and slavery, see the classic by Richard Price, ed., *Sociedades cimarronas: Comunidades esclavas rebeldes en las Américas* (Mexico: Siglo XXI, 1981). For other contributions along these lines, see N. E. Whitten Jr. and A. Torres, eds., *Blackness in Latin America and the Caribbean*, 2 vols. (Bloomington: Indiana University Press, 1998).

4. On slavery in Honduras after the sixteenth century, see the pioneering work of Melida Velásquez, "El Comercio de esclavos en la Alcaldia Mayor de Tegucigalpa, siglos XVI al XVIII," *Mesoamerica* 42 (2001): 199–222.

5. Specialists on blackness in Central American argue that mulattoes represented the larger group of African ancestry at the end of the colonial period. See the pioneering work of Rina Cáceres, "Indígenas y africanos en las redes de la esclavitud en Centroamérica," in *Rutas de la esclavitud en África y América Latina*, ed. Rina Cáceres (San José, Costa Rica: EDUCA, 2001), 83–100.

6. Víctor F. Ardón, *Datos para la historia de la educación en Honduras* (Tegucigalpa, Honduras: Imprenta "La Democracia," 1957), 19–39.

7. Juan Ramón Martínez, "Canción de amor para una ciudad exigente," in Fúnez, *Historia de San Jorge*, 11–18.

8. Martínez, "Canción de amor."

9. Martínez, "Canción de amor."

10. Fúnez, *Historia de San Jorge*, 155.

11. Max Sorto Batres, "Francisco Murillo Soto: Gran impulsor de la cultura en Olanchito," *Revista Aguán* (Olanchito) 4 (1998): 46–47.

12. Francisco Guevara-Escudero, "Nineteenth-Century Honduras: A Regional Approach to the Economic History of Central America, 1839–1914" (PhD diss., New York University, 1983), 205.

13. Guevara-Escudero, "Nineteenth-Century Honduras," 92.

14. William M. Denevan, *The Native Population of the Americas in 1492*, 2nd ed. (Madison: University of Wisconsin Press, 1992), xviii.

15. Linda Newson, *El Costo de la conquista* (Tegucigalpa, Honduras: Editorial Guaymuras, 1992), 488.

16. Newson, *El Costo de la conquista*.

17. Murdo J. MacLeod, *Historia socio-económica de la América Central Española: 1520–1720*, 2nd ed. (Guatemala: Editorial Piedra Santa, 1990), 50–51; Newson, *El Costo de la conquista*, 444.

18. Newson, *El Costo de la conquista*, 299–300.

19. Dario A. Euraque, "Zonas regionales en la formación del estado hondureño: 1830s–1930s: El Caso de la Costa Norte," *Historia y sociedad* (Puerto Rico: Universidad de Puerto Rico) 6 (1993): 112.

20. "Informe de don Ramón de Anguiano, Gobernador Intendente de la Provincia de Honduras, 1 de junio de 1788," in Leticia Oyuela, *De la Corona a la libertad: Documentos comentados para la historia de Honduras, 1778–1870* (Tegucigalpa, Honduras: Ediciones Subirana, 2000), 10–23.

21. Marvin Barahona, *Evolución histórica de la identidad nacional* (Tegucigalpa, Honduras: Editorial Guaymuras, 1991), 64–66, 184–88.

22. Fúnez, *Historia de San Jorge*, 26.

23. The data presented in this paragraph come from Newson, *El Costo de la conquista*, 469; Linda Newson, *The Cost of Conquest* (Boulder, CO: Westview Press, 1986), 306; and Héctor Leyva, ed., *Documentos coloniales de Honduras* (Choluteca, Honduras: Ediciones Subirana, 1991), 288.

24. Manuel Chávez Borjas, *Identidad, cultura y nación en Honduras* (Tegucigalpa, Honduras: Ediciones Librería Paradiso, 1990).

25. Mario F. Martínez Castillo, *Apuntamientos para una historia colonial de Tegucigalpa y su alcaldía mayor* (Tegucigalpa, Honduras: Editorial Universitaria, 1982), 56.

26. On Márquez and the mulattoes of Tegucigalpa, I consulted Rolando Sierra, *Iglesia y liberalismo en Honduras en el siglo XIX* (Tegucigalpa, Honduras: Centro de Publicaciones Obispado Choluteca, 1993), 23; and Leticia de Oyuela, *José Miguel Gómez: Pintor Criollo* (Tegucigalpa, Honduras: Banco Atlántida, 1992), 86–87. The famous painter José Miguel Gómez had to endure legal proceedings associated with his racial heritage.

27. For the abolition decree, see Antonio R. Vallejo, *Compendio de la historia social y política de Honduras* (Tegucigalpa, Honduras: Tipografía Nacional, 1882), 376–78. General considerations about the slave trade, its colonial legislation, and Central America's abolition of slavery can be found in Constantino Lascaris, *Historia de las*

*ideas en Centroamérica* (San José, Cosa Rica: EDUCA, 1982), 191–96, 272–73, 329–30, 389–92.

28. Rómulo Durón, *Biografía del presbítero Don Francisco Antonio Márquez* (Tegucigalpa, Honduras: Editorial Universitaria, 1992), 30–31.

29. John Bascom, ed., *Propaganda Pro-Honduras* (Havana, Cuba, 1930), 362.

30. Details on the Zelaya family and its colonial lineage are available in Leticia Oyuela, *Un Siglo en la hacienda: Estancias y haciendas en la antigua Alcaldía Mayor de Tegucigalpa (1670–1850)* (Tegucigalpa, Honduras: Banco Central de Honduras, 1994).

31. Medardo Mejía, *Don Juan Lindo: El Frente nacional y el anticolonialismo* (Tegucigalpa, Honduras: Editorial Universitaria, 1993), 83–95; José A. Sarmiento, *Historia de Olancho* (Tegucigalpa, Honduras: Editorial Universitaria, 1990), 31.

32. Oyuela, *De la Corona a la libertad*, 119–27.

33. Rafael Heliodoro Valle, ed., *Ramón Rosa: Oro de Honduras* (Tegucigalpa, Honduras: Editorial Universitaria, 1993), 389–90.

34. "Causa criminal a don Francisco Ferrera por su insubordinación y escándalo en estado de ebriedad en el Partido de Cantarranas," in Oyuela, *De la Corona a la libertad*, 122–24.

35. Oyuela, *De la Corona a la libertad*, 122–24.

36. Manuel Rubio Sánchez, *Historia del Puerto de Trujillo*, vol. 3 (Tegucigalpa, Honduras: Banco Central de Honduras, 1975), 515–85.

37. "Repatriación de morenos," *Revista de la Biblioteca y Archivo Nacionales* (Tegucigalpa) 2, no. 3 (1988): 44. I am grateful to the late Ramón Oquelí for sharing this important document with me.

38. Libros de Baptismo, Archivo de la Parroquia Católica de Trujillo. Thanks to Monsignor Virgilio López Carías for permission to examine these baptismal records in August 1999.

39. For a broad review of the literature on the Garífunas, see Fernando Cruz Sandoval, "A 200 años de historia garífuna en Honduras: Bases para una periodización," YAXKIN: Revista del Instituto Hondureño de Antropología e Historia 11 (2002): 89–111.

40. Elizet Payne, "El Puerto de Trujillo: Espacio, economia y sociedad (1780–1870)" (PhD diss., University of Costa Rica, 2005).

41. Documents of that period register the use of the term *moreno*, referring to Garífunas, Vallejo, *Compendio*, 313–17.

42. Mario A. Bueso Yescas, *Santa Rosa de los Llanos: Cuna de la República* (Tegucigalpa, Honduras: n.p., 1996), 60.

43. Douglas A. Tompson, "Frontiers of Identity: The Atlantic Coast and the Formation of Honduras and Nicaragua, 1786–1894" (PhD diss., University of Florida, 2001), 144. Tompson also addresses the civilizing discourse of Central American elites in this period. See Tompson, "Frontiers of Identity," 169–72.

44. Relationships between *cimarrones* and *pueblos de indios* in other regions of Latin America are explored in Jonathan D. Hill, ed., *History, Power and Identity: Ethnogenesis in the Americas, 1492–1992* (Iowa City: University of Iowa Press, 1996).

45. My thinking here has recently been influenced by Mathew Restall's consideration of one of the myths of the Spanish conquest, the notion that all the conquer-

ors were white. See Mathew Restall, *Seven Myths of the Spanish Conquest* (Oxford: Oxford University Press, 2003), 44–63.

46. For the missions in Honduras in the seventeenth and eighteenth centuries, see Newson, *El Costo de la conquista*, 390–99, 436–38, 440–41; and Newson, "La Población indígena de Honduras bajo el regimen colonial," *Mesoamerica* 9 (1985), 8–9. See also Jesús María García Anoveros, "Presencia franciscana en la Taguzgalpa y la Tologalpa (la Mosquitia)," *Mesoamerica* 15 (1988): 47–78.

47. Ann Chapman, *Masters of Animals: Oral Traditions of the Tolupan Indians* (Amsterdam: Gordon and Breach, 1992), 15.

48. Chapman, *Masters of Animals*, 13.

49. Ernesto Alvarado García, *La Legislación indigenista de Honduras* (Tegucigalpa, Honduras: Instituto Indigenista Interamericano, 1958), 95.

50. Julio Rodriguez Ayestas, comp., *Adolfo Zúñiga: Selección de escritos: El Progreso democrático* (1968; repr., Tegucigalpa, Honduras: El Ahorro Hondureño, 1976).

51. Adolfo Zuniga, "Inmigracion," and "Nuestra Riquesa Mineral: Su Rol Civilizador," in Rodriguez Ayestas, *Adolfo Zúñiga*, 19–32, 193–96.

52. Fúnez, *Historia de San Jorge*, 120–21.

53. "Relación hecha a su Majestad por el Gobernador de Honduras, de todos los Pueblos de dicha Gobernación: Años 1582," in Leyva, *Documentos coloniales de Honduras*, 67.

54. William V. Davidson, "Geografía de los indígenas toles (jicaques) de Honduras en el siglo XVIII," *Mesoamérica* 6, no. 9 (1985): 65.

55. Davidson, "Geografía," 74; "Población de las provincias de Honduras: Matrícula del año 1801," in Leyva, *Documentos coloniales de Honduras*, 288.

56. Antúnez, *Monografía*, 65, 71–72.

57. Correspondence, Municipality of Olanchito, 1867. These and subsequent related documents from the Historical Archives of Olanchito are deposited in the town's Casa de la Cultura de Olanchito. I examined the documents during research trips there in 1995 and 1999. I was ably assisted by Yesenia Martínez; my stay was funded by Honduras's National Institute of Anthropology and History, then under the direction of Dr. Olga Joya.

58. The renowned American anthropologist Richard Adams visited Agalteca in the 1950s. He recorded some elements of this story. Richard Adams, *Cultural Surveys of Panama, Nicaragua, Guatemala, El Salvador and Honduras* (Washington, DC: U.S. Government Printing Office, 1957), 653–54.

59. Acta de Sesión de la Alcaldía de Olanchito, April 1, 1901. Alcaldía municipal de Olanchito, 1867. Archivo Historico, Municipalidad de Olanchito.

60. Águeda Cáceres Delarca, interview, Agalteca, Olanchito, August 8, 1999.

61. Antonio Canelas Díaz, *La Ceiba, sus raíces y su Historia, 1810–1940* (La Ceiba, Honduras: Tipografía Renacimiento, 1999), 63–64.

62. Águeda Cáceres Delarca, interview.

63. Ernesto Alvarado García, *El Misionero español Manuel Subirana* (Tegucigalpa, Honduras: Imprenta Calderon, 1964).

64. Alvarado García, *El Misionero*, 104.

65. A recent interpretation of Subirana can be found in Rolando Sierra, "Manuel

Subirana como personaje mesiánico," *Paraninfo* (Tegucigalpa) 7, no. 14 (1998), 58–78.

66. Alvarado García, *El Misionero*, 85–86.

67. Alvarado García, *El Misionero*, 53. Documents of this period register aspects of this situation. See José Ignacio Milla, "Estado que el Infrascrito Cura de Este Beneficio protector de las Tribus incivilizadas Comprendidas en el distrito parroquial exhibe al Sr. Jefe Político," Olanchito, October 16, 1856, National Archive of Honduras, Tegucigalpa. I am grateful to Porfirio Pérez Chávez, a Honduran historian currently writing a biography of President Santos Guardiola, for sharing a copy of this document and other manuscripts found by him during his research in the National Archive of Honduras in Tegucigalpa.

68. Alvarado García, *El Misionero*, 52–53, 90–94.

69. Molina, "Del Gobierno político del departamento de Yoro al sr. ministro general del supremo gobierno del estado de Honduras," Yoro, October 27, 1856, Archivo Nacional de Honduras.

70. One Marxist historian welcomed Subirana's project as a contribution to developing capitalism in Honduras. Medardo Mejia, "El Misionero Subirana," *Boletín de la Academia Hondureña de la Lengua* 5, no. 6 (1959): 57–69.

71. Loose correspondence, Alcaldía Municipal de Olanchito, 1896, Archivo Historico, Municipalidad de Olanchito.

72. Max Sorto Batres, "Vidas ejemplares, apuntamientos biográficos del General Purificación Zelaya" (unpublished manuscript, Olanchito). I am grateful to Professor Sorto Batres for sharing this manuscript with me and for allowing me to interview him in August 1999.

73. Loose correspondence, Alcaldía Municipal de Olanchito, 1898, Archivo Histórico de Olanchito.

74. Michel Taussig, *Shamanism, Colonialism and the Wild Man: A Study in Terror and Healing* (Chicago: University of Chicago Press, 1987), 179, 373.

75. William Stokes, "The Racial Factor in Honduran Politics," *Modern Language Forum* 29 (1944): 25–30.

76. Dario A. Euraque, "The Threat of Blackness to the Mestizo Nation: Race and Ethnicity in the Honduran Banana Economy, 1920s and 1930s," in *Banana Wars: Power, Production, and History in the Americas*, ed. Steven Striffler and Mark Moberg (Durham, NC: Duke University Press, 2003), 229–49; Dario A. Euraque, "The Banana Enclave, Nationalism and Mestizaje in Honduras, 1910s–1930s," in *At the Margins of the Nation-State: Identity and Struggle in the Making of the Laboring Peoples of Central America and the Hispanic Caribbean, 1860–1960*, ed. Aviva Chomsky and Aldo Lauria (Durham, NC: Duke University Press, 1998), 151–68.

77. Dario A. Euraque, "Negritud garifuna y coyunturas políticas en la costa norte de Honduras, 1940–1970," in *Memorias del mestizaje: Política y cultura en Centroamérica, 1920–1990s*, ed. Charles Hale, Jeffry Gould, and Dario A. Euraque (Guatemala: CIRMA, 2004), 295–323.

78. The 1934 Immigration Law is available in National Archives, record group 84, *Confidential U.S. Diplomatic Post Records, Honduras: 1930–45* (Washington, DC, 1985), microfilm reel 9, 148–56.

# II

## DIALOGUES AND CHALLENGES TO FULL CITIZENSHIP

# 5

# Black Abolitionists in the *Quilombo* of Leblon, Rio de Janeiro

## Symbols, Organizers, and Revolutionaries

*Eduardo Silva*

*Eduardo Silva's chapter on the* quilombo *of Leblon builds on the rich scholarship on slave maroonage in Latin America. Maroons in the English-speaking Caribbean basin,* palenques *in Spanish America, and* quilombos *in Brazil constituted important options for African resistance in the colonial and the early modern era. But not all escaped slave communities were alike. Historically, self-manumitted Africans and Afro-Latin Americans established communities in rural or secluded areas away from the major urban concentrations and easy military attacks. As the abolition movements gained force in the second half of the nineteenth century, distinct types of communities emerged, often in close contact with urban centers and abolitionist intellectuals and liberal politicians. These abolitionist* quilombos, *as the author calls them, played important roles in shaping Brazil's abolitionist movement. Silva's study points to the need to explore the connections between runaway slave communities, which survived on the margins of society, and those abolitionists who worked within the system. His work suggests the need for further research not only on alliances among* quilombos *and abolitionists in Brazil but also between Maroons and abolitionists in Jamaica,* palenques *and intellectuals in Spanish America, and the Quakers and the escaped slaves of the Underground Railroad in the United States.*

## BACKGROUND

Since the introduction of slavery in the Brazilian territory in the early six-teenth century, there have always been multiple forms of active resistance on the part of enslaved Africans and their descendants throughout Brazil. In addition to suicide, sabotage, and the preservation of African religious customs in the face of Portuguese Catholicism, Africans often escaped the injustices of slavery by fleeing and creating escaped slaves communities known as *quilombos* or *mocambos,* many of which have continued to survive as communities well into the twenty-first century. According to R. K. Kent, there were three basic forms of active resistance by the enslaved: fugitive settlements, attempts at seizures of power, and armed insurrections, which sought neither escape nor control but often represented calls for better working or living conditions or responses to specific grievances.[1] Of the three types of resistance, the *quilombos* were probably most frequent and came the closest to re-creating free African societies in Brazil, even though they were almost always quickly destroyed and never allowed to fully develop.

A number of scholars have focused on *quilombos* as centers of resistance, particularly in the colonial era. Among the most famous centers was that of the *quilombo* of Palmares, often referred to as the Republic of Palmares because it functioned as an independent state within Brazil. Brazilians con-tinue to view Palmares in mythic, often romanticized terms, because it resisted Portuguese authority for almost a century. Scholarly and popular literature continues to explore Palmares's relevance to Brazil's past. Fewer scholars have examined *quilombos* in the modern era, particularly after independence and their role in the abolitionist movement. This essay tells the story of the *quilombo* of Leblon and its role in the abolitionist move-ment in Rio de Janeiro, the imperial capital of Brazil.[2]

## TERMINOLOGY AND CULTURAL RELEVANCE

*Quilombos* developed as a natural evolution of a group of runaway slaves who banded together in a collective process in order to survive outside the plantation system. Although most of the *quilombos* lasted for only a very short time, they were still considered threats to the establishment. The Por-tuguese were quick to respond, finding them and destroying them in order to deter other slaves from fleeing and to severely punish those who did. Yet the formation of *quilombos* challenges Seymour Drescher's claim of a "lack of a tradition of mobilization" in Brazil. Many *quilombos* became such an integral part of Brazilian society that the Portuguese authorities often signed treaties of nonaggression with *quilombo* leaders.[2]

The term *quilombo* only became commonplace after the dawn of the twentieth century. Prior to that time, Portuguese officials and escaped Africans referred to fugitive slave settlements as *mocambo*, a term derived from the Ambundu term *mu-kambo*, which meant "hideout."[3] Stuart Schwartz reports that a variety of terms were used, including *ladieras*, *mocambos*, and *quilombo*s, although *mocambo* was by far the most popular term used.[4] The application of the word *quilombo* seems to imply a more active resistance, something more reactionary than a hideout. According to Father João Antonio (de Montecúccolo) Cavazzi, *quilombo* comes from the Jaga word *Chi-lambo Plan*, which denoted a Jaga war camp. Although there is no clear historic-linguistic link between the Brazilian *quilombo* and the Jaga *chi-lombo*, the shift to the use of this word in the literature may indicate a changing perception of the nature of these settlements at the end of the nineteenth century, that is to say, the view of a *mocambo* as a slave hideout and *quilombo* as a war camp. Even so, *quilombos* in the late nineteenth century functioned around different goals depending on several factors, including location. In the midst of the abolitionist movement, *quilombos* such as the *quilombo* of Leblon played critical roles in the movement to abolish slavery.[5]

Whatever the terminology or the place, the Portuguese settlers in Brazil and the Brazilian elite viewed the *quilombo* with suspicion because their very existence undermined established authority. In 1597 this would lead a Jesuit father to write, "The foremost enemies of the colonizer are revolted Negroes from Guiné in some mountain areas, from where they raid and give much trouble, and then will come when they will dare to attack and destroy farms as their relatives on the island on São Thomé."[6]

Richard Price notes, "Maroon societies dotted the map of Brazil from the forest to the interior, where they often merged with bands of Indians, to the outskirts of major urban centers."[7] According to Roger Bastide, the fleeing slaves encountered Indians but also brought to the *quilombo* elements of Portuguese culture, including the language and elements of Catholicism.[8] Thus from this emerging historiography we see a *quilombo* that, like the institution of slavery itself, was not a static settlement, but a dynamic system in which various intercultural interactions were taking place.

Although many historians indicate that the *quilombo* seemed to be a return to the African tradition of communal life, the amount of authentic (pure) African culture depended not only on the degree of acculturation of the enslaved Africans, but also on the presence of particular Brazilian factors such as the Indians and the land. In many areas we see fusion of the Indian and the African customs, particularly in the preparation of food and the use of the local building materials. We also see slaves interacting with freed men and women, mulattoes, and even white men. White women were rarely present, although Portuguese society often feared that they would be captured and taken to the *quilombos* by fugitive slaves. Thus, as Bastide asserts, "Maroonage cannot be separated from the total social context in which it arose, which is that of the struggle of an exploited group against the ruling class."[9] In other words, enslaved Africans formed *quilombo* and organized their political, economic, and cultural activities based on the political climate, location, and their relationship to allies and foes outside of their hideout. On the eve of abolition, for example, the *quilombo* of Leblon had successfully cultivated relationships with the freed people of color and with the progressive elements of the liberal abolitionist movement. As the nineteenth century progressed and the pressures of abolition grew, Brazil also saw an intensification of the rates of manumission. In 1798, while the African traffic was still in progress, slaves made up the majority of the population (1,582,000 people). The free sector was composed basically of whites (1,010,000) and, way down the scale, of an intermediate population of freedmen and women of color (not more than 406,000). By the time of the 1872 Census, Brazil was a different country, with a total population of 9,930,000, the majority of whom were free blacks and those of mixed race (4,245,000), followed by whites (3,787,000), and, finally, by a declining population of slaves (1,510,000) and nonacculturated Indians (387,000).[10] On the eve of abolition, the province of Rio de Janeiro registered more free people of color than enslaved blacks.[11] Ironically, *quilombos* played an important role in affecting this change. Indeed, residents of the *quilombo* of Leblon, as we will see, played an active role in abolition while maintaining close contacts with other *quilombos* as far afield as the northeast.

## ABOLITION AND THE PROVINCE
## OF RIO DE JANEIRO

In colonial times, the *quilombo*'s primary aim was survival. Residents were militarily prepared to defend their dwellings and often worked out complex relationships with freed blacks, the indigenous peoples, and local whites to supply them with food and materials. In the post-1850 period, however, *quilombos* played a more active role in resistance through a variety of legal venues. Maroonage no longer represented a nostalgia for Africa but a concerted effort to play a political role in the development of a free Brazil. The *quilombo* of Leblon followed the tradition of creating their center, or sanctuary, in areas that were close to urban populations but quite inaccessible. The reason for this was simple. The *quilombos* were not as self-sufficient as poets like Joaquim José Lisboa would suggest, but rather the internal economy was based closely on urban trends, trade, and the like. In the nineteenth century, *quilombos* emerged around the state of Rio de Janeiro. In his book *História do negro brasileiro*, Clóvis Moura documents at least eight major *quilombos* from the outskirts of urban areas to more rural localities. The *quilombo* de Manuel Congo, for example, was located on the margins of the Paraíba River, while others formed in the mountain ranges of Órgãos. Diverse *quilombos* were located in the region of Inhaúma, Campos de Goitacazes, in the Morro do Desterro, in the town of Campos, and in the region now called Leblon.[12] Both the *quilombo* of Leblon and those organized in Campos were closely connected to the growing abolitionist movement of the late nineteenth century.

## THE *QUILOMBO* OF LEBLON AND THE SYMBOL OF THE CAMELLIA

When contemporary *cariocas*, the residents of Rio de Janeiro, speak of Leblon, they think about one of the most exclusive neighborhoods of the *Zona Sul* (southern zone) of the city. Leblon and Ipanema share the same coastal real estate, for example, and are divided only by the Jardim de Alah (Allah's Gardens), a canal that links the ocean to the Lagoa Rodrigo de Freitas, the lake in the center of the *Zona Sul*. At the turn of the century, however, the area of difficult access originally belonged to the Frenchman Charles Le Blond. Owner of the Aliança fishing company, Le Blond's property stretched from what is now Niemeyer Avenue, which wraps around the mountain, to Bartolomeu Mitre Avenue. Le Blond later sold sections of this property to the Portuguese merchant José de Seixas Magalhães, who installed his *chácara* (a term that refers to a rural residence or property in the country), on which the *quilombo* functioned.

The *quilombo* of Leblon, as people whispered, was a sanctuary that specialized in the production of camellias. For that very reason, these flowers were transformed into the greatest of all symbols, the icon of the radical abolitionist movement.[13] During the abolitionist campaign, especially during the difficult years, when the pro-slavery residents fought back under the conservative cabinet of the Baron of Cotegipe, nothing could be compared to the symbolic force of the camellias produced in the *quilombo*, which were also known as *camélias da liberdade* (camellias of liberty). It is enough to remember that Princess Isabel, when she came down from Petrópolis, the imperial city outside of Rio, on May 3, 1888, to read her speech from the throne, was welcomed at the Pharoux Quay, in the city center, by an extraordinary manifestation, with a band playing music and a beautiful bouquet of camellias from the *quilombo* of Leblon. The great black abolitionist André Rebouças documents the scene in his diary: "Extraordinary ovation to Isabel I and the Cabinet; President Clapp's offering of camellias from *quilombo* of Leblon (owned by Seixas); delightful speeches by Dantas,

Nabuco and Patrocínio from the Senate's windows and the surrounding streets; all of Rio de Janeiro in celebration."[14] Ângelo Agostini, the famous Italian graphic artist, aptly captured the significance of the symbol of the camellia in a lithography that depicted a boy presenting a camellia bouquet to Princess Isabel "on behalf of the fugitive slaves." The image also tied the *quilombo*, symbolized by the flowers, to the intellectuals of the abolitionist movement, since the boy was the son of João Clapp, one of the leaders of the abolitionist movement.[15]

On May 13, 1888, at the exact time that the law was signed, the president of the Abolitionist Confederation, João Clapp, again came up to the princess and, in the name of the historically victorious movement, presented her with an "exquisite bouquet of artificial camellias." Soon afterward, the Portuguese immigrant José de Seixas Magalhães, considered head of the *quilombo*, also approached her and handed the princess another bouquet of camellias. These were, however, real blooming camellias straight from the *quilombo* of Leblon.[16] This bouquet, and its origins, bore a special symbolism and represented, in the opinion of the abolitionist Rui Barbosa, "the most exquisite of the popular offerings."[17]

In truth, the now apparently innocent camellia, be it natural or artificial, was one of the most powerful symbols of the abolitionist movement in Brazil. It was the symbol of the movement's radical wing: the group that, in the 1880s, embarked on a direct action program against the regime, encouraging escapes and setting up *quilombo*s. The camellia was also used as a type of password by which the abolitionists could be identified, especially when they were engaged in dangerous, or illegal, activities such as supporting escapes and finding hiding places for the fugitives. A slave who had escaped from São Paulo, for example, and came to hide in Rio de Janeiro could immediately identify possible allies when he stepped onto the platform at the central railway station, by their wearing of one of these flowers on the left-hand side of the chest.[18] If the fugitive could not identify allies or did not know the meaning of this symbol, it would be harder for him to be able to count on the protection of the Abolitionist Confederation, a political organization founded in 1883 whose program was, simply, to fight against the slave-labor regime.[19] If he knew the symbolic language of the camellias, he would end up being housed in the *quilombo* of Leblon.

We can say that the very idea of immediate and unconditional abolition—that is, abolition without compensation for the owners—was born (or took its first steps) at the Leblon sanctuary and at other *quilombos* politically aligned with the abolitionist movement. The camellias gained their symbolic power because of the very existence of a *quilombo* that specialized in the production of camellias and its ties with the abolitionist political movement. The status of the *quilombo* as an extralegal organization meant that symbols were important for communication among escaped slaves and between the residents of the *quilombo* and abolitionists within the political system. Indeed, others, including the black social movement, abolitionists, and sympathizers among the general population, relied on the symbolism as well.

Archival research indicates that the *quilombo* of Leblon, as far as the camellias are concerned, was not an isolated or merely folkloric phenomenon but was part of a new paradigm of black resistance to the pro-slavery system, which we could call the abolitionist *quilombo*, to differentiate it from the breakaway *quilombo*, the traditional *quilombo* whose classical model is the *quilombo* of Palmares.[20]

A closer look at the Leblon sanctuary in the history of the abolitionist movement reveals the decisive role that was played by the slaves themselves and the black abolitionists in achieving abolition. In fact, without the unreserved, conscious adherence of the captive people, as shown by their mass escapes—escapes that were impossible to suppress or control—the abolitionist project would not have had the slightest chance of success.

The *quilombo* of Leblon made the idea of the immediate and unconditional abolition without compensation for the owners palpable. Politicians were not averse to evoking the *quilombo* or its symbol to further their ends. While abolitionists utilized the camellia as a symbol for their cause, conservatives such as the slaveholding Baron of Cotegipe called abolitionists with suspected ties to residents of the *quilombo* "a communist class of abolitionists." Cotegipe, the leader of the conservative cabinet in government, was attempting to cause panic by pointing out the negative and potentially catastrophic impact of abolition on the social order.[21]

Moving from one end of imperial society to the other, we can see that the symbolism of the Leblon camellias provides a window onto three key moments in Brazilian history: the role of Princess Isabel, the part played by the black intellectuals, and, especially, the part played by the enslaved individuals of African descent. The group of black intellectuals included men who garnered great respect from fellow abolitionists and who made names for themselves in other areas of Brazilian society. One such man was Luís Gama, a former slave who had become a journalist and then a type of lawyer known at that time as a *rábula*, a man who made a living from bringing lawsuits by slaves against their masters. Gama managed to set more than five hundred slaves free through existing legal channels. Luís Gama died in 1882 and did not live to see abolition, but his work in São Paulo demonstrates connections to the black brotherhood of Our Lady of Remedies, the militant black abolitionist center in São Paulo, and to the abolitionist *quilombo* of Jabaquara in Santos.[22]

The connections between the residents of the *quilombo* and leading abolitionists are clearer in the case of José Carlos do Patrocínio. Patrocínio was the leader of the abolitionist campaign in the press, and one of the secret supporters of the *quilombo* of Leblon. He was respected in the publishing world as well as figurehead of the intellectual bohemia of Ouvidor Street, the center of the literary world. Patrocínio was not opposed to using his newspaper, the *Gazeta da Tarde*, to promote liberal causes, especially abolition. He was also an innovator and had introduced the passenger car to the streets of Rio de Janeiro. This invention would have a transforming affect on the city and would help bring places on the outskirts of Rio de Janeiro, like the *chácara* of Leblon, within the city's growing boundaries.[23]

Men of the stature of André Rebouças, the first black man in Brazil to graduate with a degree in engineering, the king of the sciences in the nineteenth century, and the basis for everything that was considered to be a mark of "progress," was intimately aware of the activities of the *quilombo* of Leblon. A scientist, a great scholar, and one of the most illustrious examples of Brazilian intelligence, he later became a professor at the Escola Politécnica (Polytechnical School), in São Francisco Square.[24]

In view of the agreements and social alliances between leading intellectuals and residents of the *quilombo*, it was almost impossible to fight openly against an abolitionist *quilombo*, as had been the case with the *quilombo* of Palmares. The *quilombo* of Jabaquara in Santos, which was probably the largest colony of fugitives ever, was never really challenged, nor were the countless *quilombo*s supported by the Clube do Cupim (Termite Club), in Pernambuco or the *quilombo* of Leblon, in Rio, which was the apple of the eye of the true abolitionists—who simply thought that "slavery was stealing" and therefore needed to be fought in any way possible.[25]

In fact, in the 1880s, a modern young person with advanced ideas, whether he or she was an abolitionist or a republican, could not avoid knowing about at least one abolitionist *quilombo*. Rui Barbosa, a staunch abolitionist and antimonarchist who was also an affiliate of the Masons Society, knew the *quilombo* of Leblon very well. Important national writers such as Coelho Neto also had contact with the *quilombo* of Leblon, and the young Osório Duque-Estrada, who later wrote the words to the national anthem, supported the *quilombo* as well. Medical student Brício Filho, later a politician and journalist, knew about it also. Silva Jardim, who was a proud republican, knew of both the *quilombo* of Leblon and the *quilombo* of Jabaquara, in Santos.[26]

On the birthday of the leader of the *quilombo* of Leblon on March 13, 1887, almost all the important abolitionists in the capital of the empire were present. Certainly, Joaquim Nabuco and José do Patrocínio, the men who symbolized the abolitionist campaign, were there. João Clapp, the president of the Abolitionist Confederation, the organization that gave behind-the-scenes support and political influence to the *quilombo*s, was there. The young Ernesto Senna, José do Patrocínio's brother-in-law, was also present. The black attorney Domingos Gomes dos Santos, whose nickname in the abolitionist movement was simply "the Radical," was there.[27]

We cannot comment with any certainty on the identities of the members of the *quilombo*. Their secret and clandestine nature meant that documents were either destroyed or not kept. But we do know that the *quilombo* leaders were important enough to bring important abolitionists to a birthday celebration on March 13, 1887. Indeed, there were so many abolitionists in one place that, according to witnesses at the time, they packed the horse-drawn tram that attended the Parish of Gávea, leaving no room for anybody else, and disturbing the lives and the peace and quiet of the residents of the tranquil Parish of Gávea with their shouting, late at night, of "Long live the fugitive slaves!" and other equally subversive statements.[28]

Evidence suggests that Princess Isabel supported the *quilombo* of Leblon. On several occasions the princess had the courage to appear in public with camellias from Leblon adorning her dresses. The imperial family, under Isabel's leadership, was so committed that the imperial palace itself was eventually transformed into a kind of branch of the *quilombo* of Leblon, and there was even a fine plantation of camellias in Petrópolis. White camellias and nearly red camellias that have lasted until the present day are found at the princess's palace and at the imperial palace itself. The Museu Imperial (Imperial Museum) in Petrópolis keeps a curious blue paper envelope with old dry flowers in it. These are certainly the remains of a genuine bouquet of camellias from the *quilombo* of Leblon that was offered by the Confederação Abolicionista to senator Affonso Celso de Assis Figueiredo, Viscount of Ouro Preto, a well-known supporter of abolitionist ideas, and one of the people responsible for the exceptionally fast passage of the abolition project in Parliament. The camellias were sent to him on May 6, 1888. The following day, the project began its quick course in Congress, reaching its final signing within just five days on May 13, 1888. Historians are fortunate to have access to the records left by the Viscount of Ouro Preto. Other "abolitionist gifts" such as these probably were also sent to other members of Parliament. On his envelope, the viscount wrote the following reminder: "May 6, 1888/Flowers offered by the Abolitionist/commission on the occasion of the presentation/of the Project." Inside the envelope, together with the camellias, was a sheet of paper with only one phase: "Echoes of the Abolitionist Campaign."[29]

André Rebouças, the most influential black intellectual of the time, acted as a bridge between the escape system put together by the princess in Petrópolis and the high command of the abolitionist movement in Rio de Janeiro, the people in the Abolitionist Confederation, with João Clapp and José Carlos do Patrocínio at the forefront.

## CELEBRATING THE END OF SLAVERY

It all began on February 12, 1888, with the first flower show openly put on by the regent princess. In spite of the torrential rain that was falling in Petrópolis, the party was considered magnificent. The princess, the Count of Eu, and three boys went through the streets of the city in an open carriage at the front of an abolitionist procession, encouraging the group of supplicants who went from door to door beating drums and asking for donations to help set the captives free.[30]

The princess, who had up until then been an educated, religious, and reserved young lady, revealed herself to be openly abolitionist. She surrounded herself with other abolitionists and shattered all the political conventions of neutrality. Let nobody be fooled by that sweet, motherly air that is displayed in the pictures of the time; the young princess had strong opinions. Her intervention in political life with the Leblon camellias and flower shows simply destroyed the conservative ministry that was fighting, with the greatest difficulty, to contain precisely those abolitionists who were considered republican troublemakers. The reaction was enormous because, at that time, everybody knew what the flowers meant. André Rebouças wrote in his diary on the same day, "February 12. The first flower show in Petrópolis. Isabel I's first abolitionist declaration." André Rebouças knew the meaning of those flowers. Observe how he wrote "Isabel I"—after the battle of flowers and of camellias from Leblon, the princess took the reigns of history and made herself queen. (Beforehand, she was already Isabel I, the Redeemer.)[31]

Toward the end of the regime, it became a public and widely known fact that Princess Isabel was hiding slaves in the Petrópolis Palace, a fact that was mentioned repeatedly not only in André Rebouças's private diaries, but also in the political speeches of liberals such as Rui Barbosa, and republicans such as Silva Jardim. Rui Barbosa said as much in the speech he gave at a political event sponsored by the Sociedade Libertadora Bahiana (Freedom Society of Bahia) in the São João Theater in Salvador on April 29, 1888. "Today the regent [Isabel] openly admits, in public events, to sheltering slaves," he said, as a simple aside, as if he were speaking about a subject that was more or less common knowledge.[32]

Even Silva Jardim, Isabel's most radical and vehement critic, recognized this fact on many occasions. In Silva Jardim's opinion it really was widely known that Princess Isabel "was sheltering blacks in her palace in Petrópolis." He couldn't, however, see any merit or advantage to be gained from this fact because, or so he thought, as Isabel was a princess, she "could, using her personal authority, free them all at once." On another occasion, Silva Jardim openly criticized Princess Isabel, who, in his opinion, "was turning the Petrópolis Palace into the second example of a *quilombo* in the province of Rio de Janeiro."[33] We can deduce that the first example would be the emblematic *quilombo* of Leblon.

The princess's behavior could be interpreted in many different ways and caused dramatic divisions in the abolitionist ranks. The black intellectuals (among them André Rebouças and José do Patrocínio) literally threw themselves at the feet of the princess, to whom they gave their unconditional support and called "Isabel I, the Redeemer" long before she signed the Abolition Law.

Another one of Isabel's critics, Rui Barbosa, adopted a completely different point of view. In Rui Barbosa's opinion, the princess's "change of course" to abolitionism and her "evolution" toward radical abolitionism could not be understood as a simple matter of generosity or royal munificence. To him, it was a political issue, such that the princess had only accepted a de facto situation, a new situation, created by the abolitionist popular movement. Together, abolitionists and slaves—especially the slaves—forced the princess to "evolve" toward the idea of immediate and unconditional abolition, an idea that was defended and even brought about by the Leblon sanctuary. In Rui Barbosa's opinion, the firm attitude of the slaves, the mass escapes, and the setting up of abolitionist *quilombos* played a truly fundamental role in changing the princess's attitude.

> The truth in this *quinquennium*, which marks the agony of the slavery, is that the country has always moved ahead of the throne and the throne delayed, as much as it could, the advent of redemption, being condescending with the Sebastianist Cabinet of slavery through the most hideous means. Today the regent openly admits, in public events, to sheltering slaves. . . . But this is only after the black avalanche has cascaded down from the mountain tops of Cubatão to freedom, and the *"I don't want to"* of the slave has imposed abolition on the slave owners [*fazendeiros*]."[34]

Rui Barbosa was one of the first intellectuals to affirm that the abolition of slavery was not a gift from the imperial princess regent but was won by the slaves themselves. While many only praised the princess, her kindness, and her camellias, Rui Barbosa argued that rather than praise God or dignitaries, Brazilians should have the faith to trust themselves.[35] On several occasions, Barbosa hammered away at this point. It was the abolitionist propaganda, supported by the abolitionist *quilombos*, that "obliged" the princess to openly declare herself abolitionist and to put on her abolitionist concerts and flower shows and adorn her royal dresses "with the camellias from the *Quilombo* of Leblon."[36]

It is worth repeating that the *quilombo* of Leblon did not exist in isolation but was part of a huge network of abolitionist *quilombos* that we are only now starting to catalog and study properly. Those linked to the Abolitionist Confederation include the Clube do Cupim in Recife, the Carlos de Lacerda *quilombo* in Campos; the Senna and Patrocínio *quilombo*s, which were both in São Cristóvão, under the nose of the emperor; the Raymundo *quilombo* in Engenho Novo; the Miguel Dias *quilombo* in Catumbi; the Padre Ricardo *quilombo* in Penha; the Camorim *quilombo* in the parish of Jacarepaguá; the Clapp *quilombo* on the shore of São Domingos, in Niterói; the Jabaquara *quilombo*; and the Pai Filipe *quilombo* in Santos. These sanctuaries and many others were abolitionist *quilombo*s. They emerged in the modern and their focus differed from that of the great *quilombo*s of the colonial period. In many ways they were influenced by the ideas of the French Revolution and Brazilian republicanism. We may not yet know the names of the men and women who populated *quilombo*s like the one in Leblon, but we do know that they were part of a transitional political environment and pointed toward the importance of the black abolitionists, both enslaved and free, and the fundamental part they played in dismantling slavery in Brazil.

## NOTES

1. See R. K. Kent, "An African State in Brazil," in *Maroon Societies*, ed. Richard Price (New York: Anchor Books, 1973), 170–90.

2. Seymour Drescher, "Brazilian Abolition in Corporate Perspective," in *The Abolition of Slavery and the Aftermath of Emancipation in Brazil*, ed. Rebecca J. Scott (Durham, NC: Duke University, 1988), 429–60.

3. Ambundu Tribe is an African ethnic group located in the Congo-Angola region. See Benjamin Nuñez, ed., *Dictionary of Afro-Latin American Civilization* (Westport, CT: Greenwood Press, 1980).

4. Stuart Schwartz, "The Mocambo: Slave Resistance in Colonial Brazil," in Price, *Maroon Societies*.

5. João Antonio (de Montecúccolo) Cavazzi, *Descrição histórica dos três reinos do Congo, Matamba e Angola* (1687; repr., Lisbon, Portugal: Edição da Junta de Investigações do Ultramar, 1965), 2 vols. Quoted in Kent's "An African State in Brazil," 170–90. The Jaga were an African tribe from Angola.

6. Kent, "An African State in Brazil," 174.

7. Richard Price, *Maroon Societies*, 169. In *A Hidro e os pântanos: Mocambos, quilombos e comunidades de fugitives no Brasil* (séculos XVII–XIX) (São Paulo, Brazil: Editora UNESP, 2005), Flávio dos Santos Gómes explores the relationship among Africans and natives in various states in Brazil.

8. Roger Bastide, "The Other *Quilombos*," in Price, *Maroon Societies*, 196.

9. Bastide, "The Other *Quilombos*," 199.

10. For a case study on this process of transition, see Eduardo Silva, *Prince of the People: The Life and Times of a Brazilian Free Man of Colour* (London: Verso, 1993), mainly chap. 7.

11. Hebe María Mattos de Castro, "Beyond Masters and Slaves: Subsistence Agriculture as a Survival Strategy in Brazil during the Second Half of the 19th Century," in Scott, *The Abolition of Slavery*.

12. Clóvis Moura, *História do negro brasileiro* (São Paulo, Brazil: Editora Ática S. A.).

13. Eduardo Silva, *As Camélias do Leblon e a abolição da escravatura: Uma Investigação de história cultural* (São Paulo, Brazil: Companhia das Letras, 2003).

14. André Rebouças, *Diário e notas autobiográficas: Texto escolhido e anotações por Ana Flora e Inácio José Veríssimo* (Rio de Janeiro, Brazil: José Olympio, 1938), 2:312.

15. *Revista illustrada* (Rio de Janeiro) 13, no. 495 (1888): 4. On Angelo Agostini (1843–1910), see Nelson Werneck Sodré, *História da imprensa no Brasil* (Rio de Janeiro, Brazil: Civilização Brasileira, 1966), 232–53.

16. *Gazeta de notícias* (Rio de Janeiro), May 14, 1888: 2.

17. Rui Barbosa, "A Lição da hora," *Gazeta da tarde* (Rio de Janeiro), May 19, 1888: 1. Reprinted in Barbosa, *Trabalhos diversos* (Rio de Janeiro, Brazil: MEC/FCRB, 1965), 143–47.

18. Eduardo Silva, *As Camélias do Leblon*, op. cit., 43.

19. On Confederação Abolicionista, see Robert Conrad, *Os Últimos anos da escravatura no Brasil: 1850–1888* (Rio de Janeiro, Brazil: Civilização Brasileira, 1975), chap. 12, item: "O Movimento é reavivado no Rio de Janeiro."

20. For the development of the concepts of the abolitionist quilombo and breakaway quilombo, see João José Reis and Eduardo Silva, *Negociação e conflito: A Resistência negra no Brasil escravista* (São Paulo, Brazil: Companhia das Letras, 1989), chap. 4; and E. Silva, *As Camélias do Leblon*, op. cit., chaps. 1 and 2.

21. Brasil, *Anais do Senado Federal* (Rio de Janeiro, Brazil: Typ. Nacional, 1888); June 19, 1888: Sessão de June 19, 1888: 107.

22. On Luiz Gama, see Sud Mennucci, *O Precursor do abolicionismo no Brasil: Luiz Gama* (São Paulo, Brazil: Companhia Editora Nacional, 1938); Elciene Azeredo, *Orfeu de carapinha: A Trajetória de Luiz Gama na imperial cidade de São Paulo* (Campinas, Brazil: Editora da Unicamp/Centro de Pesquisa em História Social da Cultura, 1999). Isabela was the daughter of Brazil's emperor, Pedro II.

23. On José Carlos do Patrocínio, see Osvaldo Orico, *O Tigre da abolição* (1931; repr., Rio Janeiro, Brazil: Civilização Brasileira, 1977); R. Magalhães Júnior, *A Vida turbulenta de José do Patrocínio* (Rio de Janeiro, Brazil: Sabiá, 1969); Humberto Fernandes Machado, *Palavras e brados: A Imprensa abolicionista do Rio de Janeiro, 1880–1888* (Tese de Doutorado, Brazil: USP, 1991).

24. On André Rebouças, see Ignácio José Veríssimo, *André Rebouças através de sua auto-biografia* (Rio de Janeiro, Brazil: José Olympio, 1939); Joselice Jucá, *André Rebouças: Reforma e utopia no contexto do segundo império. Quem possui a terra possui o Homem* (Rio de Janeiro, Brazil: Odebrecht, 2001); Sydney M. G. dos Santos, *André Rebouças e seu tempo* (Rio de Janeiro, Brazil: n.p., 1985); Maria Alice de Carvalho, *O Quinto século: André Rebouças e a construção do Brasil* (Rio de Janeiro, Brazil: Revan, 1998); Andréa Santos da Silva Pessanha, *Da Abolição da escravatura à abolição da miséria: A Vida e as idéias de André Rebouças* (Rio de Janeiro, Brazil: Quartet, 2005); Leo Spitzer, *Lives in Between: Assimilation and Marginality in Austria, Brazil, West Africa, 1780–1945* (Cambridge: Cambridge University Press, 1989).

25. Eduardo Silva, *As Camélias do Leblon*, op. cit., chap. 5.

26. Antônio da Silva Jardim, *Memórias e viagens: Campanha de um propagandista (1887–1890)* (Lisbon, Portugal: Typ. Da Companhia Nacional Editora, 1891), 86–87.

27. Eduardo Silva, *As Camélias do Leblon*, op. cit., 24. The *solicitador* in Portuguese was a type of lawyer or lawyer's assistant who did not have a degree in law but was a "practicing lawyer" in the legal system.

28. Pedro Calmon, *A Princesa Isabel, a redentora* (São Paulo, Brazil: Companhia Editora Nacional, 1941), 153–54; Lourenço Luiz Lacombe, *Isabel: A Princesa redentora; Biografia baseada em documentação inédita* (Petrópolis, Brazil: Instituto Histórico de Petrópolis, 1989), 223–24.

29. Museu Imperial (Petrópolis, Brazil: RJ), "Envelope com flores secas," reg. 62.572, proc. 366/57, vol. 3.784, L. 7, fls. 80. My thanks to Dora Maria Pereira Rego Correia for this important historical document.

30. F. D. [Franklin] Dória, "As Festas da emancipação," *Correio miriam* (Rio de Janeiro), February 20, 1888: 1.

31. Eduardo Silva, *As Camélias do Leblon*, op. cit., 36.

32. Rui Barbosa, "A Lição da hora," op. cit., 138–39.

33. Antônio da Silva Jardim, *Propaganda republicana (1888–1889): Discursos, opúsculos, manifestos e artigos coligidos, anotados e prefaciados por Barbosa Lima Sobrinho* (Rio de Janeiro, Brazil: Ministério da Educacão e Cultura, FCRB, 1978), 208, 234.

34. Rui Barbosa, *Trabalhos diversos*, 139.

35. Rui Barbosa, *Trabalhos diversos*, 139.

36. Rui Barbosa, *Queda do Império: "Diário de notícias"* (Rio de Janeiro, Brazil: MEC, 1947), 35.

# 6

# To Be Black and to Be Cuban

## The Dilemma of Afro-Cubans in Post-independence Politics

*Aline Helg*

*Cuba, like Haiti, was one of the few countries that abolished slavery before it emerged on the world stage as an independent nation. Although Cuba declared independence in 1902, Cuban revolutionaries had been fighting for more political autonomy since the middle of the nineteenth century. Cubans of all races and backgrounds contributed to the struggle against the Spaniards, although after independence Afro-Cubans were largely absent from the important political and economic institutions on the island. This chapter's main purpose is to document the contribution and marginalization of blacks in the period following Cuban independence in 1902. It also highlights the continued tensions among racial and national identities at the turn of the century when the United States emerged as the preeminent military and economic power in the Western Hemisphere.*

*Latin American patriots and nationalists have often persuaded peoples of African descent to ascribe to given national programs. In many cases, such identifications have done little to ameliorate pervading social, political, and cultural marginalization for the vast majority of poor blacks. Uncritical nationalists of all backgrounds have, nonetheless, continued to label Afro-Latin American protests and attempts at organization as unpatriotic. The lack of strong democratic traditions in Latin America before the 1980s restricted the activities of civil society and stymied black mobilization. Based on archival material, Helg demonstrates how the Cuban state and society collaborated to stymie the emergence of independent black voices in the first few decades of the twentieth century.*

After achieving independence, most Latin American nations banned references to race in their constitutions and laws and claimed to be racial democracies. However, at the same time that they promoted myths of racial equality, ruling white elites embraced ideologies positing whites' superiority and blacks' and Indians' inferiority and designed policies aimed at maintaining the sociomacial hierarchies inherited from colonialism. Such conditions confronted Latin American blacks with an unsolvable dilemma. If they denied the veracity of their national myths of racial equality, they exposed themselves to accusations of being racist and unpatriotic. If they subscribed to the myths, they had to simultaneously conform to negative views of blacks. Indeed, the myths made it blasphemous for people of African descent to proclaim their blackness along with their patriotism.

This chapter focuses on the dilemma faced by Afro-Cubans in the 1900s. After explaining Cuba's belated independence in 1902, it describes continuing racial inequalities and examines how Afro-Cubans were underrepresented and marginalized in politics, in sharp contrast with their massive participation in the armies that previously fought against Spain. The chapter then turns to a discussion of the formation and ideology of the first black party in the Western Hemisphere, Cuba's Partido Independiente de Color. Founded in 1908, the party was exterminated in 1912 by the Cuban army and white Cuban volunteers in a bloody racist massacre that wiped out not only hundreds of *independientes* but thousands of Afro-Cuban men, women, and children as well. The chapter concludes by briefly examining the long-lasting effects of the 1912 massacre and the continuing difficulties faced by Afro-Cubans who identify themselves as black and Cuban.[1]

## CUBA'S BELATED INDEPENDENCE

Unlike most of Latin America, Cuba only achieved independence in 1902. Moreover, its independence was drastically limited by the U.S. imposition of the Platt Amendment and by the Unites States' growing domination of Cuban economy. Three main factors explain the island's belated and restricted independence.

First, since the 1804 Haitian Revolution, Cuba had developed the most successful sugar plantation economy in the Western Hemisphere—but an economy so dependent on slavery that it continued to import slaves in massive quantities from Africa until 1860. As a result, throughout the nineteenth century enslaved and free people of African descent comprised between 33 and 58 percent of the island's population. Obviously, Afro-Cubans were far from being a homogeneous group. Although all probably shared the experience of some kind of white racism, broad cultural, educational, class, sexual, and regional differences divided them. No common

Afro-Cuban culture or subculture united them against the dominant Spanish-Cuban culture. Rather, African and Spanish traditions blended to produce a continuum of subcultures.

At one end of the continuum were the African-born and those women and men deeply attached to African cultures (notably the Yoruba or Lucumí and the Congo traditions and their respective religions, *santería* and *palo monte*). At the other end were those with long-standing free status and residence, especially in western port cities, who identified with the dominant Eurocentric culture. Some mulattoes among the latter also assimilated prevailing racial prejudices and distanced themselves from blacks, former slaves, and Africans. Socioeconomic differences among the various regions of Cuba affected Afro-Cubans as well. Not surprisingly, the racial barrier was stronger where slavery and the sugar latifundios dominated, particularly in Matanzas and Santa Clara. In Oriente, in eastern Cuba, the existence of an important free population of color together with a slave population distributed in smaller plantations tended to blur the racial barrier.

Second, such a high proportion of blacks made many whites fear a revolution along Haitian lines in Cuba, a fear astutely sustained by Spain in order to prevent any movement of independence. In 1844, in particular, the discovery of an alleged conspiracy by slaves and free people of color to abolish slavery and end colonialism led to the indiscriminate and bloody repression of blacks and mulattoes. Known as the Conspiracy of *La Escalera* because suspects were tortured, tied to a ladder; it left a deep impression on Afro-Cubans, who since then have remembered 1844 as the Year of the Lash. At the same time, fear of a black revolution, dependency on slave labor, and hatred of Spain prompted repeated attempts by elite white Cubans to promote annexation to the United States.[2]

Third, even after the launching of Cuba's first war of independence in 1868 (not coincidentally after slavery had been abolished in the southern United States), the issue of slavery confined the conflict to Oriente, where the rebels emancipated the slaves in 1869. Nevertheless, the fear of some whites of a black takeover continuously debilitated the anticolonial movement. Simultaneously, the increasing participation of freedmen and other free people of color in the Liberation Army—not only in the lower ranks but also as military chiefs—heavily contributed to the white leadership's decision to negotiate with Spain the Pact of Zanjón, which ended the Ten Years' War in 1878. When mulatto general Antonio Maceo and a few other leaders rejected the pact and started the *Guerra Chiquita* (Short War) in August 1879, again racism played a major role in their defeat by Spain.[3]

Afterward Cuba's independence process was halted for fifteen years. In 1886 the Spanish monarchy abolished slavery, but Cuban society remained divided along racial lines. Blacks and mulattoes continued to be destined to the lowest-paid jobs and discriminated against in all aspects of their lives. There followed several years during which the pro-independence movement struggled to reconstitute itself. In this process, José Martí, a white Cuban journalist and writer in exile, acquired the conviction that if so far Cubans had failed to achieve independence, it was mainly due to whites' fear of a black takeover after victory. From the United States, he initiated a campaign to dismiss such a possibility by magnifying the importance of the 1869 abolition of slavery in the eastern liberated territories and by idealizing race relations in the Liberation Army that fought from 1868 to 1878.[4] Inside Cuba, mulatto journalist Juan Gualberto Gómez paralleled Martí's propaganda of racial harmony in his Afro-Cuban newspaper *La Igualdad* (Equality).

On February 24, 1895, a new war of independence was launched, but the problem of racism among the patriot army remained unsolved. Significantly, the supreme military command of the new Liberation Army was entrusted to the white Dominican general Máximo Gómez rather than to the Afro-Cuban general Antonio Maceo. In addition, the *Manifiesto de Montecristi* announcing the renewal of hostilities against Spain, written by Martí, addressed the risk of a race war in Cuba with troubling ambiguity: it denied such a threat while simultaneously contemplating its very possibility. In May 1895, shortly after landing in Cuba, Martí was killed in a Spanish ambush.[5]

The patriot rebellion fully succeeded only in Oriente, the region with a significant population of African descent and a tradition of struggle against Spain. Blacks joined the insurgency en masse from its beginning for a variety of reasons, ranging from the need to flee from Spanish repression to the possibility of improving their personal lives or contributing to the fight for a just Cuba. In the process, many of them acquired greater expectations regarding their position once independence was achieved, despite the fact that, not surprisingly, racism did not vanish from social relations among rebels. However, Afro-Cuban overrepresentation in the Liberation Army revived the specter of a black dictatorship along Haitian lines in Cuba. Throughout the War for Independence (1895–1898), white leaders used the threat of another Haiti to limit the power of Maceo and other Afro-Cubans and to keep blacks "in their place." Conversely, other Afro-Cuban leaders were praised for their modesty and held up by whites as an example of the "good black" who did not seek prestige and popularity. More dramatically for the outcome of the struggle against Spain, when Maceo completed the most successful campaign of the war, the invasion of western Cuba that gave the independence movement a truly national dimension, the all-white provisional government of *Cuba Libre* interpreted it as further evidence of Maceo's supposed plan to transform Cuba into a black dictatorship. They ignored Maceo's conviction that, with supplies and fresh troops from the east, the Liberation Army could soon beat the Spaniards, and they kept his troops isolated in the west. As a result, they jeopardized the most decisive insurgent victory over Spain and indirectly caused Maceo's death in combat in late 1896.

Afterward, neither the patriots nor the Spaniards achieved any major military breakthrough. In this context, it is no surprise that some elite white Cubans welcomed the U.S. intervention in 1898 and the subsequent U.S. occupation until 1902. Drawing on Cuba's deeply rooted patterns of racial differentiation, the U.S. military government imposed policies that often discriminated against Afro-Cubans.

## RACE IN THE FIRST REPUBLIC

In 1902, far from making a sharp break with the U.S. administration, the first elected Cuban government carried on several of the latter's discriminatory policies. Presided over by the Moderate Tomás Estrada Palma, it continued to marginalize blacks in politics and public employment. In addition, it launched a campaign to repress traditions of African origin under the label of witchcraft as a means of denigrating all Afro-Cubans while simultaneously promoting the "whitening" of Cuba through subsidized Spanish immigration: 128,000 Spaniards, mostly young men entering the labor force, migrated to Cuba between 1902 and 1907, 70,000 of them on a permanent basis. These were significant figures for a total population of about 2,000,000.[6]

By the time of the second U.S. occupation (1906–1909), Cuban society was still deeply divided along racial and social lines, with whites having better positions in all sectors than Afro-Cubans. According to the U.S.-sponsored census of 1907, Afro-Cubans made up less than 30 percent of Cuba's total population of 2,048,980, with 274,272 blacks and 334,695 mulattoes, a rapid proportional decline from the mid-nineteenth century. Black and mulatto men continued to be overrepresented in subordinate occupations, such as agricultural work, day labor, domestic service, and construction. Commerce was almost closed to Afro-Cubans. Because few of them had been able to attend school beyond the elementary level, and because their access to the university had been virtually prohibited by racial discrimination, they were excluded from the most prestigious professions: of 1,240 physicians and surgeons, only 9 were Afro-Cuban, and of 1,347 lawyers, only 4 were Afro-Cuban. In 1907, central, provincial, and municipal administrations employed only a small proportion of Afro-Cubans, mostly as messengers, porters, and office boys. There were only 439 Afro-Cubans among 5,964 teachers, and 9 Afro-Cubans among 205 government officials. They were even underrepresented in the security forces, despite their outstanding participation in the Liberation Army. Out of 8,238

policemen and soldiers, 21 percent were Afro-Cuban, and they were generally restricted to the lower ranks.[7]

At the same time, the number of Spaniards with a gainful occupation
increased from 103,912 in 1899 to 146,831 in 1907. Spaniards dominated
all the expanding sectors of labor. They controlled domestic trade and
transportation. They had the highest positions in the tobacco factories, and
they represented 90 percent of the island's miners and quarrymen. Even in
the distribution of public jobs with salaries paid by the Cuban state, Spaniards were in a good position compared with blacks: In 1907 there were
20 Spanish government officials (compared with 9 Afro-Cubans), and 377
Spanish male teachers (compared with 113 Afro-Cubans).

Another indication of the importance of race in employment was provided by the overrepresentation of Afro-Cuban women in the female labor
force. In 1907, 65 percent of 73,520 women with a gainful occupation were
of color. In other words, 20 percent of Afro-Cuban women over fourteen
years of age had a gainful occupation, as opposed to only 6 percent of white
Cuban women. Women of color had a long history of working outside their
homes, dating back to the time of slavery, and many had supported their
family during the War for Independence. They also overwhelmingly outnumbered white women in the workforce because racial difference
matched social difference: in many cases, Afro-Cuban families could not
survive without the work of the women. Women were often the heads of
households, as widows, single mothers, or the companions of poor, jobless,
or absent men.

In sum, the position of Afro-Cubans in the labor force had changed little
since Spanish rule. They were generally confined to certain kinds of manual
labor and were blocked from access to the expanding sectors of trade, communication, and state employment. In the early 1900s, the economy was
still deeply shaken by the war and was subjected to growing U.S. penetra-
tion. Spanish immigrants competed with Cubans for labor, which helped
to depress wages. According to a French diplomat, foreign interests dominated the economy so much that the Cuban government "only commands
public employees."[8] Indeed, state employment was the principal domain in
which an antidiscrimination policy could have been initiated in 1902. But
since it was the main opportunity for Cuban socioeconomic advancement,
many white Cubans were not ready to share public office with more than a
handful of prominent Afro-Cubans.

Additional factors also explain continuing Afro-Cuban marginalization
after independence. First and foremost, it corresponded to a long tradition
of racism and Spanish colonial policies accepted by most elite white
Cubans. However, these patterns were strengthened during the U.S. occupation, when Cubans—regardless of color—were affected not only by the
occupation's socioeconomic and political impact, but also by the racist

contempt many North Americans felt for all Cubans. Middle-class and elite Cubans who had always thought of themselves as white and superior to Afro-Cubans were troubled by the U.S. obsession with "the single drop of black blood." They were particularly upset at being labeled so-called whites and Negroid by North Americans.[9]

U.S. racism induced several elite white Cubans to reassert their whiteness and to claim membership in the "Latin race." Influenced by social Darwinian theories of the survival of the fittest, they interpreted the Cuban postwar process as a racial struggle between Anglo-Saxons and Latins, and between whites and blacks. Only by promoting European, especially Spanish, immigration, they believed, could Cuba simultaneously resist the pressure of the United States and reduce the proportion of blacks in its population.[10]

The assertion of Cuba's Latin heritage against the Anglo-Saxons also affected the construction of *cubanidad* (the essence of the Cuban nation) by the elite. Because the "true Cubans" were considered to be whites of Spanish origin, Afro-Cubans were pushed to the fringe of *cubanidad*, as a kind of "bastard" people—part African and part Cuban, remnants of slavery, doomed to decrease, if not to vanish in the long term. Mainstream newspapers promoted in fiction and in cartoons the character of Liborio, a white Latin *guajiro* (peasant), as the typical Cuban personifying the national good sense. The Cuban nation, in addition, was always represented as a white woman with straight black hair and wearing the Phrygian cap of the French republic.[11]

The construction of the Cuban national identity as white and Latin was nevertheless in sharp contradiction to Cuban history. As already mentioned, during the War for Independence, from all accounts, Afro-Cubans were overrepresented in the army that fought for a free Cuba, while white Cubans, especially in the west of the island, often remained neutral or supported Spain. Afro-Cubans also died for independence in larger numbers than whites.[12] Once Cuba became independent, the constitution stated the principles of equality and democracy (through universal male suffrage). However, no specific social policies were designed for Afro-Cubans, many of whom had been slaves, while Spanish immigration was subsidized. As a result, black Cubans continued to be discriminated against and further marginalized in the economy and society, most notably in politics and state employment.

In order to conceal this contradiction, the Cuban elite, as in other Latin American nations with a significant population of African descent, cleverly resorted to a myth claiming the existence of racial equality in the nation to justify the current socioracial order. In general, Latin American myths of racial equality built up images of lenient slavery, mulatto (not black) social mobility, the absence of legal segregation, and racial promiscuity in their countries that transformed blacks into passive recipients of whites' generosity. Simultaneously, the official ideology promoted social Darwinism, white superiority, and black inferiority as well as various stereotypes denigrating blacks. Governments reflected the ideology of white superiority in policies of subsidized European immigration aimed at progressively whitening their countries' populations. In addition, the official ideology defined equality as "equality based on merit," which conveniently ignored the fact that all individuals, for historical reasons depending on their race, did not originate from equal conditions. Moreover, such a definition implied that merit could be fairly estimated within an ideological framework positing white superiority.[13] The ultimate function of Latin American myths of racial equality, thus, was to place the blame for blacks' continuing lower social position entirely on themselves: if most blacks were still marginalized despite the existence of legal equality, it was because they were *racially* inferior.

Cuba's myth of racial equality was founded principally on Martí's pre-1895 propaganda in favor of independence. It reproduced Martí's misrepresentation of slave emancipation in Cuba as a benevolent gesture of Cuban masters and transformed Martí's vision of the War for Independence and its egalitarian outcome into reality. Accordingly, the legacy of the Liberation Army was not only to have eliminated racial discrimination in its ranks, but to have banned it forever in Cuban society. The myth highlighted the fraternity between whites and blacks in the army's leadership and troops, rather than Afro-Cuban overrepresentation and whites' attempts to keep them in the background. It attributed blacks' marginalization after armistice only to their lack of merit, without taking into account the effects of subsidized Spanish immigration as well as the legacy of slavery and racial discrimination in depriving Afro-Cubans of formal education, training, and access to prestigious professions.

Cuba's myth of racial equality exempted whites from making restitution for slave exploitation and compensating Afro-Cubans for past mistreatment. It allowed the elite to ignore blacks' overrepresentation in the war, thus denying them a full political and economic share in the republic. Moreover, the myth served to brand as racist attempts by blacks to organize separately to protest racial discrimination. Any expression of black consciousness could be stigmatized as a racist threat to national unity and could be repressed on this basis.

The dogma of equality based on merit required that inequalities founded on race be attributed to the lesser capacities of blacks. Thus, negative images of Afro-Cubans were perpetuated by the dominant ideology. Many white Cuban intellectuals still described blacks as a pernicious and degenerate race that needed to be kept in check. The threat that Afro-Cubans allegedly represented to whites and the Cuban nation was embodied in stereotypical images of Afro-Cubans as rebel savages, rapists, and witches built on the

fear of African religions and of an Afro-Cuban uprising that would transform Cuba into another Haiti.[14]

## AFRO-CUBAN RESPONSES

Afro-Cuban responses to this dominant ideology were diverse and often
informed by one's class, gender, age, culture, and regional origin. Self-
perception and strategies to realize expectations divided Afro-Cubans at the
individual level. Not without connection to one's length of free status and
Cuban residence, the spectrum ranged from those who felt deeply attached
to their African cultural origins and held to a reconstructed African world,
to those who thought of themselves as Latin (or Hispanic) and opted for
full integration in the dominant world, and to those with long-standing
free lineage who claimed full participation in mainstream society. No
option was safe. Expression of African culture and religion was barely toler-
ated and often demanded concealment. Assimilation required heavy sacri-
fices but did not eliminate the racial barrier. Full participation was, in fact,
impossible. However much Afro-Cubans assumed the religious beliefs, history, literature, music, entertainment, dress, public behavior of Spanish
Cubans, they remained discriminated against in many ways. In addition,
Afro-Cuban loyalty toward white society was constantly questioned. Thus,
those seeking assimilation or claiming full participation had to deny their
blackness and their African heritage. As a result, numerous Afro-Cubans
opted for partial integration: they conducted most of their public life in
mainstream partly segregated society, and their private life in an Afro-
Cuban subculture permitting unlimited participation.

Afro-Cubans' frustration when the racial barrier blocked their social rise
was proportionate to the unrealized expectations that had fueled their
endeavors. Some abandoned the individual struggle and withdrew from the
dominant world. Others accommodated themselves to the barrier and the
position it allowed them. Still others perceived it as an injustice and fought
against it. Among the latter were those who came to identify their fate with
that of Afro-Cubans in general and transformed their personal struggle into
a collective one. They challenged the dominant racial ideology and sought
to produce a counterideology asserting the positive value of their race. They
attempted to solidify links with their community of origin and to increase
awareness. A few capitalized on collective frustration to promote actions of
protest.[15]

Given the dominant ideological context, it is no surprise that the most
prominent Afro-Cubans at the turn of the century were neither veterans of
the Liberation Army nor supporters of African-based culture, but the
middle-aged intellectuals already famous before 1895 who had spent the

War for Independence in exile, particularly Juan Gualberto Gómez and another journalist, Martín Morúa Delgado. Both Morúa and Gómez became the living symbols of black social mobility based on merit, although their culture and experience exceeded that of several white Cubans in positions superior to theirs. They, as well as martyrs such as Maceo, came to embody the myth of Cuban racial equality. They served as evidence to other Afro-Cubans that if the latter were unable to progress socially and economically, they owed it to their own lack of ability, not to racial discrimination. Having attained the highest honors with their election as the only two nonwhites in the thirty-one-member Constituent Assembly during U.S. occupation, Gomez and Morúa Delgado further spread the myth of racial equality among Afro-Cubans, which legitimated their own power and representativeness.

After independence, Juan Gualberto Gómez, the leader of post-slavery Afro-Cuban mobilization for racial equality, entered mainstream politics and committed himself to the Liberal Party. His favorite themes were the Afro-Cuban political and cultural assimilation into the dominant society, nationalism, and opposition to the Platt Amendment. With equality guaranteed by the Cuban constitution, Gómez lost interest in the specific plight of Afro-Cubans and used his political skills mostly to preach resignation to impatient Afro-Cubans.[16]

Until his death in 1910, Morúa continuously opposed the separate organization of Afro-Cubans to defend their rights. He also associated his political future with the Liberal Party. Despite his acceptance of the Platt Amendment, he was the only Afro-Cuban elected senator. In this capacity, he tackled racial barriers in Cuban society with mixed success. As we will see later, he became famous, however, for having drafted an amendment to the electoral law that banned black political parties on the grounds that, in representing only the interests of the Afro-Cubans, they discriminated against whites and thus violated the equality guaranteed by the constitution.[17]

During the first postwar decade, Juan Gualberto Gómez and Martín Morúa were the most powerful black politicians moving in high political circles. Despite the similarity of their views on racial issues, their continuing personal feud and their membership in two rival factions of the Liberal Party prevented them from uniting their forces to promote racial equality. In addition, both refused to act in the name of Afro-Cubans and instead used their influence to build up their respective patronage networks by providing Afro-Cuban supporters with jobs in the public service.

More generally, with universal male suffrage, Afro-Cubans became an essential factor in the elections. Yet at the same time, their votes were controlled and had little effect on policy. The two dominant political parties, the Liberals and the Moderates, continued to carefully ignore the race issue and worked to attract black voters through clientele networks. Even the mostly white Socialist Workers Party (the precursor of the Communist Party) did not include anti-discriminatory policies and racial equality in its program but recommended the immigration of whites families. As a result, Afro-Cuban partisan leanings followed regional rather than ideological patterns.[18] Afro-Cuban leaders capable of draining thousands of votes if denied the usual patronage received a share of public office positions. These leaders were also offered status, privileges, and participation in the clientele networks for lesser jobs in the public service. They too became living symbols of the myth of racial equality. In return, they provided black voters for the dominant political parties. The integration of the followers of Afro-Cuban leaders into mainstream politics strengthened the power of the two major parties. At the same time, it neutralized Afro-Cubans' demands and circumvented structural change. In 1904, whereas Afro-Cubans made up 33 percent of Cuba's population, of sixty-three congressmen, only four were Afro-Cuban. Of twelve senators, only one, Morúa, was of African descent.[19] Afro-Cuban congressmen, so greatly outnumbered, remained obedient to party discipline and served mainly personal and partisan interests, avoiding the problem of racial discrimination.

Yet few black politicians opposed racial discrimination after independence. The most articulate of them was Rafael Serra, a companion of José Martí in exile in New York. Upon his return to Cuba, Serra, a representative for the Moderate Party, denounced continuing racism in Cuban society and actively campaigned for racial equality until his death in 1909. He published *El Nuevo criollo*, a weekly newspaper whose slogan was "Strength through unity, but no unity without justice." Serra's paper protested the underrepresentation of Afro-Cubans—male and female—in the public service and discrimination in public places and in education, the state-sponsored promotion of Spanish immigration aimed at "destroying the blacks" by means of demography, and the selling of Cuban land to U.S. and other foreign companies.[20]

To these problems, *El Nuevo criollo* offered several solutions. It emphasized the need for Afro-Cuban education and training. But it also considered economic responses to inequality, such as the distribution of unappropriated state lands to Cuban peasants and the creation of savings banks to finance black businesses. If blacks wanted their say in Cuba, a contributor to the paper wrote, they needed "to have weight economically on the social scale."[21]

Serra's *El Nuevo criollo* undermined the dominant ideology of white supremacy and questioned the myth of racial equality. It denounced the fact that independence had not led to an equal distribution of the nation's wealth, but on the contrary to Afro-Cuban marginalization. Under the pretext of their supposed lack of ability, blacks had been excluded from many jobs and "thrown away to rot," despite their merit and their immense service to the homeland. In addition, the paper asserted, whites were quick to stigmatize as racist Afro-Cubans who expressed their desire for equality. Furthermore, whereas other social strata could freely join forces, each time blacks organized to defend their legitimate rights, they were accused of threatening Cuban society. "Racism," the paper stated, "precisely consists in keeping in a shameful degree of perpetual inferiority the black citizens of the republic they have equally helped to conquer."[22]

However, lacking an organization to propagate his ideas beyond the paper's readers, Serra was unable to effectively channel individual Afro-Cuban frustrations into a collective movement. His membership in the Moderate Party alienated the support of Liberal blacks, while he did not rally a sufficient following among his own party to significantly pressure the government for change. Nevertheless, his newspaper circulated demonstrable information on continuing racial discrimination, and his analyses provided arguments and a theoretical framework to other Afro-Cubans challenging the social order.

## THE CHALLENGE OF THE PARTIDO
## INDEPENDIENTE DE COLOR

Black discontent grew and became vocal during the second U.S. occupation of 1906–1909, as an increasing number of Afro-Cubans began to perceive political assimilation as a trap. Some, particularly veterans of the War for Independence, formed associations and committees to defend their rights in various provincial towns. The movement's focus was the distribution of a proportional part of public offices to blacks justified by their overrepresentation in the Liberation Army, as well as the creation of a black party. Militants reportedly had ceased to entrust the cause of Afro-Cubans to Gómez and Morúa. This mobilization culminated in the successful creation in 1908 of the first black party in the Western Hemisphere, the Partido Independiente de Color, which challenged Cuba's political, social, and ideological structures. Founded by Evaristo Estenoz, Pedro Ivonnet, and other veterans of the War for Independence, the Afro-Cuban party rapidly achieved nationwide membership, linking the countryside to the cities and including thousands of day laborers, peasants, workers, and artisans and a few middle-class individuals in a program focusing on racial equality and working-class demands.

Despite its name, the Partido Independiente de Color was not racially separatist but sought the integration of Afro-Cubans in society and their participation in government "in order to be well governed." Its political program and ideology, diffused in a well-distributed newspaper, *Previsión*, addressed only a few issues directly related to race: they demanded an end to racial discrimination; access for Afro-Cubans to all jobs in the public sector, including those in the government and the diplomatic corps; and an end to the ban on nonwhite immigration. Most of the other demands aimed at improving the socioeconomic conditions of peasants and workers, regardless of race.[23]

More importantly for the problematic of this chapter, the *independientes* diffused a message of black racial pride that challenged the ideology of white supremacy and the myth of Cuban racial equality. They wanted Afro-Cubans to be recognized as a full component of Cuban nationality. Cuba was to be not only "for whites and for blacks," as Martí had written, but it was to *be black and white*. The party's demand for jobs in the diplomatic corps was a symbol of the world visibility and representativeness they hoped to acquire as Afro-Cubans. To that effect, their newspaper challenged the cartoon representation of the typical Cuban as the white Liborio and created the character of the black José Rosario to personify Cuban common sense and nationalism: "José Rosario, first names of his father and mother that he uses in remembrance of his parents. This Cuban is *a man as black as a Cuban*, young, of regular stature, of very sturdy constitution . . . of energetic character and of a worth close to foolhardiness, with little education but very good practical sense, of extremely simple habits and with no pretension whatsoever."[24] The newspaper used the characters of José Rosario and Liborio to explain the party's view of the history of black and white relations in Cuba. It told the story of José Rosario's sufferings in slavery, commitment and sacrifice in the wars for independence, and exclusion in the republic. It was also the story of Liborio's cruelty during slavery, cowardice in the wars, and betrayal after independence. According to the party, there had been a pact of honor between the two men to fight together for Cuba's freedom and to share benefits in the new republic. But the ambitious and avaricious Liborio had betrayed his comrade at the end of the war. For fear of José Rosario's revenge, he abandoned him, turned to the United States for protection, and sought alliance with the former Spanish enemy.

The theme of whites' betrayal after independence was not limited to the story of José Rosario, but it pervaded the rhetoric of the party. Afro-Cubans made up more than 80 percent of the Liberation Army and died for Cuba's freedom in much larger numbers than whites, the party repeatedly claimed. Thus, Afro-Cubans had proven their patriotism and leadership better than white Cubans. But the latter had deprived the former of the fruits of victory. Now Afro-Cuban commitment to independence demanded that they pursue, in Martí's words, "the revolution until the disappearance of the smallest injustice."[25]

Independiente leaders did not hesitate to refute the myth of racial equality in Cuba. Without directly questioning Martí's representation of slavery and abolition, they denounced white Cubans' mistreatment of slaves. Rather than emphasizing blacks' and whites' fraternity in the struggle for independence, they stressed Afro-Cubans' overrepresentation in the Liberation Army. They also showed how elite white Cubans' fear of blacks after independence had prompted some of them to seek alliance with the United States and with Spanish residents. Conscious that, by challenging the founding myth of the Cuban nation, they exposed themselves to accusations of being unpatriotic or even racist, they carefully substantiated their claims with quotations on equality from Martí.

Nevertheless, in order to rally black supporters, they also built on Afro-Cuban collective memory of white repression and exploitation, two themes avoided by Martí. They repeatedly resorted to the symbolism of slavery and of 1844 (the year of the alleged Conspiracy of *La Escalera*) to show continuities in whites' attitudes toward blacks. One cartoon, for example, ridiculed Cuba's current democracy and portrayed Afro-Cubans who had conformed to compliant assimilation into the Liberal and Conservative parties as handcuffed cabbies, their feet confined in stocks, who were subjected to the whip of a white Cuban man. Paraphrasing Martí, the caption read:

> Union . . . we are all equal.
> Long life to Democracy!
> Put up with a little more
> And you will save the fatherland,
> "With all . . . and for all."[26]

By late 1909, *Previsión*'s tone had turned virulent as it became obvious that the new Liberal administration that followed the second U.S. occupation would not bring fundamental change for Afro-Cubans. Continued racial discrimination now became the major target of the Independiente newspaper, which increasingly focused on cases of Afro-Cubans being turned down for jobs, denied service in restaurants and shops, and unfairly arrested or sentenced. *Previsión* labeled these incidents "moral lynchings" and included them on the long list of crimes against free blacks that started in 1844. It argued that Cuban racism was particularly ugly because it was based on fear of blacks and was thus hidden. This characteristic implied permanent white control of blacks designed to prevent Afro-Cubans from thinking and acting on their own, the paper asserted. Any sign of Afro-Cuban independent initiative terrified whites and servile blacks, who would immediately respond, "Racism! Don't divide the races!" The time had now arrived to act. Afro-Cubans were summoned anew, in the name of those who had fallen in the War for Independence, to oppose racism— even, if necessary, with violence.[27]

In the face of the Independiente challenge, the government and white politicians used the myth of Cuban racial equality to stigmatize their mobilization as racist and anti-white. On this basis, in early 1910 the party's newspaper was seized, and the leaders and hundreds of members of the party were arrested and persecuted for allegedly conspiring to transform Cuba into a black republic. Simultaneously, Senator Morúa proposed his amendment to the electoral law banning black parties, which was approved.[28]

The government, by resurrecting the scarecrow of Cuba becoming another Haiti, secured approval for the repression from mainstream Afro-Cuban politicians. Although found not guilty in the trial that followed, the *independientes* were disorganized by repression. Moreover, their party had been banned. After 1910, they strove to regain legality. By May 1912, their leadership, borrowing a strategy already used successfully by other political groups, decided to organize an armed protest that would force the re-legalization of their party before the November 1912 national election. By showing their force, however, the *independientes* prompted an outburst of racism that swept the entire country, unmasking the mythical character of Cuba's racial equality. The *independientes'* protest was immediately misrepresented as a race war similar to the Haitian Revolution. This allowed the government to send the army and zealous volunteers against them in the name of Cuban unity: because they had allegedly taken up arms against their white brothers, these blacks threatened the basis of the Cuban nation and thus needed to be physically eliminated. In Oriente, the only region in which the *independientes* actually demonstrated, the armed protest resulted in the death of 2,000 to 6,000 Afro-Cubans, among them the top leaders of the party and hundreds of other *independientes*. Most victims, however, were black peasant families.[29] The massacre by the Cuban army put a definitive end to the Partido Independiente de Color and made clear to all Afro-Cubans that any further attempt to challenge the political and social order would be crushed.

## AFTER THE MASSACRE OF 1912

The 1912 massacre of blacks momentarily rendered the Cuban myth of racial equality ideologically useless. Indeed, in 1912 several newspapers and social essays gave free rein to questioning the ways whites dealt with blacks in Cuba. Some even looked toward the southern United States for a blueprint for race relations. Several essayists interpreted the events in Oriente as an episode of the ongoing race struggle ruling the history of humanity. They claimed that in Cuba "one of the two [opposed races] forcibly has to succumb or to submit: To pretend that both live together united by bonds of brotherly sentiment is to aspire to the impossible."[30] All social

essayists stressed that white immigration once again needed to be promoted, and the immigration of blacks, especially from Haiti and Jamaica,
strictly prohibited because they jeopardized the whitening and the civilization of Cuba.

Some principles of the Cuban constitution were questioned—notably,
equality and universal male suffrage—on the grounds that they did not suit
a people as racially diverse as Cubans. It was time that black Cubans knew
and accepted "their true place" in society, one intellectual said. The most
racist essays also used the events of 1912 to deny Afro-Cubans a decisive
role in Cuban history. They exploited the pacifism of the Independiente
protesters in 1912 to destroy "the legend," presumably created during the
independence wars, "that blacks are more courageous, more ardent, and
more impervious to strains and hardships than whites."[31] Blacks were
described as cowards without white leadership, and General Antonio
Maceo as a mediocre military strategist. Afro-Cuban contributions to the
island's development were downplayed. In sum, one author wrote, "in no
class of human activities does Cuba owe elements of progress to the black
race."[32] To this display of white elite racism, whites from the popular classes
generally reacted with active support, indifference, or resignation. Afro-
Cubans felt too threatened to raise their voices in protest; black congressmen restated their commitment to national unity by condemning the
armed protest but also expressed concern with the resurgence of white
racism.[33]

Indeed, the 1912 massacre cast a gloomy light on Cuba's myth of racial
equality. Certain segments within the white Cuban elite and popular classes
did not hesitate to respond with massive killings to Afro-Cuban demands
for sociopolitical equality in independent Cuba. Such a response showed
that Cuba was a nation in which race remained a fundamental social construct and in which racism was still enough of an ideology to galvanize people into action. Moreover, such a massacre of thousands of men, women,
and children, most of them only because they were of African descent, has
few parallels in the post-slavery Western Hemisphere: the 1865 repression
of the Morant Bay rebellion in Jamaica and the massacre of some 12,000
Haitian settlers in the Dominican Republic in 1937.[34]

From an Afro-Cuban perspective, the tragedy of 1912 was indeed a land-
mark. The severity of the punishment inflicted that year upon Afro-Cubans
clearly indicated that they were still considered unequal to other groups
and somehow less human. The killings defined the rules of the Cuban
republican game and considerably reduced the strategies available to
blacks. From that experience, Afro-Cubans learned that to form a political
party or to threaten the government with force would only provoke racist
repression.

It is beyond the scope of this chapter to analyze in depth the development of race politics in Cuba after 1912. But, to summarize the situation succinctly, Morúa's amendment prohibiting black parties remained in force. At the same time, no legislation to guarantee racial equality and to ban discrimination in employment and social institutions was passed before the 1940s. However, changing conditions allowed the coincidence of a specific Afro-Cuban agenda with the needs of the broader society. Leftist parties and labor unions, in particular, made the struggle against U.S. imperialism one of the main issues of their propaganda, and the *cubanización* of the economy its corollary. Because Afro-Cubans were overrepresented in key sectors of labor undergoing modernization and mergers, such as agriculture, construction, the waterfront, and the tobacco industry, their integration into labor unions and leftist parties was necessary to achieve gains. As a result, black workers were able to force white-dominated leftist organizations to take into account their specific claims and to support their demands for equality. In other words, after 1920, a nationalist and anti-U.S. line of action made cross-racial unity a necessity, which advanced the Afro-Cuban cause. Anti-black racism, however, did not vanish but found new targets in the low-paid Afro-Caribbean workers from Haiti and Jamaica.[35]

In the cultural sphere as well, Afro-Cubans benefited from changes taking place in the broader society. In the face of U.S. imperialism, some white Cuban elite ideologues began to advocate national unity and to acknowledge part of the Afro-Cuban contribution to the nation. White and black Cuban intellectuals, poets, and artists, influenced by the new interest in African-influenced art taking place in Paris and elsewhere, started to look for *cubanidad* in the island's African roots. As a result, by the 1930s, an expurgated version of the counterculture and counterreligion transmitted by lower-class Afro-Cubans entered the mainstream.[36]

Integration in unions and leftist parties and partial cultural recognition, however, did not mean the achievement of racial equality. Although with time open racial discrimination declined, blacks' socioeconomic and political participation remained limited. In addition, Afro-Cubans were repeatedly blamed for attempting to represent their interests separately, and they were banned from organizing a distinct party. Blatant ideology of white supremacy slowly disappeared, but racist stereotyping still continued.

Furthermore, the myth of Cuban racial equality has proved remarkably enduring, even since the revolution of 1959. From the beginning, the government of Fidel Castro opted to tackle the problem of race indirectly by promoting egalitarian policies without raising racial tensions. The revolution desegregated the public sphere without intervening in the private sphere and banned any debate on race and racism. Interestingly, no mass organization was formed to struggle against racism (although the Federation of Cuban Women was founded to help women's integration). Up to the early 1980s, Afro-Cubans, largely lower class, benefited from the revolution's social policies, which reduced racial differences and enabled the government to claim that socialism had resolved definitively the problem of racism.[37]

However, since the collapse of the Soviet Union, Afro-Cubans have been disproportionately hit by the market-oriented measures of the special period, which have dramatically increased socioeconomic differences and aggravated race relations. At the same time, the current promotion of tourism by the government, including the commodification of part of Cuba's African heritage, has multiplied diasporic exchanges among Afro-Cubans, African Americans, Afro-Caribbeans, and Africans. As a result, interest in racial issues, particularly in the history of the Partido Independiente de Color, its demands, and its massacre in 1912, has grown among Afro-Cuban scholars, artists, filmmakers, and musicians.[38] Of course, this interest is expressed discretely and individually, and no black or antiracist movement has been formed, as it would immediately face harsh repression. Nevertheless, after over four decades of erasure, racial marginalization of Afro-Cubans and white racism have begun to be recognized as major social problems not only by some Afro-Cubans, but by the Cuban government as well.

## NOTES

From Aline Helg, *Our Rightful Share: The Afro-Cuban Struggle for Equality, 1886–1912* (Chapel Hill: University of North Carolina Press, 1995). Used by permission of the publisher.

1. According to sources, there were no blacks among the volunteers but mostly white Cubans and Spaniards, whose illegal enlistment the Spanish minister of state pretended to ignore so that they could keep their Spanish citizenship (Ciphered telegram from Cárdenas to *ministro de estado*, May 26, 1912, and ciphered telegram from ministro de estado Alhugemas to chargé d'affaires, May 31, 1912, Ministerio de Asuntos Exteriores, Madrid, Sección Histórica, legajo 1431. The Cuban army also included Afro-Cubans (21 percent, according to the 1907 Census, thus below their demographic proportion), but certain units, such the artillery that tested new machine guns against peasant families, were only made up of whites. Among the sixteen reported dead in the army, eight were Afro-Cubans.

2. Robert L. Paquette, *Sugar Is Made with Blood: The Conspiracy of La Escalera and the Conflict between Empires over Slavery in Cuba* (Middletown, CT: Wesleyan University Press, 1988).

3. Jorge Ibarra, *Ideología mambisa* (Havana, Cuba: Instituto Cubano del Libro, 1972).

4. See particularly José Martí, *Discurso en el liceo cubano*, Tampa (1891), in José Martí, *Obras completas*, 27 vols. (Havana, Cuba: Editorial de Ciencias Sociales, 1975), 4:269–79; Martí, "Mi raza" (1893), in *Obras completas*, 2:298–300; and "Los

Cubanos de Jamaica y los revolucionarios de Haití" (1894), in *Obras completas*, 3:103–6.

5. José Martí and Máximo Gómez, "Manifiesto de Montecristi," in Martí, *Obras completas*, 4:94–95.

6. For all demographic statistics, see U.S. War Department, *Censo de la república de Cuba bajo la administración provisional de los Estados Unidos, 1907* (Washington, DC: Government Printing Office, 1908).

7. U.S. War Department, *Censo*.

8. Cited in Helg, *Our Rightful Share*, 103. On the role of state employment see Louis A. Pérez Jr., *Cuba under the Platt Amendment, 1902–1934* (Pittsburgh: University of Pittsburgh Press, 1986), 89–90.

9. Irene A. Wright, *Cuba* (New York: MacMillan, 1910), 89.

10. Francisco Carrera Jústiz, *El Municipio y la cuestión de razas* (Havana, Cuba: Imprenta "La Moderna Poesía," 1904); Fernando Ortiz, "La Immigración desde el punto de vista criminológico," *Derecho y sociología* 1 (1906): 55–57.

11. See for example the cartoons in the newspapers *El Triunfo* (Havana), February 18, 1910, and *La Lucha* (Havana), April 28, 1910.

12. See Helg, *Our Rightful Share*, 278, n. 64.

13. See notably Emília Viotti da Costa, *The Brazilian Empire: Myths and Histories* (Chicago: University of Chicago Press, 1985), 234–46; Thomas E. Skidmore, *Black into White: Race and Nationality in Brazilian Thought* (New York: Oxford University Press, 1974), 11, 17–19; Winthrop R. Wright, *Café con Leche: Race, Class, and National Image in Venezuela* (Austin: University of Texas Press, 1990), 5–6, 43–46, 54–59, 73–75, 84–85.

14. See for example Francisco Figueras, *Cuba y su evolución colonial* (Havana, Cuba: Imprenta Avisador Comercial, 1907); Fernando Ortiz, *Hampa afrocubana: Los Negros brujos (Apuntes para un estudio de etnología criminal)* (1906; repr., Madrid, Spain: Editorial América, n.d. [1917?]).

15. This typology is inspired by Barrington Moore Jr., *Injustice: The Social Bases of Obedience and Revolt* (New York: M. E. Sharpe, 1978).

16. Leopoldo Horrego Estuch, *Juan Gualberto Gómez: Un Gran inconforme* (Havana, Cuba: Editorial Mecenas, 1949).

17. Leopoldo Horrego Estuch, *Martín Morúa Delgado: Vida y mensaje* (Havana, Cuba: Editorial Sánchez S. A., 1957).

18. In Oriente, Afro-Cubans tended to support the Moderate party for its stand in favor of the Liberation Army veterans' pay; on the rest of the island, they generally favored the Liberals.

19. *El Nuevo criollo* (Havana), November 18, 1905.

20. "Immigration," *El Nuevo criollo* (Havana), January 1, 1904; Rafael Serra, *Para blancos y negros: Ensayos políticos, sociales y económicos* (Havana, Cuba: Imprenta "El Score," 1907), 89–90.

21. El Negro Falucho, "Carta abierta," *El Nuevo criollo*, October 8, 1904; Francisco Valero Cossío, "El Derecho a la patria," *El Nuevo criollo*, February 3, 1906; Lorenzo Despradel, "Reflexiones," *El Nuevo criollo*, January 3, 1906.

22. Serra, *Para blancos y negros*, 89–90; and several articles in *El Nuevo criollo*, January 1, 1904, to February 17, 1906.

23. For the integral program of the Partido Independiente de Color see Causa 321/1910 por conspiración para la rebelión contra Evaristo Estenoz y 79 otros, Archivo Nacional de Cuba (hereafter ANC), Fondo Audiencia de la Habana (hereafter AH), *legajo* (bundle, hereafter leg.), 228-1, fol. 392.

24. Julián V. Sierra, "Presentación importante: Liborio y José Rosario," *Previsión* (Havana), December 30, 1909 (my emphasis).

25. *Previsión*, September 15, 1908.

26. *Previsión*, December 25, 1909.

27. Various articles in *Previsión*, November 5, 1909, to January 25, 1910.

28. Causas correccionales 210/1910 and 246/10, in Causa 321/1910, ANC, AH, leg. 228-1, fol. 1281.

29. Evidently, the exact balance of the 1912 "race war" will never be known. Official Cuban sources put the number of dead rebels at more than 2,000. U.S. citizens living in Oriente estimated it at 5,000 to 6,000. See Helg, *Our Rightful Share*, 193–226.

30. Rafael Conte and José M. Capmany, *Guerra de razas (negros y blancos en Cuba)* (Havana, Cuba: Imprenta Militar Antonio Pérez, 1912), 7–8. See also Gustavo Enrique Mustelier, *La Extinción del negro: Apuntes político-sociales* (Havana, Cuba: Imprenta de Rambla, Bouza y Cía., 1912), and several articles by prestigious intellectuals in the Havana journal *Cuba contemporánea* 1 to 9 (February 1913–November 1915).

31. Conte and Capmany, *Guerra de razas*, 11.

32. Mustelier, *La Extinción del negro*, 31.

33. "A nuestro pueblo," June 1, 1912, in *La Discusión* (Havana), June 4, 1912.

34. On the Morant Bay rebellion see Thomas C. Holt, *The Problem of Freedom. Race, Labor, and Politics in Jamaica and Britain, 1832–1938* (Baltimore: Johns Hopkins University Press, 1992), 263–309. On the massacre of Haitians, see Eric P. Roorda, *The Dictator Next Door: The Good Neighbor Policy and the Trujillo Regime in the Dominican Republic, 1930–1945* (Durham, NC: Duke University Press, 1998), 127–48.

35. On post-1920 developments, see Alejandro de la Fuente, *A Nation for All: Race, Inequality, and Politics in Twentieth-Century Cuba* (Chapel Hill: University of North Carolina Press, 2001).

36. See Robin Dale Moore, *Nationalizing Blackness: Afrocubanismo and Artistic Revolution in Havana, 1920–1940* (Pittsburgh: University of Pittsburgh Press, 1997).

37. This is the title of the first book published in Cuba since the early 1960s on the issue of race: Pedro Serviat, *El Problema negro en Cuba y su solución definitiva* (Havana, Cuba: Empresa Poligráfica del CC del PCC, 1986).

38. In 2000 Helg's *Our Rightful Share* was published in Cuba as *Lo que nos corresponde: La Lucha de los negros y mulatos por la igualdad en Cuba, 1886–1912*, trans. José Antonio Tabares del Real (Havana, Cuba: Imagen Contemporánea, 2000).

# 7

# Pan-Africanism, Negritude, and the Currency of Blackness

## Cuba, the Francophone Caribbean, and Brazil in Comparative Perspective, 1930–1950s

*Darién J. Davis and Judith Michelle Williams*

*Despite the national ideologies that attempted to co-opt, silence, and marginalize black voices at the beginning of the twentieth century, black people in Latin America and the Caribbean continued to express their discontent with national politics and their lack of civil rights when they could. From the end of World War I to the 1950s, black intellectuals and artists played important roles in calling for full citizenship and promoting black culture in nations in Europe and the Americas. While these intellectual and artistic movements may not have immediately promoted large-scale black mobilizations, they provided blacks throughout the diaspora with a new mode of thinking and acting and created several forums for dialogue across national boundaries.*

*Although separated by language, culture, and a host of other obstacles that prohibited cross-cultural communication, blacks throughout the African diaspora learned from one another and began to respond to discrimination and marginalization in similar ways. Moreover, blacks in Europe, the United States, the Caribbean, and South America utilized similar discourses of empowerment while celebrating blackness. This chapter examines the parallels and the convergences of black protest in three cultural movements. The authors emphasize the similarities in black cultural production across the African diaspora while noting how those productions were tailored to meet specific national needs.*

Pan-Africanism began at the beginning of the twentieth century as a political project by British and American intellectuals and activists who were motivated by the belief that the peoples of the African diaspora had endured a similar set of social experiences resulting from the trans-Atlantic slave trade. Early pan-Africanists aimed to provide a forum for conversation and action among people of African descent across cultures, although the "criterion of unity" often overlooked issues such as imperialism, class, and national sensibilities.[1] The varied social experiences of people of African descent outside Africa are as distinct from one another as they are from those of Africans on the continent. Local, regional, and national politics and economics, not to mention culture and language, have shaped and molded the lives of millions of individuals so as to make mobilization across the miles that separate peoples of African descent complex. Yet people of African descent responded to their local contexts in similar ways.

Political and cultural movements that challenged white oppression and colonialism while celebrating blackness and promoting black solidarity emerged from cultural contexts in which they interacted with other pan-African trends. In the wake of World War I, when the world saw the colonization of Africa, and when the nation-state became the preeminent body for global discourse, pan-Africanists from the Francophone, Spanish, and Lusophone Americas articulated political and cultural agendas that challenged Western domination and affirmed the cultural capital of blackness. This chapter documents the emergence of three major movements created by intellectuals, artists, and activists from Latin America and the Caribbean—the Negritude movement of Francophone intellectuals who hailed from the Caribbean, the Negrista movement of the Spanish Caribbean, and the Black Experimental Theater of Brazil—while highlighting their connections to Anglophone pan-Africanism and to Garveyism in particular. While these movements articulated specific grievances and agendas from their distinct colonial and postcolonial experiences, each movement defined the terms of blackness and pan-Africanism to suit the social and political contours of its own society. In *The Practice of Diaspora: Literature, Translation, and the Rise of Black Internationalism*, Brent Edwards argues that the only way to contemplate transnational black discourses such as Negritude is " by attending to the ways that discourses of internationalism travel, the ways they are translated, disseminated, reformulated, and debated in transnational contexts marked by difference."[2] Moreover, it is essential to consider how these discourses and movements influenced one another across the diaspora despite the linguistic and cultural barriers that inhibited the emergence of a global pan-African alliance.

## HISTORICAL ANTECEDENTS IN THE
## ANGLOPHONE ATLANTIC WORLD

For most of the twentieth century, the nation-state served as the basic paradigm for international communities. Thus, the idea of nation has played a primordial role in shaping the consciousness of individuals—including those of African descent—since World War I. Examples of pan-African resistance and solidarity across multiple ethnic lines abound throughout the Americas from the beginning of the slave trade. Yet modern pan-African struggles may have begun as early as the 1780s, when African Americans attempted to return freed Africans to Africa, illustrating a solidarity that transcended nation-state issues. Coming at the end of the nineteenth century, when most African nations had fallen to European colonialism, the triumph of Ethiopian forces over Italian invaders in 1895 was also an important moment that many in the diaspora viewed as victorious and that made Ethiopia an important reference point for people of African descent for years to come.

Henry Sylvester Williams, a Trinidadian-born lawyer based in London, convened the first Pan-African Conference in 1900. This conference saw the participation of African Americans, including W. E. B. DuBois, who eventually drafted the most important document to come out of the congress. "The Address to the Nations of the World" universalized the plight of people of African descent in the face of Western imperialism. Despite the all-embracing goals of early pan-Africanists, which Anglophone activists and intellectuals had constructed, people of African descent in the French and former Spanish and Portuguese colonies, though recognized, were largely absent from discussions. Only at the fifth congress in 1945, at the end of World War II, did leading English-speaking pan-Africanists issue an explicit call to all the colonial subjects of the world. Utilizing their relatively advantageous economic position, blacks in the United States and Britain called for political equality. Afro-Latin American[3] participation in pan-African forums might have been limited due to political and economic disenfranchisement, but these constraints did not mean that they did not engage in struggles of their own and that they did not support pan-African ideals.

In the wake of the first Pan-African Congress in London in 1919, when DuBois and his cohorts met to assert their vision of pan-African unity, the Jamaican-born Marcus Garvey's United Negro Improvement Association (UNIA) asserted his own diasporic vision. First founded in Jamaica, the UNIA gained a mass appeal, after Garvey's relocation to New York in 1917. Whereas DuBois had called the problem of the twentieth century that of the color line, Garvey said that the problem for Africans of the past five hundred years was that of disunity, and he set out to solve it. In 1920 the UNIA's weekly periodical, the *Negro World*, called for its first international convention to be held in August of that year. Garvey boasted a membership of four million for the UNIA and a circulation of millions for its periodical—its reach extended by publication of sections in Spanish and French. In Garvey's opinion, the earlier Pan-African Congress had no concrete achievements. His movement, however, had propagated a black capitalism that, along with its pageantry and grand rhetoric, had created an international shipping line. The first UNIA convention brought together 25,000 people in Madison Square Garden and was in some ways a repudiation of what Garvey saw as an elite and ineffectual mulatto movement more interested in itself than in the masses of blacks that they claimed to serve. John Henrik Clark succinctly recalls Garvey's thoughts: "Where is the black man's government? Where is his king and kingdom? Where is his president, his ambassador, his army, his navy, his men of big affairs? He could not answer the question affirmatively, so he decided to make the black man's government, king and kingdom, president and men of big affairs. He taught his people to dream big again; he reminded them that they had once been kings and rulers of great nations and would be again."[4] It was not in Garvey's power to actually convey the powers of these titles and offices on his followers; however, he could create the performance of such roles through the elaborate costumes, pageants, and parades that the UNIA sponsored. The UNIA conventions continued yearly until 1925, when Garvey was jailed for mail fraud.

Garvey's conventions created a performance of black pride and demonstrated the potential strength of the black masses. According to Robert Brisbane, "During that last days of July 1920, African tribesman, some in their native dress, Negroes from South and Central America, Canada and the West Indies as well a others representing the forty-eight states enthusiastically greeted each other in Harlem on what was for them a momentous occasion."[5] In addition to their thirty days of meetings, John Henrik Clark describes the delegates, dressed in the bold blue and red uniforms of the African Legion and the stunning white uniforms of the black cross nurses, parading through the Harlem streets singing the UNIA anthem, "Ethiopia, Thou Land of Our Fathers." They carried the UNIA flag with them as they sang, the colors still part of the Jamaica flag and black nationalist flags throughout the diaspora—black, the color of black skin; green for black hopes; and red for black blood. In *Black Moses*, Edmund Cronon suggests that "all the splendor and pageantry of a medieval coronation were present at this greatest of Negro shows."[6] Garvey's own dress at the convention reflected this flair for the performative and included many gold braids and an elaborate hat accented with a plume. Garvey, a skilled and dynamic orator, costumed himself in that elaborate uniform when he stood up to be proclaimed "provisional president" of Africa. This title, like so many others in the UNIA, was purely ceremonial—a pageant to impress his followers and to celebrate blackness visually. Critics and many of his contemporaries denigrated Garvey for his pageantry and spectacle, as well as his financial mismanagement and open criticism of what he called the mulatto face of black leadership; however, the visual display was always part of his mass appeal and entered into the currency of blackness that remains today. We see this remnant in the flag still lifted by blacks throughout the diaspora, even if its historical connections to Garvey's great mobilization have been lost.

As the creator of "the greatest surgence of black nationalism the civilized world has ever witnessed" Marcus Garvey proposed an alternate solution to racial conflict to deal with the imperialist threat: a return to Africa.[7] For the most part, pan-Africanists dismissed Garvey as impractical, but Garvey's UNIA associations sprung up throughout the Americas, including Cuba.[8] Many argue that Garvey was an adamant capitalist, nonetheless, his importance in shaping African American attitudes toward the state cannot be understated. Black capitalism emphasized the fact that the present American capitalist system would never reserve a proper place for Africans. Many turned to communism precisely for this reason, although Garvey himself criticized the Communists for their typical racist attitudes and paternalism.[9]

Even though there were UNIA chapters in places such as Panama, Cuba, and Costa Rica, although mostly among English-speaking Caribbean immigrants, when Garvey proposed separation as the solution to racial conflict in the Americas, Latin Americans hardly took notice. Garvey coined the slogan "Africa for Africans, those at home and those abroad," which became a cry for its members and encapsulated his ultimate program. Garvey's eloquent articulation of Africa as a historically civilized birthplace of kings, his pageantry and performance of such elevated titles, and his assertive capitalist project echoed through the diaspora, and its subtle influences can be seen in movements as diverse as the Harlem Renaissance and Francophone Negritude, Cuban Negrismo, and the Brazilian Teatro Experimental do Negro.

In general, while Afro-Latin Americans' political participation has not necessarily been explicitly or officially restricted by race in the postabolition era across Latin America, the legacy of slavery and economic deprivation have inhibited the forging of a coherent black middle class.[10] Because of the profound economic inequalities in Latin American societies, lower-income classes, in general, had less discretionary time to invest in national, much less international, enterprises. In addition, widespread political disenfranchisement of other groups, including indigenous peoples and poor whites, meant that political access was not only an Afro-Latin American issue. As a rule, however, when examining socioeconomic dynamics, Latin Americans have traditionally overlooked racial issues in favor of class inequalities. Moreover, in addition to the challenges of communication across linguistic

and cultural borders, the politics of racial and national identities has traditionally represented the most formidable challenge to pan-Africanism. Syncretism, miscegenation, patriotism, and nationalism that celebrated either
whiteness or the mestizo/*metiço* nature of Latin American societies often
recognized the historical contributions of people of African descent while
prohibiting solidarity among people of African descent within individual
countries. In many cases, national ideologies rendered black Latin Americans invisible, and thus the mere articulation of blackness and the promotion of black culture constituted a challenge to the established order both
nationally and internationally. It is within this context that the Francophone movement dubbed Negritude can be best understood.

## NEGRITUDE AND THE
## FRANCOPHONE CARIBBEAN

Negritude became one of the most important cultural revolutions of black
intellectuals in the twentieth century. This cultural and political movement
advocated human rights for blacks globally, although it did not necessarily
engender a mass following. While championing the black race in global
terms, the Francophone architects of Negritude took the negative term *nègre*
(or nigger), which denigrated blacks, and reconfigured it into a philosophy
that celebrated blackness and highlighted the contributions of blacks to
Western civilization. In the wake of the 1929 stock market crash and the
destruction of European societies in the 1930s, many intellectuals, including the French-speaking black intellectuals of Negritude, saw black culture
in messianic terms. They emphasized the cultural and spiritual contributions of Africans as an antidote to European degeneracy and insisted that
the value of black culture be recognized globally.[11]

The movement, which was inspired by the French Caribbean experience,
spread out to include blacks in all strata of society all over the world.
Despite the anti-imperialist rhetoric of its writers, Negritude ideologues
such as Aimé Césaire and the future president of Senegal, Léopold Sedar
Senghor, both students in Paris, were greatly affected and transformed by
European Marxism and surrealism. The British- and American-directed pan-
African movement and Garvey's UNIA had inserted aesthetic and political
models of blackness in the global arena of ideas that were clearly present
in the Francophone Negritude movement. These contentions, which we can
collectively interpret as a "currency of blackness" circulated in the works of
black artists from the Harlem Renaissance, and were also expressed by other
Francophone writers such as the Haitian Jacques Roumain and Jean Price-
Mars, and the French Guiana native Léon Damas.

Negritude's aim had much in common with the goals of the pan-African movement. Its ethical and aesthetic focus followed in the vein of the Harlem Renaissance, which used art, literature, and poetry as media of protest and rebellion. Indeed, the cultural movement of their counterparts in the United States would have a profound effect on the direction of the Caribbean writers, although the French Caribbean islands were much more dependent and culturally tied to Europe. Not surprisingly, the ideology of Negritude was constructed in Paris, the capital of the Francophone world. With the 1932 publication of the journal *Légitime défense* (Legitimate Defense), Negritude set out to attack the colonial culture of France imposed and copied by the conservative Antilleans. Organizers called upon Antilleans to recognize and celebrate their African roots in the face of French colonialism and white racism, citing writers such as Langston Hughes as models worthy to be followed.[12]

Young writers and students from the French Caribbean as well as students from Africa were not interested in real knowledge of their African roots. Léopold Senghor would bring to the movement an understanding of African history and society at a time when European artists including Picasso and Jean Cocteau had already begun to incorporate African aesthetics into primitivism, cubism, and other aspects of the avant-garde.[13] The black artists and activists in Paris were indebted to intellectuals from the French Caribbean such as Jacques Roumain, Jean Price-Mars, and Léon Damas.

Jacques Roumain (1907–1944), a writer, Haitian diplomat, and militant Communist, played an important role in the Negritude movement before his death. Like Garvey, Roumain was interested not only in blacks' relations with whites and their contribution to Western society but in justice and economic well-being for the proletariat.[14] Between 1927 and 1928, Roumain and Jean Price-Mars published the journal *Revue indigène* in Haiti, which aimed to promote Haitian culture and resist the cultural dominance of the United States. Although the *Revue indigène* predated the Paris-based Negritude movement, Roumain's poem "Bois D'ébène," which was printed in the *Revue*, constitutes a classic of the Negritude movement. His most important novel, *Gouverneurs de la rosée* (Masters of the Dew), likewise illustrated the trans-Atlantic links of Negritude and its fusion of ideology and artistic creativity.[15]

Although most scholars consider Césaire the major spokesman of Negritude, Léon Damas, born in Cayenne, French Guiana, deserves credit for publishing the first major works of the movement. At the Université de Paris, he studied African culture in Africa and in the diaspora, including African Caribbean countries and Brazil, before serving in the French Academy and moving to the United States.[16] His *Pigments* (1937), for example, reflected this education. In it, Damas compared Africa's present situation to Africa before slavery, emphasizing the destructive nature of the European colonial enterprise. Like Césaire, he viewed enslavement as the beginning of the decline and eradication of African culture by imperialist interests. As early as 1934, Damas's poems appeared in the French periodical *Esprit.*

While the avant-garde, and surrealism in particular, allowed Negritude writers to promote the ways black writers could help free the Western imagination from mechanisms of psychic and social repression, French Marxism also influenced Negritude. Unlike the early pan-Africanist support of the free market system and Garvey's outright rejection of communism, Negritude supporters such as Césaire, who was a member of the French Communist Party and participated in international congresses organized by the Soviet Union, consistently defended the perspectives of proletarian internationalism. Césaire, for example, joined the Communist Party because, as he reported, "In a world not yet cured of racism, where the fierce exploitation of colonial populations still persists, the Communist Party embodies the will to work effectively for the coming of the only social and political order we can accept because it will be founded on the right of all men to dignity without regard to origin, religion or color."[17]

Initially, Marxism had become a powerful tool important to the writers of Negritude in the wake of the success of the Soviet Revolution. Thus, *Légitime défense* celebrated black art while directing harsh criticism at the French government's exploitative racial policies in the Caribbean.[18] Haitian writers like Roumain differed slightly in their attacks largely due to two factors: the United States occupation of Haiti from 1915 to 1930 and the collaboration of the Haitian elite with American authorities. The U.S. occupation provoked a renaissance in Haiti of the idea of the homeland and forced intellectuals to rethink their moral, intellectual, and social values. The elite collaboration with the occupation provoked a serious consideration of Haitian folk and popular cultural forms of the country.

Although it is important to recognize that the majority of the leaders of the movement came from privileged or middle-class backgrounds, Negritude nonetheless became a valid tool for the Francophone Caribbean, as it directly attacked the legacy of slavery and the evolution of a distinct caste system characterized by miscegenation, which favored mulattoes over blacks. Negritude's main goal was to raise consciousness to promote the ultimate and equal integration of blacks into French society at a time when France still possessed colonies (rather than departments, as it now does) in the Caribbean.[19]

Throughout the forties, Césaire traveled throughout the Eastern Bloc to represent the French Communist Party. As a result, in 1949, he would be declared persona non grata in the United States, owing to the anticommunist atmosphere there. He joined a twentieth-century list of black men whom the United States considered radical and undesirable, including Franz Fanon, Marcus Garvey, and Malcolm X. Between 1946 and 1956, Cés-

aire represented Martinique in the French legislature as a Communist deputy. At home he was instrumental in urban renewal projects, but his overall
political impact at home and in France was limited.[20] Unlike many of the
French Communists who adopted an uncompromising Stalinist line in the
1950s, Césaire later broke away from the Communist Party for its rigidity
in perceiving racial realities. In 1956, Césaire argued in his letter to Maurice
Thorez that official communism was cutting Martinique off from Africa and
the rest of the Caribbean. For Césaire, imperialism was always connected
to colonialism, and colonialism implied racism. He had always hoped that
Marxism would be able to be more broadly interpreted by his colleagues.
Two years later in 1958, he founded the independent Socialist Martinican
Progressive Party (PPM).[21]

Césaire's work reflected a frustration with the state of colonialism and
Marxism's official response to racial oppression. He attempted to integrate
a racial analysis into his views on class oppression, particularly as it affected
the underdeveloped reality within French colonies. In an interview with
Lillian Kesteloot in 1971, Césaire, now a consecrated statesman, recognized
the limitations of both the writer and the politician to transform reality:
"The writer is alone with his mind, with his soul; the politician, not to mention the party hack, unfortunately has to take contingencies into
account."[22] For Césaire, however, the state of black people was different
from the other exploited masses of the world owing to the legacy of slavery.
They were ashamed of the history of enslavement and had to be liberated
from the colonial mentality. Art and culture were to play an important role
in that liberation.

In many ways, Césaire's ideas concerning black culture were essentialist.
In his attempt to celebrate and glorify African traits in his *Cahier d'un retour
au pays natal*, for example, he depicts blacks in romantic, if not stereotypical,
terms, relegating the African contribution to culture and the European to
science or reason. Yet Césaire's call was for spiritual and economic liberation, thus circumventing traditional Marxist economic materialist theory.
Only as an attack against colonialism and racism, which denigrated and
made black contributions to the Western world invisible, does Césaire's
essentialist articulation make sense. Moreover, Césaire's views must be
understood in the wake of views expressed by Oswald Spengler's *Decline of
the West*; intellectuals from the 1920s and 1930s who scorned rationality
and reason; and surrealists in particular, who called for a return to the pre-
Cartesian paradise. Césaire seized this opportunity to articulate a positive
role for people of African descent.[23] He called upon the black Egyptian gods
and on the strength of other black heroes such as the Haitian Toussaint
Louverture, which resonated with Garvey's own African hero making. Borrowing from Marxism, Césaire called for the rebuilding of a society in
which each individual will be free to develop his or her talents. Moreover,

in the *Cahier*, he likens the fate of blacks in Martinique to the fate of the proletariat and the oppressed all over the world, including Jews, Hindus, and the disenfranchised blacks of Harlem.[24]

In his political essay after the war, *Discourse on Colonialism* (1955), Césaire further indicts European civilization and harks back to Spengler, who predicted a "Decline of the West," asserting "that no one colonizes innocently, that no one colonizes with impunity either; that a nation which colonizes, that a civilization which justifies colonization—and therefore force—is already a sick civilization, a civilization which is morally diseased, that irresistibly, progressing from one consequence to another, one repudiation to another, calls for its Hitler, I mean its punishment."[25] Césaire also attacked the current state of European civilization precisely because of the failure of social transformation on a global level, ideas also found in the writings of his fellow Martinican Franz Fanon and the Haitian Jacques Roumain.[26] Césaire believed that culture could, nonetheless, be used as a political tool. Roumain, like Fanon, believed that blacks were an integral part of the international proletariat. Blacks' marginal status was not a matter of culture, but a matter of a deprivation and social and economic conditions.[27]

Negritude's racial focus would develop, overlap, and often conflict with class analysis and the emancipation of the international proletariat, a tension that would reverberate throughout the social movements of Latin America. For many such as Roumain and Fanon, the suffering of blacks was related to capitalist exploitation of poor whites. Yet Negritude, which began as a celebration of blackness, evolved into a call for inclusion, self-awareness, and attention to the black's role in international struggles. These preoccupations would be shared with others throughout the diaspora and would take diverse directions, as the philosophers of Negrismo in the Spanish-speaking Caribbean attest.[28]

## PAN-AFRICANISM, NEGRISMO, AND CUBA

Influenced by Negritude, *Negrismo* was a term commonly used in Spanish American intellectual circles of the 1930s and 1940s. Negristas, as members of this intellectual movement were called, emphasized the contribution of the African to Western culture. The Negristas in Cuba did not claim, as did the followers of Negritude, however, that the African element was the center and the redemption of Caribbean culture. They considered it *as* important as the Spanish in the forging of *cubanidad*, or Cuban-ness. Moreover, Negristas argued that the exclusion of blacks from mainstream culture was a disservice to all Cubans. Their agenda was to emphasize the unity of blacks and whites in the forging of the Cuban community—a community that was culturally mulatto. This perspective diverged from that of Césaire and other Negritude writers, and the movement included whites. At the same time, this message implied a celebration of blackness in a country in which African influences were marginalized on the national level.

In the Cuban populist tradition, Negristas saw themselves as spokesmen and guides of blacks, and as patriots of the Cuban nation. Their aim was to combat the ethnocentrism that persisted in Cuban society and allowed important elements of Afro-Cuban history to be ignored. The Sociedad de Estudios Afrocubanos (Society for Afro-Cuban Studies), for example, aspired to become the instrument for the advancement of racial unity through the publication of information that served that end. Negrista writers wanted to promote the appreciation of the Cuban past, encourage patriotic sentiments, and unite the Cuban people.[29]

Cubans heeded the Negristas not only because they included patriotic intellectuals of color such as Nicolás Guillén, but also because white scholars and ethnographers such as Fernando Ortiz and Lydia Cabrera joined their cause.[30] The prominence of white intellectuals such as Ortiz and Cabrera in the realm of a black ideological and cultural movement, while not unique to Cuba, warrants further study. Ortiz, like Nina Rodrigues and Gilberto Freyre in Brazil and French intellectuals such as Jean-Paul Sartre, played important roles in identifying black culture as an important subject of research. Unlike Sartre, who demonstrated solidarity with the Negritude writers, Ortiz's early views on African culture were not uniformly positive. Moreover, in his early works such as *Los Negros brujos* (*The Black Witches*, 1906), Otriz describes black culture in Cuba in ethnocentric terms. Robin Moore has convincingly argued that, early on, Ortiz vacillated between ethnocentricity and fascination, but that by the 1930s he both praised and promoted Negrista ideas and poetry, particularly the work of Eusebia Cosme.[31]

In an effort to present a more popularly nuanced Cuban history, the Negristas boasted of the African past as well as the African's natural cultural ability, sense of patriotism, and endurance in ways similar to the writers of Negritude. Typically, Negrista writings dealt with a folklorist element such as music, dance, or art in which African contributions were central. Negristas promoted patriotism among blacks, attempted to educate whites (in a program that would have parallels with the Black Experimental Theater in Brazil), and stressed the importance of blacks to the nation in an effort to avoid conflict.[32]

The Negristas developed a double-voiced commentary that tried to balance the dual ends of affirming blackness and asserting the importance of Cuba's national identity. Within this union, however, Negristas focused on the patriotism of blacks, emphasizing the black contribution to Cuban society in similar ways to the Negritude movement. Enslaved Africans, the Negristas argued, were forcibly bound to the Cuban soil. While Spaniards and other Europeans came and left, Africans, who could not leave, were the first to acquire a sense of homeland, which bound them to the Caribbean nation, in ways that Spaniards had not been. Therefore, in direct contrast to W. E. B. DuBois's ideas of the African American's double consciousness discussed in *The Soul of Black Folks* (1903), the Society of Afro-Cuban Studies argued that "Blacks should feel, not with more intensity, but perhaps sooner than whites, the emotion and consciousness of Cuban-ness."[33]

Many Afro-Cubans echoed these beliefs, some equating Cuban-ness with being mulatto. Elías Entralgo reported, for example, that Cuba's mulatto nature represented an equilibrium in its history, liberating the black and the white. Whites should feel, according to Entralgo, "less absolute" and blacks should feel "less inferior" in relation to the mulatto.[34] Comparing Cuba to those countries with more indigenous roots, Entralgo noted that national unity was lacking in them compared to the intensification of the national consciousness in Cuba.[35] Despite the essentialism inherent to their discourse, the overwhelming desire for the promotion of Cuban nationhood was paramount in their minds. Negristas avoided any antagonism between races by employing rhetoric similar to that of Cuba's national hero José Martí: "There is no conflict or race in Cuba because there are no races." They preferred to perceive Cuba as a unified culture, but they shrewdly let Cubans know that they were indebted to Africans and their descendants. This was a strategy that directly responded to the legacies of the race wars at the beginning of the century that resulted in the massacre of hundreds of black Cubans.[36] (See chapter 6.)

The Negristas saw their role as cultural leaders as a didactic one. They were prepared to guide Cuban society toward consolidation through common knowledge and awareness of a shared heritage. Cuban history, Ortiz reported, had been characterized by four stages: the hostile, the "transient" period of *mestizaje*, the adaptive second generation of Creoles, and, finally the vindication and recuperation of dignity by the people of color and the acceptance of the mulatto as a national symbol.[37] The Negristas also cited other black intellectuals of the diaspora and, like their French counterparts, forged alliances with the Communist Party. For example, committed Communist Nicolás Guillén was a friend of Jacques Roumain and referenced the African American writer Langston Hughes. Moreover, many of Guillén's works illustrate an awareness of and identification with the struggles of African Americans. This is seen vividly in Guilléns poem about the 1955 racist slaying of Emmett Till, a fourteen-year-old black teenager from Chicago. Guillén's *West Indies Limited* (1954) also forged bonds between Cuba and other Caribbean nations.[38]

At the same time, Afro-Cubans like Guillén and Blas Roca saw the contradiction in the rhetoric of members of the Cuban upper classes who spoke out against racial discrimination but continued to attend social bourgeois clubs that often denied entrance to Afro-Cubans.[39] Other intellectuals such as Salvador García Aguero demanded that Cubans be held accountable for unpatriotic actions, urging the government to enforce the antidiscrimination laws of the 1940 constitution.[40] Still, Afro-Cubans' attempts to organize exclusively along racial lines met with opposition, and many Cubans saw such endeavors as counterproductive and as negative as white prejudice. Others were clearly afraid of being labeled unpatriotic. Not surprisingly, when Enrique Andreu attempted to create a Federation of Societies of Color, other Afro-Cubans criticized him. Prominent journalist Gustavo Urrutía, for example, claimed that such associations should be formed on the basis of their character and not of their color.[41] Although Negrismo shared many of the same goals as the Francophone Negritude movement, Cuban patriotism played an important role in shaping Afro-Cuban consciousness and the way in which Cubans celebrated blackness and promoted black rights. Moreover, the Negristas responded to and "cashed in" on the currency of blackness in ways that corresponded to the social and political climate of the Spanish Caribbean in general and Cuba in particular. In many ways the Negrista approach was much more cautious than that of the Negritude writers. In Brazil, the pan-Africanist Black Experimental Theater would also begin cautiously but would develop to fully embrace the afrocentricity of Negritude.

## PAN-AFRICANISM, AND THE STAGING OF NEGRITUDE IN BRAZIL: THE CASE OF THE TEATRO EXPERIMENTAL DO NEGRO

Brazil received the largest number of slaves in the transatlantic slave trade and it was the last nation in the Americas to end slavery in 1888. Despite these facts, the country maintained a reputation as a racial paradise for much of the twentieth century. Brazilians and foreigners often categorized Brazilian race relations as free of the polarizations present in U.S. society. However, racial interactions in Brazil, while complex, still follow distinct ideological forms that, more or less, separate black from white or divide people into white and nonwhite. After emancipation Brazil did not see waves of violence against blacks, nor did Brazilian government pass draconian laws to oppress blacks, but the state did nothing to help integrate them into the changing economy. Moreover, rather than employ blacks in newly emerging industries, they subsidized the immigration of European laborers. Furthermore, in the years following emancipation, developing narratives of national identity in both popular and intellectual circles created a vision of a mixed-race Brazil and celebrated the mulatto as the image of the new nation. The rhetoric of the era encouraged miscegenation as part of a process of "whitening" that would strengthen the national character.

Figure 7.1.    Abdias Nascimento and Ruth de Souza, founders of
the Teatro Experimental do Negro, performing a scene from
Shakespeare's *Othello*. Source: Funarte, Rio de Janeiro

Despite this veneer of peaceable interactions, black Brazilians continually
organized to advocate for greater access to opportunity. The strongest of
these efforts emerged in the large southern cities of Rio de Janeiro and São
Paulo. In the earliest years of the twentieth century in São Paulo, Afro-
Brazilians created scores of black periodicals that were often linked to social
clubs and in which discriminatory acts and black Brazilian aspirations were
recorded. Also in the rapidly industrializing city of São Paulo in 1930

emerged the Frente Negra Brasileira (Black Brazilian Front), the largest mass mobilization of black Brazilians, which eventually developed into a political party. The activities of the Front ceased in 1937, however, when Getúlio Vargas abolished all political parties. The Teatro Experimental do Negro (TEN) in Rio de Janeiro only emerged on the Brazilian national scene when Vargas began dismantling his dictatorship in 1944. TEN turned to Negritude as an alternative to the national narratives that privileged mulattoes over blacks and promoted the advantages of whitening. TEN was certainly a theater—and, one might argue, primarily one—however, it had the aspirations to form a political movement and to affect social, economic, and cultural practices in Brazil.

At the closing session of TEN's first Afro-Brazilian Congress, TEN member Aguinaldo Camargo saluted the presiding officer of the session, the black senator Hamilton Nogueira, and then addressed the following exaltations to each of the three organizers of the Congress: "The Illustrious, Dr. Abdias do Nascimento, 'Negritude' in person. Esteemed Prof. Guerreiro Ramos! The thinker of 'Negritude.' Esteemed Professor Édison Carneiro—the researcher of 'Negritude.'"[42]

Camargo's opening suggests the depth of the commitment of TEN and its followers to the ideology and practice of its distinctly Brazilian implementation of Negritude. Sociologist Guerreiro Ramos called TEN the practice of the theory of a Brazilian sociology that he had developed, a theory that reached far beyond the limits of the theater. In TEN's nearly twenty-five years of existence it not only produced plays, held conferences, created literary art, and held group therapy classes, but it also created a discourse that reconceptualized the idea of Brazilian-ness through the filter of Negritude.

Following those who participated in the French intellectual movement in the 1930s that gave birth to Negritude, Nascimento, and other Afro-Brazilians were interested in access to full citizenship. Like the French Caribbean artists looking toward recognition as French citizens, Nascimento and other Afro-Brazilians wanted all the rights of citizens. They looked to creative expression as the tool to gain entry to this milieu. Moreover, the Brazilian articulation and celebration of blackness through TEN included a strategy of symbolic politics that relied on a set of images and signs or "a shared international iconography" that had a currency within the context of the international struggle for black self-determination.[43]

While Garveyism and his physical return to Africa found few voices in Brazil or Spanish-speaking America, TEN posited a symbolic return to African culture that played an essential if not fundamental part in the construction of modern Brazil. Poetry and, to a lesser extent, poetic prose were the forms that the Francophone activists used to express their connection to an African rather than a European tradition. In Cuba, Afro-Cubans used a blending of music and poetry and were aided by social scientists and historians interested in recovering the African past. Theater was TEN's artistic basis, and Nascimento, TEN's major spokesman and architect, looked for roots of Afro-Brazilian performance traditions in African, rather than Portuguese, forms. TEN was deliberate in maintaining its connections with the international context of Negritude, while using the theatrical form to create a vision of the black man as tragic hero. Rather than the festive or comic ideas of blackness that had emerged within the popular spheres of Brazilian entertainment, TEN demanded that blacks receive serious treatment on the stage and be given tragic proportions. In his history of black theater in Brazil, Péricles Leal argued that because of stereotypes of blacks in Brazil and the United States, it was practically impossible in either country "to conceive of an actor of color representing the great human sufferings, putting him in the skin of a character complex in his pain, in his love, in his anguish in his despair and his hope."[44]

TEN's project was to place images of black dignity on the stage, a process in which, according to Júlio César Tavarez, "the bodies of those subjects socially rejected by the racist structure were transformed by TEN into archetypes of resistance."[45]

TEN's own sense of Negritude, its articulation of blackness, and its place in the Brazilian nation may have been influenced by French and North American thinkers, but Nascimento and the actors and activists who comprised TEN were responding to a uniquely Brazilian reality that gave lip service to the fraternity of blacks and whites, celebrated the mulatto as symbolic of racial union, and marginalized black voices. Indeed, the emergence of TEN in the mid-1940s vividly illustrates the force of Negritude, not only as a historical movement with a particular history arising from a particular moment in the Francophone world, but also as a transnational ideology that traveled and became a liberating set of ideas for blacks in other regions. TEN's local adaptation of Negritude reflected the Brazilian situation and served the political ends of the group within the local context.

In the preface to *Dramas para negros e prologo para brancos* (Dramas for Blacks and Prologue for Whites), published by the theater in 1961, Nascimento articulated TEN's project and proposed a guide to reading its plays. In so doing, Nascimento created the basis for a distinctly Afro-Brazilian dramaturgy that dialogued and resonated with peoples throughout the African diaspora while specifically and explicitly addressing whites in didactic terms. As Nascimento explained, "Our anthological work for the black Brazilian drama reveals another dimension, in which surges the authentic black voice, as a race and as a man of color: the social life: Living as a black man is not a common perception of the western mind. Race and color differentiate themselves and turn to a specific sensibility that developed a new creative dimension in the century of Negritude."[46]

In Nascimento's vision TEN described the everyday lives of black Brazilians and emphasized that those life stories were worth telling despite having been both distinct and unknown to white Brazilians. Nascimento searched for a creative force that would guide the theatrical work of TEN, and that force was a Brazilian rearticulation of Negritude.[47] For Nascimento, Negritude was an idea that was both essentially black and unintelligible to whites. This contention provided a specific criticism of white intellectuals who had researched and published about the lives of blacks Brazilians without engaging with actual blacks voices, or allowing blacks to represent themselves in national and international forums. Indeed, Nascimento not only revolutionized Brazilian theater, but he also reordered traditional constructions of theater history when he argued that the theater of peoples of color preceded Greek theater. Like Garvey's hailing of Ethiopia or Césaire's proclamation of a black Egyptian God, he integrated the theater of the Egyptian as part of the African heritage and created a model of origin that centers on Africa.[48]

Nascimento understood black Brazilians' need to connect to the international black struggle, which arose in societies that played prominent roles on the international world stage such as France and the United States. He was acutely aware of Brazil's status as a developing country and searched for strategies that would help overcome black Brazilians' invisibility in a country already marginalized from world affairs. "Even separated by the injunctions of history and by the languages and cultures of each new nation," Nascimento announced to Brazilians, "the blacks from the exodus indicated in 1501, route to the new world, maintained the unity implanted by color and the common heritage of collective memory.[49] Nascimento affirmed not only links to Negritude but foreshadowed his later commitment to a more defiant pan-Africanist discourse. The allegiances that he detailed were essential to the picture of black Brazilian drama that he illustrated in Brazilian society in the post–World War II era. For Nascimento the genealogy of black Brazilian theater moved from Africa to the Americas, and thus, it was important for him to incorporate the black theater of Cuba and the United States into his worldview. In Cuba, he saw the importance of ritual dances, and in the United States he understood the significance of African American pioneers such as James Hewlett and Ira Aldridge, as well as white writers such as Eugene O'Neill and Ridgely Torrance. Nascimento also claimed black musical idioms such as jazz, blues, spirituals, and ragtime as a part of a common African diasporic heritage.

Nascimento wanted to make clear to his critics that all blacks share not only a common origin in Africa, but that that commonality extended to culture and shaped experience, which meant that the experiences of Africans in the United States were congruent with those of Africans in Brazil. Thus when he employed the currency of blackness to reformulate ideas such as Negritude or produce plays such as Eugene O'Neill's *Emperor Jones* or Langston Hughes's *Mulatto*, it was a legitimate act, and one that was not without context. He was using those ideas to reflect on another manifestation of their common heritage rather than claiming these examples as Brazilian, as many of his detractors claimed. Ironically, many critics considered Nascimento's affirmation of his blackness as racist, although he succinctly explained that

> As Negritude is an affirmation that is particular to one color and of one race, it constitutes an anti-racist gesture. She belongs, as we have already said with regard to TEN, not to the order of ends but to the order of means. One day Negritude will not have any reason to exist. It will die to give up its place to another type of human relations. But until that day, while the black [man] continues as "a mere object of verses in whose elaboration he does not participate," Negritude will stay alive and active.[50]

Nascimento understood Negritude as a tactic born out of necessity rather than a permanent statement of a separatist ideology. Thus, Nascimento carefully positioned himself both inside and outside of the ideologies of Brazil, wanting both to assert the primacy of blackness but also argue for its full inclusion into the rights and privileges of citizenship. One could argue that these views moderated his militancy and anticipated criticisms of TEN's project, however, it is more accurate to say that he was incredibly strategic in his language and tactics, as he realized that he relied on the very establishment that he criticized for the financial support that allowed for TEN's continued existence.

Examining the revolutionary actions of TEN in hindsight, Nascimento explained that "in Brazil, the flag of Negritude was grasped by TEN, since its foundation in 1944."[51] He also set out a concise history of the role of blacks in the Brazilian theater before detailing some of TEN's early successes and laid out the importance of the theater's work in developing plays with roles for blacks. Nascimento cited O'Neill as an inspiration and asserted the need for texts written by black authors. "The author of *Emperor Jones* . . . supports the claim, that the author of plays for black actors should be black himself," although he recognized many white collaborators and sympathizers.[52] Even as TEN attempted to replace the vision of the mulatto nation with Negritude, the realities of Brazil's artistic and intellectual class prevented this and reflected a somewhat uneasy accommodation that even in TEN, images of blackness had mixed-race birth. Despite these tensions, Nascimento upheld Negritude as an oppositional strategy to that of assimilation: "Assuming in Brazil, the consequences and the implications that Negritude contains, it sharpens the instruments of its refusal, produced in the spoilage and in the suffering; refusal of cultural assimilation; refusal of compulsory assimilation; refusal of humiliation; refusal of misery; refusal of servitude."[53]

Nascimento was attempting to dialogue with whites (and blacks who were also unconvinced by Negritude), but he still wanted to maintain the distinctiveness of the project and the primacy of a separate black identity.

One of the key extra-theatrical weapons in TEN's arsenal was the organization of various conferences and meetings to discuss the "negro problem" in Brazil. Starting in 1945 TEN launched a series of black conferences, conventions, and congresses, which, while including whites, allowed a space for blacks to theorize about themselves and to replace the dominant ideology with their own. TEN's assemblages followed a history of conferences in which Brazilian blacks had been discussed by theorists and academics as objects. These meetings functioned both as performances in which educated blacks were able to assert themselves for the academics present and for the larger public who would read about them in the media, and as platforms where TEN was able to propose its own racial orthodoxy.

TEN's 1950 First Congress of the Black Brazilian was scheduled so as to commemorate the one hundredth anniversary of the abolition of the slave trade in Brazil and to intervene in the creation of the UNSECO studies on race in Brazil, originally intended to explain the exceptional harmony of Brazil's race relations. Several of the principal authors and researchers of those studies were active participants in TEN's conventions who presented theses for debate and presided over some discussions that were published in the hope of influencing the UNESCO report.[54] Guerreiro Ramos, a sociologist and member of TEN, submitted the thesis "A UNESCO e as relações de raça" (UNESCO and Race Relations), in which he suggested that UNESCO study TEN's attempts to change racial attitudes using theater, beauty contests, group therapy, museums, and films.[55] At this conference the speakers addressed the social problems of blacks rather than solely cataloging their culture.

Published eighteen years later, the proceedings of the convention, *O Negro revoltado* (The Rebellious Black), lost much of the optimism of the convention. Instead, the work served as a cry of frustration and, as the title indicates, revolt. Although it included a report of the proceedings of the 1950 black congress, the first seventy pages encompass a fiery address by Abdias do Nascimento and is TEN's angriest discourse. Between the 1950 congress and the 1968 publication of this book, Brazil had moved from a constitutionally elected government headed by the sympathetic Vargas to a repressive military regime that viewed ethnic mobilization as a threat to the goals of the nation. Nascimento had suffered through personal scandals, electoral defeats, and a long censorship battle over his play *Sortilégio*. Ramos had gone into exile in the United States in 1966, after his election to Congress and threats of persecution by the military dictatorship, and

Nascimento would soon follow. All these disappointments provide the backdrop for that text.

In *O Negro revoltado*, Nascimento demanded the rejection of miscegenation as a strategy for racial improvement and the end to the objectification of the black Brazilian as historically quaint, folkloric, colorful, or the font of Brazilian culture. The alternative he suggested was Negritude. In his later vision of Negritude, Nascimento also moved away from attempting to engage and educate white Brazilians in a strident support of pan-Africanism and the heroes who represented it. This pantheon included many African Americans and Negritude figures such as Aimé Césaire and Léopold Senghor but also extended to black Brazilians such as Chico Rei, Luís Gama, José do Patrocínio, Cruz e Sousa, and Lima Barreto." Whereas in 1961 before the military coup of 1964, which stymied Brazilian democracy, Nascimento had called Negritude a tactic that would one day be obsolete, in his later articulations, he argued that "the values of Negritude are thus perpetual, perennial, or permanent, in the measure that being the perpetual, perennial or permanent the human race and its historic/cultural sub-products."[56] He posited a historical contour of the struggle when he suggested the *quilombo*, or Maroon community, as the model of revolt and mobilization of Afro-Brazilians, foreshadowing his later work *Quilombismo*. Nascimento was interested in the independent and oppositional spirit of the *quilombos* and the ability of Africans to maintain aspects of their culture and sovereignty.[57] Indeed, Nascimento saw the founders of the *quilombos* are the precursors of the contemporary Brazilian struggle today. When enslaved men and women risked their lives, "they rejected the forced work, of the cultural values, new gods, new language, new style of life."[58]

There is no denying the fact that TEN's work changed the face of the Brazilian stage. TEN's most active period as a theater was from its birth in 1944, when it debuted as part of the Teatro Estudantil production of *Palmares*, until 1957, when it produced Nascimento's own *Sortilégio: Mistério negro*. In that period it produced six plays, many of which were repeated, and four reviews, recitals, or compilation shows. It also participated in four productions by mainstream groups, including the famous *Orfeu da conceição* by Vinicius de Moraes. Prior to TEN's ideological and stage work, blacks were seldom present on the Brazilian stage, and when they were, they were relegated to comic figures, and in a country with a significant population of African descendants, these characters were played by whites in blackface. After TEN's intervention, mainstream authors began to write complex, if at times still stereotypical, black characters, and blackface was no longer acceptable. Without the marriage of TEN's version of Negritude and its political component, it would not have been as successful in its challenge to Brazilian stage practices. As an ideology of aesthetics, Negritude was a powerful tool; however, as a means for access to political inclusion, both the ideology and TEN were less successful. In addition to TEN's theatrical work the group produced a magazine, hosted conferences, created literacy classes, held programs in group therapy, and supported candidates for office.

TEN began during an important period of national identity formation in Brazil, and it demanded that race be part of that discussion. The ideology of Negritude provided the discursive base of all their actions, helping them to tap into the international currency of blackness for their own struggles of self-determination. The activities of the Teatro Experimental do Negro were varied and had lasting impact. If one looks at easily measurable ends like laws passed or persons elected to office, TEN was not a successful political mobilization. However, one must look not just at what TEN did, but how those acts were employed and read after its demise; if one looks to the power of its discourse and the discourse that arises around it was very effective. It changed the terms of racial debate in Brazil.

The Teatro Experimental do Negro, like the other movements discussed in this chapter, capitalized on the transnational rhetoric of black pride and social equality that arose within the pan-African movements and Garveyism of the first half of the twentieth century. Its task was distinct from that of the U.S. civil rights movement that targeted specific North American legislation that mandated segregation and prohibited black voting, for example. In Brazil, Cuba, and the Francophone Caribbean, racism was a matter of custom, not law, and the waves of discrimination were regionally unequal. Mobilizing blacks in Brazil, where Brazilians were encouraged to believe that there were no racial problems in the country, for example, would prove an exceptionally difficult task.

Cultural, linguistic, and historical differences among peoples of African descent in the diaspora constituted de facto barriers to communication as well as to political, economic, and other programs across national lines. During slavery, African families were torn apart and condemned to lives of servitude in diverse regional and cultural eras where they adapted, assimilated, and influenced emerging customs. The diversity of languages, customs, and religions—not to mention class distinctions among Africans—urges us to carefully define and distinguish "African-ness" in Africa and in the diaspora. As Sidney Mintz and Richard Price aptly explain in *The Birth of African-American Culture*, however, the birth of African diasporic culture and consciousness emerged as a result of a hybridization, syncretism, and cultural exchange, first among many African ethnic groups living in close quarters, from the bowels of slave ships to slave quarters throughout the Americas, and then through cohabitation with indigenous and diverse European groups.[59]

While male writers, artists, and activists were largely responsible for articulating the diverse politics of blackness of Negritude in the French Caribbean, Cuba, and Brazil, women and gender played important roles in each region. Men and women of African descent routinely protested the exploitation and stereotyping of black women, particularly in sexual terms. Others highlighted the importance of women to pan-African struggles against slavery in maroonage and in the creation of modern nation-states. Women such as Paulette Nardell, and her sisters Alice and Jane, played significant roles in the Francophone Negritude movement of the 1930s and 1940s. Contemporaries in Cuba praised Eusebia Cosme's poetry, while others recognized the scholarship of Lydia Cabrera to Negrista thought. Actress Ruth de Souza, along with Abdias do Nascimento, was one of the cofounders of the Black Experimental Theater.[60] María Nascimento edited a column in *Quilombo* dedicated to the woman's voice in Brazil entitled "Fala Mulher" (Women Speak Up).[61] Integrating women fully into the histories of black movements in Latin America warrants further investigation, yet equally important is the study of black women in pan-African movements and as transnational promoters of the currency of blackness.

The decline of empire and the institutionalization of the nation-state at the beginning of the twentieth century encouraged black identification with nationhood rather than race. Ironically, across the diverse national discourses of race-nation, the struggles and strategies of peoples of African descent show remarkable similarities. These similarities constitute part of the currency of blackness and included three basic tenets: the call for equal rights, the edification of the black race, and the celebration of blackness. Black art, literature, poetry, and theater played pivotal roles in the articulation of blackness in all spheres of society. Indeed, cultural production became a conduit for the celebration of black culture and the expression of discontent, and the springboard for participation into the political and economic spheres precisely because Africans and their descendants had been barred from representing American nations and from attaining footholds in national political circles. The pioneers of the French-speaking community articulated their dual agenda of protest and celebration in remarkably essentialist terms. Yet the Francophone idea of Negritude evolved from its historical essentialism and embraced broader meanings for the diaspora. That black intellectuals in the so-called peripheral areas of the West, specifically Latin America and the Caribbean, shared similar preoccupations with blacks who lived closer to the centers of power in England and the United States affirms an implicit pan-African currency across class and national lines.

## NOTES

1. Ronald W. Walters, *Pan Africanism in the African Diaspora* (Detroit, MI: Wayne State University Press, 1993), 326.

2. Brent Hayes Edwards, *The Practice of Diaspora: Literature, Translation, and the Rise of Black Internationalism* (Cambridge, MA: Harvard University Press, 2003), 7.

3. For purposes of clarity and consistency, the term "African Americans" will refer to people of African descent in the United States. "Afro-Latin American" and "black" will be used interchangeably.

4. John Henrik Clarke, "Marcus Garvey: The Harlem Years," *Transition*, 46 (1974): 15.

5. Robert H. Brisbane, "His Excellency: The Provincial President of Africa," *Phylon* 10, no. 3 (1949): 261–62.

6. Edmund David Cronon, *Black Moses: The Story of Marcus Garvey and the United Negro Improvement Association* (Madison: University of Wisconsin Press, 1955), 63.

7. Brisbane, "His Excellency," 262.

8. DuBois famously called Garvey a "little fat black man; ugly, but with intelligent eyes and a big head," Garvey used this quote repeatedly to show that the mixed-race DuBois was not proud of his African heritage. See Elliott M. Rudwick, "DuBois versus Garvey: Race Propagandists at War," *Journal of Negro Education* 28, no. 4 (1959): 428.

9. See *New Jamaican*, September 5, 1932.

10. The Caribbean islands represent an exception to this generalization insofar as strong Afro-Caribbean middle classes have emerged in all the English- and French-speaking islands, but people of African descent make up the majority of these populations.

11. Oswald Spengler, The *Decline of the West*, trans. Charles Francis Atkinson (New York: Alfred A. Knopf, 1926–1928).

12. A. James Arnold, *Modernism and Negritude* (Cambridge, MA: Harvard University Press, 1981), 27–33.

13. Léopold Senghor is also considered one of the founders of the movement, who would later distance himself from many of the Negritude writers of the Caribbean. Maurice Delafosse was a white Frenchman who did extensive studies in Africa. He helped dispel many myths on African primitivism and the notion that Africans did not have any true religion. See *The Negroes of Africa: History and Culture* (Washington, DC: Associated Publishers, 1931).

14. Henock Troullot, *Dimension et limites de Jacques Roumain* (Port-au-Prince, Haiti: Les Etudes Fardin, 1981), 9–11.

15. Selvyn Cudjoe, *Resistance in Caribbean Literature* (Athens: Ohio University Press, 1980), 116–20.

16. Hal May and Susan M. Trotsky, eds., *Contemporary Authors* (Detroit: Gale Research, 1989), 125:82–83.

17. André Breton, *What Is Surrealism?* ed. Franklin Rosemont (New York: Monrad Press, 1978), 1–3.

18. Lewis Nkiosi, "Negritude: New and Old Perspectives," in *Tasks and Masks* (Essex, UK: Longman, 1981), 11–27.

19. Arnold, *Modernism and Negritude*, 46–48.

20. Aimé Césaire, *Aimé Césaire, the Collected Poetry*, ed. and trans. Clayton Eshleman and Annette Smith (Berkeley and Los Angeles: University of California Press, 1983), 4–12. The quote is taken from "Why I Am a Communist?" published origi-

nally by the Communist Party in France. See Oswald Spengler, *The Decline of the West*, trans. Charles Francis Atkinson, 2 vols. (New York: Arnold A. Knopf, 1926).

21. Arnold, *Modernism and Negritude*, 169–77; also Gregson Davis, *Non-vicious Circle* (Stanford, CA: Stanford University Press, 1984), 3–24.

22. Quoted in Arnold, *Modernism and Negritude*, 177–79.

23. Thus, Negritude is connected to the twentieth century dialogue on modernity.

24. See Césaire, *Cahier d'un retour au pays natal*, trans. Abiola Irele, 2nd ed. (Columbus: Ohio State University Press, 2000), 20–25; Césaire, *Discourse on Colonialism*, trans. Joan Pinkham (New York: Monthly Review Press, 1972), 65–78.

25. Césaire, *Discourse*, 17–18.

26. Césaire, *Discourse*, 17–18, 60–61.

27. Troullot, *Dimension et limites*, 9–12.

28. Jacques Roumain, *Gobernadores del rocio* (Santo Domingo, Dominican Republic: Ediciones de Taller, 1981); also for an analysis of the novel, see Cudjoe, *Resistance in Caribbean Literature*, 126.

29. Fernando Ortiz, "La Cubanidad y los negros," *Estudios afrocubanos* 3 (1939): 4–6. Because of the war, paper shortage was a problem. The journal stopped publication between 1941 and 1945 but resumed in 1946. It published volume 1940–1946 in 1946. See introductory article in *Estudios afrocubanos* (1940–1946).

30. *Cuba en la mano* (Havana, Cuba: Imprenta Ucar, García y cia, 1940), 736–68. See also Instituto de Literatura y Lingüística de la Academia de Ciencias de Cuba, *Diccionario de la literatura cubana* (Havana, Cuba: Editorial de la Havana, 1980), 321; Fernando Ortiz, *Hampa afrocubano. Los Negros esclavos: Estudio sociológico y de derecho público* (Havana, Cuba: n.p., 1916). In order to trace African elements in Cuba, Ortiz had to delve back into the colonial era, which only ended in 1898. *Los Negros esclavos* is good general study of slavery's role in Spain's most lucrative colony from its origins to abolition. His best-known work outside of Cuba is the classic *Contrapunteo cubano del tobaco y del azúcar* (1940; repr., Caracas, Venezuela: Biblioteca Ayacucho, 1978).

31. Robin Moore, "Representations of Afrocuban Expressive Culture in the Writing of Ferando Ortiz," *Latin American Music Review/Revista de música lationoamericana* 15, no. 1 (1994): 32–54.

32. "El Emblema de la Sociedad de Estudios Afrocubanos," *Estudios afrocubanos* 1 (1937): 11–14.

33. "El Emblema."

34. "El Emblema," 185.

35. "El Emblema," 188. Other writers such as Alcides Arguedas from Bolivia seemed to corroborate this view. See *Pueblo enfermo* (La Paz, Bolivia: Libreria Editorial Juventud, 1982), published for the first time in 1909 and republished in 1936.

36. See José Martí, "Mi raza" (Patria, 16 de abril de 1893), *in Obras Completas* (Havana, Cuba: Editorial Nacional de Cuba, 1963–1973), 2:298–300.

37. Ortiz, "La Cubanidad y los negros," *Estudios afrocubanos* 3 (1939): 3–15.

38. Nicolás Guillén, "Elegía a Emmett Till," in *Las Grandes elegías y otros poemas* (Caracas, Venezuela: Bibleoteca Ayacucho, 1982), 21–22.

39. Blas Roca, "El Decreto sobre la discriminación racial," *Hoy* (Havana), December 6, 1951: 2.

40. "La Discrimination la ley y la trampa," *Fundamentos* 10, no. 95 (1950): 128–34. In *El Negro en Cuba*, Robaina uses Aguero's statement to foreshadow the need for a revolution as well as to justify the gains of the revolution.

41. P. Portuondo Calá, introduction to "Palabras," *Atenes: Revista de afirmación Cubana* 2, no. 14 (1931): 4; Juan Gualberto Gómez, "Las Soluciones: La Identidad," *La Fraternidad*, September 15, 1890. Reprinted in Gómez, *Por Cuba libre* (Havana: Oficina de Historiador de la Ciudad, 1954), 230–34.

42. Abdias do Nascimento, *O Negro revoltado* (Rio de Janeiro, Brazil: Edições GRD, 1968), 285.

43. The term "symbolic politics" and its definition are taken from a seminar at the American Seminar at the University of Kansas on March 5, 2003, by Maylei Blackwell.

44. Péricles Leal, "Teatro negro do Brasil," *Quilombo* 6 (February 1950): 11.

45. Júlio César Tavares, "Teatro Experimental do Negro: Context, estructura e ação," *Dionysos* 28 (1988): 84.

46. Abdias do Nascimento, "Prólogo par brancos," *Dramas para negros e prólogo para brancos* (Rio de Janeiro, Brazil: Edicão de Teatro Experimental de Negro, 1961), 9, 10.

47. Nascimento, "Prólogo para brancos," 10.

48. Nascimento, "Prólogo para brancos," 11.

49. Nascimento, "Prólogo para brancos," 15.

50. Nascimento, "Prólogo para brancos," 19.

51. Nascimento, "Prólogo para brancos," 19.

52. Nascimento, "Prólogo para brancos," 24.

53. Nascimento, "Prólogo para brancos," 25.

54. These include Charles Wagley, who produced a volume on rural areas in the state of Bahia; Roger Bastide, who produced the volume on São Paulo with Florestan Fernandes; Oracy Noguera, who contributed to the volume on São Paulo; Thales Azevedo, who wrote the text on elites in Salvador; and Luis Aguiar Costa Pinto, who wrote text on Rio de Janeiro.

55. Nascimento published the proceedings of the congress in 1968 under the title *O Negro revoltado*. Discussion of Ramos's thesis appears on pages 154–57.

56. Nascimento, "Prólogo para brancos," 51.

57. Palmares was the largest and most well known of Brazil's Maroon communities, which withstood fourteen attacks by the Portuguese authorities before being destroyed in fifteen and its leader Zumbi killed. See Edson Carneiro, *O Quilombo de Palmares* (Rio de Janeiro, Brazil: Civilização Brasileira, 1966).

58. Nascimento, "Prólogo para brancos," 53.

59. Sidney Mintz and Richard Price, *The Birth of African-American Culture* (Boston: Beacon Press, 1992). This classic was originally published in 1976.

60. "Romances de Jorge Amado," *Quilombo* 1, no. 1 (1948): 6.

61. María Nascimento, "Crianças racistas," *Quilombo* 1, no. 1 (1948): last page.

# III

DISPLACEMENT,
TRANSNATIONALISM, AND
GLOBALIZATION

# 8

# The Logic of Displacement

## Afro-Colombians and the War in Colombia

*Aviva Chomsky*

*Colombia is the only country in Latin America that mandates black political representation in the National Congress. Federal Law 70 (ratified in 1993), which assigns seats in its National House of Representatives to Afro-Colombians, guarantees Afro-Colombian political participation on the national level, although not all black communities are represented. At the same time, Colombia's civil war and large-scale economic plans in rural areas traditionally occupied by black Colombian peasants have led to widespread economic problems and displacement. Afro-Colombian dislocation constitutes the latest tragic example of the dispersion of people of African descent that began centuries ago. Not surprisingly, Afro-Colombians have joined together to protest these injustices.*

*Chomsky's chapter not only provides an analysis of the government and business policies that have led to dislocation, but it also documents Afro-Colombian international and national strategies in the face of crisis. She carefully places Afro-Colombian displacement into the broader social and political history of Colombia and highlights the role of U.S. and multinational political and economic interests in the turmoil. Displacement is not unique to Colombia, however. Nor is it a phenomenon only experienced by peoples of African descent. This chapter also raises questions about how government and corporate policies often lead to the displacement of disenfranchised people in general.*

Colombia has one of the largest populations of internally displaced people in the world, and Afro-Colombians are disproportionately represented among the displaced.[1] While the half-century of war in Colombia and the terror that has become part of the fabric of everyday life, for many Colombians, may seem anarchic and incomprehensible, there is, in fact, a logic to the process. Or rather, there are several competing logics. Taking a long historical view of the plight, and the activism, of Colombia's African-descended communities can help to illuminate these logics.

The first strand in the story is gold. Gold motivated the first large-scale displacement of Africans, on Portuguese, Spanish, and British slave ships, to the Pacific Coast regions of Colombia. Gold extraction has also destroyed the land over the centuries. Tropical forests have been felled, and soil and water have been contaminated by mercury. Increasingly mechanized mining techniques have exacerbated the environmental depredations of mining. Communities formed by the descendants of the slaves brought to mine the gold have then been forced off their land to accommodate further mining. The second strand in the story is race. In their encounters with Asia, Africa, and the Americas, especially after 1492, Europeans developed ideologies of racial difference that justified conquest, genocide, and exploitation. In the nineteenth century these ideologies were codified into pseudo-scientific dogma. The dogma justified systems of social and economic exclusion after the abolition of slavery and permeated the institutions of newly independent nation-states. The third strand in the story is violence. Violence uprooted Africans from their homes in Africa, and it uprooted them again and again from the lands and homes that they established in Colombia.

Closely related to all of these strands is the issue of labor. After serving as a source of forced labor in the colonial period, Afro-Colombians in the twentieth century found three different socioeconomic roles open to them. Some still worked at backbreaking, mostly agricultural, labor to supply profits for the export economy. Some escaped from the export economy, creating a Colombian version of Sidney Mintz's "reconstituted peasantry," which had roots in the *cimarronaje* of those who escaped slavery generations before.[2] And some were expelled from their land to make room for a new export economy that did not need their labor. If the old economy was utterly dependent on the labor of African-descended people, the new economy rendered many of them superfluous.

Another aspect of the Afro-Colombian experience is invisibility. From official statistics and government policies, to academic studies, to the popular imagination, people of African origin have been systematically excluded and ignored by the Colombian mainstream. Yet people of African origin comprise over 20 percent of Colombia's population, making the country home to the largest African-origin population of the Americas, after Brazil.[3] The final strand is resistance. The struggle to pursue spaces to create and maintain individual and collective identities, and for individual and collective survival, has been central to Afro-Colombian existence. Displaced and dispossessed generation after generation, Afro-Colombians have nonetheless survived, created a vibrant cultural identity, and reinvented their struggle for dignity in a social order endlessly redesigned to deny it.

## RACE AND REGION IN COLOMBIA

Numerous studies have emphasized the extent to which race has been associated with region in Colombian history, and the quasi-colonial relationships established inside the country between the whiter central regions and the predominantly black and indigenous peripheries.[4] Like colonies everywhere, the peripheral regions have been characterized by forced labor, extractive industries, poverty, lack of social services, violence, and derogatory attitudes shaped by racism from the center.

If any region in Colombia best represents the center, it is Antioquia's coffee-growing and industrial highlands, with their reputation for being white, Catholic, and industrious. Recent studies have emphasized the quasi-colonial relationship between the heartland of Antioquia and its multira-

**Figure 8.1.   Many Afro-Colombians live in poor communities without basic services. Here two women use the waters of a river as a makeshift laundry. Source: Garry Leech**

cial tropical peripheries.[5] This chapter will focus on three of these tropical peripheries that are home to large Afro-Colombian populations: the Chocó, Urabá, and the Guajira. While the history of each region is unique, they share some tragic similarities.

Colombia's 1991 constitution is a unique document in Latin America in that it recognizes Afro-Colombian communities as distinct, like indigenous communities, with common rights to land. This construction is complicated by two factors. First, the recognition and granting of communal land titles was one factor leading to the massive displacements of the 1990s. For along with the tentative recognition of land rights came a neoliberal economic onslaught that created new opportunities for profit. Investors, speculators, and the armed groups allied with them saw more lucrative uses for the land on which communities were growing yams, yucca, rice, and plantains for their subsistence. Second, the legal identification of Afro-Colombian communities as rural and land-based excluded large numbers of Afro-Colombians from the very category. Collective landholding communities have indeed historically been an important element of Afro-Colombian survival, social identity, and collective existence. Yet they are also an expression of particular forms of historical development that do not incorporate all Colombians who are of African descent. Most African-descended Colombians form part of a rural proletariat or belong to marginalized urban populations, and some, though disproportionately few, have joined the urban working, middle, and even upper classes.

## *LA VIOLENCIA*: RACIALLY STRUCTURED VIOLENCE

Most studies trace the violence that has shaken Colombia in recent decades to the 1940s, when the assassination of a populist politician, Jorge Eliécer Gaitán, unleashed a popular uprising and a violent reaction that subsequently deepened and became entrenched in many regions of Colombia. Traditional histories of *la violencia*, as the phase of the violence that lasted from 1948 through the 1950s came to be called, saw it in partisan terms, as a battle between liberal and conservative factions of Colombia's traditional elite, with each side mobilizing peasant clients on its behalf.

Recent studies, however, have focused on the economic, social, cultural, and racial aspects of the violence and have discerned clear patterns that transcend the liberal-conservative explanation. Mary Roldán argues that *la violencia* in Antioquia was in large part an effort on the part of Antioquia's white elites to establish control over the province's primarily Afro-Colombian and indigenous peripheries and their populations. According to Roldán, "For Antioquia's elite and political authorities, the limits of a regional community were drawn around spaces that were long-held objects of desire. . . . These were areas of strategic importance, characterized by natural resources and economic potential to enrich and extend Antioqueño power, but which, for various reasons, had historically proven difficult to control or resistant to Antioqueño cultural, political, and economic domination. Peripheral areas were the sites in which the parameters of regional identity and authority were fought over and shaped and where violence became endemic and widespread."[6]

The smallholder coffee-producing center of Antioquia, where most of the population of the province lived, largely escaped the worst of *la violencia*. Instead, the more lightly populated peripheral regions, including the tropical lowlands to the west and north, and the area along the Magdalena River to the east, saw the greatest levels of violence. There, Roldán shows, partisanship expressed a cultural and economic struggle as government forces used violence to establish control over the populations of regions that had heretofore maintained a degree of independence.[7]

In the Chocó too, partisanship had much to do with economic and cultural identification. As in Antioquia, the violence consisted primarily of conservative attacks on liberal towns. A government study published in 1963 estimated that some four hundred people died in the Chocó as "the violence descended there from Antioquia, affecting the banks of the Atrato, Carmen del Atrato, Napipí, Naurití, Urequí (Juradó, Cupica), and Quibdó (Bebará, Bojayá)." Several towns, including Bojayá, went up in flames.[8] Most of the region's Afro-Colombian population chose to flee, rather than join, the struggle.[9]

## FORTY YEARS OF VIOLENCE AND DISPLACEMENT

In 1958 the Liberal and Conservative parties joined forces to alternate power in the National Front. Some analysts have seen the formation of the National Front as the end of *la violencia*, but Roldán argues that far from ending, the violence "took on a distinctly social and economic cast by the later years of the 1950s, giving rise in some areas to the nucleus of what would constitute insurgent, leftist guerrilla groups in the 1960s. It appeared that *la violencia* had not ended, but simply evolved."[10]

In 2003, the United Nations Development Program (UNDP) published an analysis of the recent violence in Colombia that almost eerily reflected what Roldán had argued about the 1940s and 1950s. The UNDP report concluded that "the conflict has unleashed itself primarily in the peasant 'periphery' of Colombia, and has been marginal to the center."[11] The results of this long history of violence and displacement can be seen in the migra-

**Figure 8.2.    An Afro-Colombian child appears in the foreground. Behind him are two soldiers from the Colombian army. The Colombian army is a constant presence in many Afro-Colombian communities in the Chocó region on the Colombian Pacific coast. Source: Garry Leech**

tion patterns of Colombia's African-origin population, inside and outside the Chocó. Many of today's Afro-Colombian peasant communities in the Chocó have their origins in the 1930s, 1940s, and 1950s, when they were founded by refugees of *la violencia* or migrants impelled by economic desperation as their lands were taken over by the process of concentration that accompanied it.[12] Dozens of these communities were forcibly displaced in the paramilitary incursion of the region in the 1990s. In Urabá, Afro-Colombian peasants, fleeing violence elsewhere, migrated into the region in the 1940s and 1950s and then were displaced again by violence in the 1960s, after they had cleared the land. A new wave of migrants into the region has since created a labor force for the banana plantations, and many of them have in turn been displaced by violence. The Afro-Colombian community of Tabaco, in the Guajira coal-mining region, was likewise displaced in 2001.

## THE WAR ESCALATES: THE 1991 CONSTITUTION VERSUS NEOLIBERAL PROJECTS

Two apparently contradictory trends coincided at the beginning of the 1990s, with complex but disastrous results for Colombia's African-descended populations. First a long process of negotiation resulted in the formulation of the constitution of 1991, a strikingly progressive document that enshrined the state's commitment to protecting the social welfare of its inhabitants and acknowledged the specific rights of Afro-Colombian communities. The constitution went far beyond traditional liberal documents, which define rights primarily in negative terms, in defining Colombia as a social state of law and enshrining the role of government as promoting the political, social, and economic rights of its citizens. At the same time, however, the government embarked on a process of neoliberal economic reform imposed by the World Bank and the International Monetary Fund, which on many levels created a direct contradiction to the spirit of the constitution.

Transitory Article 55 of the 1991 constitution required Columbian Congress to implement legislation "recognizing the rights of black communities that have been occupying untitled lands in the rural river-basin zones in the Pacific in accordance with their traditional patterns of production, and their right to collective ownership of the land" as well as "protecting these communities' cultural identity and their rights, and fostering their economic and social development." The legislation, passed as Law 70 of 1993, created the legal category of "Lands of Black Communities" and enabled Afro-Colombian communities to gain collective legal title to the lands they inhabited and worked. Funded in part by the World Bank and carried out by the Colombian agrarian reform institute INCORA, the process of titling began in 1996, and by 2003 over 4.5 million hectares had been titled to Afro-Colombian communities.[13]

This legislation paralleled laws elsewhere in Latin America and Colombia recognizing collective land rights of indigenous communities but is very unusual in acknowledging the collective identities and rights of African-descended people in the Americas. Its passage is testimony to both the unique historical trajectory of people of African origin in Colombia, and to their activism in promoting their rights.

At the same time that these rights were being granted on paper, however, they were disappearing on the ground. A series of national-level economic reforms, along with development plans specifically aimed at the Pacific region, and the responses of multinational corporations involved in logging, mining, and African palm production to these developments and to growing global demand and opportunity, brought a tidal wave of unwanted and destructive economic activity to the region. As communities tried to exercise their new legal rights, they found themselves confronted by two forces operating outside the Colombian state, but with its tacit collaboration: the multinationals and the paramilitaries. While the state recognized and promoted the rights of Afro-Colombian communities with one hand, it was undermining them in a devastating way with the other.

## EL CHOCÓ: "THE AFRICAN
## HEART OF COLOMBIA"[14]

In many ways, the Pacific Coast province of Chocó was and is, in both demographic and cultural terms, the heartland of Afro-Colombia. Chocó's population of 1.31 million is over 90 percent Afro-Colombian, and many people of African origin elsewhere in Colombia trace their origins to the Chocó. "Some historians saw Chocó as a very big *palenque*," explained the province's former governor, Luis Gilberto Murillo.[15] Freed and escaped slaves established communities along the many rivers of the Pacific region, establishing social, economic, and cultural patterns that became the basis for today's communities and identities.[16] When the region was granted departmental status in 1947, political structures for Afro-Colombian local governance were created.

Despite El Chocó's poverty and apparent isolation, various outside actors have been extracting resources from the area for hundreds of years. Gold was what enticed the Spanish to the region and prompted them to import thousands of African slaves. Gold still lures outside investors and companies to the Chocó, and some descendants of those slaves still work at mining it. The Chocó is one of the poorest regions of Colombia, but as in so much of Latin America, it is a poverty created by the extraction of wealth.[17]

From the beginning of the twentieth century, U.S. and British mining companies have moved in to extract gold and platinum in the Chocó. Under various names (Consolidated Goldfields, Anglo-Colombian Development Company, Pacific Metal Company, South American Gold and Platinum Company, International Mining Corporation), Chocó Pacífico established its headquarters at Andagoya, constructing a typically segregated area called "Andagoyita" where its Afro-Colombian workers lived. Between 1948 and 1972, the company extracted $196 million worth of gold and platinum, most of the profits of which ended up in New York. Along the Timbiquí River, Timbiquí Gold Mines displaced large numbers of people and created its own enclave, first under British control, then French, before the company closed down operations at the end of World War I.[18] Popular protests against Chocó Pacífico and other foreign mining companies erupted in the 1970s, and the company was nationalized. Until 1989, when it dropped to third place, Chocó was the second-largest gold-producing department in the country. It has continued to produce 97 percent of the country's platinum.[19]

The Atrato River in the Chocó contributed to a Latin American rubber boom after the development of the vulcanization process in the 1850s created a huge demand for tropical rubber. By the 1860s, eighty tons of rubber were being shipped annually to New York through Turbo and Cartagena. Like other boom-and-bust areas, the Atrato was depleted of indigenous rubber, and plantations were established with 1.5 million trees in the

Atrato and Baudó regions. These were abandoned after 1913, replaced by more profitable southeast Asian sources of rubber, only to be revived in the 1940s when Asian sources were cut off during World War II.[20]

The National Front government that took power in 1958 took a major step in inviting international capital into the Pacific region with Law 2 of 1959, which declared the lands there a national forest reserve, untitled and open for development. The regional development corporation, Codechocó, was charged with granting licenses to mining, lumber, and other companies wishing to operate there.[21] "With this step, it opened the doors for the lumber industry to take over territory, expel its ancestral inhabitants. This begins the history of the destruction of the rainforests."[22]

Starting in the 1950s, various U.S. and Colombian companies became involved in logging in the region. Wood was processed in plants in the cities of Barranquilla, Buenaventura, Tumaco, and Cali for domestic use, for paper production, and for export to the United States and Canada.[23] Two companies linked with U.S. capital, Pizano S. A. and the Dago Group, used the wood of *cativales* and *guandales* for export from Barranquilla in the production of their products. The Idaho-based Boise Cascade Corporation purchased a 75 percent interest in Pizano in 1969, as well as a plywood and particleboard plant; by 1972, Boise, through Pizano, was operating two plywood and veneer plants, in Barranquilla and Turbo, and a particleboard plant in Barranquilla. It was also engaged in extensive logging in the Atrato River basin until the end of the 1970s and continued to import lumber from Colombia through the 2000s.[24]

The Chocó accounted for 60 percent of the wood consumed in Colombia by the year 2000. According to the Critical Ecosystem Partnership Fund, "Illegal logging is stimulated by short-term licenses, often granted for just one year, and also by the fact that autonomous regional corporations have been allowed to selectively log certain very valuable species. The logging sector also tends to the exploitation by intermediaries, who benefit from the industry at the expense of the poor. Although the poor do the work of cutting and transporting trees (some 70% of the poor in Chocó work at this), they receive only minimal benefit or income from this activity."[25]

International agencies have played a major role in promoting large-scale agricultural production in the Chocó. The first World Bank mission to Colombia in 1950 urged such development; in 1958 the UN Food and Agriculture Organization sent Maurice Ferrand to Colombia to help the government implement a program of African palm oil production. The project began in the Tumaco region in the 1960s but did not take on its current huge scale until the 1980s. African palm plantations occupied 960 hectares of land in 1970, 14,000 in 1989, and 30,000 in 1996.[26] The U.S. Andean Trade Preference Act of 1991, expanded into the Andean Trade Promotion and Drug Eradication Act in 2002, helped to fund African palm production, supposedly as an alternative to coca growing.[27] Anthropologist Arthur Escobar aptly sums up the plight of displaced Colombians: "Land for African palm plantations has been seized from black farmers by force or purchase, causing massive displacement from the land and intensive proletarianization. Displaced people now work for meager wages in the plantations. [African palm production] has transformed the biocultural landscape of the area, from small patches of land cultivated by local people in the midst of the forest to the interminable rows of palm trees so characteristic of modern agriculture."[28]

In the 1970s, the biodiversity of the Chocó and its potential for tourism created another lure for outsiders. In 1973, the government created the 72,000-hectare Parque Nacional Los Katíos in the northern Chocó, along the border of Panama and bordered also by the Cacarica and Atrato rivers. The government touted the park as an example of its commitment to environmental preservation, and for its potential for ecotourism.[29] For the Afro-Colombian communities of the area, however, the park had a very different meaning.

In describing the growth of the community of Puente América, one refugee explained, "In 1975, when the government used tricks and money to expel the people from the Parque Nacional Los Katíos, more people came."[30] Another stated, "After fifty years of no state presence in our communities, this presence materialized at just two points in time: in 1973, to displace us from our lands that today form part of the Parque Natural Katíos, and since December of 1996 when the army and paramilitaries arrived, leading up to our forced displacement during the last week of February 1997."[31]

From the 1980s on, successive Colombian administrations have worked to implement development plans for the Chocó region. Belisario Betancur (1982–1986) developed Pladeicop, which was replaced with Plan Pacífico in 1992, to be in turn supplemented by the Proyecto Biopacífico (1993–1998), which was urged and supported by the United Nations Development Program, the World Bank, and the Global Environmental Facility, aimed at protecting the biodiversity of the region.[32] These plans proposed a series of megaprojects including the construction of a naval base in Bahía Málaga; ports, highways, and railroads, including the connecting of the Panamerican Highway through the Darién Gap; hydroelectric plants; and an oil pipeline, all of which have threatened both the fragile environment of the Chocó and the communities that live there.[33]

## RESISTANCE: AFRO-COLOMBIAN SOCIAL ORGANIZATIONS

The African-descended communities of the Chocó have been at the forefront of black political and social organizing in Colombia. During the

1980s, in the face of the increasing incursion of extractive industries in the region, members of the communities began to organize for the defense of their lands and the survival of their ecological environment.[34] Catholic missionaries involved in liberation theology were instrumental in founding base communities and peasant associations "to create consciousness and critically examine their own situation, especially the impact of the big logging companies operating in the area on the environment, the labor force, and the black community."[35] In the Atrato River region of the Chocó, the Asociación Campesina Integral del Atrato (Atrato Integral Peasant Association, or ACIA), with support from a Dutch development project (DIAR) as well as the church, was organized "to improve social and economic conditions by means of sustainable management of local natural resources, including forests, fish, and minerals. One of the main goals was to control the large-scale extractive industries from outside the region, which were seen as being responsible for severe environmental damage as well as the low wages and precarious working conditions of the local communities."[36] A fundamental point of reference for the ACIA was the Chocó indigenous organization Organización Regional Embera Wounaan (OREWA), with which the organization worked closely. By the end of the 1980s some thirty-five community organizations had joined ACIA.[37]

Finding their attempts to pressure Codechocó on the issue of its concessions, especially to logging companies, fruitless, ACIA turned to the national level. A general strike in May 1987 brought a national government delegation to the Chocó to investigate conditions, and ACIA also sent a delegation to Bogotá to meet with various government agencies to protest the environmental consequences of logging in the region. The following month, representatives of Codechocó and the National Planning Department attended a conference organized by ACIA, with the participation of the DIAR, the church, and other black and indigenous organizations, which resulted in an agreement revising Law 2. As a result, the peasant communities of the Chocó were granted, at least in theory, the right to collective title and management of part of the Pacific forest reserve.[38] "With this step ACIA turned the traditional position of black organizations on its head. Instead of claiming rights on the basis of equality—a civil rights perspective—it changed to claiming rights on the basis of difference—ethnic rights."[39]

In urban areas also, Afro-Colombian organizing took root in the 1970s and 1980s. One of the first black organizations in Colombia was Centro de Investigación y Desarrollo de la Cultura Negra (CIDCUN), founded in 1975.[40] This was followed a year later by a student group, Soweto, which sought to understand and create consciousness of people of African origin in Colombia as part of the global struggle for African rights.[41]

Out of Soweto, in 1982, a group in the Chocó city of Buenaventura founded Cimarrón, the name of which was a reference to the runaway slaves of the past, which looked more to the specificity of the Afro-Colombian experience. Members of Cimarrón also traveled to rural areas to participate in church-sponsored courses, workshops, and meetings to promote Afro-Colombian consciousness and organizing.⁴² Along with ACIA, Cimarrón was instrumental in pressing for Afro-Colombian territorial and cultural rights to be incorporated into the 1991 constitution, in Transitory Article 55.⁴³ In the Chocó, ACIA, OREWA, and other base organizations, with the support of the European missionary teams in the Atrato, coordinated a highly visible takeover of the Quibdó cathedral, the mayor's office, and the office of INCORA, as well as the Haitian Embassy in Bogotá, to press for the article's inclusion in the constitution.⁴⁴

The public recognition of Afro-Colombian rights, the creation of institutional means for agitating for them, and the availability of resources for organizations led to a proliferation of black organizations in the early 1990s. The various organizations came together in what came to be known as the Proceso de Comunidades Negras, based in Buenaventura, to focus specifically on the enactment of Afro-Colombian land, cultural, and social rights guaranteed by the 1991 constitution. By 1994 the Ministry of the Interior had recognized 350 black community organizations.⁴⁵

This wave of activism among the rural communities of the Chocó coincided as well with global stirrings of mobilization for indigenous rights, as well as environmental organizing and consciousness around issues of biodiversity. Colombia's PCN (Proceso de Comunidades Negras) was able to draw on, and contribute to, both global dialogues. The anthropologist Peter Wade puts the actions of the PCN into perspective: "It is not surprising that the official representation of black identity has taken this form, if one considers the role played by indigenous organizations, the Church (whose experience has been above all with indigenous communities) and the State in the formulation of Transitory Article 55 and the Law 70, although it is important to recognize that black organizations too have played an important role."⁴⁶ The PCN has drawn strength from its ability to engage with these global movements and has succeeded in putting Afro-Colombian issues on the political agenda both nationally and worldwide. International NGOs and scholars have been impressed with the ways it has pushed theoretical and organizational boundaries in conceptualizing issues of community, racial and ethnic identity, land, and the environment. Anthropologist Arturo Escobar, for example, emphasizes the ways that the PCN has contributed to the global debate on biodiversity: "Activists have introduced a number of important conceptual innovations such as biodiversity as 'territory plus culture,' and entire Pacific rainforest region as a 'region-territory of ethnic groups'; that is, an ecological and cultural unit that is woven together through the daily practices of the communities. Moreover, nature is not an entity 'out there' but is associated with the collective practice of humans who see themselves connected to it."⁴⁷

At the same time, however, the PCN has been criticized for privileging one aspect of the Afro-Colombian experience and neglecting others. The majority of Colombia's African-descended people do not, in fact, live in rural communities in the Chocó, but rather in urban areas. While they may share a common history, their present realities have diverged, and the kinds of political and social change they desire are complementary rather than identical. While Colombia's economic development model, foreign investment, neoliberal reforms, cutbacks in social services, and state-sponsored violence affect the vast majority of Afro-Colombians, and in fact are in large part responsible for the rural-to-urban migration that has contributed to these differentiations, the process of community recognition and land titling carried out through Law 70 leaves many Afro-Colombians unaffected. A 2000 study showed that some 80 percent of displaced Afro-Colombians in Bogotá came from rural communities in the Chocó, but only 23 percent planned or hoped to return to their communities.[48]

## THE LOGIC OF VIOLENCE AND DISPLACEMENT

Precisely the region where black peasant organization had its roots and its greatest strength, the Medio and Bajo Atrato region, where ACIA was founded, was where a violent military reaction swept through first, and with greatest force. Although launched by the supposedly illegal paramilitary AUC (Autodefensas Unidas de Colombia), the devastating incursion, which displaced thousands of inhabitants, was clearly supported by both the Colombian army and the logging companies whose concessions were threatened by the titling of communal lands and by peasant mobilization in general.

In 1992, before Law 70 went into effect, two of the companies involved in logging in the Atrato region, Maderas de Darién and Pizano S. A., collaborated to receive license to carry out logging in the Cacarica, Salaquí, and Truandó river basins, in the *municipio* of Riosucio. Ignoring its previous commitments to ACIA about protecting the communities and environment of the area, Codechocó granted these two companies rights to log on 38,629 hectares and extract 972,672 cubic meters of lumber over a period of ten years.[49]

The communities protested, and a prolonged series of judicial proceedings followed. When Law 70 went into effect, the communities began to petition for legalization of their titles. Then in 1996, the government revived a plan to build a "dry canal" with port facilities in the Gulf of Urabá and Cupica Bay, connected by a railroad. Coinciding with this discussion, paramilitary forces began to move into the area in December 1996, taking over the community of Riosucio. They were soon followed by a massive army incursion.[50]

In February 1997, only days before the land claims were to be awarded to the Cacarica communities, the paramilitaries killed or "disappeared" some seventy community members. This was the opening salvo of Operation Genesis, carried out by the infamous 17th Brigade of the Colombian army, beginning with an aerial bombardment campaign that displaced some 3,700 people over the course of a few days,[51] along with thousands of others displaced in the following months. It was years before they could return.

Ominously symbolic of what has been happening in the Chocó since Law 70 was passed has been the transformation of ACIA from a militant peasant organization fighting proactively for land rights in the 1990s to one that works primarily among urban refugees from those same lands, in the city of Quibdó, in the 2000s.[52] One of the newest organizations is AFRO-DES, the Association of Displaced Afro-Colombians, based in Bogotá, whose shantytowns are now home to thousands of those displaced from the Chocó. AFRODES was founded in 1999 to work with families displaced by the 1996–1997 paramilitary incursion in Riosucio/Cacarica, which drove some 10,000 to 20,000 from their homes. Marino Córdoba of AFRO-DES estimated in 2003 that some 900,000 Afro-Colombians were among Colombia's two to three million internally displaced people.[53] In November 2000, AFRODES and the PCN sponsored the First National Meeting of Displaced Afro-Colombians in Bogotá.[54]

For AFRODES, the logic of violence and displacement is clear. Córdoba explains:

> I was displaced from my village of Riosucio (Chocó Department) in 1996 as a result of a bombing jointly undertaken by the paramilitaries and the Colombian military (17th Brigade). Riosucio was the first place in the Colombian Pacific region where Afro-Colombian persons were granted communal rights to their lands under Law 70 (1993). In this part of the country the lands and natural resources (wood and minerals) belonging to the native communities have been appropriated by businesspeople, politicians and settlers. There are economic interests in this area as well as plans to construct an inter-oceanic canal that will link the Pacific and Atlantic oceans. This activity has led to displacement of Afro-Colombians and the impoverishment of native communities.[55]

Or, in the words of Libia Grueso, one of the founders of the PCN, "armed conflict exists in this area because of a dispute over who owns the land. The area where armed conflict can be found coincides with areas where major projects are being proposed."[56]

Likewise, after a paramilitary attack in the Afro-Colombian community of Zabaletas in Valle del Cauca, in which twelve were killed, four kidnapped, and many houses burned, the PCN protested: "The ancestral rights of the Black and Indigenous Communities recognized in the Constitution are seen as an obstacle to this exploitation and development. Under the false pretext of community collaboration with the guerrilla, they use violence and intimidation to forcibly displace them and weaken their base organizations."[57]

The role of the guerrillas in the region is somewhat different. They are not involved in the larger project of promoting the neoliberal/multinational agenda of facilitating logging, African palm production, and mining (although they have been involved in the use of land for coca production).[58] Unlike the paramilitaries, the guerrillas have no interest in displacing the population. Prior to the paramilitary takeover of the region, the guerrilla presence consisted primarily of brief incursions into communities to organize revolutionary meetings, making their presence known and then disappearing.[59]

Since the paramilitary takeover, however, guerrilla attacks on civilians have increased. One of the largest single civilian death tolls came in May 2002, when a guerrilla-launched cylinder bomb killed over a hundred residents who had sought refuge in a church during a confrontation between the guerrillas and the paramilitaries in Bojayá. Although the guerrillas claimed, probably truthfully, that the church was not the target, their extensive use of weapons like cylinder bombs and land mines that disproportionately affect noncombatants undermines their claims to endorse a social agenda in support of peasant communities. Communities often fear the guerrillas not because the guerrillas have a history of coming in and driving out inhabitants, as the paramilitaries do, but because a guerrilla presence is likely to be used as an excuse for a paramilitary incursion.[60]

The Cacarica communities continued to press for legal rights and protections to return to their lands, and finally in 1999 the government granted them collective title to 103,024 hectares of land and promised protection for the construction of two new communities, Nueva Vida and Esperanza de Dios. The government promised to guarantee that no armed actors would enter the area, as well as funding for community development projects and, as "moral reparations," committed to prosecute those accused of the attacks that had forced the communities to flee.[61]

At the same time, however, Codechocó granted Maderas del Darién and Pizano S. A. an extension on their logging permits, on the grounds that the military situation had prevented them from taking advantage of them. Paramilitary bases protect Pizano's operations in La Honda and La Balsa, where the wood is processed before transport to Pizano's plant in Barranquilla. By 2002, eighty more members of the community had been killed.[62]

African palm producers have also been poised to take advantage of the paramilitary takeover of the region. Undermining the legal authority of the community councils created by Law 70 to manage the collective economy of the communities, companies like Urapalma S. A. have offered credit and technical assistance to individual families to encourage them to convert to African palm production. Since 2001, Urapalma, protected by the continuing presence of the 17th Brigade and the paramilitaries, has managed to plant some 1,500 hectares of African palm inside lands titled to Afro-Colombian communities. According to the Inter-American Human Rights Court, "The armed operatives and incursions in this area have had as their objective to intimidate the members of the communities, to make them either join in the palm production, or leave the territory."[63]

In the words of the Diocese of Quibdó,

> Using the pretext of trying to solve the problem of poverty, the government and economic groups are trying to impose a model of development that is unsustainable and that threatens our national sovereignty. Huge infrastructure and agro-industrial projects are designed and executed without consultation with or agreement from the affected communities, and imposed at the cost of war, death and displacement. This is exactly what is happening in the Bajo Atrato with the cultivation of African Palm. The communities and their organizations are never opposed to development, but they want their own goals to be taken into account, and to be able to participate in the design, execution, and benefits of this development.[64]

To residents of the communities, the complicity of the state in the paramilitary/economic project is self-evident. As of 2003, only two people had been convicted in the dozens of murders and thousands of displacements that took place in El Chocó.[65] In the words of one Cacarica community member, "They say that they are trying to put an end to drug trafficking but I don't see that they are trying to stop it. Army officers out of uniform come and tell everyone to come to their farms and that they would give them land to grow coca and African palm. How is this trying to stop drug trafficking?"[66]

In the Solidaridad Chocó Interethnic Forum in Turbo in November 2003, the participating organizations, the Diocese of Quibdó and Apartadó, ACIA, OREWA and ASCOBA (Association of Community Councils and Organizations of Lower Atrato), issued a call to the many different entities that have played a role in the violence in Chocó: the Colombian state and its agencies, the guerrillas, the businesses investing in the region, and the foreign governments and agencies involved. "We warn you that to be in the business of life, not of death, and you must stop sponsoring violence," the investors were told. "We ask that you respect our rights and our territory, and that you make an effort to understand our way of thinking, and not impose your own beliefs about development."[67]

## MORE DEVELOPMENT, MORE DISPLACEMENTS:
## THE TOWN OF TABACO AND THE URABÁ
## BANANA ZONE

One of the largest new development projects that the Colombian government undertook in the 1980s, with heavy funding from the United States, international agencies, and foreign capital, was the Cerrejón Zona Norte coal mine, now the largest strip mine in the world, in the northern Guajira province. The small mostly Afro-Colombian farming communities in the vicinity of the mine were distant from the political organizing that was growing in the urban areas and in the Chocó.

The town of Tabaco, on the periphery of the mine, was founded by several interrelated extended families of Afro-Colombian migrants and refugees. Over the decades the residents, with little help from the state, built their houses, a church, a school, and a health center. By the 1990s some seven hundred people made their lives there, farming, fishing and hunting, and working for pay on neighboring ranches.[68]

The Cerrejón mine, however, then operated as a joint venture between Exxon and the Colombian government, had other plans for the land where Tabaco was situated. As the company itself explained, "it needed to acquire possessions located at Tabaco, in order to continue with the development of the mining plan."[69] Residents found themselves increasingly isolated as the roads leading to their community were shut down, dust and blasting from the mine destroyed hunting and fishing grounds and made daily life intolerable, and mounted private security forces incessantly patrolled their village.

The company began individual negotiations with the residents of Tabaco, and also with the community's priest, Marcelo Graziosi. Distant from the process of community organizing that had taken place in Afro-Colombian villages in the Chocó, and without the support of the church, which had proven so instrumental there, Tabaco residents nonetheless quickly organized themselves into the Committee for the Relocation of Tabaco, requesting that the company find a suitable spot where the community as a whole could be relocated. Under increasing company pressure, however, some residents agreed to sell their homes and land, and, to the dismay of the community, the priest agreed to sell the church, pocketing the money. Meanwhile, the municipal government withdrew the teacher from Tabaco's school, and the personnel who staffed the health center. Finally, on August 9, 2001, company bulldozers, backed by police and company security forces, entered the town, dragged the remaining residents from their homes, and razed it to the ground.[70]

Even the small Committee for the Relocation of Tabaco, though virtually unknown inside Colombia, has found some international allies. The international Mines and Communities network and the Mineral Policy Institute in Australia have sought to work with communities that have suffered from multinational mining development worldwide. Representatives of Tabaco have visited London and Salem, Massachusetts, whose power plant is one of the major U.S. consumers of El Cerrejón's coal. In Nova Scotia, another major purchaser, the Atlantic Regional Solidarity Network has sent representatives to the Guajira to meet with people from Tabaco and other Afro-Colombian and indigenous communities threatened by the mine.

As in the Chocó and the Guajira, in the northern region of Urabá, the Colombian state was virtually absent, and the region had long been the object of foreign-controlled extractive industries. Since the 1960s, the expulsion of Urabá's peasants and the conversion of the land into a sea of cattle ranches and banana plantations perhaps portend the future that awaits much of the Chocó province. In Urabá, the paramilitaries have played a somewhat different role in the 1980s and 1990s. Rather than clearing the land and forcing peasants into the export economy—a process that had already been accomplished much earlier there—a campaign of paramilitary terror systematically eliminated the Left from the local geography.

In Urabá too, social movements, in particular leftist unions, had arisen to struggle for a more equitable distribution of the region's wealth. Starting in the late 1980s, however, union organizers and members, human rights and peace activists, and members of the Unión Patriótica political party were slaughtered in an approximately ten-year bloodbath that left the unions and the local governments of the region decimated, and the banana growers, the paramilitaries, and those willing to collaborate with them firmly in control of the region.

In the nineteenth and early twentieth centuries some of Urabá's few inhabitants—mostly Afro-Colombian migrants from the Caribbean coast—engaged in subsistence production, but more worked for U.S. and English buyers for rubber, tagua (a palm nut that resembles marble and was used in button making), and hardwoods. Up to 10,000 people worked in tagua collection in Urabá, some through a system of contracted labor, during the height of this industry at the end of the nineteenth century. Boston's George D. Emery Company had "immense operations" there between 1883 and 1929, which brought a flow of migrant workers from Sinú. Turbo was founded in 1847, and Chigorodó in 1912, as centers of the extractive industries.[71] The United States Rubber Development Corporation also established rubber plantations in Urabá in the mid-1940s. Inhabitants periodically protested concessions that the government made to foreign companies in the region.

When *la violencia* struck in the 1940s, Urabá quickly became the site of active guerrilla control and extraordinarily high levels of violence. Between 1938 and 1951 the population shrank by 16 percent, to 49,160. By 1953 the region was essentially in the hands of the paramilitaries, as the guerrillas had either been captured or taken amnesty. In conjunction with the violence came the construction of a highway through the region (finished at the end of World War II, but not opened to automobile traffic until 1954), and the expulsion of 5,000 squatters. The Carretera del Mar "emerged as a central locus of violence" in the late 1940s and early 1950s.[72] *Colonos* (tenant farmers) also attacked the rubber plantations in Villa Arteaga in 1950, causing 60,000 pesos' worth of damage. Although Roldán concludes that "it is impossible to draw an absolute correlation between paramilitary violence, land concentration, the growth in property values, and the expansion of large-scale commercial production of sugar and cattle" in Urabá, it is clear that property values and land concentration both increased dramatically between the early 1940s and the early 1960s.[73]

The banana industry was poised to take advantage of this situation, moving into Urabá beginning in 1952. The United Fruit Company's Frutera de Sevilla began to shift operations from Santa Marta to Urabá in the early 1960s. The company extended credit and loans to Colombian investors on the condition that they acquire and title land and fulfill the company's requirements as far as improvements, drainage, roads, and the like. *Colonos* who had cleared the land without title generally lost it during this process in the 1960s, and small banana fincas were gradually swallowed up by larger ones through the 1970s and 1980s.[74]

Employment in the banana industry, and the completion of the Carretera al Mar, attracted a new wave of migrants; from 1951 to 1964 the population grew 204 percent to 149,850, and by 1985 to 249,239.[75] Most of these migrants (50 percent in 1979) came from Chocó.[76] By 1984 Urabá was producing 92 percent of Colombia's banana exports, and Colombia had gone from providing 4.5 percent of the world's banana production in 1974 to 11.5 percent in 1985, making it one of the four largest exporters in the world.[77] With the expansion of the banana industry came the army; radical unions and peasant organizations; armed guerrillas, at the end of the 1970s; and paramilitaries, in the mid-1980s.[78]

By 1995, Urabá had a population of 350,000, with 29,000 hectares planted in bananas, in 409 farms belonging to 310 owners. Sixteen thousand people, many of them newcomers to the region, worked on these farms; 24 percent came from Córdoba, 23 percent from Chocó, 23 percent were native to Urabá, and 17 percent came from elsewhere in Antioquia and Colombia.[79] Poverty, violence, and the spread of ranching continued to push migrants from Córdoba and Chocó into Urabá into the 1990s, while the expansion of ranching and of violence in rural Urabá has pushed migrants into its inadequate urban centers.[80]

Conditions on the banana plantations in the 1960s and 1970s were widely acknowledged to be horrendous. Two-thirds of the workers were

Afro-Colombians who had previously been peasants, small miners, or fishermen. The workday lasted up to eighteen to twenty hours; workers lived in camps on company property, with no water or electricity, sometimes sleeping in cardboard boxes. In the 1960s, 72 percent of workers lived in these camps, and in 1979, 89 percent. Even in 1979, very few of these barracks had running water, electricity, or latrines. Urban centers were practically nonexistent in Urabá, and housing and public services were scarce.[81] Housing conditions in Apartadó were even worse than on the plantations in 1979, and even in 1993 only 31 percent of houses in Apartadó had access to running water.[82]

For William Ramírez, the combination of workers' campesino origins, the exploitative working conditions on the plantations, the region's history of campesino and *colono* organizations and guerrilla activism, and the growth of marginal barrios in which workers lived in increasing numbers made the banana proletariat "an actor who is socially and culturally torn by heterogeneous and even contradictory tensions, and by an uneven and rocky political evolution."[83] The dispersal of the workers was social and cultural as well as geographical. In a period of rapid immigration, workers initially "tend to form into cultural 'ghettos' where they conserve their customs, traditions, eating habits, and where they spend their free time."[84]

Fifteen years later, in 1993, a human rights commission found a similar lack of collective identity in the region, but divisions were now based more on politics than cultural/regional identities.

> The region's paramount problem is the lack of any social base that is not polarized in one of the manifestations of the political/military conflict in Urabá. There is no base with a regional identity and rooted in the zone. Thus, in the midst of polarized actors who participate in, support or stimulate the military confrontation, any community that could mediate or not take sides, and thus have the independence to criticize or point out the attacks against human dignity committed by either of the two sides, is still incipient.[85]

The 1980s and 1990s were extraordinarily bloody decades in Urabá, as workers struggled to organize unions on the plantations, two competing guerrilla organizations vied for workers' loyalty and influence in their unions, and, by the late 1980s, paramilitary organizations came in, at the invitation of some of the large landholders in the region and with the open approval of the army, to destroy not only the guerrillas, but any independent or progressive political organization in the area. Hundreds of banana workers were killed and thousands displaced, including virtually all of the left-wing leadership of the union. By the end of the 1990s, the union, having severed all ties with the Left, had entered into a "social pact" with the banana growers, with the blessing of the paramilitaries, who retained a strong presence in the region.[86]

Although many of Urabá's banana workers are of Afro-Colombian origin, they have not been in a position to benefit from Law 70. Their struggles have been framed in different terms. Yet they are also victims of the same war in Colombia, in which the government, with ample backing from the United States, has pursued a development model heavily reliant on foreign investment and has relied on military and paramilitary force to create the conditions desired by foreign investors. In the Urabá banana zone, the clearing of the land to allow for export agriculture took place decades ago, while in Chocó it is happening today.

In many ways, the historical trajectory of Colombia's African-origin population is depressingly familiar and suggests that the particular characteristics of today's neoliberal globalization are only a contemporary reincarnation of very old historical patterns. For at least five hundred years, economic "development" has been a process that has enriched a few at the expense of the many, and people of African origin have been dispossessed of their lands and forced to labor under horrific conditions to support the export economy.

In other ways, the experiences and actions of Afro-Colombians are refreshingly unique and suggest the resilience and creative capacity of the human spirit under even the most adverse of circumstances. As the global economy has evolved and created new means of exploitation, people have developed new means of resistance. In struggling to maintain their land and livelihoods, Afro-Colombians have intersected with social actors and movements ranging from liberation theology, to Black Power, to Marxist guerrillas, to environmentalists, to unions, to anthropologists, to international solidarity and anticorporate globalization activists.

Globalization and neoliberalism may have facilitated corporate power in remote regions of the world like the Chocó, Urabá, and the Guajira, but they have also created new avenues for constantly reinvented identities, solidarities, and grassroots resistance.

## NOTES

1. The number of displaced people is subject to debate. The governmental Red de Solidaridad Social estimated the number of displaced persons at approximately one million in mid-2003; the nongovernmental Consultoría para los Derechos Humanos y el Desplazamiento (CODHES) placed the number at 2.9 million.

2. For an explanation of Mintz's reconstituted peasantry see the classic essay, "The Question of Caribbean Peasantries," *Caribbean Studies* 1, no. 3 (1961): 31–41, and Mintz's *Caribbean Transformations* (Chicago: Aldine, 1974).

3. Juan de Dios Mosquera Mosquera cites a figure of 25.6 percent of the population, or 6,500,000 people, based on an estimation of the proportion of black population in different regions. See *Las Comunidades negras de Colombia: Pasado, presente*

*y futuro* (Pereira, Colombia: Movimiento Nacional por los Derechos Humanos de las Comunidades Negras de Colombia-Cimarrón, 1985), 29. Afro-Colombian organizations cite from 30 to 40 percent. See Luis Gilberto Murillo, speech at the American Museum of Natural History, New York, February 23, 2001, http://isla.igc.org/SpecialRpts/SR2murillo.html (accessed June 15, 2005); Minority Rights Group, *No Longer Invisible: Afro-Latin Americans Today* (London: Minority Rights Publications, 1995), xiii, cited in Ulrich Oslender, "La Lógica del río: Estructuras espaciales del proceso organizativo de los movimientos socials de communidades negras en el Pacífico colombiano," in *Acción colectiva: Estado y etnicidad en el Pacífico colombiano,* ed. Mauricio Pardo (Bogotá, Colombia: ICANH), 127.

4. See, for example, Peter Wade, *Blackness and Race Mixture: The Dynamics of Racial Identity in Colombia* (Baltimore: Johns Hopkins University Press, 1993). More recently, Mary Roldán and Nancy Applebaum have built on this concept. See Mary Roldán, *Blood and Fire: La Violencia in Antioquia, Colombia, 1946–1953* (Durham, NC: Duke University Press, 2002), and Nancy Applebaum, *Muddied Waters: Race, Region, and Local History in Colombia, 1846–1948* (Durham, NC: Duke University Press, 2003).

5. James Parsons first suggested the concept of colonization to explain highland Antioquia's relationship with its peripheries in *Antioqueño Colonization in Western Colombia,* 2nd ed. (1949; repr., Berkeley and Los Angeles: University of California Press, 1968).

6. Roldán, *Blood and Fire,* 40.

7. Roldán, *Blood and Fire,* 41.

8. Oscar Almario, "Dinámica y consecuencias del conflicto armado colombiano en el Pacífico: Limpieza étnica y desterritorialización de afrocolombianos e indígenas y 'multicultralismo' de Estado e indolencia nacional," in *Conflictos e (in)visibilidad: Retos en los estudios de la gente negra en Colombia,* ed. Eduardo Restrepo and Axel Rojas (Cauca, Colombia: Editorial Universidad de Cauca, 2004), 81, 83.

9. William Villa, "La Sociedad negra del Chocó: Identidad y movimientos sociales," in Pardo, *Acción colectiva,* 218.

10. Roldán, *Blood and Fire,* 22.

11. Programa de las Naciones Unidas Para el Desarrollo, *El Conflicto: Callejón con salida* (*Informe Nacional de Desarrollo Humano-Colombia*), 2003, Chapter 1, 21, www.pnud.org.co/2003/full/capitulo_1.pdf (accessed June 13, 2005).

12. See CAVIDA, *Somos tierra de esta tierra: Memorias de una resistencia civil* (Cacarica, Colombia: CAVIDA, 2002), chap. 1; Programa de las Naciones Unidas Para el Desarrollo, *El Conflicto.*

13. Twenty-seven of these titles were in Nariño, totaling 721,000 hectares, as of July 2003. Odile Hoffman, "Espacios y región en el Pacífico Sur: ¿Hacia la construcción de una sociedad regional?" in *Gente negra en Colombia: Dinámicas sociopolíticas en Cali y el Pacífico,* ed. Olivier Barbary and Odile Hoffman (Cali, Colombia: Centro de Investigaciones y Documentación Socioeconómicas, Facultad de Ciencias Sociales y Económicas de la Universidad del Valle, 2004), 213; William Villa, "El Territorio de comunidades negras, la guerra en el Pacífico y los problemas del desarrollo," in *Panorámica afrocolombiana: Estudios sociales en el Pacífico,* ed. Mauricio Pardo Rojas, Claudia Mosquera, and María Clemencia Ramírez (Bogotá, Colombia: ICANH, 2004), 333, cites over two million hectares in 2001.

14. Murillo, speech.

15. Murillo, speech.

16. Oslender, "La Lógica del río," 126, citing 1998 figures; Mauricio Pardo, "Aproximaciones al análisis histórico del negro en Colombia," in Pardo, Mosquera, and Ramirez, *Panorámica afrocolombiana*, 81–83; Jacques Aprile-Gniset, "Apuntes sobre el proceso de poblamiento del Pacífico," in Pardo, Mosquera, and Ramirez, *Panorámica afrocolombiana*, 276–77, 279–81.

17. See Orián Jiménez Meneses, "Esclavitud y minería en Antioquia," in VI Cátedra Anual de Historia, *150 años de la abolición de la esclavización*, 192–222; Sergio Mosquera, "Los Procesos de manumisión," in *Afrodescendientes en las Américas: Trayectorias sociales e identitarias. 150 años de la abolición de la esclavitud en Colombia*, ed. Claudia Mosquera, Mauricio Pardo, and Odile Hoffmann (Bogotá, Colombia: Universidad Nacional de Colombia/Instituto Colombiano de Antropología e Historia ICANH, 2002), 99–119. See also Wade, *Blackness and Race Mixture*, chap. 8.

18. See Alfredo Vanín Romero, "Lenguaje y modernidad," in *Pacífico: ¿Desarrollo o diversidad?* ed. Arturo Escobar and Alvaro Pedrosa (Santafé de Bogotá, Colombia: CEREC, ECOFONDO, 1996), 47–48; William Villa, "La Sociedad negra del Chocó," 218 n. 14; Mosquera, *Las Comunidades negras de Colombia*, 41.

19. See Hernán Cortés and Eduardo Restrepo, "Deforestación y degradación de los bosques en el territorio-región de las comunidades negras del Pacífico colombiano," www.wrm.org.uy/deforestation/LAmerica/Colombia.html (accessed June 12, 2005).

20. See Warren Dean, *Brazil and the Struggle for Rubber: A Study in Environmental History* (Cambridge: Cambridge University Press, 1987), for a classic study of this phenomenon. Robert West details the Colombian rubber cycles in *The Pacific Lowlands of Colombia* (Baton Rouge: Louisiana State University Press, 1957), 166–68; 247, nn. 77, 78, 79, 80.

21. Mauricio Pardo, "Estado y movimiento negro en el Pacífico colombiano," in Pardo, *Acción colectiva*, 235.

22. William Villa, "Movimiento social de comunidades negras en el Pacífico colombiano: La Construcción de una noción de territorio y región," in *Los Afrocolombianos: Geografía humana de Colombia*, ed. A. Maya (Bogotá, Colombia: Instituto Colombiano de Cultura Hispánica, 1998), 436–37, cited in Orlando Jaramillo Gómez, "Del tiempo cambiado a la titulación colectiva: Movimiento social y comunidades negras del alto San Juan," in Pardo, *Acción colectiva*, 179.

23. See Cortés and Restrepo, "Deforestación y degradación de los bosques." West says that two companies, one with U.S. financial backing, began exporting the tropical wood cativo in 1953. West, *The Pacific Lowlands of Colombia*, 170.

24. Bernardo Pérez Salazar, "Acondicionamiento territorial en curso: El Caso de la cuenca baja del Río Atrato, Chocó," www.planetapaz.org/regiones/pacifico/Defensa_atrato.pdf (accessed June 20, 2005); Boise Cascade, *Annual Reports*, 1969–1979. The Turbo plant was closed in 1974, and the equipment moved to Barranquilla (*Annual Report*, 1974).

25. Critical Ecosystem Partnership Fund, "Perfil del ecosistema: corredor de conservación Chocó-Manabí, ecorregión terrestre prioritaria del Chocó-Darién-Ecuador Occidental (Hotspot), Colombia y Ecuador," December 2001, www.cepf.net/Image

Cache/cepf/content/pdfs/final_2espanish_2echoco_2ddarien_2dwestern_20ecuador _2eep_2epdf/v1/final.spanish.choco_2ddarien...2dwestern_20ecuador.ep.pdf (accessed June 13, 2005), 17–18.

26. Arturo Escobar, "Viejas y nuevas formas de capital y los dilemas de la biodiversidad," in Escobar and Pedrosa, *Pacífico: ¿Desarrollo o diversidad?* 109, 111–12; see also Cortés and Restrepo, "Deforestación y degradación de los bosques."

27. Office of the United States Trade Representative, "Second Report to Congress on the Operation of the Andean Trade Preference Act as Amended," April 30, 2005: 30. www.ustr.gov/assets/Trade_Development/Preference_Programs/ATPA/asset...up load_file337_7673.pdf (accessed May 28, 2005).

28. Arturo Escobar, "Cultural Politics and Biological Diversity: State, Capital, and Social Movements in the Pacific Coast of Colombia," in *Between Resistance and Revolution: Cultural Politics and Social Protest*, ed. Richard G. Fox and Orin Starn (New Brunswick, NJ: Rutgers University Press, 1997), 47. Escobar cites local informants who refer to "many deaths" along the Tumaco-Pasto highway, as palm growers resorted to violence to drive out small farmers. "These deaths, say the locals, were orchestrated by the large palm-growers in collaboration with the [Departamento Administrativo de Seguridad]." Escobar, "Viejas y nuevas formas de capital," 113, n. 4.

29. See Juan Tamayo, "El Territorio negro en el Golfo de Tribuga-Chocó," in William Villa, *Comunidades negras: Territorio desarrollo* (Medillín, Colombia: n.p., 1996), 61–62, 66, for a description of the tourist industry in the 1990s; "Parques nacionales de Colombia: Parque Nacional Natural los Katíos," www.parquesnacionales .gov.co/areas/lasareas/katios/katiintro.htm (accessed June 20, 2005).

30. CAVIDA, *Somos tierra de esta tierra*, 28.

31. "Desde las comunidades de autodeterminación, vida, dignidad de Cacarica, hasta los humanos del mundo: Nueva presencia militar en nuestro territorio," no. 140 (October 14, 2001), www.nodo50.org/derechosparatodos/Areas/AreaCOLOM -8.htm (accessed June 8, 2005).

32. Mauricio Pardo, introduction to *Acción colectiva*, 8; Alvaro Pedrosa, "La Institucionalización del desarrollo," in Escobar and Pedrosa, *Pacífico: ¿Desarollo o diversidad?* 84–87. Escobar describes the Plan Pacífico as even more explicitly promoting capitalist development than Pladeicop, although it included a (severely underfunded) environmental component (46).

33. For a summary of these projects, see Mieke Wouters, "Derechos étnicos bajo fuego: El Movimiento campesino negro frente a la presión de grupos armadas en el Chocó. El Caso de la ACIA," in Pardo, *Acción colectiva*, 273–74, n. 41.

34. Villa, "La Sociedad negra del Chocó," 224, n. 24.

35. Pardo, "Iniciativa y cooptación: Tensiones en el movimiento afrocolombiano," in *150 años de la abolición de la esclavización en Colombia* (Bogota: Ministerio de Cultura, 2003), 662.

36. Pérez Salazar, "Acondicionamiento territorial en curso." The Dutch-Colombian project, Desarrollo Integral Agrícola Rural (DIAR), worked in the Atrato Medio region from 1976 to 1984 in conjunction with Codechocó to improve agricultural production techniques (Alvaro Pedrosa, "La Institucionalización del desarrollo," 82–83). DIAR joined with the CEBs to oppose logging concessions in the Atrato

region. See Stefan R. F. Khittel, "Uso de la historia y la historiografía por parte de las ONG y OB de las comunidades negras en el Chocó," in Pardo, *Acción colectiva*, 76.

37. Pardo, "Iniciativa y cooptación," 663; Carlos Rúa, "Territorialidad ancestral y conflicto armado," in Mosquera, Pardo, and Hoffmann, *Afrodescendientes en las Américas*, 561–72; José Isidro Cuesta, "¿Qué es la Ocaba?" in *Contribución Africana a la cultura de las Américas: Memorias del Coloquio Contribución Africana a la Cultura de las Américas*, ed. Astrid Ulloa (Bogotá, Colombia: Proyecto Biopacífico/Instituto Colombiano de Antropología, 1993), 139.

38. Pardo, "Estado y movimiento negro," 237–38; Pardo, "Iniciativa y cooptación," 662.

39. Pardo, "Estado y movimiento negro," 238.

40. Teodora Hurtado Saa, "La Protesta social en el norte del Cauca y el surgimiento de la movilización *étnica* afrocolombiana," in Pardo, *Acción colectiva*, 97.

41. Khittel, "Uso de la historia y la historiografía," 72.

42. Khittel, "Uso de la historia y la historiografía," 84.

43. See Pardo, "Iniciativa y cooptación," 661.

44. Khittel, "Uso de la historia y la historiografía," 77. This process is also described in CAVIDA, *Somos tierra de esta tierra*, 230.

45. Pardo, "Estado y movimiento negro," 245. ACIA and the other Chocó base organizations, however, maintained some distance from this national-level organizing (246–47). Oslender, "La Lógica del río," 135.

46. Peter Wade, "Identidad y etnicidad," in Escobar and Pedrosa, *Pacífico: ¿Desarrollo o diversidad?* 291.

47. Arturo Escobar, "Bio-diversity: A Perspective from Within," *Seedling: The Quarterly Newsletter of Genetic Resources International*, June 1999. Escobar first formulated this argument in his coauthored essay with Libia Grueso and Carlos Rosero, two PCN activists. See Grueso, Rosero, and Escobar, "The Process of Black Community Organizing in the Southern Pacific Coast Region of Colombia," in *Cultures of Politics/Politics of Cultures: Re-visioning Latin American Social Movements*, ed. Sonia E. Alvarez, Evelina Dagnino, and Arturo Escobar (Boulder, CO: Westview Press, 1998), 196–219.

48. AFRODES and CODHES, "Estudio a hogares y familias de afrocolombianos en situación de desplazamiento residentes en Bogotá," October 16, 2000, www .derechos.org/nizkor/colombia/doc/afro.html (accessed June 28, 2005).

49. Pérez Salazar, "Acondicionamiento territorial en curso."

50. Pérez Salazar, "Acondicionamiento territorial en curso"; Wouters, "Derechos étnicos bajo fuego," 268.

51. Pérez Salazar, "Acondicionamiento territorial en curso." The story of the displacement and its aftermath is extensively documented with testimonies in CAVIDA, *Somos tierra de esta tierra*.

52. Wouters, "Derechos étnicos bajo fuego," 280.

53. Marino Córdoba, interview with Gimena Sánchez-Garzoli, senior research analyst, Brookings/SAIS Project on Internal Displacement. In *Refugee Watch* 20 (December 2003), www.brookings.edu/fp/projects/idp/articles/20031230sanchez .htm (accessed June 8, 2005).

54. The proceedings of the meeting were published as AFRODES, *Forjamos Esperanza*.

55. Córdoba, interview with Sánchez-Garzoli.

56. Michelle Nijhuis, "Libia Grueso Advocates for Afro-Colombians and Their Land," *Grist*, April 22, 2004, www.gristmagazine.com/maindish/grueso042204.asp (accessed June 15, 2005); "Espacios y región en el Pacífico Sur," 213, 219, 221.

57. PCN communiqué, May 12, 2000, reprinted in Oslender, "La Lógica del río," 138.

58. However, some residents believe that the FARC tacitly supported the activities of the logging companies, because they were able to extort money from them. See Mieke Wouters, "Comunidades negras, derechos étnicos, y desplazamiento forzado en el Atrato Medio: Respuestas organizativas en medio de la Guerra," in Mosquera, Pardo, and Hoffmann, *Afrodescendientes en las Américas*, 377, n. 31.

59. See Wouters, "Derechos étnicos bajo fuego," 269. Displaced residents blame the EPL for a 1993 attack that displaced them from Alto Baudó (Chocó), and an unidentified guerrilla group for a 1999 attack that displaced others from Juradó (Chocó). See AFRODES, "Chocó: Desinterés official y desintegración comunitaria," in *Forjando esperanza* ed. AFRODES (Bogotá, Colombia: AFRODES, 2001), 16–17. These cases, however, appear to be more the exception than the rule.

60. A study carried out among displaced Afro-Colombians in Bogotá by AFRODES and CODHES in 2000 found that 55.26 percent were displaced by paramilitary attacks, 19.30 percent by the guerrillas, 3.51 percent by the army, and 9 percent by others; 14 percent did not know the identity of their attackers. AFRODES and CODHES, "Estudio a hogares." These figures correspond to those arrived at by the United Nations, which found the paramilitaries responsible for 57–63 percent of forced displacements in 2000, with the guerrillas blamed for 12–13 percent, and the rest blamed on the state or unidentified forces. Arturo Escobar, "Desplazamientos, desarrollo y modernidad en el Pacífico colombiano," in Restrepo and Rojas, *Conflictos e (in)visibilidad*, 57.

61. Pérez Salazar, "Acondicionamiento territorial en curso." The repopulation of the Cacarica communties is described in detail through testimonies in CAVIDA, *Somos tierra de esta tierra*, chap. 6.

62. Pérez Salazar, "Acondicionamiento territorial en curso."

63. CIDH, "Resolución de la Corte Interamericana de Derechos Humanos de 6 de marzo de 2003, Medidas provisionales solicitadas por la Comisión Interamericana de Derechos Humanos respecto a la República de Colombia. Caso de las comunidades de Jiguamiandó y Curbaradó," in Noche and Niebla, "El Modelo de violencia estructural sigue intacto en el Chocó," anexo 1 to "Caso tipo: Bojayá." *Revista por la vida*, 2004, www.nocheyniebla.org (accessed June 15, 2005), 59.

64. Pastoral letter, Diocese of Quibdó, Easter 2002, quoted in Noche y Niebla, "El Modelo de violencia estructural sigue intacto en el Chocó."

65. Noche y Niebla, "Caso tipo: Bojayá/Bojayá: La Tragedia continúa," *Revista por la vida*, 2004: 23, www.nocheyniebla.org (accessed June 15, 2005).

66. CAVIDA, *Somos tierra de esta tierra*, 299.

67. Noche y Niebla, "Caso tipo: Bojayá/Bojayá," 51–52.

68. Remedios Fajardo Gómez, "Violación sistemática de los derechos humanos

de indígenas, negros y campesinos por parte de la multinacional minera Intercor, filial de la Exxon, en el departamento de La Guajira, Colombia," August 9, 2001; Untitled transcript of video footage taken by several Colombian journalists interviewing residents of Tabaco in August, 2001, in the author's possession (hereafter, Tabaco video transcript). See also Gilma Mosquera Torres in "Sobre los poblados y la vivienda del Pacífico," in Pardo, Mosquera, and Ramirez, *Panorámica afrocolombiana*, 291–329, especially 307.

69. "Case Study: Tabaco-Case Study of a Negotiation and Recent Events," www .cerrejoncoal.com/social/Tabaco.html (accessed June 15, 2005).

70. Tabaco video transcript.

71. James Parsons, *Antioqueño Colonization in Western Colombia*, 2nd ed. (Berkeley and Los Angeles: University of California Press, 1949), 44–49, cited in Fernando Botero, *Urabá: Colonización, violencia, y crisis del Estado* (Medellín, Colombia: Universidad de Antioquia, 1990), 22. Botero further notes that when Emery pulled out in the 1930s, some of its overseers became landlords.

72. Gerard Martin and Claudia Steiner, "El Destino de la frontera: Urabá en los años noventa," in *Urabá*, ed. Centro de Investigación y Educación Popular (Bogotá, Colombia: CINEP, 1995), 52. Roldán cites the 1951 census as listing an even smaller population of only 17,000 in Urabá. Roldán, *Blood and Fire*, 171, 223–27; Botero, *Urabá*, 25, 31.

73. Botero, *Urabá*, 25, n. 34; Roldán, *Blood and Fire*, 225.

74. Medófilo Medina, "Violence and Economic Development: 1945–50 and 1985–88," in *Violence in Colombia: The Contemporary Crisis in Historical Perspective*, ed. Charles Bergquist, Ricardo Peñaranda, and Gonzalo Sánchez (Wilmington, DE: Scholarly Resources, 1992), 162; Botero, *Urabá*, 73–77, 88–89.

75. Martin and Steiner, "El Destino de la frontera," 52; Botero, *Urabá*, 81. Botero cites a figure of 82,969 in 1964, saying this was five times the population in 1950.

76. Fernando Botero Herrera and Diego Sierra Botero, *El Mercado de fuerza de trabajo en la zona bananera de Urabá* (Medellín, Colombia: Universidad de Antioquia, 1981), 106.

77. Jenny Pearce, *Colombia: Inside the Labyrinth* (London: Latin America Bureau, 1990), 250; William Ramírez Tobón, *Urabá: Los Inciertos confines de una crisis* (Bogotá, Colombia: Planeta, 1997), 33.

78. Mauricio Romero says that the FARC and the EPL both became active in the region at the end of the 1970s. Mauricio Romero, "Los Trabajadores bananeros de Urabá: De 'súbditos a ciudadanos'?" mansucript, 3, www.ces.fe.uc.pt/emancipa/ research/pt/ft/uraba.html (accessed June 8, 2005); Botero, *Urabá*, 36.

79. Martin and Steiner, "El Destino de la frontera," 71; "Informe de la Comisión Verificadora de los Actores Violentos en Urabá," in Centro de Investigación y Educación Popular, *Urabá*, 14.

80. Martin and Steiner, "El Destino de la frontera," 64.

81. Romero, "Los Trabajadores bananeros de Urabá," 5–6; Pearce, *Inside the Labyrinth*, 251; Botero, *Urabá*, 81; Botero Herrera and Sierra Botero, *El Mercado de fuerza de trabajo*, 93; Martin and Steiner, "El Destino de la frontera," 63.

82. Botero Herrera and Sierra Botero, *El Mercado de fuerza de trabajo*, 150; Comisión Andina de Juristas/Seccional Colombia, *Informes regionales de derechos humanos: Urabá* (Bogotá, Colombia: Comisión Andina de Juristas, 1994), 44.

83. Ramírez Tobón, *Urabá*, 43.

84. Botero Herrera and Sierra Botero, *El Mercado de fuerza de trabajo*, 108.

85. Comisión Andina de Juristas/Seccional Colombia, *Informes regionales de derechos humanos*, 159.

86. See Aviva Chomsky, "What's Old, What's New? Globalization, Violence, and Identities in Colombia's Banana Zone," paper presented at the Latin American Studies Association/Labor Studies preconference Las Vegas, October 2004; Aviva Chomsky, *Linked Labor Histories: The United States and Colombia in the Long Twentieth Century* (Durham, NC: Duke University Press, forthcoming), chap. 5.

# 9

# Hip-Hop and Black Public Spheres in Cuba, Venezuela, and Brazil

*Sujatha Fernandes and Jason Stanyek*

*A study of transnational black culture would be incomplete without an examination of the emergence and proliferation of hip-hop. Born in the urban centers of North America, the language and aesthetics of hip-hop have not only transformed contemporary popular music but have influenced styles and politics around the globe. This chapter explores the emergence and significance of hip-hop in Cuba, Brazil, and Venezuela as a medium of self-expression and as a vehicle for black political protest. Latin American artists often make explicit references to hip-hop's North American roots. Nonetheless, the authors argue that artists in Latin America continue to represent marginalized and disenfranchised black communities in ways that are specifically tailored to Latin American realities.*

The rising popularity of hip-hop culture in countries across Latin America and the Caribbean coincides with the politicization of ethnic and racial cleavages, as marginalized groups forge new social identities and demand their political rights.[1] Cuba, Venezuela, and Brazil are three Latin American countries where hip-hop has been particularly important. As new forms of inequality and hierarchy develop in Cuba as a result of the growth of tourism and gradual integration into a market economy, black Cuban youth appeal to the promises of racial egalitarianism and employment enshrined in socialist ideology. Social movements in Venezuela that began to gain momentum after the street riots of the late 1980s have reached fruition in the current moment, as the impoverished and marginalized majority demands their share in the wealth of the nation. And in Brazil, the commu-

199

nities of black activists that began to organize during the unraveling of the military dictatorship in the late 1970s have continued to wage a public struggle against the racist structures of a society in which inequality has intensified during twenty years of democratic governance.

In these three countries, rap music has become an important vehicle for the expression of political demands, the construction of new social identities, and the creation of alternative modes of leisure, survival, and transformation. Hip-hop emerged from the experiences of urban black communities in the United States, and in diverse contexts it has retained its role of documenting struggle and survival at the margins. Urban culture sometimes gives rise to new forms of social identification, often based in figures from the past, social stereotypes, or symbols that are reclaimed by black and marginalized youth. Contemporary contestation is framed in terms of historical struggles for independence and is defined against constraining social norms. The partial snapshots that we provide here of hip-hop culture in three Latin American countries should serve to highlight the positive role that cultural production can play when creative and conscious people use music as part of an effort to reimagine and restructure the very political fabric of everyday life.

In this chapter we explore the resonances and parallel development of hip-hop as a musical form in Cuba, Brazil, and Venezuela, but we also address the distinct ways in which rap music takes shape in these various contexts. We invoke the concept of "black public spheres" to call attention to the substantial transnational and diasporic connections that link black communities throughout the diaspora. Hip-hop culture is just one mode of articulation that dispersed members of these communities can use to engender such links. At the same time, by consciously talking about "spheres" (and not a single "sphere") we want to suggest that there are substantial differences in the way that black culture is used and produced in particular locations. Sentiments of pan-African belonging are not enough to do away with the crucial lineaments of national, ethnic, and linguistic difference. Showing how hip-hop culture simultaneously forms the basis for transnational *and* local conceptions of raciality is one of our principal goals here.

The idea of the public sphere is also appropriate as we highlight hip-hop's function as a vehicle for civic dialogue. When hip-hop culture emerged in the Bronx in the 1970s it existed as a form of public utterance, as a way of reconstituting space and reconfiguring history, a creative methodology for subverting regimes of dominance and marginalization.[2] Communities of diasporic black youth, children of migrants from the southern part of the United States, and immigrants from Jamaica, Puerto Rico, and other parts of the Caribbean used aerosol technology to turn subway cars into canvases that traveled the breadth of New York City; they gave new meanings to old albums by alchemically transforming the turntable from a playback device into an instrument out of which they coaxed innovative musical languages and sounds; they used microphones to baptize themselves with names that spoke of individual and collective social identities that had never before existed; they devised kinesthetic moves that defied the scripted logics of human anatomy. And to do all these things they drew on the corporeal, sonic, and philosophical foundations of African diasporic culture, using strategies that circulated globally to reenvision the very structure of their own local environment. Remarkably, this all happened as the postindustrial Bronx, ravaged by racist social policies that caused the flight of jobs, capital, and people from the inner city, was quite literally burning. In "the most destitute corner of Babylon" a culture of creativity and optimism emerged out of the intercorporeal collective gestures of African-diasporic youth.[3]

When hip-hop went global in the early 1980s, a particular strain of the culture retained this critical conception that held public life to be fundamentally transformable. In some of its guises, hip-hop culture in Cuba, Venezuela, and Brazil has been used by young people as a portal for entering into the very deliberations over identity and power that constitute the public sphere. Hip-hop culture, in its most liberatory manifestations, is used by marginalized and conscious youth as both a mode of analysis and a program for action. Given the new and highly specific kinds of racial and ethnic cleavages that characterize the Cuban, Venezuelan, and Brazilian public spheres, hip-hop is an important tool that has been used to create rejoinders to the forces that would have communities of color remain on the political margins.

## LOCAL RACIAL POLITICS IN CUBA, VENEZUELA, AND BRAZIL

Members of hip-hop communities often use critical analyses of local experience as scaffolding for creative and political action. In fact, one might say that at the aesthetic center of hip-hop creativity is a view that the transmission of ideas and material culture is fundamentally linked to rather radical processes of translation and recontextualization. Hip-hop artists value what is often referred to as *signifyin'*, the out-in-the-open manipulation of cultural codes and artifacts according to local needs and sentiments. As Livone Sansone has suggested, "Global black symbols are selectively reinterpreted within national contexts—each informed by class, age, gender, and local circumstances—and what can't be combined with one's own situation is discarded. . . . The meaning of black objects is not universal and is often contested.[4] While there is a transnational history that links all African diasporic communities—what Sidney Lemelle and Robin D. G. Kelley have called the "critical matrix of forced labor, European hegemony and racial capitalism"[5]—the black public spheres of Cuba, Venezuela, and Brazil are marked by rather divergent social histories. The particular (and shifting) ways that racial politics play out in these three countries has an enormous effect on how hip-hop is produced, disseminated, and consumed in each location.

Hip-hop culture in Cuba is shaped by a highly specific set of social and economic conditions, including the demographic restructuring of the urban metropolis and increasing racial inequalities in the so-called special period of economic hardships. Hip-hop culture grew rapidly in housing projects such as Alamar and other areas of high-density housing, occupied by mainly black working-class communities such as Old Havana, Central Havana, Santos Suárez, and Playa. Rapping became especially popular in the context of Cuba, while DJing and graffiti writing have been more difficult due to the lack of turntables, records, spray cans, and other resources. Until the collapse of the Soviet Union, black and poorer communities in Cuba were relatively protected from neoliberal processes of economic restructuring. However, the crisis of the special period forced the Cuban government to adopt policies of austerity in order to increase the competitiveness of the Cuban economy in the global economy. Although policies of austerity and restructuring have affected Cuban society as a whole, Alejandro de la Fuente argues that there have also been various racially differentiated effects. The legalization of dollars has divided Cuban society according to those who have access to dollars and those who do not.[6] Family remittances are the most important source of hard currency for most Cubans, and since the majority of Cubans in the diaspora tend to be white, it is white Cuban families who benefit most from remittances.[7] Racial prejudice has become increasingly visible and acceptable in the special period.

In a period of increasing racial tensions and racial inequalities, Afro-Cubans find themselves deprived of a political voice. Drawing on discourses of racial democracy, the Cuban revolutionary leadership attempted to eliminate racism by creating a color-blind society in which equality between blacks and whites would render the need for racial identifications obsolete. While desegregating schools, parks, and recreational facilities, and offering housing, education, and health care to the black population, the revolutionary leadership simultaneously closed down Afro-Cuban clubs and the black press.[8] De la Fuente sees the possibility for racially based mobilization emerging from the contradictions of the current special period: "The revival of racism and racially discriminatory practices under the special period has led to growing resentment and resistance in the black population, which suddenly finds itself in a hostile environment without the political and organization tools needed to fight against it."[9] Afro-Cuban religious forms such as Santería have begun to gain popular support in this period, but rap music has taken on a more politically assertive and radical stance as the voice of black Cuban youth. Although some older black Cubans cannot relate to the militant assertion of black identity in Cuban rap, it is becoming increasingly relevant to Cuba's youth, who did not live through the early period of revolutionary triumph and are hardest hit by the failure of the institutions established under the revolution to provide racial equality in the special period.

North American rap music is the original source of Cuban rap music, and from the early days Cuban rappers have maintained close ties with rappers in the United States. While the early waves of hip-hop music that came to Cuba were more commercial, by the time of the first rap festival in 1995, Cubans were hearing African American "conscious" rap music. Like the African American activists who visited Cuba during the 1960s and 1970s from Stokely Carmichael to Angela Davis and Assata Shakur, who is currently in exile in Cuba, African American rappers such as Paris, Common Sense, Mos Def, and Talib Kweli spoke a language of black militancy that was appealing to Cuban youth. In an interview, rapper Sekuo Umoja from Anónimo Consejo said that "We had the same vision as rappers such as Paris, who was one of the first to come to Cuba. His music drew my attention, because here is something from the barrio, something black. Of blacks, and made principally by blacks, which in a short time became something very much our own, related to our lives here in Cuba."

Venezuelan rap has also emerged from a distinct set of conditions brought about by a growing process of urban segregation, a deterioration in the urban services, and a crisis of the state. As the impending collapse of the Soviet Union in 1989 precipitated a major crisis in the Cuban socialist system, so too, the introduction of neoliberal market measures in Venezuela led to spontaneous protests, rioting, and looting around the country on February 27, 1989, followed by a massive crackdown by police and the military. As in Cuba, the gradual insertion of Venezuela into a neoliberal global order required new forms of efficiency and competition that put pressure on the state-based developmental model pursued by previous governments. The shift of resources away from infrastructure, health care, education, and other social services led to a sustained increase in social inequality during this period.[10] These changes were also racialized, with those at the bottom of the social scale—mostly the black, indigenous, and mixed race Venezuelans, who form the majority of the population—hit hardest by the changes. The social disjunctures, atomization, and crisis in governance that began in 1989 led to a spiraling in violence, crime, and urban tension. Ana María Sanjuán comments that in 1999, the homicide rate in Venezuela had risen 20 percent from the previous year.[11] This number was greater in Caracas, where the number of homicides sometimes reached the one hundred mark on weekends.[12] In this context of general disorder and crisis of authority, alternative systems of justice such as street gangs and urban mafias grow in importance, contributing to a growing cycle of violence.[13]

The period of the early 1990s also saw the growth of local popular movements in the barrios, shantytowns that ring the hillsides of Caracas. These nonpartisan movements reached a peak in 1998 when the Polo Patriótico, an alliance led by Hugo Chávez Frías, won the general elections and came into power on a platform promising to fight corruption, break away from the U.S.-supported neoliberal agenda, and rewrite the constitution.[14] The political mobilization fostered by Chávez has led to a deepening societal divide, as the lower classes increasingly identify along race and class lines. Juan Carlos Echeandía, a Venezuelan rap producer, said in an interview that the emergence of rap music in Venezuela coincided with the increasing importance of the popular masses in the political process of the country: "In some ways, the popular masses begin to have voice and vote . . . they begin to have much more importance in politics and society. And this is also what happens via the discs." The appearance of a racially and politically conscious discourse in Venezuelan rap has been partly related to a more general emergence of a marginalized minority demanding its social and political rights.[15]

Yet the forms of consciousness that are reflected and created through Venezuelan rap are less of the militant black nationalist variety predominant in Cuban rap music and more related to the continuing urban reality of crime, extreme poverty, and death by gang violence. Echeandía has a label called Venezuela Subterránea (Venezuela Underground), and two of the main groups signed to the label are Guerrilla Seca and Vagos y Maleantes. In interviews, rappers Colombia and Requesón, members of Guerrilla Seca, talk about their musical inspiration as coming from African American gangsta rappers such as Tupac. Although Colombia and Requesón do not understand the English lyrics, they say that it is the dark and ominous tones of American gangsta rap that speak to their experiences of a kind of gang life that breeds nihilism, vacancy, and despair among youth in the barrios. In Venezuela, rap music has also given voice to a new kind of racial consciousness among black youth. For instance, Requesón argues for the superiority of the black race: "We are a great race, I think we are a superior race." In a shift from popular historical views of race that denied the existence of racial divisions in Venezuela and placed more importance on national rather than racial identity,[16] rappers have begun to reclaim black identity.[17]

Despite the language of a racial democracy that has dominated political rhetoric in Venezuela, rappers point to the underlying racism that exists in Venezuelan society and is now the basis for the politicization of racial and class cleavages. However, unlike in Cuban rap, these reflections on race do not become demands for racial equality, as people of color in Venezuela still do not have the tendency to see themselves as distinct groups, less still political groupings. These differences are related to distinct histories, particularly the absence of race-based organizing in postcolonial Venezuela. While in Cuba, there were several experiments in racial mobilization, such as the Partido Independiente de Color (see chapter 6), formed in 1908, there have been no corresponding organizations in Venezuela. Race in Venezuela exists less as a category for political mobilization and more as what Raymond Williams refers to as a "structure of feeling."[18] As Echeandía said, "It exists as a reality . . . but it is not openly described as such." Being black or of mixed-race in Venezuela is not generally seen in terms of a political identity; rather it is associated with the lived experience of poverty, violence, and marginality.

Hip-hop culture arrived in Brazil in the early 1980s just as the military regime that had seized power in a 1964 coup began to loosen its brutal hold on Brazilian society. It was during the *abertura* (opening) that marked the transition away from the military dictatorship that Brazilians of African descent, using critical notions of African heritage and black solidarity, created vivid rejoinders to *branqueamento*, or whitening, and racial democracy, the twin ideological pillars of the vast de-Africanization project undertaken by the white elite during the century that followed the formal emancipation of African slaves in 1888. Responding to persistent, heavily racialized inequalities—differential access to basic rights and services, residential segregation, lopsided incarceration rates—black activist groups such as the Movimento Negro Unificado (formed in 1978) began to create what Michael Dawson has referred to as a "black counterpublic," one that promoted an alternative civic dialogue on racial issues.[19] While there had been precedents for race-based organizing and resistance prior to the *abertura* period, Edward Telles has argued that it wasn't until the 1990s that Brazil made a tentative first step away from the debilitating, coded racism of the racial democracy paradigm toward a social system that implemented affirmative action programs as curatives for racial inequalities. "The black movement," according to Telles, "made racial democracy a hopelessly inappropriate concept."[20]

In many ways, it has been music that has provided a particularly powerful voice for this new articulation of a black public sphere. Using sounds both as a register of black marginalization and as a catalyst to promote social change, black Brazilians have blurred the lines between activism and creative work. Beginning in the mid-1970s in the city of Salvador, *blocos afros* (black carnival organizations) such as Ilê Aiyê and Olodum created socially conscious songs that invoked a pan-African sensibility drawn from knowledge of the anticolonial struggles taking place in Lusophone Africa and the philosophy and sounds of reggae music from Jamaica and black soul music from the United States. Both of these *blocos* also devoted serious energy to community projects—they founded schools, started newspapers, and labored to give aggrieved black youth a political voice. The use of black music imported from other locations in the diaspora was also a defining characteristic of the funk movement that emerged in Rio de Janeiro in the early 1970s and had an enormous impact on urban black populations all over Brazil. George Yúdice has called Brazilian funk a challenge to "the symbolic production of a 'cordial' Brazil"[21] and, in some cases, funk performers introduced "didactic" political material into their shows in Rio's clubs.[22] The diasporic, antihegemonic political edge of Brazilian hip-hop has crucial precedents in the funk movement of Rio and the *blocos afros* of Salvador.

Brazilian hip-hop developed principally in the favelas of São Paulo, and over its almost twenty-five-year history it has become an important cultural form in many urban areas of Brazil. As in the United States, hip-hop in Brazil is marked by an enormous diversity of styles and political perspectives; not all hip-hop in Brazil is socially engaged, and some of it is plagued by the same crass materialism, misogyny, and stale beats that characterize some mainstream U.S. hip-hop. Members of the hip-hop community in Brazil have, however, consistently placed a strong emphasis on grassroots social activism; in fact, one might say that a principal characteristic of Brazilian hip-hop has been its concern with progressive politics. By the late 1980s in São Paulo, hip-hop manifested itself as a significant channel through which black Brazilians could exert pressure on the dominant public sphere for full citizenship and equal rights. In 1990, only two years after *Hip-hop cultura de rua* and *Consciência black*, the two most important early compilations of rap music, were released, members of the hip-hop community in São Paulo formed the Movimento Hip Hop Organizado, a coalition of local "posses" that mobilized on a neighborhood basis, giving lectures and workshops for schools and nongovernmental organizations and connecting themselves with political parties and the local black movement.[23] This type of articulation between cultural production and political mobilization is extremely common in Brazilian hip-hop.

Hip-hop groups in major Brazilian cities have used rather stark verbal and sonic imagery to reflect the escalating conditions of violence and denigration that black youth face on a daily basis. Between 1988 and 2002, for example, almost 4,000 people under eighteen were killed by firearms in Rio de Janeiro, a number that is higher than in many areas engaged in war (for example, fewer than five hundred children were killed in the fighting between Palestinians and Israelis during the same fourteen-year period).[24] In 1988, at the beginning of the real ascendancy of hip-hop in Brazil, 66 percent of blacks in Brazil lived in conditions of "miserable poverty," while only 14.7 percent of white Brazilians lived in the same conditions. Blacks have higher rates of unemployment and illiteracy; lower rates of school enrollment (at all education levels); lower life expectancy; less access to potable water and sewage systems, garbage collection, and electricity; and lower rates of ownership of television sets and refrigerators. The list could go on.[25] In these circumstances, album and song titles such as *Holocausto urbano* (Urban Holocaust), *Direto do campo de exterminio* (Direct from the Extermination Camp), "Bem vindos ao inferno" (Welcome to Hell) and "Saída de emergência" (Emergency Exit) represent all-too-real evocations of how life is actually lived in contemporary urban Brazil.

## HIP-HOP IN CUBA

Afro-Cuban youth have used rap music as a means of contesting racial hierarchies and demanding social justice. Paul Gilroy sees the transference of black cultural forms such as hip-hop as related partly to its "inescapably political language of citizenship, racial justice, and equality," a discourse that speaks to the realities and aspirations of black youth globally.[26] Through their texts, performances, and styles, Cuban rappers demand the inclusion of young Afro-Cubans into the polity and they appeal to the state to live up to its promises of egalitarianism. Cuban rappers, particularly those who identify as "underground," point out the race blindness of official discourse and the invisibility of the experiences and problems of marginalized communities in a society that has supposedly "solved" questions of race. Given the lack of forums for young Afro-Cubans to voice their concerns, rap music provides an avenue for contestation and negotiation within Cuban society.

Rappers are critical of the silencing of questions of race in Cuban society. In their song "Lágrimas negras" (Black Tears), the group Hermanos de Causa challenges the claims that in Cuban revolutionary society, racism has been eradicated. "Lágrimas negras" is a famous Cuban song, which was created by the Matamoros Trio in the 1920s and has been performed by many other groups since. Hermanos de Causa sample the song, introducing particular racial implications not present in the original song. They say, as long as racist attitudes exist, racism still exists: "Don't say that there's no racism, where there's a racist." The song brings the reality of lived experience to bear on the rhetoric of racial egalitarianism:

| | |
|---|---|
| *No me digas que no hay* | Don't tell me that there's no racism |
| *Porque yo sí lo he visto* | Because I've seen it |
| *No me digas que no existe* | Don't tell me that it doesn't exist |
| *Porque lo he vivido* | Because I've lived it |

The rappers point to the exclusion of blacks from the tourist industry, Cuba's fastest growing source of hard currency, as well as their ongoing absence from television programming and cinema. When blacks do appear, it is in "secondary roles of last resort" or the "classic role of slave: faithful, submissive or the typical thief without morals." Hermanos de Causa expose the absence and stereotypes of Afro-Cubans in the media, which is particularly ironic in a society that has claimed to have seen the end of racism.

The group Anónimo Consejo draws links between a history of exploitation and a present of racial inequality. According to Gilroy, one of the core themes of African diasporic musical forms is history, a concern that "demands that the experience of slavery is also recovered and rendered vivid and immediate."[27] Slavery becomes a metaphor for contemporary injustice and exploitation. In "A Veces" (At Times), Anonimo Consejo connects the history of Cuban slaves with the situation of contemporary Afro-Cubans. The rapper begins with his geographical location, identifying himself as "a Cuban from the East," which is considered less cultured than Havana. He is lying in his "poor bed" thinking about slavery and the struggle of black people in his country, when the similarities of the present situation occur to him:

| | |
|---|---|
| *Hoy parece que no es así,* | You think it's not the same today, |
| *El oficial me dice a mí,* | An official tells me, |
| *"No puede estar allá,* | "You can't go there, |
| *Mucho menos salir de aquí,"* | Much less leave this place," |
| *En cambio al turista se la trata* | In contrast they treat tourists |
| *diferente,* | differently, |
| *Será posible gente que en* | People, is it possible that in |
| *mi país yo no cuente?* | my country I don't count? |

The rapper uses the critique of racial hierarchies in the past as a way of identifying contemporary racial issues such as police harassment of young black people and the preferential treatment given to tourists over Cubans by officials. He identifies himself as "the descendent of an African," a *cimarron desobediente*, or runaway slave, drawing his links to an ancestral past rooted in a history of slavery and oppression.

While male rappers speak about historical problems of slavery and marginality, women rappers talk about how black women face forms of enslavement and marginalization from black men. In "Eres bella" (You Are Beautiful), Las Krudas point to machismo as an "identical system of slavery" for women. Just as male rappers point to the exclusion of rap from major media programming, venues, and state institutions, Las Krudas challenge male rappers for their exclusion of women: "I have talent and I ask, how long will we be the minority onstage?" Black women have been made invisible, objectified, and silenced in the historical record, and popular culture is no exception. In "Amiquiminongo," Las Krudas argue that since the time of slavery black women and men have been stereotyped as "a beautiful race," "so strong" and "so healthy," but they point out that black women have never been given a voice: "When I open my mouth, 'poof!' raw truths escape from it, they don't talk of this, they want to shut me up." Women rappers demand inclusion in the hip-hop movement and society more generally. As Las Krudas claim, "There is no true revolution without women." Women rappers are "ebony guerrillas" who are fighting for a place in the struggle alongside black men.

## HIP-HOP IN VENEZUELA

Cuban rappers promote certain ideals associated with the Cuban Revolution and make demands on the state to meet the promises of the revolution, particularly regarding racial equality. By contrast, Venezuelan youth from poor backgrounds have lost faith in the previous ruling parties to provide social services and protection for their communities and have come to rely on their own forms of survival in the familiar yet increasingly violent terrain of the barrio. Through their music, rappers reflect on the conditions and experiences that force them into a life of crime and violence. Guerrilla Seca, in "Malandrea negro" (Black Delinquency), argues that it is the poverty, hunger, and desperation of the barrios that produce the resort to crime as a means of survival. Trying to find meaningful work for unskilled black youth is practically impossible: "I go on desperately, looking for work is a joke." Even for those who want to find work in the formal economy there are few opportunities: "I look for legal cash, but destiny is changing me." If one needs money and there are no legal opportunities, then they turn to crime and the informal underground economy is the only path, according to the rapper, especially when one has children to support.

Similarly, in their chronicle of street life, "Historia nuestra" (Our History), Vagos y Maleantes relate that they began dealing drugs, *empecé en el jibareo*, at the age of seventeen. While the parents of the rapper dreamed of him being an engineer, he dreamed of being a criminal. Scholars have pointed to the decline in stable employment in manufacturing, which was available to a greater extent to working classes in previous decades across the Americas; the rise in unemployment; the growth of an informal economy; and the shift to temporary part-time work.[28] It is this lack of viable legal employment that spurs the growth of crime as one of the only options for survival available to marginalized urban youth in Venezuela.

In contrast to the principled gangsters of the past, what the informant Comegato calls "a real *malandro*, a gentleman" who participates in crime for the benefit of his family and his community,[29] what dominates today is *chigüirismo*, or killing for money without regard for the other members of the barrio. In "Cuando hay droga y dinero" (When there are drugs and money), Guerrilla Seca describes the *malandro* (delinquent), as a kind of cold-hearted, malevolent individual:

| | |
|---|---|
| *En negocios de droga y dinero* | In the business of drugs and money |
| *No hay panas ni nada* | There are no friends or nothin' |
| *Esto es malandreo, puro lacreo.* | This is delinquency, pure trouble. |
| *El que menos tú piensas* | The one who you least suspect |
| *Te mata por plata mi pana,* | Will kill you for cash, homie, |
| *Esto es malandreo, es lo que veo.* | This is delinquency, it's what I see. |

The *malandro* is motivated by a desire for consumer goods and a jealousy of those who have more than oneself. *Malandro*s will kill one another for money, fashionable clothes, and Nike shoes. In their negotiations over drugs, nobody can be trusted, and the *malandro* has no friends, as this world is dominated by cruelty and self-interest. Robin D. G. Kelley notes that in the case of Los Angeles's gangsta rappers, the absence of socially responsible criminals is related to the structural absence of job opportunities and is not due to a pathological culture of violence. Yet Kelley acknowledges that at times these distinctions between socially conscious and malevolent gangsters are blurred, and the same voices describing "black-on-black" crime may call for action against dominant institutions.[30] Likewise, Guerrilla Seca states in "Cuando hay droga y dinero:" "I have my morals high, assaulting banks and leading the way." Compared with the *malandro* who steals from his own community and would even assault his neighbor, in this part of the song the rapper targets wealthy corporate institutions and rich people, like a modern-day Robin Hood.[31]

Rappers seek to reclaim the social stereotypes of the *malandro* and the *maleante*. The name of the group Vagos y Maleantes comes from a 1956 law entitled *Ley sobre vagos y maleantes* (Law against vagrants and undesirables). According to Patricia Marquez, the law was devised during the military regime of Marcos Pérez Jiménez in order to imprison dissidents and opponents of the regime, but it came to be used as a way of incarcerating those who were considered "undesirables" by the authorities.[32] Vagos y Maleantes appropriate this name as a way of revindicating themselves and their lifestyle. Echeandía claims that "In Venezuela, blacks are *malandros* or delinquents, and the rappers via their discs and their music say that: 'Yes, we are, and here we express it, here we scream it.'" Both Vagos y Maleantes and Guerrilla Seca have parental advisory labels on the covers of their discs. On the cover of Guerrillas Seca's disc "La Realidad mas real," an English-language label reading "Parental Advisory, Explicit Lyrics" is superimposed over the tip of Colombia's middle finger, which is being raised in an obscene gesture. On the Vagos and Maleantes disc, "Papidandeando" there is a label in Spanish, which reads *Pendiente Activo, Grado Maloso* (Attention, Bad Rating). These labels, which originated in North America after senate committee hearings that required the labels for all nationally distributed hardcore rap albums,[33] have come to provide a stamp of authenticity or street credibility in the Venezuelan context.

The traditional figure of the warrior as symbolized in religious imagery is also used as a way of reimagining the role of the modern-day *malandro*. In their song "Destino" (Destiny), the group Santuario describes the world of contradictions that they inhabit, and within this world they imagine themselves as descendents of mythic religious warriors and gods:

| | |
|---|---|
| *¡Yo era valentía de Ochun aja!* | I was a warrior of Oshun! |
| *Yo era la valentía* | I was the warrior |
| *Del tronco de Legua* | Of the arm of Elegua |
| *Yo era Orosineima, Aquereful* | I was Orosineima, Aquereful, |
| *Y si están en mi camino de aquí* | And if they are in my path, |
| *No van a escapar.* | They're not going to escape. |

Oshun, Elegua, and Orosineima refer to *orishas*, or deities of the religion of Santería, which has come to Venezuela mainly via Cuba. "Legua" refers to Elegua, the deity who opens paths. The "arm of Elegua" is an allusion to the symbolic arm of the deity. The rapper, Black Soul, seeks to identify his own experiences of street fighting with the bravery of the orishas, thereby increasing his own moral authority. In contrast to the derogatory associations of terms such as *malandro*, *vago*, and *maleante*, rappers reclaim these terms and infuse them with older meanings of bravery and justice.

## HIP-HOP IN BRAZIL

Michael Hanchard has suggested that "the 1988 commemoration of abolition in Brazil was the single most important event for the black movement in the post–World War II era,"[34] and while scholars have cautioned against ascribing too much influence to black activist organizations in Brazil,[35] there is little doubt that the substantial protests and demonstrations by the black movement that year marked a new phase in the public recognition of the racist foundations of Brazilian society. Organizers called for an acknowledgement that the *Lei Áurea* (Golden Law), the decree of abolition issued by Princess Isabel in 1888, did little for black Brazilians in their quest for equal rights and the benefits of full citizenship. Musicians in particular did much to articulate to a wide audience the ironies of the centennial celebrations. In the nationally televised carnival of Rio de Janeiro, two *escolas de samba* (samba organizations), Mangueira and Vila Isabel, devoted their parade themes to critiquing the commonly held conception that Brazil was a racial democracy. Mangueira, Rio's oldest *escola de samba*, paraded to a song entitled "100 anos de liberdade, realidade ou ilusão" (100 Years of Freedom: Reality or Illusion), which questioned the notion that oppressive conditions faced by black Brazilians were substantially transformed by abolition.

| | |
|---|---|
| *Será que* | I wonder whether |
| *Já raiou a liberdade* | Freedom already dawned |
| *Ou se foi tudo ilusão* | Or if it was all an illusion |
| *Será, que a Lei Áurea* | Could it be that the "Golden Law" |
| *Tão sonhada* | Our big dream |
| *Há tanto tempo assinada* | Which was enacted a long time ago |
| *Não foi o fim da escravidão* | Wasn't the end of slavery |

As in the Anónimo Consejo example from Cuba presented above, Brazilian rappers have also sought to examine the continuity between the history of slavery and contemporary conditions in black Brazilian communities. The past is offered up not so much as "what happened already" but as "what is happening still." At times, the superimposition of different historical moments—much like the dense layering of sonic sources that characterizes rap production—is used to highlight the unending crisis facing people of African descent in Brazil. When the group Face da Morte (Face of Death) raps that "they freed the slaves and threw them into misery" (*libertaram os escravos e jogaram na miséria*) on "Mudar o mundo" (Change the World), they too activate a link between past injustice and contemporary desolation and call attention to the false promise of post-abolition "liberation."

In other cases, Afro-Brazilian rappers configure the past as a site of strength, not powerlessness, and look to the long history of black resistance during the slave period to provide inspiration for current battles against the forces that contribute to racial marginalization. For example, the song "Antigamente quilombo, hoje periferia" (Yesterday *Quilombo*, Today Periphery), by the São Paulo-based group Z'Africa Brasil, draws a correspondence between the struggle for black autonomy waged by Zumbi, the leader of the Palmares *quilombo* in the late seventeenth century, and the battles against poverty and inequality undertaken by inhabitants of the favelas of the late twentieth century:

| | |
|---|---|
| *Zumbi, o redentor* | Zumbi, the savior |
| *Agora o jogo virou* | Now the game has changed |
| *Quilombos guerreou* | *Quilombos* fought |
| *Periferia acordou* | The periphery woke up |
| *Cansamos de promessas* | We are tired of promises |
| *Volta pro mato capitão* | Go back to the jungle captain |
| *Pois já estamos em guerra* | Because we're already at war |

In this song, historical continuity is not only realized through the complex textual alignment of past and present; there is also a sonic dimension that speaks to a rich diasporic understanding of African musical traditions from outside Brazil. In the beat that accompanies the verse above, there is an extended slide guitar solo in the gritty delta blues style that originated in the state of Mississippi during the Jim Crow period. Black Brazilian history is sonically extended by Z'Africa Brasil to include the histories of people of African descent throughout the diaspora.

The mining of black music from the United States has been a common strategy for invoking an African identity in Brazilian rap. In their song "Rap do trem" the group RZO makes great use of the sitar sample from A Tribe Called Quest's 1990 hit "Bonita Applebum" (later used by the Fugees for their remake of Roberta Flack's "Killing Me Softly"). In the same song RZO offers up another pan-African link (quite similar to the Vagos y Maleantes example from Venezuela cited above), this one with Yoruba and the Afro-Brazilian religion *Candomblé*, when they ask the *orixá* (*oricha* or *orisha* in Spanish), or African deity, Oxalá to give them the strength to fight (*E eu peço a Oxalá e então, sempre vai nos guarder / Dai-nos forças pra lutar*). And, to cite another example, in their "Sr. Tempo Bom" (Mr. Good Time), Thaíde and DJ Hum, two of hip-hop's biggest stars in Brazil, employ a looped beat and the "Oh yeah" from Jean Knight's "Mr. Big Stuff," released in 1971.[36]

Thaíde and DJ Hum, still major figures on the Brazilian rap scene, appeared on *Hip-hop cultura de rua*, one of the two major compilations released in 1988, the year that rap music made a forceful entry into the Brazilian public sphere. On *Consciência black*, the second compilation released that year, the group Racionais MCs (Rational MCs), which would soon become the most important hip-hop act in the country, debuted their "Pânico na Zona Sul," a song that charted out a diasporic connection with the blacks in the United States through the use of a sample from James Brown's 1974 hit "The Payback." The Godfather of Soul's influence on the group was so strong that one of its members, Mano Brown, went as far as to appropriate Brown's surname. In an interview from a program aired on TV Cultura, a São Paulo-based television station, Mano had this to say about hearing James Brown's music when he was a kid:

Man, James Brown . . . It was the most powerful music that I had heard, it really made us proud. Everything that you heard in school about blacks, everything you heard about the neighbors or the wide world in general, when you heard James Brown, you forgot everything. You start becoming proud, you become strong, no? I think this made the blacks at that time in the 1970s in Brazil leave the club feeling like superman after hearing James Brown.[37]

But "Pânico na Zona Sul" cannot only be reduced to a statement of Afro-diasporic connections and transnational black pride. It also bears witness to the very pervasive local forms of violence that characterize life in the periphery of São Paulo. The sampled sound of a gunshot that explodes out of the middle of the second verse might seem to draw an expressive parallel to NWA's "Straight Outta Compton" (also released in 1988), but there are limits to the kinds of translation that are possible when rap is evaluated cross-culturally; Compton is not Capão Redondo, the favela Mano Brown is from, and the type of escalating racial violence that affects young blacks in Brazil is of an order of magnitude different than that in the United States. Teresa Caldeira has written that in 1999 a full 10 percent of all deaths in the city of São Paulo were homicides, compared with 1.44 percent of deaths in 1984.[38] Her research has also shown that in the twenty-year period between 1981 and 2001, the police in São Paulo killed 11,692 people; some years the number was over 1,000, an astonishing average of three murders per day by the police.[39] In "Pânico na Zona Sul" the members of Racionais use hip-hop as a potent global methodology for taking stock of local conditions.

This is not to imply that this methodology leads Brazilian hip-hop artists to create uniform depictions or offer up standardized responses. As in the United States, hip-hop culture in Brazil is characterized by divergent depictions of "the real." Facção Central (Central Faction), another hip-hop crew from São Paulo, provides a more gruesome accounting of the violence of the black periphery than Racionais does in "Pânico na Zona Sul." The video to their song "Isso aqui é uma guerra" (This Here Is a War), banned from television by the Ministério Público (district attorney) of São Paulo, graphically shows two murders, a carjacking, and numerous armed robberies. In response to the censoring of their work, Eduardo, one of the members of the group says, "The video doesn't talk about Disneyland, but Brazil, the country with the most deaths from firearms. If it had been made in Sweden then it could have caused surprise. The surprising thing is that someone here would be shocked by this content."[40]

| | |
|---|---|
| *Isso aqui é uma guerra* | This here is a war |
| *Onde só sobrevive* | In which only those |
| *Quem atira . . .* | Who shoot survive . . . |

| | |
|---|---|
| *Infelizmente o livro não resolve* | Sadly, the law is useless |
| *O Brasil só me* | Only with a gun does Brazil |
| *Respeita com um revolver . . .* | Show me respect . . . |
| *Eu quero roupa, comida* | I want clothes, food |
| *Alguém tem que sangrar* | Someone has to bleed |
| *Vou enquadrar uma burguesa e* | I'm gonna aim at a bourgeoisie and |
| *Atirar pra matar* | Shoot to kill |

And the song continues, emphasizing the relation between the images conjured up in the lyrics and the way life is lived in urban Brazil: "This is no soap opera / There's no love on the screen / The scene exists" (*Aqui não é novela, Não tem amor na tela / A cena existe*).

Of course, rappers need not only *depict* reality; they have also developed substantial tactics for *transforming* it. In "Pânico na Zona Sul" Racionais advocates a different method for dealing with the violence faced by black Brazilians. After saying that "Racionais is going to talk about the reality of the streets" (*Racionais vão contar a realidade das ruas*), they go on to emphasize how a critical sensibility can mutate fear into a positive force for change, into self-reliance and what they broadly label "consciousness." In this song Racionais makes a proposition that knowledge can enable survival by prompting citizens to engage actively in the public sphere. As the French philosopher Maurice Merleau-Ponty wrote, "Consciousness is in the first place not a matter of 'I think that' but of 'I can.'"[41] When rap groups in Brazil talk about consciousness they are not just referring to a state of mind, a filling up of gaps in understanding, but a way of translating knowledge into action. Racionais MCs have been involved in substantial social campaigns for victims of AIDS and for alleviating hunger and the notion that consciousness of social problems can be turned into counter-hegemonic action is a key part of their creative work. "Pânico na Zona Sul" continues:

| | |
|---|---|
| *A mudança estará* | The change will be |
| *Em nossa consciência* | In our consciousness |
| *Praticando nossos atos* | Practicing our actions |
| *Com coerência* | With coherence |
| *E a conseqüência será* | And the consequence will be |
| *O fim do próprio medo . . .* | The end of our own fear . . . |
| *A nossa filosofia* | Our philosophy |
| *É sempre transmitir* | Is to always transmit |
| *A realidade em si* | Reality the way it is |

This transmission of reality "the way that it is" becomes pure pedagogy on "Capítulo 4, versículo 3" (chapter 4, verse 3), a song from Racionais MC's 1997 album *Sobrevivendo no inferno* (Surviving in Hell) the largest-selling independent record in Brazilian recording history. Making a cameo appearance on the introduction to the track, Primo Preto (Black Cousin), a hip-hop producer in São Paulo, gives this eye-opening rundown of the social conditions facing blacks in Brazil:

| | |
|---|---|
| *60% dos jovens de periferia* | 60% of the youth of the periphery |
| *Sem antecendências criminais* | Without police records have |
| *Já sofrerarm violência policial* | Already suffered police violence |
| *A cada quatro pessoas mortas* | Out of every four people killed |
| *Pela polícia três são negros* | By the police, three are black |
| *Nas universidades brasileiras apenas* | In Brazilian universities, only |
| *2% dos alunos são negros* | 2% of the students are black |
| *A cada quatro horas um jovem negro* | Every four hours a young black man |
| *Morre violentamente em São Paulo* | Dies violently in São Paulo |
| *Aqui quem fala é* | The person speaking here is |
| *Primo Preto, mais um sobrevivente* | Primo Preto, one more survivor |

Much like KRS One's notion of "edutainment," members of Racionais have presented eloquent and critical statements that inform their listeners of the problems facing black youth in the favelas of São Paulo. However, as in Cuba and Venezuela, blackness in Brazil cannot be thought as a homogenous, stable identity; class, gender, location, and generation all play an important role in how race is lived in contemporary Brazil. In "Biografia feminina," Cris, a woman rapper from the group Somos Nós A Justiça (We Are Justice), adds a level of gender awareness not often heard in Brazilian rap, speaking against biological determinism and imploring women to create polemics and then turn rhetoric into action:

| | |
|---|---|
| *Mulheres escravizadas á sua* | Women, enslaved to their |
| *Condição biológica* | Biological condition |
| *Isso não tem lógica* | This doesn't make sense |
| *Bendita sejam aquelas* | Bless those women |
| *Que geraram polêmica* | Who create polemics |
| *Atitude idealista tem que lutar* | Idealistic attitude, you have to fight |
| *Para obter conquistas* | To get what you want |
| *É preciso reivindicar* | It's necessary to protest |
| *Desigualdade, chega, chega* | Inequality, it's enough already |
| *Mas que absurdo 129 mulheres* | How absurd, 129 women |
| *Morreram em busca de* | Died trying to get |
| *Melhores condições de trabalho* | Better working conditions |
| *Pensamento falhos não estáo nos livros* | Faulty thoughts are not in books |

| | |
|---|---|
| *Basta procurar, pesquisar e* | You just have to look, research, and |
| *Achará escrito* | You'll find it written |

Perhaps the most powerful moment of the above excerpt comes when Cris unleashes the salvo about the important role "research" plays for women who want to mobilize. Reaching into the history of the labor struggle in the United States, she presents the example of the Triangle Factory fire that took place in New York City on March 25, 1911, which claimed the lives of 129 young immigrant women, many of whom were part of the unionization movement that sought to correct the deplorable labor conditions of sweatshops like the Triangle Factory. For Cris, local gender politics has an extensity that pushes beyond the geographic limits of São Paulo. Later in the song, saying that she's going to "localize in geography, teach in practice" (*localizar na geografia, ensinar na prática*), Cris brings it all back home, referencing Zezé Motta, Clementina de Jesus, Dona Ivone Lara, and Alcione, all pioneering black women musicians in Brazil. The idea of speaking, of bearing witness to the varied contours of the everyday lives of black Brazilians, becomes a crucial part of the production of counter-hegemonic action, of "teaching in practice."

## CONCLUSION

This chapter offers sketches of three immensely complex communities that have organized themselves around hip-hop culture. We have aimed to provide a window into how black youth in Cuba, Venezuela, and Brazil use hip-hop in their daily lives, rather than giving a broad accounting of the contested and always-shifting relationships among race, culture, and politics in these countries. Our intention was to project onto these pages a few of the traces that hip-hop has left in the black public spheres of three Latin American countries with vastly different yet interconnected histories. Hopefully, what we have presented will be enough to spur a dialogue on a number of vital issues: how cultural forms are localized in an epoch that has witnessed ever-increasing global flows of products, information, and people; how unequal access to the privileges of full citizenship can prompt young people of color to use the cultural resources they have at their disposal to create critical responses to their own marginalization; how diasporic connections function, always simultaneously, on local and transnational levels; and how the aesthetic dimensions of hip-hop culture can never be disembedded from the valences of racial politics.

All over the world young people use hip-hop to help make sense of, and sometimes reimagine, the very political contours of their daily lives. Capi-

**Figure 9.1.    Hip-hop artist painting graffiti in São Paulo, Brazil. Source: Sujatha Fernandes**

talizing on hip-hop's elegant aesthetic arsenal, its history of transformation and resistance, they can ask tough questions and provide eloquent responses, always taking advantage of a critical methodology developed by marginalized black and Latino youths from the United States and the Caribbean. While hip-hop culture is an ever-mutating, heterogeneous set of practices, the history of the African diaspora is never absent from any hip-hop utterance. As Raquel Z. Rivera has said about the sonic dimension of hip-hop culture, "Rap, therefore, must be understood through the recognition of its intense technological and industrial mediation, its international popularity, its historical context and its continued rootedness in poor communities of color across the United States."[42] Although hip-hop is a remarkably flexible form, created in vastly divergent circumstances by people with sometimes radically different identities and needs, its primary reference points still derive from the experiences and histories of African-diasporic youth.

Given the legacy of brutal enslavement and enduring forms of oppression and subjugation in Latin America, the articulation of hip-hop culture with blackness takes on heightened resonance for people of African decent in this region. To be sure, there are substantial differences in the way blackness is lived Cuba, Venezuela, and Brazil; but we want to suggest that the members of hip-hop communities in these countries are all engaged in creating strategies that help render the public sphere more open and pliable for people of color who have been disproportionately hit with the burdens of partial citizenship. Hip-hop is nowhere in the world an endpoint or a final resolution to crisis, but it has been used, at times quite successfully, by young blacks to help forge a critical dialogue within the public spheres to which they have been denied full access.

## DISCOGRAPHY

### Cuba

Anónimo Consejo. "A Veces." Lyrics obtained from artist, 2001.
Hermanos de Causa. "Lagrimas negras." *Cuban Hip Hop All-Stars, Vol 1*. Papaya Records, 2001.
Las Krudas. "Amiquimiñongo." *CUBENSI*. Demo, 2003.
Las Krudas. "Eres bella." *CUBENSI*. Demo, 2003.
Papo Record. "Prosperaré." Recorded by Sujatha Fernandes, Cubadisco festival, May 16, 2001.

### Brazil

DMN. "Saída de emergência." *Saída de emergência*. Sky Blue Music, 2001.
Facção Central. *Direto do campo de extermínio*. Unimar Music, 2003.
Facção Central. "Isso aqui é uma guerra." *Versos sangrentos*. Sky Blue Music, 2000.
Faces da Morte. "Mudar o mundo." *Manifesto popular Brasileiro*. Sky Blue Music, 2001.
Racionais MCs. "Capítulo 4, versículo 3." *Sobrevivendo no inferno*. Cosa Nostra, 1997.
Racionais MCs. "Pânico na Zona Sul." *Holocausto urbano*. Zimbabwe, 1992.
RZO. "Rap do trem." *Rap & Hip-Hop #01* [DVD]. Rhythm and Blues, 2004.
Sistema Negro. "Bem vindos ao inferno." *Poetas de rua, Vol. 1*. Zambia, 2000.
Somos Nós a Justiça. "Biografia feminina." *Se tu lutas tu conquistas*. Vibrato, 2001.
Thaíde and DJ Hum. "Sr. Tempo Bom." *Preste atenção*. Eldorado, 1996.
Various Artists. *Hip-hop cultura de rua*. Eldorado, 1988.
Various Artists. *Consciência black*. Zimbabwe, 1988.
Z'Africa Brasil. "Antigamente quilombo, hoje periferia." *Agosto negro*. ST2 Music, 2004.

### Venezuala

Guerrilla Seca. "Cuando hay droga y dinero." *La realidad mas real*. Caracas, Venezuela: Subterraneo Records, 2002.

Guerrilla Seca. "Malandreo negro." *Venezuela subterranea*. Caracas, Venezuela: Subterraneo Records, 2001.
Santuario. "Destino." Andromeda Productions, 2000.
Vagos y Maleantes. "Historia nuestra." *Papidandeando*. Caracas, Venezuela: Subterraneo Records, 2002.

## NOTES

1. In this chapter we view hip-hop as a constellation of aesthetic and political approaches to cultural production and consumption. This constellation is an always shifting articulation of a number of overlapping dimensions, or elements: the visual (graffiti, fashion, video, advertisements), the sonic (rap, DJ culture, studio techniques, spoken language), the kinesthetic (break dancing, gestural language), the philosophical/ideological (lyrical content, political activism), and the economic (entrepreneurial activity, "bling"). The authors are responsible for all translations into English of the original Spanish and Portuguese texts and lyrics found in this chapter.

2. For recent books on the emergence of hip-hop culture in the United States, see Jeff Chang, *Can't Stop, Won't Stop: A History of the Hip-Hop Generation* (New York: St. Martin's Press, 2005); Raquel Z. Rivera, *New York Ricans from the Hip Hop Zone* (New York: Palgrave Macmillan, 2003); Jim Fricke and Charlie Ahearn, eds., *Yes Yes Y'All: The Experience Music Project Oral History of Hip-Hop's First Decade* (New York: Da Capo Press, 2002).

3. Craig Werner, *A Change Is Gonna Come: Music, Race and the Soul of America* (New York: Plume, 1999), 236.

4. Livio Sansone, *Blackness without Ethnicity: Constructing Race in Brazil* (New York: Palgrave Macmillan, 2003), 87.

5. Sidney J. Lemelle and Robin D. G. Kelley, "Imagining Home: Pan-Africanism Revisited," in *Imagining Home: Class, Culture, and Nationalism in the African Diaspora*, ed. Sidney J. Lemelle and Robin D. G. Kelley (London: Verso, 1994), 8.

6. In October 2004, Fidel Castro once again banned the circulation of the U.S. dollar in Cuba. The dollar has been replaced by the convertible peso, which is equivalent to the dollar but has no value outside Cuba.

7. Alejandro de la Fuente, *A Nation for All: Race, Inequality and Politics in Twentieth-Century Cuba* (Chapel Hill: University of North Carolina Press, 2001), 319.

8. De la Fuente, *A Nation for All*, 280.

9. De la Fuente, *A Nation for All*, 329.

10. Yves Predrazzini and Magaly Sanchez, *Malandros, bandas y niños de la calle: Cultura de urgencia en la metropoli latinoamericana* (Caracas, Venezuela: Vadell Hermanos Editores, 2001).

11. Ana María Sanjuán, "Democracy, Citizenship, and Violence in Venezuela," in *Citizens of Fear: Urban Violence in Latin America*, ed. Susana Rotker (New Brunswick, NJ: Rutgers University Press, 2002), 87.

12. Sanjuán, "Democracy, Citizenship," 87.

13. Authors' interview with Juan Carlos Echeandía, Caracas, Venezuela, January 13, 2004.

14. Margarita López Maya, David Smilde, and Kate Stephany, *Protesta y cultura en Venezuela: Los Marcos de acción colectiva en 1999* (Caracas, Venezuela: Consejo Latin-oamericano de Ciencias Sociales, 2002).

15. Authors' interview with Colombia and Requeson, Caracas, Venezuela, January 13, 2004.

16. Winthrop R. Wright, *Café con Leche: Race, Class, and National Image in Venezuela* (Austin: University of Texas Press, 1990).

17. Authors' interview with Echeandía.

18. Raymond Williams, *Marxism and Literature* (Oxford: Oxford University Press, 1977).

19. Michael Dawson, *Black Visions: The Roots of Contemporary African-American Political Ideologies* (Chicago: University of Chicago Press, 2003), 23.

20. Edward E. Telles, *Race in Another America: The Significance of Skin Color in Brazil* (Princeton, NJ: Princeton University Press, 2004), 53.

21. George Yúdice, "The Funkification of Rio," in *Microphone Fiends: Youth Music and Youth Culture*, ed. Andrew Ross and Tricia Rose (New York: Routledge, 1994), 196.

22. Yúdice, "Funkification of Rio," 206.

23. Elaine Nunes de Andrade, "Hip hop: Movimento negro juvenil," in *Rap e educação, rap é educação*, ed. Elaine Nunes de Andrade (São Paulo, Brazil: Summus, 1999), 88–89.

24. Tom Gibb, "Rio: Worse than a War Zone," September 9, 2002, http://news.bbc.co.uk/2/hi/americas/2247608.stm (accessed August 5, 2005).

25. Abdias do Nascimento and Elisa Larkin Nascimento, "Dance of Deception: A Reading of Race Relations in Brazil," in *Beyond Racism: Race and Inequality in Brazil, South Africa, and the United States*, ed. Charles Hamilton et al. (Boulder, CO: Lynne Rienner, 2001), 111–20.

26. Paul Gilroy, *The Black Atlantic: Modernity and Double Consciousness* (Cambridge, MA: Harvard University Press, 1993), 83.

27. Paul Gilroy, "One Nation under a Groove: The Cultural Politics of 'Race' and Racism in Britain," in *Becoming National: A Reader*, ed. Geoff Eley and Ronald Grigor Suny (New York: Oxford University Press,1996), 363.

28. Philippe Bourgois, *In Search of Respect: Selling Crack in El Barrio* (Cambridge: Cambridge University Press, 2003); Predrazzini and Sanchez, *Malandros, Bandas y Niños de la Calle.*

29. Jose Roberto Duque and Boris Muñoz, *La Ley de la calle: Testimonios de jóvenes protagonistas de la violencia en Caracas* (Caracas, Venezuela: Fundarte, 1995), 108.

30. Robin D. G. Kelley, "Kickin' Reality, Kickin' Ballistics: Gangsta Rap and Post-industrial Los Angeles," in *Droppin' Science: Critical Essays on Rap and Hip Hop Culture*, ed. William Eric Perkins (Philadelphia: Temple University Press, 1996), 124.

31. Authors' interview with Echeandía.

32. Patricia Marquez, *The Street Is My Home: Youth and Violence in Caracas* (Stanford, CA: Stanford University Press, 1999), 229. The law has recently been suspended under Chávez.

33. Eithne Quinn, *Nuthin' but a "G" Thang: The Culture and Commerce of Gangsta Rap* (New York: Columbia University Press, 2005), 88.

34. Michael Hanchard, *Orpheus and Power: The Movimento Negro of Rio de Janeiro and São Paulo, Brazil, 1945–1988* (Princeton, NJ: Princeton University Press, 1994), 142.

35. Michael Hanchard, *Orpheus and Power*, 21; Yúdice, "The Funkification of Rio," 211; Howard Winant, "Racial Democracy and Racial Identity: Comparing Brazil and the United States," in *Racial Politics in Contemporary Brazil*, ed. Michael Hanchard (Durham, NC: Duke University Press, 1999), 104.

36. In the video to "Sr. Tempo Bom," Thaíde and DJ Hum invoke the visual side of African American soul culture, with their use of clothing and hairstyles from the early 1970s. Incorporation of black fashion from the United States was crucial for the Brazilian funk movement mentioned earlier in this chapter.

37. *Ensaio*, TV Cultura, January 27, 2003. The original text, spoken in Portuguese by Mano Brown, follows: "Nossa, o James Brown. . . . Foi a música mais forte que eu ouvi . . . que deu orgulho mesmo. Tudo que você ouviu na escola sobre preto, tudo que você ouviu sobre os vizinhos ou do mundão geral, quando você ouve James Brown você esquece tudo. Você passa a ter orgulho, você fica forte, né? Eu acho que isso aí fazia os pretos daquela época dos anos 70 no Brasil sair do salão se sentindo superman depois de ouvir James Brown."

38. Teresa Caldeira, "Police Violence in Democratic Brazil," *Ethnography* 3, no. 3 (2002): 244.

39. Caldeira, "Police Violence," 245.

40. Ivan Claudio, "Máquina de escândalos," *Istoé*, www.terra.com.br/istoe/1609/artes/1609maquinas.htm (accessed August 5, 2005). The original text in Portuguese follows: "O clipe não fala da Disneylândia, mas do Brasil, o país onde mais se mata com arma de fogo. Se tivesse sido feito na Suécia, poderia até causar espanto. O espantoso é alguém daqui se chocar com o seu conteúdo."

41. Maurice Merleau-Ponty, *Phenomenology of Perception* (London: Routledge, 1989), 137.

42. Rivera, *New York Ricans*, 12–13.

# 10

## Unfinished Migrations: From the Mexican South to the American South

### Impressions on Afro-Mexican Migration to North Carolina

*Bobby Vaughn and Ben Vinson III*

*The histories of the United States and Latin America have been intertwined since the colonial era. In the modern and contemporary eras, that history has been dominated by U.S. military and political intervention, economic expansion, and investment. Latin America has also influenced the United States, but as in the case of African legacy, that impact has mostly come from below, from conquered or deterritorialized people such as Mexicans and Puerto Ricans. By the 1970s, the Latino population in the United States (immigrant and native born) was so large that the United States institutionalized a new ethnic category in its natural census.*

*In 2003, Latinos officially became the largest "minority community" in the United States, and a host of media outlets reported this data in highly divisive and competitive language vis-à-vis African Americans. Few highlighted the fact that Latinos, who are of many races and ethnicities, are culturally or nationally defined. Indeed, until recently, studies of the Latino populations have largely failed to examine race relations within the Latino community or how the African legacies within Latino communities interact with the African legacies within the African American communities. Students of Latino history are more likely to recognize the African influences among U.S. residents with backgrounds from the Caribbean or from*

*Brazil, where African influences are well known, but do not associate blackness with countries such as Mexico.*

*Bobby Vaughn and Ben Vinson III's preliminary ethnography on Afro-Mexicans in North Carolina will begin to change that. This chapter represents a fresh step into a new field of research that combines the literature on immigration and trans-nationalism in the United States with that on race and identity in Latin America. This chapter not only questions issues of racial solidarity and perceived identity but provides readers with a number of insights into cross-diasporic relations in general, and between African Americans and Afro-Mexicans in particular. Poor Afro-Mexicans, who faced discrimination and marginalization at home in Mexico, con-front new questions of identity and class when they enter communities in the United States. Vaughn and Vinson also remind us of the limits of racial categories in the United States such as "white," "Hispanic," and "black" to identify a diverse pool of immigrants with multiple backgrounds and national and ethnic allegiances. Despite its inadequacies, states and individuals still use national origin as a con-struction that determine life experiences.*

The rapid growth of Latinos has sparked a reengagement with the question of what it means to be a "minority" in the United States and whether the traditionally conceived boundaries of the terms "black" and "white" are in need of significant revision. Other migrant streams that qualify for minority status, such as those from Asia, Africa, the Caribbean, and the Middle East, have certainly been important to the overall social landscape of the United States, but arguably, the recent dramatic increase of Latinos has outpaced all the other groups with potentially deeper cultural effects. In the southern United States in particular, the Latino surge has begun to challenge the long-standing primacy of African Americans as the region's predominant minority population. As the fates of both groups increasingly converge, the challenge to Latinos and African Americans lies in their mutual effort to understand each other while respecting and appreciating their differences.

Issues of black-Latino relations are generally thought about in mutually exclusive terms—with "blackness" typically being relegated solely to the domain of African Americans. Until recently, there has been little interroga-tion as to the "race" of Latinos.[1] This chapter engages the question of Afro-Latino identity in the United States by focusing on the racial and ethnic landscape of North Carolina, particularly the Raleigh-Durham and Winston-Salem metropolitan areas, while unraveling some of the assumed racial biases that accompany traditional discussions of black-Latino rela-tions. During the 1990s, North Carolina possessed one of the fastest-growing Latino populations in the United States, growing by 500 percent according to some estimates.[2] Latinos currently constitute nearly 6 percent of the state's eight million inhabitants, up from 1.2 percent in 1990.[3] The largest areas of growth and concentration have been in the areas of Greensboro, Charlotte, and Raleigh, and a significant proportion of the Latino immigrant group has come from Mexico.[4] As of 2002, nearly 41.5 percent of the state's immigrant population was of Mexican origin, making Mexicans the largest single immigrant group in the state.[5] Settling in the South, they have arrived to areas that have long been zones of African American residency. In 2000, during part of the peak period of Latino migration, the African American population in North Carolina represented a full 21.6 percent of the state's population.[6]

## MEXICO: HISTORICAL BACKGROUND AND BLACKNESS

Mexicans, like most Latin Americans, are not a homogeneous racial group. Mexico has a long history of grappling with racial discrimination as well as its own blackness and ethnic diversity. Indeed, anti-black racism is not a phenomenon that is foreign to Mexicans. During colonial times (1521–1821), peoples of African descent in Mexico struggled to seek liberty from slavery, and once free, they had to deal with navigating through the political, economic, and social discrimination that enveloped them by means of the Spanish American caste system.[7] Although the caste system was abolished in the 1820s, thanks in no small part to the military efforts of Afro-Mexicans, for the rest of the nineteenth century, Mexico's vigorous effort to modernize meant deep engagement in a series of debates about the nature of national order and progress. In the process, both Mexican blackness and indigenousness became problematic categories that jeopardized the health of the nation-state. While intellectuals and political actors eventually embraced indigenousness, the topic of blackness, despite enjoying moments of vogue in political circles in the late 1870s, became viewed as antithetical to national ambitions.[8]

These attitudes have a sinuous history. From the end of the nineteenth century into the early twentieth century, Mexico extended an ambivalent attitude toward blacks. With an alternating tempo, between the 1850s and 1910 government officials and businessmen actually proceeded to invite small numbers of foreign blacks, particularly African Americans and Afro-West Indians, into the nation. In an inversion of modern U.S.-Mexican border relations, these immigrants were summoned to help establish agricultural colonies in remote and underproductive areas; provide labor on important projects of national significance (such as railroads); and, in the case of a community of Afro-Seminoles, provide military support against aggressive frontier indigenous groups like the Apaches.[9] While never amounting to more than several thousand individuals, as black immigrant streams flowed in, Mexico's national discourse on race strove to distance itself from the nation's black heritage. It was decreed repeatedly in public and private settings that Mexico's blacks (the descendants of slaves) were but a small marginal population, near extinction and on the brink of being fully assimilated into the nation.[10] Such rhetoric was familiar in nineteenth-century Latin American circles and was even heard in countries with far greater numbers of blacks.[11] By using this discourse to influence ideologies, perceptions, and attitudes, Mexico strove to relegate its black presence to a distant colonial past; blacks were a contributor to the nation's history, but not necessarily (save foreigners) to its climb into modernity.

Little changed during the Mexican Revolution (1910–1920). In fact, given the hard times that struck the country between 1926 and 1931 and the global depression of the 1930s, new immigration laws focused hard on barring even the foreign blacks who had once been welcomed into Mexico just decades earlier. Although immigration impediments were lifted in 1935, by and large, the tenor of blackness as a theme in national history had been exposed. It might be best to characterize the immediate post-revolutionary era as one when blackness was tangentially, at best, embraced into the idea of nationhood. In the 1920s, as Mexico searched for symbols and images by which to unify a nation that had been ripped apart by civil unrest, a handful of intellectuals considered Afro-Mexicans an important component toward the shaping of a new political and social order. Alfonso Toro, writing in 1921, was a principal thinker in this regard. While espousing the popular and widely held view that blacks had virtually "vanished" into the national population due to centuries of racial mixture, he was still one of the first to express the idea that specific patterns of black settlement in the colonial period, combined with the legacy of slavery, had created a unique character amongst Afro-Mexicans that was subsequently transmitted into the broader population upon assimilation. In fact, he believed that the proclivity for Mexicans to participate in revolutionary movements was due to the black heritage. Consequently, he conceived both the struggle for independence from Spain (1810–1821) and the Mexican Revolution as being the direct results of African ancestry.[12] José Vasconcelos, popularly considered to be one of the primary intellectual voices of the cultural arm of the Mexican Revolution, spoke about blacks too, but in far less flattering terms. In his classic tome on racial mixture, *La Raza cósmica*, he elaborated the theory of a new and improved race in the tropics; but blacks were conspicuously seen as a negative stain on racial progress.[13] Although he was not alone in his thinking, a few others were less sure of such conclusions. Heeding Alfonso Toro's call to pursue further scholarship on blacks, throughout the 1930s and 1940s, scholars like Carlos Basauri, Gabriel Saldívar, Nicolas León, Joaquín Roncal, and eventually Gonzalo Aguirre Beltrán proved influential in studying the "folkloric" impact of the black population, their ethnography, their historical contributions to the evolution of specific Mexican regions, and ultimately, their relevance to the new model and symbol of Mexican identity—*mestizaje* (racial mixture).[14] While the majority of their works were small-scale studies, their body of research constitutes the genesis of what has become the modern field of Afro-Mexican studies. Indeed, their research has been foundational toward the greater recovery of Afro-Mexican history and current works of anthropology.

Yet, during the early twentieth century, there was a perceptible disconnect between Mexico's political and scholarly discourse, and the invisibility of Afro-Mexicans on the national stage. Frozen in time, except in a few key anthropological works,[15] intellectual ideas contributed to the perception of blacks as playing a minimal role in modern life. A few foreign correspondents did a somewhat better job of acknowledging the contributions of contemporary Afro-Mexicans. Carleton Beals, writing for the *Crisis* in 1931, authored a story on the Afro-Mexican town of Valerio Trujano, citing its participation in the revolution and commenting on local political struggles against corrupt politicians and wealthy hacienda (estate) owners.[16] Apart from references to race, the article reads as if it were discussing the plight of peasant communities anywhere in Mexico. On the other hand, a later article appearing in *Ebony* about the same town showed that even the foreign media could be easily seduced into the trap of depicting black communities as "lost in time," ripe for recovery.[17]

The truth of the matter is that Afro-Mexicans have left a lasting legacy in the past and present. They continue to inhabit certain areas of the country, specifically the Pacific Coast, albeit in numbers that represent small fractions of the national population.[18] At the dawn of the twenty-first century, as with their non-black compatriots, the lure of a better life northward during times of economic hardship has led many to settle in the United States, if only temporarily. For a number of reasons, ranging from family and friendship networks to lucrative employment opportunities and an appealing climate, Afro-Mexicans have chosen North Carolina as one of their primary destinations and have made Winston-Salem and parts of Raleigh their home.

Can the blackness of some of these immigrants serve as an important rallying point toward engendering community ties and solidarity among African Americans and Mexicans in North Carolina? Does the blackness of these immigrants create additional challenges for them with respect to their dealings with whites, African Americans, or other Latinos? These vital questions not only provide a break from the confining black-white framework of contemporary race relations, but they also interrogate different ways of being Latino. Latino and Mexican identities are multivalent, and an exploration of the uniqueness and particularities of these identities is essential if the South is to truly understand its newest residents.

## ORIGINS: BEING BLACK IN
## SOUTHERN MEXICO

For at least three hundred years, Mexico's southern Costa Chica region has held one of the highest concentrations of Afro-Mexicans. These blacks descend from African slaves who were transported by the Spanish as part of a slave trade that was most active from the 1580s to the 1640s. The historical record suggests that the slaves were initially used as laborers in the busy port of Acapulco, as well as in colonial cattle enterprises in the more rural regions.[19] By the twentieth century, although *mestizaje* started to slowly influence the region, published accounts continued to highlight the Costa Chica's blackness. Oral histories taken amongst elders in the Costa Chica's towns confirm these perceptions.[20]

Most Costa Chica towns are commonly categorized by locals as either *pueblos negros* (black townships), *pueblos indios* (Indian townships), and *pueblos mestizos* (mestizo townships). These lines are clearly drawn in the minds of local people of all colors, notwithstanding the national myth of Mexico being a mestizo nation in which racial distinctions are meaningless.[21]

It was not until 1966 that the Pacific Coast highway succeeded in bringing the Costa Chica's towns and villages into much closer communication with Acapulco, the principal metropolitan center of the southern coast.[22] The highway ushered in the arrival of large numbers of outsiders and their families who, in contrast to the old entrenched landed elite, were more inclined to raise their families alongside the locals, intermarry with them, and integrate themselves into rural communities, albeit in a more privileged class position. This post-1960s and 1970s migration precipitated a profound *mestizaje* that has only intensified over the past decade. As the Costa Chica's Afro-Mexican population experiences increased racial mixture and marital exogamy, the members of their population who migrate to North Carolina will likely exhibit fewer phenotypic markers that are commonly interpreted as black in the United States. Clearly, this is not to say that one must exhibit certain phenotypic characteristics in order to *be* black; that involves a complex process of identity construction that we do not purport to predict. It is important, nonetheless, to entertain the possibility that as Afro-Mexican transmigration ensues, an increased *mestizaje* in Mexico—in addition to other social, cultural, and economic forces—may play an important role in the *costeños'* experience with racial formation in the United States.

## BEING BLACK TOGETHER: AFRO-AMERICAN
## AND AFRO-MEXICAN RELATIONS

The onerous INS and border patrol presence in California has served as one of the principal motivating factors for shifting previous Costa Chica

**Figure 10.1.  Costa Chica convenience store on East Sprague Street in Winston-Salem. Photographed by Bobby Vaughn**

migrant flows to southeastern portions of the United States. Undocumented Afro-Mexicans who lived in California prior to arriving in North Carolina reported that their blackness was of particular value out West, where they were more preoccupied with evading the authorities: "[In California] we could walk around a little more comfortably [than other Mexicans] because the *migra* would think that we are African Americans and not look twice at us."[23] The notion that Afro-Mexicans are better able blend into the U.S. population than their mestizo counterparts can also be found in New York City, where Afro-Mexicans are frequently mistaken for Puerto Ricans, Dominicans, or other Afro-Caribbean ethnicities that do not raise much suspicion.[24] But in North Carolina, the advantage of passing as African American or Puerto Rican seems muted, since Mexican immigrants on the whole are far less fearful of the *migra* than they are in California. This is despite the possibility that over half of North Carolina's Latino population is undocumented.[25]

Overall, the Latino population of Forsyth County, where Winston-Salem is located, represents one of the most dynamic and growing demographic sectors within the state. Official estimates from the 2000 census placed their numbers at 16,043, or roughly 8.6 percent of the county's total population of over 185,000. Mexicans comprised the majority, numbering 11,908 individuals, representing just under three-quarters of the Latino group.[26] While the number of African Americans substantially outnumbered Latinos (68,924 individuals, or 37.1 percent of the county's population), it seems fair to say that the Mexican component of the area's population was certainly significant and has definitely grown. Current unofficial estimates, including undocumented workers, place the population of Latinos at 30,000 individuals, of which Mexicans are the vast majority, and Afro-Mexicans from the Costa Chica number perhaps as many as 80 percent within that group.[27]

According to local residents, one of the first Afro-Mexicans from the Costa Chica to migrate to Winston-Salem was Biterbo Calleja-Garcia, who in 1978 crossed the border illegally to work in Texas. He was persuaded by a local coyote (a guide who assists undocumented workers) to seek employment in North Carolina, where he would earn more money. The move was a success. Shortly after arriving, he began earning $3.35 an hour cultivating seventeen acres of tobacco. His two sisters eventually joined him, and the family lived in a trailer on a tobacco farm, working grueling days from 7 a.m. until 10 p.m. Calleja-Garcia opted not to live in the United States permanently, deciding to return to Mexico during the off-season. However, his initial trip proved so successful that he returned to the same employer on an annual basis. He also spread the word of economic opportunities in North Carolina among friends and family living in the Costa Chica town of Cuajiniquilapa, as well as other friends and relatives working in California. After ten years, he became a documented worker and stopped returning to Mexico. But a lasting connection had been made. Others from the Costa Chica's towns followed his lead, fanning out throughout the greater Winston-Salem area. Calleja-Garcia himself changed his line of work, becoming a construction worker and earning up to $6.00 an hour, enabling him to move into a two-bedroom home in Waughtown.[28] While it is hard to verify if Calleja-Garcia was indeed the first Afro-Mexican in Winston-Salem, he certainly represents one of the earliest waves of immigrants, and his singular influence in paving the way for other *costeños'* migration is significant.

The personal stories of a significant number of Afro-Mexicans in Winston-Salem are similar to Calleja-Garcia's. This is to say that a significant proportion of the population consists of first-generation immigrants (some with temporary work visas) who have come seeking work in low-paying hourly wage-earning positions, particularly in the area's factories, restaurants, and bakeries. Among the industries in the area that attract labor are cigarette and T-shirt packaging factories, window frame assembly plants, and swimming pool drainage complexes.[29] Wages hover at around $6.25 an hour. A number of immigrants have been able to successfully utilize the growing Mexican demographic to their advantage. As the *costeños* solidify their presence in Winston-Salem, they have come to constitute a recognizable subcommunity among the Latino population, complete with their own identities, tastes, customs, and habits. To cater to these tastes, a number of enterprising *costeños* have opened small businesses and restaurants, where they hire others from their region. Many of these stores have names that reflect the identity of the people—such as the Costa Chica convenience store on East Sprague Street. Frequently, *costeños* prefer doing business in these settings, where they feel they are better understood both in terms of language (including local regionalisms in the Costa Chica's vernacular) as well as shared experiences. Beyond supplying merchandise, such stores can be a source of information exchange and a place to enact, forge, and cement social relationships.

It is not uncommon to find African Americans and Afro-Mexicans shopping together in a number of community stores. The interactions can range from relative indifference to polite exchanges by neighbors—some of whom are struggling with Spanish, and others who are in the process of mastering English. Generally speaking, however, the differences in everyday life experiences, buttressed by cultural and historical differences, have thus far prevented a socially viable solidarity between Afro-Mexicans and African Americans. On the other hand, while evidence of friction between African Americans and Latinos, such as gang violence and robberies targeting Latino communities, exists elsewhere in North Carolina,[30] in Winston-Salem these episodes have either been less pronounced or reported with less frequency.[31] One partial explanation for this is that settlement patterns here have tended to segregate the Latino community, keeping them at arm's length from many potentially hostile interactions.[32] While further work is needed to confirm these tentative observations, it appears that as Mexicans began arriving to Waughtown and other parts of East Winston-Salem, African Americans moved north and west to preexisting black communities. Fewer Mexicans moved to the more symbolically significant downtown areas, as opposed to other North Carolina cities, but settled in Waughtown and revitalized the area with new economic activity.[33]

African Americans interviewed during our field study in Winston-Salem expressed a range of views regarding the new Mexican immigration:

"They're taking over." African American male, teenager

"A lot of them speak English but act like they can't." African American male, thirties

"I can't blame them for doing what they have to do for their families." African American male, twenties

"They play their music too loud all night long." African American female, forties

"I don't really know any of them well, but they don't bother me." African American male, twenties

None of the African Americans with whom we spoke was aware that perhaps a majority of the Mexicans in Winston-Salem are of African descent. Typical of some of their responses is "I never really thought about it, but yeah, some of them are pretty dark. I had no idea." African Americans recognized *costeños* simply as Hispanics or Mexicans, and it is their economic impact on specific neighborhoods that figures much more prominently to African American perceptions than their blackness. For instance, a strip mall known as King's Plaza in Waughtown once housed a number of African American–owned businesses. One of the few still remaining is a black beauty-supply store. A young African American employee confirmed that a kind of "black flight" is taking shape in Waughtown, similar to the white flight that happened in East Winston-Salem when blacks moved there from the downtown tobacco factory areas during the 1940s:[34]

> Seems like [the] more they move into the area, the more we [blacks] move somewhere else. I don't really know why we move away [laughs]. I guess we just want to go where there are more black people. I've noticed that in the last year, as more Hispanics moved into the area, fewer black people come into the store, and they [the Hispanics] don't really buy what we sell here. And I tell you one thing, whenever a store goes out of business around here they buy it and open up a store for themselves. To be honest, I'll be surprised if we last more than a year here. We have to go where we can get more black customers.

This conversation exemplifies a kind of ambivalence expressed by many blacks in Winston-Salem. There is recognition that Waughtown is becoming increasingly Latino, but there has not been the kind of concern, much less, panic, that one might expect. A kind of resignation seems to have set in, and blacks appear to have no shortage of attractive predominantly black neighborhoods to which to relocate as alternatives to Waughtown.

The tendency for African Americans to move to other neighborhoods is not lost on the newly arriving *costeños*. In the Lakeside Apartment complex, a former middle-class neighborhood from the 1950s that has since become the site of numerous housing code violations, Ricardo, a young man originally from San Nicolás, was explicit in saying, "Yeah, when we moved here 2 years ago our next-door neighbors were black, and a few houses across the street were African American [too]. I don't know why they left, we got along pretty well, I thought."[35] As for where the African Americans might have gone, "I have no idea [laughs]! I guess they went wherever there aren't a lot of us; I don't know."

Whereas the Lakeside Apartment complex represents a middle-class neighborhood that has experienced an Afro-Mexican transformation, over the past several years a number of lower-class developments have also been significantly reconstituted. For instance, Columbia Terrace, constructed around 1950 as the city's first low-income housing project, was primarily occupied by blacks. But in the 1990s, dramatic increases in Latinos have brought about a situation whereby today nearly half of the units are occupied by *costeños,* and the other half by African Americans.[36]

Despite some recent complaints of discrimination reported by both African Americans and Mexicans to the city's human relations department,[37] none of our informants reported any open hostility between Afro-Mexicans and African Americans. Some *costeños* with whom we spoke expressed indifference when it came to African Americans. Apparently, part of the distance separating the two groups stems from the fact that many of the current *costeños* are undocumented, and all "Americans," black or otherwise (including some fellow Latinos), must be treated with suspicion until their true intentions are learned. Yet, even after getting closer and overcoming initial mistrust, certain levels of indifference can remain. José, from Cuajinicuilapa said, "I don't think about them [African Americans] very much. There are a few on my job and we get along fine. We don't really talk too much, though, you know . . . since I don't speak very much English. But they don't bother me, and I'm not out looking for trouble."

Refrains such as "they don't bother me and I don't bother them" and "I've never had any problems with them," in addition to being a common way to express that relations are satisfactory, may reveal something more. Responses that highlight the absence of conflict as a primary characterization of interpersonal and intergroup relations do not explicitly entertain the possibility of overtly positive, fraternal, or harmonious relationships. Solidarity with the African American community does not appear to emerge as a desire among most of the *costeños* with whom we spoke.

If a greater sense of the African diaspora and interethnic solidarity is to arise between *costeños* and African Americans, we might look to the younger generations for possibilities. Most of the examples we encountered of positive intergroup relations were developed informally, usually between young coworkers. The casual friendship that arose between Octavia and Martín (*costeños*) and two African American coworkers is illustrative of this rather coincidental and unintentional cross-cultural experience.

Octavia and Martín are a young couple in their midtwenties who have been living in the Lakeside neighborhood for five years and who describe themselves as *moreno* (black). While they did not have any African American neighbors, they did meet two African Americans from their job. Martín and Octavia spoke with us on their front porch in the early evening, and Martín recounted meeting their friends:

> We have two black [*afroamericanos*] friends that we met at work . . . they are good people. We just got to know each other at work . . . one is a man and the other is a woman. The woman speaks some Spanish so it's easy to talk to her, but the man doesn't, so we do the best we can! [laughs]. But they're good peo-

ple. They haven't come here to visit us, but we have gone over to their house a few times. . . . No, we haven't had, you know, too many black friends, but the couple from work, we like them and we have a good time with them.

Encounters such as these typified the kinds of interactions we discovered in the Winston-Salem Latino community—*costeños* who made acquaintances with African Americans without expressing any particular ethnic bond, shared heritage, or affinity. Indeed, when stepping back and looking at the broader literature on African American relations with other black immigrants, such as people from the Caribbean and Africa, we find that social interactions between the groups range widely, from intimate and supportive to tense and hostile. A number of studies suggest that any attempts to make broad generalizations or presumptions about black solidarity should be approached with care.[38]

Nevertheless, taking this into account, there were a few moments in our conversations with Afro-Mexicans when people articulated an awareness of a unity—or at least a potential unity—with African Americans. Marta, a *costeño* from Cuajinicuilapa, immediately invoked ideas of a shared heritage when we spoke with her and her husband in the corner store they own in the Waughtown neighborhood. She bemoans the lack of solidarity between the two groups: "In Mexico, we try to come together as black people and here nobody even realizes that we come from the same roots. I think that if the African Americans knew about our common history we would get along better. In Mexico we are just starting to learn about our history, but here the African Americans know their history; that's their advantage." Marta is well aware of the emerging México Negro organization in the Costa Chica—a grassroots movement that has, since 1997, attempted to engage in social action at the local level through an explicit examination and celebration of Afro-Mexican ethnic identity.[39] She suggests the prospect of mutual support: "Since they speak English, they could help us by teaching us, and we could help them by teaching them Spanish, right? I think that would be a good thing because we are all struggling and maybe that way we could both move forward [*seguir adelante*]. . . . We could at least talk to one another more!" Marta is not satisfied with the "they don't bother me" attitude that seems to characterize *costeño*-African American relations. She would like to see a much more deliberate effort to engage with African Americans. Marta realizes that hers is not the prevailing view among her *paisanos* (countrymen) and attributes this to education, explaining, "Most of us don't have much education, and we're poor and ignorant of these things."

In addition to this lack of education in Mexico about the African origins of *costeños*, a black identity has typically been downplayed among blacks and has not typically served as a source of pride. Those Afro-Mexicans, like

Marta, who have bucked the trend and have sought to embrace blackness are more often educated and professional. Social and economic conditions in the rural Costa Chica constrain the formation of a significant educated and professional class; this may help account for the uniqueness of Marta's kind of ethnic consciousness among *costeños*.

The following example involving a *costeño*'s embrace of African Americans exemplifies neither the happenstance friendship of Octavia and Martín, nor Marta's politicized desire for solidarity. Rather, it represents an Afro-Mexican encounter with African Americans that springs from commonalities of interest in popular culture, particularly hip-hop culture. Seventeen-year-old Cipriano, a *costeño* from Punta Maldonado, arrived to Winston-Salem two years ago. The tattooed young man, who admittedly struggles with English, was immediately drawn to African Americans and made friends quickly, some of them in the apartment complex where he lived. The blacks whom he met were his age, and he even dated a young African American woman for awhile. In explaining why so few *costeños* seem to hang out with African Americans, he explained, "A lot of people [Mexicans] are scared of blacks and are suspicious of them but I never was. I always liked their music, you know, like Eminem and 50 Cent. . . . Sometimes people see that I like hanging out with them, and they ask me if I know them, if they are friends of mine, and if I'm not getting into trouble [laughs]!"

Cipriano confessed a certain attraction to hip-hop culture even before arriving in the United States. In Mexico, he remembers watching dubbed movies on broadcast Mexican television—movies that depicted rap music, street gangs, and a hip and rebellious vision of black culture. He and his friends, who made up a kind of counterculture within his rural Mexican town, were drawn to those images:

> So when I got here, I was like, I want to hang out with bad-ass people [laughs] . . . you know, not really violent people, but I like that style. . . . You see how I wear my pants [baggy and low] and stuff. I feel more comfortable with African Americans, and when my English gets better it will be easier for me. . . . Of course, I hang out with people from my town [Punta Maldonado] most of the time but would like to have more African American friends because I seem to click with them.

Cipriano, like other young *costeños*, was initially drawn to the hip-hop youth culture while in Mexico, where he was exposed to images from United States television and movies. However, Cipriano was one of the few *costeños* we met who, in addition to embracing the symbols of African American youth culture, has made concrete efforts to engage with black people.

Cirpriano's father offered his assessment of the situation: "The thing is," the dark-skinned Afro-Mexican interjected, "the blacks [*negros*] think that we want to run them out of this area—that we want their jobs or something, but really, how are we going to take away their jobs when we don't even speak English?" He continued, "Where I work [a municipal sanitation plant], it's just Mexicans there because it's low-paying. I don't think you all [African Americans] want to work there for minimum wage [laughs]!"

The extent of such competition (or lack thereof) in the labor market between Latinos and African Americans deserves further study. A Latina correspondent for Winston-Salem's local Spanish-language newspaper explained that, based on her several years of working in the city, she believes that "in reality, there isn't a serious problem between the two communities, except that there is the belief among African Americans that the Mexican workers are taking away jobs."[40] She added, however, that there is no economic data of which she is aware that would support that perception. Cipriano's father's perception is certainly one of some tension, arising from misunderstandings about the role of Mexicans in the local labor force. The ways that both communities understood such perceptions suggest important questions for further ethnographic research. How, for example, might any Latino competition for jobs manifest itself to African Americans, and furthermore, how and in what contexts might feelings of uneasiness among African Americans be communicated to Latinos? The ways and extent to which these communities communicate with one another deserves detailed study.

Further research must also look to the varied experiences of Afro-Mexican youth in schools. Issues of racial identification are likely to affect Afro-Mexican youth in ways that differ from the impact felt by their parents. Such impacts are likely to correlate to whether they were born in the United States, at what age they emigrated to the United States, and their English proficiency. Deeper research in North Carolina might further illuminate the concerns and experiences of a teenage girl from Cuajinicuilapa who has lived in Chicago since age four.

> I also want to learn more in detail about my background. My mother has told me very little, but I want to find my real identity. All these years I've been mistaken for Cuban and never viewed as a Mexican. When I start speaking Spanish people are surprised I speak it very fluently. My sister and I feel sometimes out of place everywhere we go because barely nobody has the same cultural background. We feel very awkward in a group of all Mexicans, like in parties or Mexican stores. They look at us with ignorance, or I don't know how to explain it.[41]

Ethnographic research in North Carolina and other centers of Afro-Mexican migration can begin to allow this young lady, known to us as *soydecuaji* (I am from Cuaji), to better understand her heritage and make sense of it in the context of a Mexican immigrant experience in which issues of Mexican blackness are usually left out of the prevailing discourses. Such research must necessarily be placed into the broader political, economic, and cultural contexts that shape the relationship between the United States and Mexico. The racial and national controversy surrounding Mexico's 2005 release of the commemorative stamps celebrating the black comic character Memín Penguin points to the need for this contextualization and the challenges to diasporic consciousness.

## CHANGING RACIAL DEBATES AND TRANSNATIONAL BLACKNESS

In July 2005, Memín Penguin, a black Mexican comic book character who resembles Curious George, or even a little black sambo, was celebrated with a postage stamp in his honor. The stamp was well received by many sectors of the Mexican public, for whom he represented a fond image of childhood. But the stamp's image offended African Americans in the United States and a wide segment of the international community, since it smacked of discrimination. The stamp's release came only months after Mexican president Vicente Fox made disturbing public remarks that Mexican immigrants to the United States take jobs "that not even blacks want to do."[42] The public attention that both episodes garnered on each side of the border reveals interesting new dimensions of the ongoing shifting saga of race relations. For the first time, within the context of high-level forums, Mexican images of blackness were pitted against those of African Americans.

The ideas and actions behind the discourse and debate signal important differences and dynamics. On one hand, President Fox said what was perhaps on the minds of many Mexicans, immigrants and nonimmigrants alike. From his point of view, blackness served as a form of class marker. By invoking the notion that all Mexican immigrants "occupied" a space that, within the structure of the United States's hierarchical system of social relations, was traditionally held by blacks, Fox situated Mexican immigrants at the lowest rung of the social ladder. However, in perceiving race as being analogous to class, Fox made an error—essentially miscalculating the trajectory of race relations in the United States. One reason why African Americans demanded an apology and were offended by his remarks was because the civil rights movement and subsequent gains for equality have marked significant strides in helping blacks move beyond the freeze-frame lower-class stereotypes held by invocations of blackness. Jesse Jackson and Al Sharpton traveled to Mexico to help bring the leader up to speed on African American progress and diversity. Unknowingly, Fox had turned back the clock on African American history with his remarks, even though he was trying to make a comment about the plight of Hispanics.

Fox stalled before issuing an apology. Part of the delay may have come from political posturing. The Mexican leader did not want to appear malleable to U.S. whims. On the other hand, the delay may have been due to the sincere belief that his remarks were innocent, with little wide-reaching effect. The stalling did not play out well in the Mexican press, and numerous headlines and political cartoons were released on the issue.[43] As events continued to unfold, the debates about Fox's comments sparked an internal national conversation about race in Mexico that called into question the nation's race credentials. One of the premises of *mestizaje* asserts that because racial mixture is an inherent feature of national life, those who live within "racial democracies" such as Mexico are usually vigilant against racism.[44] Fox seemingly broke the principles of this idea with his comments. Opportunists critical of Fox's leadership took the incident as a chance to expose his shortcomings of leadership, even to the point of labeling him a racist both against blacks and the very Mexican immigrants he was trying to defend.[45] But there were others, less fettered by the political jockeying, who probed for deeper meaning from the event. In fact, on the airwaves and in the newspapers, a public space was opened to critically examine Mexico's own blackness. A few articles appeared on Afro-Mexicans living in the Costa Chica, as well as essays reflecting on why Mexico has been so reluctant to acknowledge its own African heritage.[46] Recent struggles by politicians to obtain communal rights for Afro-Mexicans (based on claims to ethnic status) were also featured in the press, particularly the activities of Ángel Heladio Aguirre Rivero, the ex-governor of the state of Guerrero (1996–1999).[47]

In many ways, numerous aspects of the rich discussions were short lived. With the issuance of the commemorative Memín Penguin stamp, negative U.S. responses toward the comic book image inspired some Mexicans to revert to defensive attitudes and posturing with respect to their outlook on race. According to several commentators, academics, and observers, particularly within Mexico City, the caricature should not have been understood as a racialized figure, but as a cultural emblem.[48] Created in the 1940s by Yolanda Vargas, the comic book proved instrumental in midcentury literacy campaigns. Thematically, it was a risk taker, addressing subjects such as interracial family dynamics and class disparity, but always from a humorous perspective (at least in the eyes of some Mexicans). It quickly became a success, running new story lines into the early 1970s.[49] Although repeat issues with freshly designed cover art can still be found on the streets of Mexico today, large numbers of Mexicans fondly remember Memín as an image of their childhood. On this score, shortly after the stamp was released, many pleaded for the United States to consider the broader context of the image and its production, as well as its story lines, rather than simply rushing to interpret and chastise Memín's physical features.[50] Several advisors and ministers close to President Fox conceived that it might be wise to invite Jesse Jackson and Al Sharpton down to Mexico for another visit, this time so that *they* might be able to bring these civil rights leaders up to speed on the nuances of racial sensitivities. Memín had come to demonstrate what many Mexicans had always feared about the influence of ideas from the north—a desire to overanalyze the role of race in society.

A number of critical themes can be detected in the subtext of the Memín episode and Vicente Fox's comments. First, Mexican historian Miguel Leon-Portilla has wondered why the media and others were intentionally exacerbating the relationship between African Americans and Mexicans. The question is an excellent one, with significant cross-border implications. As our research in North Carolina has demonstrated, the relationships between African Americans and Mexicans can sometimes be marked by suspicion and tension, although in Winston-Salem this was less of a factor. The high profile given to the "racist" tendencies of Fox, and the history of discriminatory caricature that the Memín image invoked, has arguably not smoothed over these relations. Secondly, both episodes call attention to the new landscape of cultural politics emerging in the United States. As Mexicans continue to increase their demographic presence, there may be more incidents like the one caused by the Memín stamp. Mexicans coming to the United States may bring with them different attitudes toward race and blackness that may not meld with ours. Theirs is a different racial history. Meanwhile, the United States will insist upon conformity to a multicultural sensitivity that may seem strange to Mexicans. This insistence upon conformity tends to permeate politics within Mexico. Interestingly, the change in political regimes in Mexico, from the PRI (which held presidential power continuously from the 1920s until 2000) to the PAN, has provided a historical break in Mexican political culture, and quite possibly an opportunity to facilitate wide changes in racial thinking. And as witnessed in 2005, Mexican politicians played the race card against Fox.

Will this translate into a new form of multicultural politics, one that evaluates a politician's success on his/her ability to maneuver successfully within the international scene of racial diplomacy?

One of the underpublicized key issues regarding the Memín/Fox episode is how it unfolded in the Costa Chica, and to what extent it has influenced Afro-Mexican perceptions of blackness. Arguably, the results of the Memín/Fox affair had the greatest impact symbolically—gesturing toward ideas of blackness rather than affecting the reality of lived conditions. While Memín's image and Fox's words certainly had real transnational effects in political circles (and in shaping attitudes among African Americans toward

Mexicans), at the same time their impact may have rung hollow in the everyday experiences of Afro-Mexican immigrants and their families in Mexico.

Indeed, in the Costa Chica during the summer of 2005, Fox's comments and the Memín controversy received little attention and were not being widely discussed. Carlos, a self-described *moreno*, for example, didn't feel personally offended by the image but could see how blacks in the United States might not like it since, as he saw it, the character is supposed to be a depiction of an African American (*un negro de allá*), and not a Mexican![51]

Afro-Mexican activists in the region, however, responded much more strongly and condemned the Memín stamp project. Representatives from México Negro called for the withdrawal of the stamp and published an open letter to the president. These black leaders see the Memín controversy as a kind of blind spot in Mexico, and one leader with whom we spoke informally mentioned that it probably never occurred to the government to ask any Afro-Mexican leaders what they thought before they introduced the stamp.[52] These dissenting voices among Afro-Mexican leaders contrasted markedly with examples of a rallying around Memín as a symbol of nationalist pride. As we drove through Mexico City, we'd glimpse a large billboard prominently situated along a major freeway. The sign featured the image of Memín, along with the words "Are you talking about me?" and "100% Mexicano." In addition, the noted Mexican historian Enrique Krauze, in a *Washington Post* column, appears to count himself among those Mexicans who see Memín not as racist, but as "a highly pleasing image rooted in Mexican popular culture."[53]

While the micro-events of race play themselves out transnationally in places such as Winston-Salem and the Costa Chica, and elsewhere in the United States and Mexico, at the same time there are macro-level changes and shifts in racial discourse that are equally transnational, and that are in a constant state of reinvention. While it is still too early to tell where these processes are headed, we can certainly surmise that the changes they bring about will have an impact on racial formation processes on both sides of the border. In the United States, blackness as a category seems poised to become stretched—inclusively bearing within it the histories and experiences of blacks throughout the greater diaspora. To some degree, this process seems inevitable, given the current flow of migrant streams. But as the Winston-Salem case suggests, if diasporic blackness is to configure into the conceptualizations of blackness in the United States, a certain amount of racial consciousness is needed from the immigrants themselves, which must then be recognized by African Americans. Specifically in the case of Afro-Mexicans, this is precisely where the power of macro-level racial discourses may prove to be a contributing factor. The Memín/Fox episodes, despite being as sinuous, complex, and problematic as they were, at the very least sensitized broad sectors of the population on both sides of the border to Mexican blackness and Mexican debates on blackness. In this fashion, the episodes may have set the stage for a possible convergence of racial histories.

Preliminary field research suggests that in Winston-Salem the Afro-Mexican heritage of new immigrants plays less of a role in their everyday lives, as contrasted with both contemporary *costeño* experiences in the Costa Chica and with historical Afro-Mexican experiences. Mexican *negros* and *morenos* become Hispanic in North Carolina, where they find that the African American experience monopolizes discussions of blackness. Indeed, it is quite possible that in the context of the New South, alternate forms of blackness, particularly forms of diasporic blackness that originate outside the United States, may be largely silenced under the weight of the legacy created by the history of African Americans in the region. But for Afro-Mexicans living in North Carolina, there is still more to the story. Patterns of increased *mestizaje* in Mexico have lessened the likelihood that *costeños* will tend to identify themselves based on physical markers, and it has made it more difficult for African Americans to even recognize Mexican blackness. Perhaps more important, however, are the significantly dissimilar life and class experiences that differentiate between the newly arrived, non-English-speaking, and often undocumented Mexican population, as opposed to the black sons and daughters of the American South. It remains to be seen how the two communities might come together in the future. While solidarity between blacks and Latinos can arise from shared social and economic interests,[54] in the case of Winston-Salem, perhaps the unique history of the *costeños* will serve as points of reflection for both communities who represent an ever-complex African diaspora.

## NOTES

The authors would like to thank the Black Diaspora Consortium at the University of Texas at Austin for support for a Rockefeller Center Grant for the Study of Diasporic Racisms. The authors would like to acknowledge support from the Institute of Latin American Studies at the University of North Carolina at Chapel Hill and the National Humanities Center, as well as the Africana Research Center at Pennsylvania State University. Furthermore, the encouragement of Edmund T. Gordon, William Darity Jr., and Althea Cravey was indispensable to this project.

1. See the entire issue of *Latino Studies* 1, no. 1 (2003).

2. U.S. Census Bureau Census 2000, summary file 1.

3. U.S. Census Bureau Census 2000, summary file 1.

4. El Pueblo, *2005 NC Latino Legislative Agenda* (Raleigh, NC: 2005); U.S. Census Bureau, "Table 4-1A, Nativity and Parentage of the Population for Regions, Divisions, and States: 2000," 2000 Current Population Survey.

5. U.S. Census Bureau, American Community Survey, 2002.

6. W. H. Frey, "Immigration and Internal Migration 'Flight' from US Metropolitan Areas: Toward a New Demographic Balkanization," *Urban Studies* 32 (1995): 733–57; U.S. Census Bureau, *North Carolina Fact Sheet 2000*, www.factfinder .census.gov.

7. For material on fighting for autonomy under slavery, see Herman L. Bennett, *Africans in Colonial Mexico Absolutism, Christianity, and Afro-Creole Consciousness, 1570–1640* (Bloomington: Indiana University Press, 2003); Javier Villa-Flores, " 'To Lose One's Soul': Blasphemy and Slavery in New Spain, 1596–1669," *Hispanic American Historical Review* 82, no. 3 (2002): 435–69; and Frank Proctor III, "Slavery, Identity, and Culture: An Afro-Mexican Counterpoint, 1640–1763" (PhD diss., Emory University, 2003). For information on dealing with liberty under the caste system, see R. Douglas Cope, *The Limits of Racial Domination: Plebeian Society in Colonial Mexico City, 1660–1720* (Madison: University of Wisconsin Press, 1994); Ben Vinson III, *Bearing Arms for His Majesty: The Free-Colored Militia in Colonial Mexico* (Stanford, CA: Stanford University Press, 2001); Nicole von Germeten, "Corporate Salvation in a Colonial Society: Confraternities and Social Mobility for Africans and Their Descendants in New Spain" (PhD diss., University of California, Berkeley, 2003); and Laura A. Lewis, *Hall of Mirrors: Power, Witchcraft and Caste in Colonial Mexico* (Durham, NC: Duke University Press, 2003).

8. For information on blacks participating in the wars of independence and in early national politics see Theodore G. Vincent, *The Legacy of Vicente Guerrero: Mexico's First Black Indian President* (Gainesville: University Press of Florida, 2001).

9. Kenneth Porter, "The Seminole in Mexico, 1850–1861," *Hispanic American Historical Review* 31, no. 1 (February 1952): 1–36.

10. Vinson, *Flight: The Story of Virgil Richardson, a Tuskegee Airman in Mexico* (New York: Palgrave Macmillan, 2004), 142–56.

11. See Winthorp R. Wright, *Café con Leche: Race, Class, and National Image in Venezuela* (Austin: University of Texas Press, 1990).

12. Alfonso Toro, "Influencia de la raza negra en la formación del pueblo mexicano," *Ethnos: Revista para la vulgarización de Estudios Antropológicos sobre México y Centro América* 1, no. 8–12 (1920–1921): 215–18.

13. José Vasconcelos, *La Raza cósmica: Misión de la raza iberoamericana* (Barcelona, Spain: Agencia Mundial de Librería, 1958)

14. Gonzalo Aguirre Beltrán, *La Población negra de México: Estudio etnohistórico*, 3rd ed. (Mexico City, Mexico: Fondo de Cultura Económica, 1989); Carlos Basauri, *Breves notas etnográficas sobre la población negra del Distrito de Jamiltepec, Oaxaca* (Mexico City, Mexico: Primer Congreso Demográfico Interamericano, 1943); Gabriel Saldívar, "La Influencia africana," in *Historia de la música en México* (Mexico City, Mexico: SEP, 1934), 219–29; Joaquín Roncal, "The Negro Race in Mexico," *Hispanic American Historical Review* 14, no. 3 (1944): 530–40; Nicolás Léon, *Las Castas del México colonial o Nueva España* (Mexico City, Mexico: Talleres Gráficos del Mueso Nacional de Arqueologiía, Historia y Etnografía, 1924).

15. Even the work of Aguirre Beltrán facilitated this process. Still, some of his research did much to call attention to contemporary Afro-Mexican populations. For some examples, see Aguirre Beltrán, *Cuijla, esbozo etnográfico de un pueblo negro*, 2nd

ed. (Mexico City, Mexico: Fondo de Cultura Económica, 1989), and Aguirre Beltrán, "La Población negra de Guerrero," *Novedades*, February 13, 1949.

16. Carleton Beals, "Valerio Trujano: Black Joy," *Crisis*, May 1931: 153–54, 174.

17. "Valerio Trujano: All-Negro Village Discovered in Mexico," *Ebony*, April 1957: 91–94.

18. In Mexico, the official census only identifies ethnically those people who speak an indigenous language. We estimate the self-identified Afro-Mexican population of that coastal region to be between 30,000 to 60,000.

19. Joan Cameron Bristol, "Negotiating Authority in New Spain: Blacks, Mulattos, and Religious Practice in Seventeenth Century Mexico" (PhD diss., University of Pennsylvania, 2001).

20. Basauri, *Breves notas etnográficas*; Roberto Cervantes-Delgado, "La Costa Chica: Indios, negros y mestizos," in *Estratificación étnica y relaciones interétinicas*, ed. M. Nolasco Armas (Mexico City, Mexico: Instituto Nacional de Antropología e Historia, 1984), 37–50; Manuel Martínez Gracida, "Estudio de la raza negra o africana en Oaxaca," in *Reseña histórica del antiguo reino de Tutupec* (n.p.: 1907).

21. Critical analyses of *mestizaje* as a powerful nationalist construction can be found in Agustín Basave Benítez, *México mestizo: Análisis del nacionalismo en torno a la mestizofilia de Andrés Molina Enríquez* (Mexico City, Mexico: Fondo de Cultura Económica, 1992); Florencia E. Mallon, "Constructing Mestizaje in Latin America: Authenticity, Marginality, and Gender in the Claiming of Ethnic Identities," *Journal of Latin American Anthropology* 2, no. 1 (1996): 170–81; and Bobby Vaughn, "Race and Nation: A Study of Blackness in Mexico" (PhD diss., Stanford University, 2001).

22. Laurentino Luna, "La Reforma agraria en Cuajinicuilapa, Guerrero: Microhistoria de una pobalción Guerrerense" (BA thesis, Universidad Nacional Autónoma de México, 1975).

23. The ethnographic research and interviews result from a ten-day period of fieldwork in and around Winston-Salem.

24. Interview with Margarita, a *costeño* in the Collantes, Oaxaca, who had recently returned from New York, July 2000.

25. Amy Frazier and Sherry Wilson, "Killers Slip behind Curtain of Silence; Crimes against Hispanics Tough for Investigators; Some Advocates Link Ethnicity to Low Arrest Rate," *Winston-Salem Journal*, February 24, 2002.

26. This information, derived from Census 2000, can be found at www.winston-salem.areaconnect.com/statistics.htm.

27. Lisa Hoppenjans and Ted Richardson, "Mexican Ways, African Roots; Most of City's Hispanic Residents Are Natives of a Region Populated by Descendants of Black Slaves," *Winston-Salem Journal*, June 19, 2005.

28. This story is recounted by Hoppenjans and Richardson in "Mexican Ways, African Roots."

29. Hoppenjans and Richardson, "Mexican Ways, African Roots."

30. Ben Stocking, "Worlds Apart," *Raleigh News and Observer*, May 4, 1997; Oren Dorell, "Latino Gang Activity Surges," *Raleigh News and Observer*, August 24, 2003.

31. Frazier and Wilson, "Killers Slip behind Curtain of Silence."

32. For a comparative look at black-brown relations in Raleigh, see Cindy George, "Moving toward Understanding," *Raleigh News and Observer*, January 23, 2004.

33. "Latin Music Fills the Air as Patrons Dance the Night Away at a Flashy New Club in City's 'Little Mexico,'" *Winston-Salem Journal*, July 7, 2002; Fran Daniel, "A True Variety Store; New Market Offers Customers a World of Choice," *Winston-Salem Journal*, December 18, 2000; Fran Daniel, "King's Full House; King Plaza Shopping Center Is Getting Three New Tenants," *Winston-Salem Journal*, October 12, 2001; "A New Language; Producers, Retailers Turning Attention to Buying Power of Hispanics," *Winston-Salem Journal*, April 28, 2002; Mike Davis, *Magical Urbanism: Latinos Reinvent the US City* (London: Verso, 2000).

34. "Where? Eastern Part of Town Isn't Definable," *Winston-Salem Journal*, August 6, 2002.

35. Carey Hamilton, "Where Home Is No Haven; Sprawling Lakeside Apartment Complex, a Portrait of Housing Decline," *Winston-Salem Journal*, August 18, 2002; and "Once Lakeside Was a Nice Place to Live," *Winston-Salem Journal*, August 31, 2002.

36. Hoppenjans and Richardson, "Mexican Ways, African Roots."

37. Hoppenjans and Richardson, "Mexican Ways, African Roots."

38. Ongoing conflicts between African Americans and African immigrants in New York City are reported in Jennifer Cunningham, "Tensions between Africans and African Americans Surface Again," *New York Amsterdam News*, February 3, 2005. Historical solidarity between African Americans and Anglophone Caribbean immigrants is highlighted in Irma Watkins-Owens, *Blood Relations: Caribbean Immigrants and the Harlem Community, 1900–1930* (Bloomington: Indiana University Press, 1996), and similar historical evidence of congenial interactions African Americans have enjoyed with Afro-Cubans is offered in Susan D. Greenbaum, *More than Black: Afro-Cubans in Tampa* (Gainesville: University Press of Florida). Additional ethnographic research on African Americans and other black immigrant groups can be found in Mary Cothan, "Black versus Black: The Relationships among African, African American, and African Caribbean Persons," *Journal of Black Studies*, 33, no. 5 (2003): 576–604.

39. See Vaughn, "Race and Nation," for more on México Negro.

40. Interview with Johanna Piñuerúa of *Qué pasa* newspaper, June 16, 2004.

41. This is taken from an e-mail written to the authors (cited with permission).

42. See "Mexican Leader Criticized for Comment on Blacks," CNN.com, May 15, 2005. www.cnn.com/2005/US/05/14/fox.jackson, and Rosa Elvira Vargas Enviada, "Realizan mexicanos trabajos que ni los negros quieren: Fox," *La Jornada*, May 14, 2005.

43. For instance, see a cartoon of President Fox dressed as a colonial viceroy, standing in front of portraits of the colonial Mexican caste system. This ran in *La Jornada*, May 17, 2005, www.jornada.unam.mx/2005/may05/050517/cartones /fisgon.jpg. *La Jornada* and other Mexican dailies ran several cartoons that week.

44. This premise is explored and tested by several contributors in Anani Dzidzienyo and Suzanne Oboler, eds., *Neither Enemies Nor Friends: Latinos, Blacks, Afro-Latinos* (New York: Palgrave Macmillan, 2005), 4–155.

45. Roberto Garduño, "Fox, inculto, racista y falto de sensibilidad: PRI y PRD," *La Jornada*, May 15, 2005.

46. Laura Castellanos, "Ignora México datos de su población negra," *La Reforma*, June 8, 2005.

47. For example, see Laura Castellanos, "Buscan volver etnia a los afromexicanos," *La Reforma*, June 8, 2005.

48. David Brooks Corresponsal, "Travesura de Memín Pinguín pone en jaque la relación bilateral entre México y EU," *La Jornada*, July 1, 2005; Pablo Espinosa, "Travesura diplomática de Memín Pinguín," *La Jornada*, July 1, 2005; Fabiola Palapa, Ericka Montaño, and Monica Mateos, "Memín Pinguín 'no es el icono popular del racismo en México,'" *La Jornada*, July 1, 2005.

49. Interview with Sixto Valencia, May 1996. Note that there was a hiatus in story lines between the mid-1950s and 1961.

50. An interesting examination of the comic book is Marco Polo Hernández Cuevas, "Memín Pinguín: Uno de los cómics mexicanos más populares como instrumento para codificar al negro," *Afro-Hispanic Review* 22, no. 1 (2003): 52–59.

51. Virtually no one we spoke with was familiar with Fox's comments. When we broached the subject with a range of people in Collantes, Oaxaca, many people reported that they had never seen the comic book character.

52. The open letter from México Negro can be found at www.equaljusticesociety .org/action_mexicanstamp.html.

53. Enrique Krauze, "The Pride in Memin Penguin," *Washington Post*, July 12, 2005.

54. Some episodes of African American and Latino solidarity can be detected in North Carolina's Spanish-language press. For instance, see "Mujeres de Wake, NC, promueven relaciones interraciales," *La Voz de Carolina*, April 1999; "Trabajadores de Carolina Turkey Se Organizan y Continuan a Proceder" and "Multan a 'Carolina Turkey' por la Muerte de Un Obrero," *La Voz de Carolina*, March 1994; "Los Sindicatos y los hispanos ofrecen sendero para ellos mismos y para la nación," *La Voz de Carolina*, February 1997; and "Trabajadores agrícolas de Carolina del Norte piden sindicato laboral," *La Voz de Carolina*, June 1997.

# IV

## MEDIA AND SELECTED RESOURCES

# 11

## Fading In

## Race and the Representation of Peoples of African Descent in Latin American Cinema

*Darién J. Davis*

*This chapter provides an assessment of the roles of black peoples in the construction of cinema in Latin America. As in other sectors of society, black Latin Americans are underrepresented in positions of power within the film industry. There are very few black filmmakers or scriptwriters, for example. This is not related to talent but rather to access to the technology. Yet Afro-Latin Americans have played important roles in front of and behind the camera. In countries with established film traditions such as Cuba and Brazil, black actors and actresses have helped bring complex images and interpretations to the cinema. In addition, this chapter argues that many non-black socially conscious feature film and documentary filmmakers have also played critical roles in bringing black characters and stories to the silver screen. As black Latin Americans raise social consciousness and conquer social and political space, black imagery in Latin American films continues to evolve from its stereotypical and one-dimensional beginnings to more complex and nuanced representations.*

Cinema has played an important role in the representation and diffusion of culture throughout the Americas. Filmmakers have utilized the silver screen for a variety of purposes from propaganda to entertainment to raising social consciousness. As in other areas of American life, Africans and their descendants have played significant roles in the development of the cinematic tradition in Latin America and the Caribbean. They have made significant contributions as scriptwriters, producers, editors, directors, researchers, and actors, despite discriminatory practices that have limited their access and opportunities. At the same time, however, weak Latin American and Caribbean economies have provided few opportunities for filmmakers of all ethnicities.

Despite these obstacles, Brazil and Cuba, two countries with significant black populations, have produced scores of feature films that have garnered national and international praise. In addition, Latin American experimental and documentary filmmakers have made a number of important works that speak to national and local experiences. Unfortunately, even high-quality Latin American and Caribbean films cannot attract the audiences that the highly advertised Hollywood blockbuster films often do. Nor has Latin America or the Caribbean developed internationally influential and visible black directors or actors similar to their North American counterparts. But this has little to do with talent and much to do with language barriers, access to global communication systems, and limited publicity.

An assessment of film production in Brazil, Caribbean Basin, and Spanish South and Central America will help us to understand the varied experience of the people of the African diaspora in film. Shaped by the social, political, and aesthetic trends from the region from which it emerges, cinema has nonetheless contributed to pan-African consciousness. Indeed, feature films and documentaries about black culture and history have also played an important role in raising the awareness of the impact of the African diaspora throughout the Americas.

## BRAZIL

The black influence in Brazil's film industry began in the industry's earliest stages, although Afro-Brazilians constitute a small fraction of the working directors, producers, technical staff, and actors. Black directors and writers have suffered from limited access to federal, state, foundation, and private funds necessary to make films in Brazil. Nevertheless, Brazil has produced several important directors. Afro-Brazilian writer, producer, and director Cajado Filho worked on a number of important films in the late 1940s and early 1950s, although the work of other black directors such as Odilon López and Waldyr Onofre deals more specifically with racial issues.[1]

At the beginning of the twenty-first century, the São Paulo group Dogma Feijoado (Bean Stew Dogma), led by Jefferson De and other black filmmakers including Noel Carvalho, Billy Castilho, Rogério, Daniel Santiago, and Agenor Alves, aims to create a black cinema that both represents the multiplicity of the black experience and speaks directly to black audiences. Although inspired by the Danish group Dogma 95 and black American directors, Dogma Feijoada is firmly routed in the Brazilian experience. Jefferson De's *Distraida a morte* (*Distracted to Death*) and Ari Cândido Fernandes's *O Rito de Ismael Ivo* (*The Ritual of Ishmael Ivo*) are two of the first films that represent Dogma Feijoada's goals. In addition, there is also a host of documentaries by Afro-Brazilians from Zózimo Bulbul to Joel Zeto Araujo on a variety of topics from slavery to modern topics.

Black actors and actresses have played important roles in both the cinema and television series and *novelas*, or soap operas. The pioneering work of Benjamin de Oliveira, one of Brazil's first clowns and a silent-movie actor, leads the list of talented Afro-Brazilians, which includes writer and producer Haroldo Costa, Lea Garcia, Ruth de Souza, Milton Gonçalves, Zezé Motta, and the new generation of artists such as Lázaro Ramos, Taís Araujo, and the young actors and actresses from the Rio theatrical group Nós do Morro.

Despite the growing opportunities, Brazilian feature films about race and the African diaspora are largely shaped by an eclectic group of white filmmakers, many of whom (including Cacá Diegues, Hector Babenco, Fernando Mirelles, and Helvécio Ratton) have garnered critical acclaim for their work. Four major categories—slavery, miscegenation and syncretism, popular culture and celebration, and class dynamics and marginality—help us to place the major Brazilian films on race and on black Brazilians into thematic perspective, although some films overlap into various categories.

Few Brazilian films on slavery were made before the 1950s, with the exception of Marques Filho's 1929 *Escrava Isaura* (*The Slave Isaura*), based on Bernado Guimarães 1875 novel of the same name (and remade in 1949 by Eurides Ramos). *Escrava Isaura* is emblematic of a host of films that purportedly support black causes, such as abolition, while not necessarily embracing the notion of black liberation and self-sufficiency. To Guimarães and other abolitionists, the case of Isaura is tragic because she is well educated and "looks white," sentiments that allow Brazilians of the time, and consequently the film, to sidestep issues of black suffering and liberation.

Some three decades later *Sinhá moça* (*The Plantation Owner's Daughter*, 1953) and *João Negrinho* (1958) provided viewers with more complex representations of abolition. Based on the nineteenth-century work by Maria Dezonne Pacheco Fernandes, *Sinhá Moça* (directed by Tom Payne and Osvaldo Sampião) is a dramatic period piece about the abolition of slavery, although the film centers on the conflict between a slave-owning father and his abolitionist daughter. At the same time, the film offers complex views and performances by many talented actors, not least of which was Ruth de Souza, one of the cofounders of the Experimental Black Theater with the Afro-Brazilian pioneer and activist Abdias do Nascimento. The film received a number of important national and international awards in 1953 and 1954 for its directors and for best actress.

The Afro-Brazilian response to slavery is the focus of three of Cacá Diegues's films: *Ganga Zumba* (1964), *Xica da Silva* (1976), and *Quilombo* (1984). A member of the socially committed *cinema novo* movement, Diegues has shown a commitment to covering black themes and employing black actors and actresses throughout his career. *Ganga Zumba*, which relies heavily on historical sources as well as myth, lore, and fantasy, re-creates the life of Ganga Zumba, nephew of Zumbi, the famous leader of Palmares, the seventeenth-century runaway slave community turned republic that is treated in Diegues's *Quilombo: Xica da Silva*, on the other hand, tells the story of the Brazilian *mulata* slave Xica (played by the black actress Zezé Motta) and her alliance with João Fernandes, a Portuguese diamond official, who lives in Vila Rica (Ouro Preto, in the state of Minas Gerais) in the eighteenth century. The film emphasizes the plight of black women held in bondage in a contradictory manner, as it utilizes the stereotype of the erotic black woman while illustrating the limits of sexual unions as a means of social ascent.[2] Also important in this category is Walter Lima Junior's *Chico rei* (*Chico, the King*, 1985). The film chronicles the capture of Galanga from a royal Congo family, his baptism in Brazil as Francisco (Chico), and his eventual liberation and challenges to the colonial government.

While slavery and abolition constitute an important theme in Brazilian historical and cultural studies, many more films have explored issues of miscegenation and/or syncretism, two forces that many scholars believe have been fundamental to the Brazilian character. At the same time, this reality has often been misused to promote patriotism and deflect attention from social change. Thus, it is not surprising then that many Brazilian films treat issues of miscegenation or syncretism de facto as a part of the Brazilian cultural landscape, while others focus on the problems and challenges of syncretism and miscegenation more explicitly, as in the case of *Xica* or *Escrava Isaura*. The complexities of miscegenation and whitening is highlighted in *Macunaíma*, Joaquin de Andrade's 1969 satirical adaptation of Mario de Andrade's work of the same name. The film employs satire to provide insight into racial attitudes and the desire of the Brazilian to become white.

Brazilian films often present racial intermingling and mixing with its class complexities rather than focusing explicitly on race, as in the U.S. film *Guess Who's Coming to Dinner?* (1967). Films such as Carlos Manga's 1953 *Dupla de barulho* (*A Great Pair*, with Grande Otelo and Oscarito) and Waldyr Onofre's *As Aventuras amorosas de um padeiro* (*The Amorous Adventures of a Baker*, 1976) lighten any possible interracial tensions with humor. Furthermore, Onofre's film about the adventures of two working-class men with a white woman from the middle class is more about class dynamics in a Rio neighborhood.

Still, as in U.S.-based movies such as Spike Lee's *Jungle Fever* (1991) and following in the tradition of Diegues' *Xica*, certain fatalism often dooms interracial relations despite historical examples to the contrary. This is the case in Odilon Lopez's *Um e pouco, dois e bom* (*One Is Not Enough, Two Is Good*, 1971); in the more complex *Tenda dos milagres* (*Tent of Miracles*, 1977); and in *Na boca do mundo* (*In the Mouth of the World*, 1979). Antonio Pitanga's *Na boca do mundo* centers on a love triangle among a black worker (Antônio), a white bourgeois woman (Clarisse) with whom he has an affair, and his mulatto girlfriend (Terezinha). Race and class intersect with urban and rural tensions in a film that ends with the death of the main character and a surprising alliance between Clarisse and Terezinha.

Intraclass racism and prejudice are not as pervasive in Brazilian films. Nelson Pereira dos Santos exposes this issue (among many) in *Tenda dos milagres* through a complex plot that deals with middle-class intermarriage and the obsession of a white professor who tries to hide his African ancestry. Paradoxically, the film also celebrates miscegenation—an ideology that has its roots in the nineteenth century and gained spokesmen in Gilberto Freyre and Jorge Amado, author of the novel *Tenda dos milagres*, on which the film is based—as a solution to racism, rather than black rights and liberation. While literature and cinematographic texts have historically focused on alliances of European men and women of color, Carlota Camuarti's 1996 dramatic farce *Carlota Joaquina* departs from this trend by reporting that Infanta Carlota Joaquina was lured by the Brazilian racial-mixing experience and took a black lover.[3]

Religious miscegenation, or syncretism, is treated in a number of Brazilian films, including *Tenda dos milagres*, Glauber Rocha's *Barravento* (1961), and *O Pagador de promesas* (*The Given Word*, 1962). *O Pagador de promesas* and *Tenda dos milagres* focus directly on syncretism while illustrating the tensions and prejudice of white society, *Barravento* examines the Afro-Bahian religion on its own terms, although not without exposing the limitations of organized religion. The Brazilian-Nigerian production of *A Deusa negra* (1979), directed by Nigerian filmmaker Olá Balogún, provides a rare cross-Atlantic glimpse into the religious and cultural continuity through the Yoruba-based religion *Candomblé*. *Samba da criação do mundo* (*Samba of the Creation of the World*, 1979) attempts to give a Yoruban rendition of the world's creation and Afro-Brazilian religious values, themes covered in a number of documentaries and shorts from Brazil, the United States, and Europe.[4]

African religious practices such as *Candomblé* and *Umbanda* have had an impact not only on religion in Brazil but also on other national and local customs from dance and music to dress and food. In the silent-film era, Afro-Brazilian musicians such as Pixinguinha and Donga played live music during screenings. Others composed and played in orchestras for the carnival revue films of the 1930s and 1940s and the melodramas and humorous *chanchadas* that showcased the talents of Grande Otelo, one of the pioneering Afro-Brazilian performers. Afro-Brazilian musicians have also been at the center of a number of documentaries such as Leon Hirszman's 1969 *Nelson Caviquino* and *Viva São João* (*Long Live St. John!* 2002), the latter of which features Gilberto Gil.

Although filmmakers recognized the contributions (if not central role) of blacks to Brazilian popular music, they were visibly absent from the 1930s carnival films such as *Alô alô carnival* and *Alô alô Brazil*. This changes somewhat with the making of Luis de Barrow's *Samba em Berlim* (1943), with Grande Otelo and Nilo Chagas, and other films such as *Rio Zone Norte* (1957), with Grande Otelo, Angela Maria, and a host of other Afro-Brazilian performers. For its time, the internationally acclaimed French production *Orfeu negro* (Black Orpheus, 1959) was a rare assembly of talented black actors and performers based on the Vincius de Morais play *Orefeu de conceião*. Only in 1999 did Cacá Diegues create his own rendition of the play, simply titled *Orfeu*, and starring Afro-Brazilian Tony Garrido, from the musical group Cidade Negra.

Black poverty and marginality also represent major themes in Brazilian cinema. While music, revelry, and religion constituted important aspects of the realist dramas of *cinema novo*, black discontent and revolt were essential in films such as Pereira dos Santos's *Rio 40 graus* (1956) and *Rio Zona Norte* (1957), as well as Roberto Farias's 1962 *Assalto ao trem pagador* (*The Pay Train Robbery or Attack on the Pay Train*), based on a 1960 train robbery. Despite the title, Farias provides an engrossing story about the relationship among the multiracial robbers, interweaving issues of race and class. Tião, one of the black thieves, stands in contrast to Grilo Peru, one of the white robbers, who not only iterates the only explicit racial slur in the film but also is able to spend his money conspicuously without drawing attention to himself. *Assalto ao trem pagador* boasts a talented multiracial cast that brought the film more critical acclaim than other films that deal with the inhabitants of the favelas. Also worthy of mention is Leon Hirszman's *Eles não usam black tie* (*They Don't Wear Black Tie*, 1980), which deals with labor conflicts in São Paulo and in which black characters play principal roles, but race does not necessarily play a factor in the drama.

The twenty-first century has brought a host of impressive films that focus critically on poverty, marginality, and black responses to them. *Uma onda no ar* (broadcast on Radio Favela, 2002) presents the development and triumph of alternative radio created by four Afro-Brazilians in the favelas of Belo Horizonte in the state of Minas Gerais. Hector Babenco's 2003 production of *Carandiru*, an epic on the São Paulo prison system of the same name, links this production to the politically committed movies of *cinema novo*. New directors include Fernando Mierelles, with his two films *Maids* (2000) and *City of God* (2002), and the New York-based Brazilian filmmaker Karim Aïnouz's *Madame Satã* (2002). Race and class are intimately interconnected in all three films, but the fact that the main characters in all three films are marginalized black characters indicates the need to explore, as Dogma Feijoada intimates, more diverse experiences of Afro-Brazilians.[5]

There are signs that this may already be taking place. Many critics regard Lázaro Ramos as one of the most important contemporary actors, for example. He has portrayed black characters in diverse and varied films, such as *Madame Satã*, as well as characters whose identities are not necessarily racially specified. This is the case of his central roles in two films by Jorge Furtado: *O Homem que copiava* (*The Man Who Copied*, 2003), *Meu tio matou um cara* (*My Uncle Killed a Guy*, 2005), and *O Homem do ano* (*Man of the Year*, directed by José Henrique Fonseca, 2003). *Meu tio matou um cara*, Sergio Goldenberg's *Bendito Fruto* (2005), and Joel Zito Araujo's *Filhas do vento* (*Daughters of the Wind*, 2005) all constitute positive developments in the representation of Afro-Brazilians on the silver screen. The subtle and often comedic *Meu tio matou um cara* is one of the few Brazilian films to focus on a black middle-class family and deals with race head-on. The main character and teenage narrator (Duca), played by the young Afro-Brazilian actor Darlan Cunha, provides comments about his life, his family, and his friends, and on being the only black student in his school. *Bendito Fruto* centers on the relationship between the white hairdresser Edigar and his relationship with his black common-law wife Maria in Botafogo. In this complex yet believable Brazilian story, Goldenberg explores the subtle relationship between race and class in Brazilian family dynamics as Edigar struggles to publicly recognize his relationship with Maria, who used to be the maid.

Meanwhile, Maria grapples with a number of her own issues, including how to let her son know that Edigar is his father. Finally, *Filhas do vento* is the first contemporary film to feature Afro-Brazilian women across multiple generations in varied and complex roles.

Afro-Brazilians such as Zito are increasingly calling for and creating their own spaces in film and television. In November 2005, the São Paulo-based *TV da Gente* (Our TV) made its historic debut by becoming the first Brazilian television station aimed specifically at black audiences. José de Paula Neto, the main creator behind the TV station, secured a national audience as a singer and then as host of the popular *TV Globo* series *Princess for a Day*. Initiatives such as Neto's, which come from the community, have historically served for multiple forms of empowerment that stretch beyond the media.[6]

## THE CARIBBEAN BASIN

Despite their shared history and parallel African influences, the multilingual and politically independent nations of the Caribbean Basin (which often include the coastal regions of South and Central America) stand in contrast to Portuguese-speaking Brazil, which is unified politically and linguistically. Moreover, of all the Caribbean nations, Cuba is the only country that has developed an important film industry, and only after 1960. The former French, English, and, to a lesser extent, Dutch island colonies, all with black majorities, have nonetheless inspired foreign filmmakers. The islands have provided exotic backdrops to a host of Hollywood films, from *The Satanic Dr. No* (1963) to the cross-diaspora *How Stella Got Her Groove Back* (directed by Kevin Rodney Sullivan, 1998). Examples that explore the autonomous cultures of the Caribbean include Robert Rossen's *Islands in the Sun* (1957); Gillo Pontecorvo's 1969 *Burn*, loosely based on the events of the Haitian Revolution; and a host of indigenous, European, and North American documentaries.[7]

The French and English Caribbean have produced few feature films, although Jamaican Perry Henzel's 1978 movie *The Harder They Come* helped to bring images of the poor black neighborhoods of Kingston to the silver screen, along with the vibrant reggae music that has inspired the world. The French Caribbean has produced a number of important filmmakers, including the Haitians Raoul Peck (*Haitian Corner*, 1988) and Rassoul Labuchin (*Anita*, 1982), and the prolific Christian Lara from Guadeloupe. Martinican director Euzhan Palcy's quiet portrayal of poverty and the lack of educational opportunities in a Martinican neighborhood in *Rue cases nègres* (*Sugar Cane Alley*, 1983) brought her wide acclaim, ultimately leading her to work in Hollywood on *The Dry White Season*, a social drama that takes place in South Africa. Guadeloupen-born Christian Grandman examines relationships among a number of marginalized Caribbean characters at the inhospitable Tèt Grenné in Pointe-à-Pitre in his 2000 film *Tèt Grenné*.

Outside Cuba, feature filmmaking in the Spanish Caribbean is rare. Nor have Dominicans or Puerto Ricans critically examined the African legacy in many other film forums. Some exceptions include Efraín López's *Isabel la negra*, the story of a Puerto Rican prostitute, filmed in English; Leon Ichaso's 2001 treatment of the Nuyorican poet Piñero, which features black Nuyoricans who knew Piñero; and the rare *Nueba yol* (directed by Angel Muñiz, 1996), inspired by the immigrant experience of Dominicans in New York.

## FILMMAKING IN CUBA

Before 1959, Cuban film production had been irregular and uneven. After the success of the Castro-led revolution, Cuba's film production was aided by the creation of the Cuban Institute of Filmic Art and Film Production and Industry (ICAIC) and the Cuban Broadcasting Institute. Inspired by revolutionary ideals, Cubans engaged intellectuals throughout Latin America and the Caribbean in forging a new Latin American cinema, and creating what filmmaker Julio García Espinosa, one of the founders of ICAIC, described as an "imperfect" and thus anti-Hollywood cinema. From the 1960s to the 1980s, the ICAIC produced a steady stream of feature films and documentaries and perfected the docudrama, which included elements of both genres, and created animated and more experimental film genres. Afro-Cubans have helped shape the Cuban film industry, although, as in Brazil, they are not as visible as one might expect.[8]

Sergio Giral and Sara Gomez, two well-known directors from the early phase of ICAIC, have been followed by an enthusiastic group of young directors and writers that includes Gloria Rolando, Tony Romero, and Rigoberto López. Actors and actresses have been equally important in bringing Cuban stories to the silver screen. Actresses such as Adelá Legrá, Assenhe Rodriguez, and Daisy Granados have played multiple roles in Cuban film since the 1960s. Granados, considered by many the grande dame of Cuban cinema, often plays roles where racial identity is ambiguous or seemingly unimportant, although she also played the *mulata* title character in *Cecilia* (1981). Afro-Cuban veteran actors such as Mario Balsameda, Miguel Benavides, and Tito Junco have made significant contributions to Cuban cinema. Unfortunately, the economic crisis and the growing number of talented Cubans who have left the island have meant that many young would-be actors and filmmakers have had to abort their careers in film or find other work abroad. Moreover, as in Brazil, few black actors have appeared in central roles in nonhistorical feature films in the last decade.

From the beginning of the revolution, however, Afro-Cubans and themes of the African diaspora have figured prominently in Cuba's film production. One important example was Sabá Cabrera Infante's 1961 short documentary film *P.M.*, which showed scenes from Havana's highlife featuring Cubans, the majority of whom were black, dancing and drinking in a local bar in Havana. The government's censoring of the film marked an important shift in the relationship between intellectuals who had supported the revolution and the Castro government. Although film production emerged under the watchful eyes of the censors bent on promoting revolutionary ideas and themes, many filmmakers succeeded in bringing their critical vision to the silver screen. Cuban films such as Tomás Gutiérrez Alea's *Cumbite* (1964), based on the Jaques Roumain novel about the life of sugarcane cutters in Haiti, also promoted third world solidarity. As in Brazil, four broad categories, with socialist modifications, help us to understand the filmography of race and Afro-Cubans in communist Cuba, although all four engage more explicitly with notions of nationhood or *cubanidad*. These categories are slavery; miscegenation/racial intermingling; music and culture; and race, class, and nationhood.

Slavery lasted longer in Cuba than in any other Spanish colony, making Cuba the most culturally African of the Spanish-speaking nations of the Caribbean Basin. Thus, as in Brazil, slavery and abolition figure prominently in the Cuban filmography. Indeed any period piece prior to the 1880s would be remiss without references to slavery. The majority of films that deal with slavery were made through a Marxist revolutionary lens with explicit class analysis, while at the same time reconstructing important Cuban historical realities.

Tomás Gutiérrez Alea's 1977 *La Última cena* (*The Last Supper*) deals explicitly with slavery and race relations. Based on an eighteenth-century incident, the film presents the story of a pious and supposedly well-meaning slave owner who decided to treat his slaves better by instructing them in the values of Christianity and by inviting them to participate in the feast of the celebration of Passover. The result is explosive as the slaves rebel, burning the plantation and attempting to escape.

Afro-Cuban director Sergio Giral began his career in the 1974 with *El Otro Francisco* (*The Other Francisco*, 1975), a film that engages the prerevolutionary official recounting of Cuban slavery while simultaneously deconstructing it. The film reinterprets Suarez y Romero's nineteenth-century antislavery romantic novel *Francisco Romero*, written some twenty years before *Uncle Tom's Cabin* (1851–1852). The film is important for emphasizing the slave's role in his own freedom. Giral also directed a number of documentaries and feature films including *Maluala* (1980) and *Maria Antonia* (1991), the latter an innovative reading of the Afro-Cuban goddess of beauty, Ochún.

The nineteenth century saw the decline of slavery at a time when most of the Latin American societies were becoming increasingly more mestizo. Syncretism and racial intermingling figure prominently in Cuban films and in many respects represent Cuban culture de facto, making the term "Afro-Cuban" problematic at best. Huberto Solás' *Cecilia* (1983), based on the nineteenth-century novel *Cecilia Valdés* by Cirilo Villaverde, points to the problems of miscegenation in a society dominated by European values in many ways similar to Brazil's *Escrava Isaura*. Cecilia represents a third-generation Cuban family that has slowly become more white and tries to escape her black past. Solás's *Miel para Ochún* (*Honey for Oshun*, 2001) examines the issue of black heritage in a more provocative way. The main character, a "white" Cuban exile, returns to Cuba to find his mother, whom he barely remembers and whom he believes abandoned him: He not only comes into contact with Afro-Cuban culture but ultimately reunites with his Afro-Cuban mother. The dialogue with earlier Cuban films such as *Lucía*, also directed by Solás, and Tomás Gutiérrez Alea's *Memorias del subde-*

*sarrollo* (*Memories of Underdevelopment*) cannot be overlooked. Particularly interesting is the choice of actress Adelá Legrá as the Cuban mother in *Miel para Ochún*. Legrá played a peasant woman who becomes a part of the 1960s revolutionary culture in the epic *Lucía*, and at the beginning of the twenty-first century, she plays the character in *Miel para Ochún* who represents the maternal figure whom the exiled protagonist seeks.

Despite Cuba's Marxist focus on class analysis and its spurring of official religion, Afro-Cuban Santeria has flourished under the revolution and has even been commodified for a growing tourist economy. Cuban films have treated Santeria, an integral part of Cuban culture, as a part of the Cuban landscape in films such as Tomás Gutiérrez Alea's *Fresa y chocolate* (*Strawberry and Chocolate*, 1995). Alea's treatment of race in *Fresa y chocolate* and *Memorias del subdesarrollo* deserves special mention. On one hand, blacks and blackness are equated with undesirable Dionysian elements of Cuban culture from which the protagonists of both films wish to distance themselves. On the other hand, black actors in Cuba and throughout Latin America are often limited to roles representing stereotypes such as the uncontrolled dancers and musicians in the opening scene of *Memorias del subdesarrollo* or the *santero* in *Strawberry and Chocolate*.

Other feature films have provided more profound or lengthy examina-

**Figure 11.1.   Afro-Cuban actress Adelá Legrá in still from *Lucía*, 1968**

tions of African cultural influences. A departure from the political and committed new cinema of Cuba is Manuel Octavio Gómez's eclectic 1982 musical *Patakín*. Otero Gómez provides a modern reading of two Yoruban deities in conflict: Changó, the god of thunder (represented by a man who lives off his wife) and Oggún, the deity of war and guardian of arms and metals (played by a hard-working machinist). Although drawing on popular idioms, the film, which was billed as Cuba's first musical, was more comedy than drama and was not successful in engaging Cuban audiences.

The 1990 films *Miel para Ochún* and *La Vida es silbar* (*Life Is to Whistle*, 1998) interject Afro-Cuban cultural influences, symbols, and icons into larger national issues in a more profound manner. In the former, the search for the character's mother is explicitly and implicitly tied to the search for Ochún, the goddess of sweetness and beauty, at a critical time in Cuba's divided history. In the multilayered *Guantanamera*, Alea integrates Afro-Cuban mythology throughout the narrative to comment critically on the Cuban political situation, death, and ultimately life in Cuba at the end of the 1990s—although the major characters are not black.

## MEXICO AND SPANISH SOUTH AND CENTRAL AMERICA

The black image and presence in feature films outside Brazil and the Caribbean Basin have not been prominent. Argentine films such as Maria Luisa Beberg's *Camila* (1984) provides a brief glimpses of black servitude in the affluent O'Gorman household under dictator Juan Manuel Rosas, but Argentine feature films rarely include or make references to Argentine blacks. In Mexico the now-classic *Angelitos negros*, Joselito Rodríguez's 1949 Mexican remake of the Fannie Hurst novel *Imitation of Life* (the Hollywood versions of which were made in 1934 and 1959) deals explicitly with race in a Mexican film, but it was not inspired by a Mexican reality but treated issues that resonated throughout the region.

Colombia, Peru, and Venezuela have all been influenced by the African diaspora, but rarely has that influence translated into a major part of national debate. Moreover, economic and civil strife has made film production difficult in all three countries over the last decade. Carlos Hugo Christensen's earlier *La Balandra Isabel llegó está tarde* (*The Isabel Docked This Afternoon*, 1949) represents an important cinematographic contribution to the filmography of the African diaspora. Adapted from the Guillermo Memeses's story of the same name, *La Balandra Isabel llegó está tarde* provides a rare portrait of urban Afro-Venzuelan culture. In addition, it re-creates scenes of black Venezuelan folklore and folk beliefs, although the narrative centers on the conflicts of the married white protagonist, who is torn between his son and wife and Esperanza, the prostitute. Although Esperanza's racial identity is often ambiguous, she is clearly a product of the Afro-Venezuelan urban scene and represents the stereotypical beautiful and seductive *mulata* who cannot be trusted.

In films from the Andean region, black characters are rare. *Pantaleón y las vistadoras* (*Captain Pantoja and the Special Services*), the 1994 film by Francisco J. Lombardi, documents the presence of Afro-Peruvians with minor characters. One important exception, however, is Alberto Durant's *Coraje* (1998), which focuses on the extraordinary figure of María Elena Moyano, an Afro-Peruvian activist from the neighborhood of Villa El Salvador, on the outskirts of Lima. Like the majority of Latin American films with central black characters, *Coraje* is not about blackness, per se, but about Moyano's role as a grassroots activist and community leader caught between the terrorist activities of the Shining Path and the inattentive government.

## A WORD ON DOCUMENTARIES

Outside of Brazil, Cuba, Argentina, and Mexico, Latin American film industries remain weak, limiting the representation of national reality in general and black issues in particular. Documentary filmmakers from inside and outside Latin America have helped to promote and explore a host of issues relevant to the black experience, although, with few exceptions, documentaries have not attracted the attention of the press or of audiences of feature films.

Many Brazilian documentary makers, for example, have exposed contemporary issues and problems related to the Afro-Brazilian in ways that feature films have not. Indeed, compared to U.S. filmgoers, contemporary Brazilian documentaries have garnered a massive following among filmgoers thanks, in part, to film festivals.

Black filmmaker Zózimo Bulbul's 150-minute film *Aboilção* (*Abolition*, 1988), which often meanders, nonetheless represents an important document that registers a personal perspective on the celebration of the one hundredth anniversary of the abolition of slavery. Sections of Orson Welles's 1992 release *It's All True*, which gave the Banco do Brasil–sponsored festival its name, deal with black influences in Brazil in the 1930s. Of the many important documentaries to come out of Brazil at the beginning of the twenty-first century, two deserve special mention. Joel Zito Araujo's *A Negacão do Brasil* (*The Negation of Brazil*, 2000) examines the struggles of black actors in Brazil while discussing how racial taboos, prejudice, and stereotypes have limited their roles in the television industry. The riveting *Bus 174* explores the tragic life of Sandro do Nascimento, a young black man who hijacked Bus 174 in Rio de Janiero on June 20,

2002. The film's innovative analysis interconnects issues of race, poverty, the media, the state, and police brutality, touching on the major issues at the beginning of a new millennium. Some of these issues are present in New York-based filmmaker Tania Cypriano's powerful *Oda Ya! Life with AIDS* (2001), which focuses on the AIDS community as well as AIDS education and positive celebrations of human sexuality. North American NGOs have also helped promote issues of race in Brazil on film. This is the case of the Global Exchange video *Benedita da Silva*, based on the life of one of Rio de Janeiro's political personalities and an important voice in Brazil's Workers' Party (PT).[9]

Afro-Cuban customs and rituals have been explored in many Cuban documentaries and shorts. Gloria Rolando's *Oggún* (1992), for example, provides viewers with an understanding of the Afro-Cuban god of the same name. Through the multilayered testimony of Lázaro Ross, the lead singer of the Conjunto Folclórico Nacional de Cuba, and a devotee of Oggún, Rolando presents viewers with stories that allow them to understand the Afro-Cuban religion that remains vital to Cubans in and outside Cuba. Afro-Cuban filmmaker Rigoberto López's *Yo soy del son a la salsa* explores the development of salsa from its beginnings in Cuba as *son*. Luis Felipe Bernaza's docudrama *Hasta la reina baila el danzón* (*Even Queen Isabel Dances the Danzón*, 1991) combines live interviews with surrealist historical reenactments, while satirizing many popular Cuban beliefs. The director includes scenes from Yoruban ceremonies and an innovative rendition of Afro-Cuban poet Nicolás Guillén's famous "Sensemayá." Especially important in helping to raise awareness of many of the forgotten Afro-Cuban musical veterans was Win Wenders's widely acclaimed 1999 documentary *Buena Vista Social Club*. The film, which followed the making of a CD and the world tour of American musician Ry Cooder with legendary but forgotten figures such as Compay Segundo, Ibrahim Ferrer, and Omara Portuondo, was responsible for reviving the careers of all the musicians involved. Other documentaries on legendary figures such as Chano Pozo and Joseito Fernandez, as well as encounters with Dizzie Gillespie and Harry Belafonte, add to Cuba's extensive list of documentaries. José Sánchez-Montes's endearing documentary *Bola de Nieve* (2002), for example, provides a brief biography of one of Cuba's musical treasures.

Cuba's first female director, Sarah Gómez, was an Afro-Cuban pioneer who had directed a number of short documentaries before her acclaimed docudrama *De cierta manera* (*One Way or Another*), with Tomás Gutiérrez Alea and Julio García Espinosa, released in 1977. Gómez provides a poignant look at the culture of marginality prior to the revolution and the challenges of the revolution in Cuba's transition to a socialist society. The film is particularly important because of its focus on the ritual of the male-only Abakua Society, which was regarded by many in the regime as anti-revolutionary.

Following in the footsteps of Gómez, Gloria Rolando's *Raíces de mi corazon* (*Roots of My Heart*, 2001) deserves particular mention because of its attempt to treat Cuba's race war of 1912, when members of a Cuban black political party (the Partido Independiente de Color) clashed with government forces when parties based on race were declared illegal. The result was the massacre of thousands of Afro-Cubans and decades of silence about the event that made discussions of racial discrimination all but taboo. Also worthy of note is Rolando's *El Alacrán* (*The Scorpion*), which traces the origins of Cuba's legendary Scorpion Parade in 1908, in the segregated setting of Old Cuba, where elegantly costumed whites in blackface paraded in carriages, and Afro-Cubans practiced their sacred drumming and dancing traditions in secret.

*Si me comprendieras* (*If You Only Understood*), the 1998 film by Rolando Díaz, is one of the first Cuban films to discuss openly and frankly Cuban racism and emigration, and Cuba's international historical and contemporary presence in missions abroad. The film begins with a Cuban director assembling his cast for a new film project. In search of a black female dancer and singer, he takes to the street with his video camera. The film follows the film crew from behind the camera as they encounter and talk with Cuban women and possible candidates. From this perspective, audiences receive a glimpse into filmmaking in Cuba as well as attitudes toward women and Afro-Cubans.

The Cuban immigrant communities in the United States and the swelling exile communities in the post-1959 era, especially on the East Coast, have meant that, as in Puerto Rico and the Dominican Republic, cultural production in Cuba cannot be limited to the island. This is particularly true of music and literature but also of film. Particularly important from the African diaspora perspective is Pam Sporn's modest but revealing documentary *Cuban Roots/Bronx Stories* (2000), which highlights the experience of one black Cuban family while underscoring the diversity in the Cuban exile community.[10]

In general, documentaries have also more successfully challenged the national myths of whiteness in South America than feature films. *Afroargentines* (directed by Diego Ceballos and Jorge Fortes, 2002) chronicles the marginalization of blacks in Argentina and their cultural legacy, for example, while *Sodad* (directed by Lorena Fernandez, 2002) focuses on the Cape Verdian community in that country. The joint Peruvian-Belgian documentary *Susana Baca: Memoria viva* (2002) on the renowned singer and activist Susana Baca places the performers' work and development into their proper historical contexts. A host of other documentaries about the African experience in the Americas provide glimpses into local enterprise. They include small-budget productions such as the sixteen-minute *Candombe* (directed by Rafael Deugenio, 1993), about the Afro-Uruguayan musical tradition. In Colombia, a handful of documentaries have explored the country's African legacy, particularly the *palenques*, or runaway slave communities. The 2002 UK-Colombian production directed by Tom Feiling, *Resistencia: Hip-Hop in Colombia*, looks at hip-hop in Colombia and the response of various artists to the civil war that has ravaged the country for decades.

U.S.-based production companies and joint Latin American-U.S. documentaries have added to the growing list of documentaries, including the Media Project's *The Panamá Deception*, which features interviews with a number of Afro-Panamanian community leaders and commentators, attesting to the varied and diverse African presence throughout the Americas. *The Promised Ship* (directed by Luciano Capelli, 2000) takes us through the paths of black people from the West Indians to Central America. Veteran settlers remember Marcus Garvey's impact on their lives. *Never Again* (directed by Marta Rodríguez and Fernando Restrepo, 2001) focuses on the stories of Afro-Colombians and their displacement from the El Chocó region of Colombia, and their struggle for justice.

There are also impressive additions to the filmography on Mexico. In *The Forgotten Roots* (2001), Rafael Rebollar examines Mexico's African roots, while *From Florida to Coahuila* (2002) tells the history of the Mascogos, known in the United States as the Black Seminoles. The Black Seminoles, the only Native American group not to sign a peace treaty with the United States, live in towns like Nacimiento in Coahuila, Mexico, and Brackette-ville, Texas. Despite these additions, there are many more issues in Spanish South America and Mexico that have yet to be explored in film.

The peoples of the African Diaspora have had an impact, directly or indirectly, on every American nation. Government commitment to funding film production has provided the necessary backbone to the Brazilian and Cuban film industry, although foreign and private investment has been critical. Documentaries, with their lower production costs, have highlighted important issues about the African experience in the Americas. Historical films aside, until recently Latin American filmmakers were not as likely as their North American counterparts to treat prejudice and racial discrimination as central issues. Ironically, this has begun to change at a time when North America has seen a number of black actors play roles that are not racially predetermined and when interracial alliances are becoming more common on the silver screen. The welcome addition of a number of Afro-Latin American filmmakers, actors, and other professionals, which has benefited the region's film production, and cross-national collaboration are two developments that will be fundamental to the exploration of black themes and issues in the future.

## NOTES

1. For an excellent overview of Brazilian cinema, see Johnson, Randall Johnson, and Robert Stam, eds., *Brazilian Cinema,* expanded ed. (New York: Columbia University Press, 1995). Also see John King, *Magical Reels: A History of Cinema in Latin America* (New York: Verso, 1990). The two most important books on blacks in Brazilian cinema are João Carlos Rodrigues, *O Negro Brasileiro e o cinema,* 2nd ed. (Rio de Janeiro, Brazil: Pallas, 2001) and Robert Stam, *Tropical Multiculturalism: A Comparative History of Race in Brazilian Cinema and Culture* (Durham, NC: Duke University Press, 1997).

2. The lesser-known film *Metiça* also focuses on the plight of a female slave in the eighteenth century in the interior of Brazil.

3. *Carlota: Princessa do Brasil* is based on several historical documents including Luiz Edmundo, *A Corte de Dom João no Rio de Janeiro 1808–1821* (1939–1940); Marcus Cheke, *Carlota Joaquina, Queen of Portugal* (1947), and Bertita Harding, *The Amazon Throne: The Story of the Braganzas of Brazil* (1941). The film is presented as a comedy, however, and ridicules both Carlota and her husband, Prince João, and describes the Brazilian aristocracy as indolent and pretentious.

4. Stam discusses the *Tenda dos milagres* and other films that celebrate Afro-Brazilian religions and culture in *Tropical Multiculturalism,* 299–307.

5. See review of *Madame Satã* in Darién Davis, "Film Review," *American Historical Review* 107, no. 5.

6. Tom Phillips, "TV Station Directed at Blacks Debuts in Brazil/Channel Hopes to Contribute to Reducing Racism," *San Francisco Chronicle,* November 27, 2005.

7. Mbye Cham, ed., *Ex-Iles: Essays on Caribbean Cinema* (Trenton, NJ: Africa World Press, 1992).

8. See Michael Chanan, *The Cuban Image: Cinema and Cultural Politics* (Bloomington: Indiana University Press, 1985); Alfonso J. García Osuna, *The Cuban Filmography, 1897 through 2001* (Jefferson, NC: McFarland, 2003).

9. After its release, Tania Cypriano's film received praise from critics and activists in addition to winning several awards, including Best Documentary at the Pan-African Film Festival in California and award for best film at the New York African Diaspora Film Festival in New York.

10. For a good historical and contextualized overview of the Latino image in film in the United States, see Charles Ramirez Berg, *Latino Images in Film: Stereotypes, Subversion, and Resistance* (Austin: University of Texas Press, 2002). Although in need of updating, an excellent reference source is Luis Reyes and Peter Rubie, *Hispanics in Hollywood: An Encyclopedia of Film and Television* (New York: Garland, 1994).

# Glossary of Terms

*Candomblé*: the thriving religion practiced in Brazil; *Candomblé* is the result of syncretism between traditional Yoruban African beliefs and the beliefs of the Catholic Church. Characteristics include a pantheon of saints (*orixás*) and the use of ritual dance, trance, and possession.

*cimarrón*: an escaped or fugitive slave in Spanish America. In contemporary Colombia, an Afro-Colombian NGO that promotes the rights of black Colombians has adopted this as a name for the group.

*Code Noir*: French colonial law enacted on March 10, 1685, that mandated baptism and conversion of African slaves.

**Garifuna**: also known as Black Caribs, the Garifuna population originated on the island of St. Vincent around 1635. African slaves shipwrecked there began to mix with the native indigenous people, giving rise to a new people and society. After being expelled from the island in 1797, the Garifuna people spread throughout Central America. The Garifuna culture includes strong traditions of dance, music, and a religion that combines African, Catholic, and Indian beliefs.

**ladino**: the Central American term for a **mestizo** (person of Spanish and indigenous heritage). In some regions it is also used to refer to Hispanicized natives.

*mestizaje*: the mixing of cultures, people, and customs.

**mestizo**: means "mixed," sometimes used as a euphemism for mulatto; a person of mixed stock.

**moreno**: brown complexion, synonym of *pardo* or mulatto in some regions. In other regions it is used as a euphemism for **mulatto**.

**mulatto (*mulato*)**: progeny of African and European union. The children of mulattos are also considered mulattos. A synonym of *pardo* or **moreno**, it is often used in Spanish and Portuguese America to refer to a skin color in between black and white (i.e., brown).

**Negrismo**: philosophical literary movement in Hispanic America that promoted the contributions of African culture to Latin America.

**Negritude**: philosophical literary movement originating in French-speaking countries in Africa and the Caribbean that celebrated the contributions of African culture to the West.

267

orisha (*orixá, oricha*): the spirit or deity of *Candomblé* in Brazil, or Santería in Cuba. Orishas are thought to be of Yoruban origin, although deities and customs from other African ethnic groups have been incorporated into the Yoruban cosmology.

*Palo Monte* **and Santería:** the two principal Afro-Cuban religions. Both are a mixture of Catholicism and African traditions, however, the emphasis is on the African religious and cultural roots. In both, large parts of the liturgy remain in African languages: Yoruba for Santeria and Kikongo for *Palo Monte*. Today hundreds of thousands of Americans participate in these traditions, making them vibrant, ever-changing expressions of the influence of African culture in the Caribbean.

*palenques*: runaway slave communities in Spanish America, equivalent to Brazilian *quilombos*, or Maroons in the English colonies.

*pardo*: synonym of **mulatto**, but indicates color. Also called **moreno**, it is the color in between the black and the white or between yellow and brown.

**peninsular:** term used to refer to persons from (born on) the Iberian peninsula to distinguish him or her from the **Creoles**.

*patria*: "homeland," often applied to a particular region within a broader national territory.

**Treaty of Rsywich:** treaty signed by Spain and France in 1697 that ceded the western part of the island of Hispaniola (today Haiti) to the French. The treaty was an attempt to put an end to the threat of French buccaneers to Spanish holdings in the Caribbean.

*trigueño*: "wheat colored." The term can be used to refer to light skinned blacks, although it has also be applied to whites.

*Umbanda*: urban Afro-Creole spiritualist religion of Brazil.

**Voodoo (*vodun*):** Afro-Creole religion originating in Haiti, but practiced throughout the Caribbean.

# Resource Sites, NGOs, and Human Rights Organizations

**Amnesty International**
International Secretariat
1 Easton Street
London WC1X 0DW
United Kingdom

United States Headquarters
5 Penn Plaza, 14th floor
New York, NY 10001
www.amnesty.org

**Committee on the Elimination of Racial Discrimination (CERD)**
**United Nations High Commissioner on Human Rights**
Secretary of the Committee on the Elimination of Racial Discrimination
Treaties and Commission Branch
Office of the High Commissioner for Human Rights
Palais Wilson
52, rue des Pâquis, CH-1201
Geneva, Switzerland
www.ohchr.org/english/bodies/cerd/index.htm

**Franklin H. Williams Caribbean Cultural Center–African Diaspora Institute**
408 W. 58th Street
New York, NY 10019
Telephone: (212) 307-7420
www.caribecenter.org

**Global Exchange**
2017 Mission Street #303
San Francisco, CA 94110
www.globalexchange.org

**Human Rights Watch, Americas Division**
350 Fifth Avenue, 34th Floor
New York, NY 10118
hrwnyc@hrw.org

**Inter-Agency Consultation on Race in Latin America**
Inter-American Dialogue
1211 Connecticut Avenue, NW
Suite 510
Washington, DC 20036
www.thedialogue.org

**Inter-American Development Bank**
1300 New York Avenue, NW
Washington, DC 20577
Section on Social Inclusion and Inequality
www.iadb.org/topics/si&e.cfm

**Minority Rights Group International**
54 Commercial Street
London E1 6LT
United Kingdom
www.minorityrights.org

**National Association for the Advancement of Colored People (NAACP)**
**NAACP Branch & Field Department**
4805 Mt. Hope Drive
Baltimore, MD 21215
www.naacp.org

**Organization of the Americas Inter-American Commission on Human Rights**
1889 F Street, NW
Washington, DC 20006
http://cidh.oas.org

**TransAfrica Forum**
1426 21st Street, NW, 2nd Floor
Washington, DC 20036
www.transafricaforum.org

# Time Line

**1791**  On August 21, a slave uprising erupts near Le Cap in St. Domingue (Santo Domingo) and spreads like wildfire—the beginning of the end of slavery in the French colony.

**1794**  The French National Convention emancipates French colonial slaves.

**1804**  On January 1, Haitians proclaim the independent Republic of Haiti.

**1805**  The Constitution of Haiti provides that any slave arriving in Haiti is automatically both free and a citizen of the country.

**1807**  England and the United States prohibit their citizens from engaging in the international slave trade.

**1813**  Gradual emancipation is adopted in Argentina.

**1814**  Gradual emancipation begins in Colombia.

**1815**  At the Congress of Vienna, Britain compels Spain, Portugal, France, and the Netherlands to abolish the slave trade (though Spain and Portugal are permitted a few years of continued slaving to replenish labor supplies).

**1817**  On September 23, Great Britain and Spain sign a treaty prohibiting the slave trade: Spain agree to end the slave trade north of the equator immediately, and south of the equator in 1820.

**1820**  Britain begins to use its naval power to suppress the slave trade.

**1822–1844**  Haiti occupies Spanish Santo Domingo.

**1823**  Slavery is abolished in Chile.

**1824**  Slavery is abolished in Central America.

**1829**    Slavery is abolished in Mexico.

**1831**    Slavery is abolished in Bolivia.

**1838**    Slavery is abolished in all British colonies.

**1842**    Slavery is abolished in Uruguay.

**1848**    Slavery is abolished in all French and Danish colonies.

**1851**    Slavery is abolished in Ecuador, and the slave trade is ended in Brazil.

**1854**    Slavery is abolished in Peru and Venezuela.

**1862**    Slave trade ends in Cuba.

**1863**    Slavery is abolished in all Dutch colonies.

**1865–1870**    The War of Paraguay results in the death of thousands of black soldiers fighting for Uruguay, Paraguay, Brazil, and Argentina

**1865**    Slavery is abolished in the United States as a result of the Thirteenth Amendment to the Constitution and the end of the Civil War.

**1871**    Gradual emancipation is initiated in Brazil.

**1873**    Slavery is abolished in Puerto Rico.

**1886**    Slavery is abolished in Cuba.

**1888**    Slavery is abolished in Brazil.

**1902**    Cuban independence is declared (although Cuba includes a provision in the constitution that gives the United States the right to intervene in its national affairs).

**1900**    The first Pan-African Congress is convened.

**1912**    Race wars in Cuba begin.

**1932**    The publication of the journal *Légitime défense* marks the beginning of the Negritude movement.

**1933**    The French Negritude movement is founded.

**1940**    The most progressive and socially responsible constitution in Cuba's history declares racism illegal in Cuba.

**1944**    The Black Experimental Theater is founded in Rio de Janeiro by Abdias do Nascimento and Ruth de Souza.

**1948**    The General Assembly of the United Nations adopts the Universal Declaration of Human Rights.

**1959** The Cuban Revolution begins.

**1960s** The civil rights movement in the United States serves as an inspiration to blacks across the Americas. In the midst of the Cold War, however, and governed by right-wing dictatorships, Latin America's black movement would not have an impact on the national or international scene until the late 1980s.

**1978** The Unified Black Movement in São Paulo is founded.

**1988** A century of Brazilian abolition is celebrated. The Palmares Foundation in Brazil is established as a project to promote black Brazilian rights. The foundation functions as a quasi-independent state institution for in the accreditation and granting of lands to *quilombos*, communities of the descendants of former runaway African slaves.

**1992** During the commemorations for the five hundred-year anniversary of the arrival of European culture in the Americas, indigenous and black organizations come together to protest genocide and European exploitation in the Americas. This year also witnesses the assassination of Maria Elena Moyana, a black Peruvian who fought for the rights of Peru's poor.

**1993** Colombia's Federal Law 70 assigns seats in its National House of Representatives to Afro-Colombians, making Colombia the only country in Latin America to adopt racial quotas.

**1996** Uruguay hosts the First Conference against Racism and Xenophobia, which becomes a catalyst for Latin American pan-Africanism.

**2000** Native and black Brazilians join together to protest and call attention to the plight of their communities during the five hundred-year anniversary of the arrival of the Portuguese in Brazil.

**2001** The World Conference against Racism, Racial Discrimination, Xenophobia and Related Intolerance takes place.

**2002** Brazil's Workers Party (PT) wins the presidency and control of Congress in Brazil. President Luis "Lula" Inácio da Silva appoints four Afro-Brazilians (Gilberto Gil, Benedita da Silva, Marina Silva, and Matilde Ribeiro) to top posts in his cabinet. PT later establishes the Ministry for the Promotion of Racial Equality (SEPPIR).

**2003** The first meeting of legislators of African descent from around Latin America is held in Brazil to plan strategies for future cross-national and regional cooperation.

# Further Readings

## HEMISPHERIC AND COMPARATIVE SOURCES

Andrews, George Reid. *Afro-Latin America, 1800–2000*. Oxford: Oxford University Press, 2004.

Cooper, Frederick, Thomas C. Holt, and Rebecca J. Scott. *Beyond Slavery: Explorations of Race, Labor, and Citizenship in Post-emancipation Societies*. Chapel Hill: University of North Carolina Press, 2000.

Hooker, Juliet. "Indigenous Inclusion/Black Exclusion: Race, Ethnicity and Multi-cultural Citizenship in Contemporary Latin America." *Journal of Latin American Studies* 37, no. 2 (2005): 285–310.

Klein, Herbert S. *The Atlantic Slave Trade*. New York: Cambridge University Press, 1999.

Linebaugh, Peter, and Marcus Rediker. *The Many-Headed Hydra: Sailors, Slaves, Commoners, and the Hidden History of the Revolutionary Atlantic*. Boston: Beacon Press, 2000.

Minority Rights Group. *No Longer Invisible: Afro-Latin Americans Today*. London: Minority Rights Publications, 1996.

Scott, Rebecca J., et al., eds. *Societies after Slavery: A Select Annotated Bibliography of Printed Sources on Cuba, Brazil, British Colonial Africa, South Africa, and the British West Indies*. Pittsburgh: University of Pittsburgh Press, 2002.

Stephens, Thomas M. *Dictionary of Latin American Racial and Ethnic Terminology*. Gainesville: University Press of Florida, 1999.

Thorp, Rosemary. *Progress, Poverty and Exclusion: An Economic History of Latin America in the 20th Century*. Baltimore: Johns Hopkins University Press, 1998.

Walker, Sheila S., ed. *African Roots/American Cultures: Africa in the Creation of the Americas*. Lanham, MD: Rowman & Littlefield, 2001.

## BRAZIL

Benjamin, Medea, and Maisa Mendonça. *Benedita da Silva: An Afro-Brazilian Woman's Story of Politics and Love*. Oakland, CA: Institute for Food and Development Policy, 1998.

Bennett, Herman. *Africans in Colonial Mexico: Absolutism, Christianity, and Afro-Creole Consciousness, 1570–1640*. Bloomington: Indiana University Press, 2003.

Bergad, Laird. *Slavery and the Demographic and Economic History of Minas Gerais, Brazil*. Cambridge: Cambridge University Press, 1999.

Butler, Kim D. *Freedoms Given, Freedoms Won: Afro-Brazilians in Post-abolition São Paolo and Salvador*. New Brunswick, NJ: Rutgers University Press, 1998.

Harding, Rachel. *A Refuge in Thunder: Candomblé and Alternative Spaces of Blackness*. Bloomington: Indiana University Press, 2000.

Hecht, Tobias. *At Home in the Street: Street Children of Northeast Brazil*. Cambridge: Cambridge University Press, 1998.

Johnson, Ollie A., III. "Racial Representation and Brazilian Politics: Black Members of the National Congress, 1983–1999." *Journal of Interamerican Studies and World Affairs* 41, no. 4 (1998): 97–118.

Kraay, Hendrik. *Race, State, and Armed Forces in Independence-Era Brazil: Bahia, 1790s–1840s*. Stanford, CA: Stanford University Press, 2001.

Lauderdale Graham, Sandra. *Caetana Says No: Women's Stories from a Brazilian Slave Society*. Cambridge: Cambridge University Press, 2002.

Lindsey, Shawn. *The Afro-Brazilian Organization Directory: A Reference Guide to Black Organizations in Brazil*. Parkland, FL: Universal Publishers, 1999.

Lovell, Peggy A., and Charles H. Wood. "Skin Color, Racial Identity and Life Chances in Brazil." *Latin American Perspectives* 25, no. 2 (1998): 90–109.

Reichmann, Rebecca, ed. *Race in Contemporary Brazil: From Indifference to Inequality*. University Park: Pennsylvania State University Press, 1999.

Sheriff, Robin. *Dreaming Equality: Color, Race, and Racism in Urban Brazil*. New Brunswick, NJ: Rutgers University Press, 2001.

Sheriff, Robin. "The Theft of Carnival: National Spectacle and Racial Politics in Rio de Janeiro." *Cultural Anthropology* 14, no. 1 (1999): 3–28.

Telles, Edward E. "Racial Ambiguity among the Brazilian Population." *Ethnic and Racial Studies* 25, no. 3 (2002): 415–51.

## SPANISH AMERICA

Applebaum, Nancy. *Muddied Waters: Race, Region, and Local History in Colombia, 1846–1948*. Durham, NC: Duke University Press, 2003.

Arocha, Jaime. "Inclusion of Afro-Colombians: Unreachable National Goal?" *Latin American Perspectives* 25, no. 3 (1998): 70–89.

Blanchard, Peter. "Miguel García: Black Soldier in the Wars of Independence." In *The Human Tradition in Colonial Latin America*, ed. Kenneth J. Andrien. Wilmington, DE: Scholarly Resources, 2002.

Bronfmas, Alejandra. "'En Plena Libertad y Democracía': *Negros Brujos* and the Social Question, 1902–1919." *Hispanic American Historical Review* 82, no. 3 (2002): 549–87.

Carroll, Patrick. *Blacks in Colonial Veracruz: Race, Ethnicity, and Regional Development*. Austin: University of Texas Press, 1991.

Casanovas, Joan. *Bread, or Bullets! Urban Labor and Spanish Colonialism in Cuba, 1850–1898*. Pittsburgh: University of Pittsburgh Press, 1998.

Chalhoub, Sidney. "Dependents Play Chess: Political Dialogues in Machado de Assis." In *Machado de Assis: Reflections on a Brazilian Master Writer*, ed. Richard Graham. Austin: University of Texas Press, 1999.

Chamosa, Oscar. "To Honor the Ashes of Their Forebears: The Rise and Crisis of African Nations in the Post-independence State of Buenos Aires, 1820–1860." *Americas* 59, no. 3 (2003): 347–78.

Chomsky, Avi. "'Barbados or Canada?' Race, Immigration, and Nation in Early-Twentieth Century Cuba." *Hispanic American Historical Review* 80, no. 3 (2000): 415–62.

Cottrol, Robert J. "The Long Lingering Shadow: Law, Liberalism and Cultures of Racial Hierarchy and Identity in the Americas." *Tulane Law Review* 76, no. 1 (2001): 11–79.

Díaz, María Elena. *The Virgin, the King, and the Royal Slaves of El Cobre: Negotiating Freedom in Colonial Cuba, 1670–1780*. Stanford, CA: Stanford University Press, 2000.

Eltis, David. *Economic Growth and the Ending of the Transatlantic Slave Trade*. New York: Oxford University Press, 1987.

Ferrer, Ada. *Insurgent Cuba: Race, Nation, and Revolution, 1868–1878*. Chapel Hill: University of North Carolina Press, 1999.

Findlay, Eileen J. Suárez. *Imposing Decency: The Politics of Sexuality and Race in Puerto Rico, 1870–1920*. Durham, NC: Duke University Press, 1999.

Fuente, Alejandro de la. *A Nation for All: Race, Inequality, and Politics in Twentieth-Century Cuba*. Chapel Hill: University of North Carolina Press, 2001.

Geggus, David P., ed. *The Impact of the Haitian Revolution in the Atlantic World*. Columbia: University of South Carolina, 2001.

Gott, Richard. *In the Shadow of the Liberator: Hugo Chávez and the Transformation of Venezuela*. London: Verso, 2000.

Graden, Dale T. "The Origins, Evolution, and Demise of the 'Myth of Racial Democracy' in Brazil, 1848–1998." In *La Reconstrucción del mundo en América Latina*, ed. Enrique Pérez Arias. Lund, Sweden: Cuadernos Heterogénesis, 1998.

Grillo, Evelio. *Black Cuban, Black American: A Memoir*. Houston, TX: Arte Público Press, 2000.

Grinberg, Keila. "Freedom Suits and Civil Law in Brazil and the United States." *Slavery and Abolition* 22, no. 3 (2001): 66–82.

Grueso, Libia, Carlos Rosero, and Arturo Escobar. "The Process of Black Community Organizing in the Southern Pacific Coast Region of Colombia." In *Cultures of Politics/Politics of Cultures: Re-visioning Latin American Social Movements*, ed. Sonia E. Alvarez, Evelina Dagnino, and Arturo Escobar. Boulder, CO: Westview Press, 1998.

Guss, David M. *The Festive State: Race, Ethnicity, and Nationalism as Cultural Performance*. Berkeley and Los Angeles: University of California Press, 2000.

Helg, Aline. "The Limits of Equality: Free People of Colour and Slaves during the First Independence of Cartagena, Colombia, 1810–1815." *Slavery and Abolition* 20, no. 2 (1999): 1–30.

Helg, Aline. *Our Rightful Share: The Afro-Cuban Struggle for Equality, 1886–1912*. Chapel Hill: University of North Carolina Press, 1995.

Howard, David. *Coloring the Nation: Race and Ethnicity in the Dominican Republic.* Boulder, CO: Lynne Rienner, 2001.

Howard, Philip. *Changing History: Afro-Cuban Cabildos and Societies of Color in the Nineteenth Century.* Baton Rouge: Louisiana State University, 1998.

Inter-American Development Bank. *Facing up to Inequality in Latin America.* Washington, DC: Author, 1998.

Jiménez, Michael. "The Elision of the Middle Classes and Beyond: History, Politics, and Development Studies in Latin America's 'Short Twentieth Century.'" In *Colonial Legacies: The Problem of Persistence in Latin American History,* ed. Jeremy Adelman. New York: Routledge, 1999.

Johnson, Paul C. *Secrets, Gossip, and Gods: The Transformation of Brazilian Candomblé.* New York: Oxford University Press, 2002.

Kelley, Robin, and Earl Lewis, eds. *To Make Our World Anew: A History of African Americans.* New York: Oxford University Press, 2000.

Lewis, Marvin A. *Afro-Uruguayan Literature: Post-colonial Perspectives.* London: Associated University Presses, 2003

Lovejoy, Paul, and David Richardson. "Trust, Pawnship, and Atlantic History: The Institutional Foundations of the Old Calabar Slave Trade." *American Historical Review* 104, no. 2 (1999): 333–55.

Lovell, Peggy A. "Race, Gender and Regional Labor Market Inequalities in Brazil." *Review of Social Economy* 58, no. 3 (2000): 277–93.

Nobles, Melissa. *Shades of Citizenship: Race and the Census in Modern Politics.* Stanford, CA: Stanford University Press, 2000.

Palmié, Stephan. *Wizards and Scientists: Explorations in Afro-Cuban Modernity and Tradition.* Durham, NC: Duke University Press, 2002.

Phillips, Kevin. *Wealth and Democracy: A Political History of the American Rich.* New York: Broadway Books, 2002.

Putnam, Lisa. *The Company They Kept: Migrants and the Politics of Gender in Caribbean Costa Rica, 1870–1960.* Chapel Hill: University of North Carolina Press, 2002.

Rodríguez, O., Jamie E. *The Independence of Spanish America.* Cambridge: Cambridge University Press, 1998.

Rout, Leslie B., Jr. *The African Experience in Spanish America.* Princeton, NJ: Markus Wiener, 2003.

Sagás, Ernesto. *Race and Politics in the Dominican Republic.* Gainesville: University Press of Florida, 2002.

Schmidt-Nowara, Christopher. *Empire and Antislavery: Spain, Cuba, and Puerto Rico, 1833–1874.* Pittsburgh: University of Pittsburgh Press, 1999.

Stallings, Barbara, and Wilson Peres. *Growth, Employment and Equity: The Impact of the Economic Reforms in Latin America and the Caribbean.* Washington, DC: Brookings Institution Press, 2000.

Stubbs, Jean, and Pedro Pérez Sarduy. *Afro-Cuban Voices: On Race and Identity in Contemporary Cuba.* Gainesville: University Press of Florida, 2000.

Twinam, Ann. "Pedro de Ayarza: The Purchase of Whiteness." In *The Human Tradition in Colonial Latin America,* ed. Kenneth J. Andrien. Wilmington, DE: Scholarly Resources, 2002.

Uribe-Uran, Victor. *Honorable Lives: Lawyers, Family, and Politics in Colombia, 1780–1850.* Pittsburgh: University of Pittsburgh Press, 2000.

Van Cott, Donna Lee. *The Friendly Liquidation of the Past: The Politics of Diversity in Latin America.* Pittsburgh: University of Pittsburgh Press, 1999.

Vianna, Hermano. *The Mystery of Samba: Popular Music and Identity in Brazil.* Ed. and trans. John Charles Chasteen. Durham, NC: Duke University Press, 1999.

Vincent, Theodore G. *The Legacy of Vicente Guerrero: Mexico's First Black Indian President.* Gainesville: University Press of Florida, 2001.

Vinson, Ben, III. *Bearing Arms for His Majesty: The Free-Colored Militia in Colonial Mexico.* Stanford, CA: Stanford University Press, 2001.

Wade, Peter. "Introduction: The Colombian Pacific in Perspective." *Journal of Latin American Anthropology* 7, no. 2 (2002): 2–33.

Wasserman, Mark. *Everyday Life and Politics in Nineteenth-Century Mexico: Men, Women, and War.* Albuquerque: University of New Mexico Press, 2000.

Whitney, Robert. *State and Revolution in Cuba: Mass Mobilization and Political Change, 1920–1940.* Chapel Hill: University of North Carolina Press, 2001.

# Index

# About the Contributors

**Aviva Chomsky** is professor of history at Salem State College, where she teaches Latin American and world history. Her most recent book is *The Cuba Reader: History, Culture, Politics* (with Barry Carr and Pamela Smorkaloff). She is currently working on a long history of globalization as it links the labor histories of New England and Colombia.

**Darién J. Davis** is associate professor of history and Latin American studies at Middlebury College. His major areas of research are twentieth-century Brazilian social and cultural history and the African diaspora in Latin America. He is author of numerous articles on race, patriotism, immigration, and nationhood in Latin America and the United States. His recent book-length manuscripts include *Avoiding the Dark: Race and the Forging of National Culture in Modern Brazil* (1999) and *Afro-Brasileiros Hoje* (2000). His latest project is about Brazilian performers in the early twentieth century.

**Dario Euraque** has taught at Trinity College in Hartford, Connecticut, since 1990. He has published articles and reviews in many academic journals in the United States, Europe, Latin America, and the Caribbean. His early work on Honduran economic and social history was published as *Reinterpreting the "Banana Republic": Region and State in Honduras, 1870s–1972* (1996). His most recent book is *Conversaciones históricas con el mestizaje en Honduras y su identidad nacional* (2004). It addresses questions of race, ethnicity, state formation, and national identity in modern Honduran and Central American history. He is currently working on a modern history of sexuality in Honduras.

**Sujatha Fernandes** is a member of the sociology department at Queens College, City University of New York. She teaches courses on Caribbean

287

politics and society, Latin American social movements, and culture and power. She is the author of *The Arts of Politics: Culture, Public Spheres and State Power in Contemporary Cuba*, forthcoming with Duke University Press.

**David Geggus** is professor of history at the University of Florida. A former J. S. Guggenheim Fellow and fellow of the Royal Historical Society, he has also held fellowships at the Woodrow Wilson Center and the National Humanities Center. His publications include *Slavery, War and Revolution* (1982) and *Haitian Revolutionary Studies* (2002).

**Aline Helg** is a professor of history at the University of Geneva in Switzerland. Her most recent books include *Liberty and Equality in Caribbean Colombia, 1770–1835* (2004) and *Our Rightful Share: The Afro-Cuban Struggle for Equality, 1886–1912* (1995), both of which have garnered several major international historical prizes. She also has published several articles and book chapters on comparative race relations in the Americas, black mobilization, independence, and racial ideas in Latin America as well as on Cuba and Colombia. She is currently writing a book on blacks in the Americas after slavery.

**Eduardo Silva** is a researcher at Fundação Casa de Rui Barbosa, in Rio de Janeiro. He has written several books on slavery and black culture in Brazil, among them *Prince of the People: The Life and Times of a Brazilian Free Man of Colour* (1993) and *As camélias do Leblon e a Abolição da Escravatura: Uma Investigação de história cultural* (2003). His recent work explores the underground abolitionist movement in Brazil.

**Ricardo D. Salvatore** is professor of history at the Universidad Torcuato Di Tella in Buenos Aires, Argentina. He has edited *Close Encounters of Empire: Writing the Cultural History of U.S.-Latin American Relations* (1998), with Gilbert Joseph and Catherine LeGrand. He is the author of *Wandering Paysanos: State Order and Subaltern Experience in Buenos Aires Province during the Rosas Era* (2003). He has written various articles on the cultural history of U.S.-Latin American relations and about imperial representations in general. He is currently completing a book manuscript entitled "The Empire of Knowledge: United States Strategies for Knowing South America, 1898–1945."

**Jason Stanyek** is assistant professor of music at New York University. His major areas of research are Brazilian music, improvisation, technologies of copresence, interculturalism, and global hip-hop. His most recent publication, "Transmissions of an Interculture: Pan-African Jazz and Intercultural Improvisation," appeared in *The Other Side of Nowhere: Jazz, Improvisation* *and Communities in Dialogue* (2004). Currently, he is writing a book on Brazilian diasporic performance in the United States.

**Camilla Townsend** is associate professor of history at Rutgers University, New Brunswick. She is the author of *Tales of Two Cities: Race and Economic Culture in Early Republican North and South America,* and of numerous articles. Currently, she is working on the history of Nahuatl-speaking indigenous people in Mexico.

**Bobby Vaughn** is assistant professor of anthropology at Notre Dame of Namur University in Belmont, California. He is coauthor of *Afromexico* (2004) with Ben Vinson. He has taught a number of classes on race and ethnicity in Mexico, blackness in Latin America, and race and nationalism.

**Ben Vinson III** is professor of Latin American history and director of the Center of Africana Studies at Johns Hopkins University. He is the author of *Bearing Arms for His Majesty: The Free-Colored Militia in Colonial Mexico* (2001) and *Flight: The Story of Virgil Richardson, a Tuskegee Airman in Mexico* (2004).

**Judith Michelle Williams** is an assistant professor in the Department of English. She is also part of the core faculty of the program in Latin American studies at the University of Massachusetts Amherst. She is presently at work on a monograph tracing the history of black theater in Rio de Janeiro, Brazil. She is also a filmmaker and theater director.